ILLICIT WORLDS OF

ANNA MORCOM

Illicit Worlds of Indian Dance

Cultures of Exclusion

OXFORD
UNIVERSITY PRESS

Oxford University Press, Inc., publishes works that further
Oxford University's objective of excellence
in research, scholarship, and education.

Oxford New York
Auckland Cape Town Dar es Salaam Hong Kong Karachi
Kuala Lumpur Madrid Melbourne Mexico City Nairobi
New Delhi Shanghai Taipei Toronto

With offices in
Argentina Austria Brazil Chile Czech Republic France Greece
Guatemala Hungary Italy Japan Poland Portugal Singapore
South Korea Switzerland Thailand Turkey Ukraine Vietnam

Published by Oxford University Press, Inc
198 Madison Avenue, New York, New York 10016

Published in the United Kingdom in 2013 by C. Hurst & Co. (Publishers) Ltd.

www.oup.com

Library of Congress Cataloging-in-Publication Data
Morcom, Anna.
Illicit worlds of Indian dance : cultures of exclusion / Anna Morcom.
p. cm.
Includes bibliographical references and index.
ISBN 978-0-19-934353-9 (alk. paper)
ISBN 978-0-19-934354-6 (alk. paper)
1. Dance—Social aspects—India. 2. Dance—Psychological aspects—India. 3. Women dancers—India—Social conditions. 4. Transgender people—India—Social conditions. 5. Marginality, Social—India. 6. India—Social conditions. I. Title.
GV1693.M67 2013
793.3'1954—dc23
2013017923

1 3 5 7 9 8 6 4 2

Printed in India
on Acid-Free Paper

CONTENTS

Acknowledgements vii
List of Images xi

Introduction: Indian Performing Arts and Modernity's Cultures of Exclusion 1
Pakeezah *and the paradigm of the traditional female public/erotic performer in South Asia* 3
Female public/erotic performers, patriarchy and transgression 6
The new order: mapping legitimate and illicit zones in Indian performing arts 11
Colonial and postcolonial modernities, collateral damage and performing arts 15
Possibilities for and signs of change in post-liberalisation India 24
Recovering histories, valuing performing arts: the aims of this book 27

1. The Creation and Recreation of India's Illicit Zones of Performing Arts: Dynamics of Exclusion in Colonial and Postcolonial India 31
Stigmatisation and the loss of status and livelihood of hereditary female performers in colonial India 32
The repetition and consolidation of history: Continued dynamics of exclusion of female erotic performers in postcolonial India 41
Conclusions 58

2. Female Hereditary Performers in Post-Independence India: Communities, Histories and Livelihoods 61
Tribes and communities: the social organisation of hereditary female performers 62
Female hereditary performing communities in contemporary India 71
Conclusions 85

3. Transgender Erotic Performers in South Asia 87
MSM transgenders and sexual minorities in South Asia 89
Erotic feminine male performers in historical sources 91
Kothis, *femininity, dance and eroticism* 96
Conclusions 107

4. The Bollywood Dance Revolution and the Embourgoisement of Indian Performing Arts 109
Classical performing arts 111
Indian/Hindi films and the film industry 113
The Bollywood dance revolution: new horizons of dance in middle class India 117
Conclusions 138

5. Mumbai Dance Bars, Anti-*Nautch* II, and New Possibilities 141
*The continuation and repetition of history: The dance bar ban as anti-*nautch II 145
New directions: The bar girls debacle as an unprecedented chapter in the history of public/erotic female performers in India 158
Conclusions 169

6. The Contemporary World of *Kothi* Performers: Changing Patterns of Livelihood and Socio-Cultural Space 171
Contexts and genres 173
The social organisation of kothi *performers* 176
Livelihoods of kothi *dancers: some glimpses* 182
New struggles for socio-cultural space 194
Conclusions 201

Conclusion 203

Notes 213
Bibliography 257
Index 281

ACKNOWLEDGEMENTS

There are innumerable people and organisations to thank who have helped to make this book possible. To begin with, I extend my thanks to the British Academy whose Larger Research Grant supported approximately sixteen months of fieldwork for this project between 2006 and 2009. I am also grateful to the Music and Letters Trust for a grant towards an invaluable top-up field trip for this book in 2010.

In terms of the core fieldwork for this book, one of the biggest votes of thanks must go to Varsha Kale, President of the Indian Bargirls Union and an activist with remarkable vision, who I met in 2006 for general enquiries about Mumbai's bar girls and dance bars. This meeting dramatically opened up the project, as she informed me that most of the bar girls were from hereditary (*khandani*) backgrounds, and hence linked to communities and lineages of courtesans and dancing girls. She was able to introduce me to *Deredar* courtesans in Mumbai, in Muzaffarpur and to performers and ex-performers from other communities, including *Nat* and *Bedia*, in Mumbai and beyond. She also introduced me to many *Kolhati Lavani* performers. I cannot thank Varsha and her husband Ankush Deshpande enough for their support, generous hospitality, and friendship. Time spent with them has been an education. Whilst all the *khandani* performers I met across Maharashtra/Mumbai, Delhi, Uttar Pradesh, Bihar and Rajasthan may not be keen to be named, I would like to extend my thanks to them for giving me their time and sharing experiences and information. I would also like to thank several of them for some absolutely unforgettable *mujra* performances involving film music, dance and *Qawwali*, in Mumbai (Fores Road and Congress House) and Muzaffarpur, which I wish more people would understand the value of. I would also particularly like to thank Pinky Madhiwal and her uncle Shyam Lacchiya for their time in educating me about the *Nat* community and *Bhatu* performers in general, and for the trip to *Nat* villages in Rajasthan which they arranged and accompanied me on.

The second dimension of fieldwork for this book has been with transgender *kothi* and *hijra* performers (many of whom I refer to with pseudonyms). I would like to thank Salman, Rajesh and Mahesh, who initially opened up this world for me when I met them at the Entertainment Workers conference in Calcutta in 2007, where they encouraged me to come to Lucknow to meet male *mujra* performers. The Bharosa Trust and Naz Foundation International (NFI) were invaluable in Lucknow in helping introduce me to *kothi* performers and for their excellent resource centre, and I would like to thank Shivanandam Khan and Imran Khan for their assistance. I would also like to thank the many *kothi*s and *kothi* performers I met in Lucknow for their openness in discussing their lives with me, their friendliness, and some wonderful dance performances, in particular, Salim, Samesh and Narendra. The biggest thank you must go to Divya Sagar in Lucknow, who was the key facilitator of my fieldwork in this city, an excellent brainstormer, and a loyal friend and sister. I would also like to thank her parents for their warmth and hospitality, and was delighted to see them win the Bharosa Trust's parents prize one year I was there. Divya, an accomplished *kothi* performer, was able to introduce me to many other performers, to accompany me on endless interviews, and also several trips to Balliya. She was particularly helpful in introducing me to some of the older generation of *kothi* performers. I would also like to extend warm thanks to Samesh, who introduced me to a range of *kothi* and *hijra* performers in Lucknow, including those involved in *Nautanki* and *Badhai*.

Research on *kothi* performers also extended to Balliya, Delhi and Mumbai. In Balliya, I am grateful for the help of Shailesh Kumar. In Delhi, I would like to warmly thank Naz India and Anjali Gopalan, and specifically the Milan project and Rahul for time, help, explanations, and support. I would also like to thank Siddharth for sharing his knowledge and stories, and hope I have the opportunity to see him perform another time. In Mumbai, I am grateful for the help of two charismatic *hijra* performers, Laxminarayan Tripathi and Simran, and for an unforgettable drop-in evening at Humsafar Trust, where I saw sizzling performances from Simran and other *kothi/hijra* performers.

The third dimension of this book is the middle class, transnational Bollywood dance scene. I would like to thank a range of dancers and choreographers for taking time out from their impossibly busy lives to talk to me and tell me about the film industry, live dance shows, and dance institutes. In Mumbai, I would like to thank the well-known singer/dancer/choreographer Ganesh Hegde, and dancers/entrepreneurs Justine, Gaysil, Anchel and Vivek. I would also like to give a big thank you to Shiamak Davar, Rajesh Mansukhani and a number of dancers at SDIPA for meeting me and for their friendliness and help in explaining about how SDIPA and also the Victory Arts Foundation (VFA) work and their own involvement in dance. In Delhi, I would like to thank Kalpana Bhushan, from whom I would have greatly enjoyed learning some dance had there been more time, and Praveen Shandilya. I am also very grateful to Gaggun Bedi, director of the Sparkling Pearlz Institute of

Fine Dances, Grooming and Fitness in Jalandhar for a particularly memorable and informative day meeting him and a number of his students, who enthusiastically shared their views on and experiences of dance, a recent discovery for the largely female, married cohort I met. Their enthusiasm and positive energy towards dance was infectious, and I left wishing I could stay on and join the institute.

Moving away from those who were a direct part of my fieldwork, I would like to say a particularly warm thank you to Rachel Dwyer, who has been as immensely generous as ever in introducing me to people and sharing contacts. Particularly supportive during this project were Talmeez Ahmed and Sunita Mainee, who are some of the most hospitable, friendly and kind people I have ever met, and to whom I owe a very big vote of thanks; and Julian Parr, who is an indefatigable source of good energy and fun, who had me to stay in Delhi for I can't remember how long or how many times, much to my general betterment.

This book has also benefitted from immeasurable amounts of input from other colleagues and friends, ranging from brief but inspiring discussion to longer term brainstorming and networking. I would like to thank the following (in alphabetical order): Ira Bhaskar, Kaushik Bhaumik, Amy Caitlin Jairazhboy, Sameena Dalwai, Angela Impey, Saleem Kidwai, Amie Maciszewski, Jerry Pinto, Shweta Sachdeva, Madhu Sarin, Katherine Schofield, Amrit Srinivasan, Shzr Ee Tan, Valentina Vitali, and Richard Widdess. Madhu Sarin I must thank also for wonderful hospitality in Chandigarh on numerous stopovers, and Shzr Ee Tan, for having me to stay in Singapore, for a brief yet very intriguing exploration into dance bars and Bollywood dance. I would also like to thank the following people who read partial or full drafts of the manuscript and offered invaluable comments and support (again, in alphabetical order): Thierry Dodin, Ananya Kabir, Tina K Ramnarine, Davesh Soneji, Richard Williams, and the second anonymous reader for Oxford University Press. I would like to give a particular vote of thanks to Michael Dwyer for believing in the project (even at the teething-problem stage), helping revise the manuscript, and seeing it through to a book. I am also grateful to the whole team at Hurst for their work in preparing the manuscript. I would also like to thank Ravinder Singh and Shweta Sachdeva (who transcribed many interviews for the book).

I am also grateful, as ever, to my parents, for their enduring interest and engagement with my work, and support of me in general. I also thank Carlo Gallo, who emerged latish in this project, for kindness, support, companionship and brainstorming too.

This book is dedicated to all the performers in this book, and those like them. In particular, it is dedicated to the disenfranchised female hereditary and *kothi* performers of India, who continue to struggle for livelihood and socio-cultural space.

LIST OF IMAGES

1. Sahib Jan performing *Inhin logon ne*. (DVD capture) 5
2. *Chalte chalte* from *Pakeezah*. (DVD capture) 8
3. Sahib Jan's final dance, *Aaj hum apni duaon ka asar dekhenge*. (DVD capture) 9
4. 'A retrospective of the films of Shahrukh Khan' film festival booklet sponsored by The High Commission of India in Nairobi and the Ministry of External Affairs, New Delhi in 2006. 13
5. Motif of a dancing girl used to illustrate an article about Calcutta sex workers with no traditional performing background. 50
6. Eighty-five-year-old *Nat* former court performer with his disused *sarangi*, Tonk, Rajasthan, 2010. (Author's photograph) 72
7. Eighty-five-year-old *Nat* former court performer shows his shield, used for hunting for Rajput patrons, Tonk, Rajasthan, 2010. (Author's photograph) 73
8. John Paul's Slum Development Project, Dr Khan, author and other staff discussion with commercial sex workers, Pune, 2010. (Author's photograph) 81
9. Divya Sagar, staff member at Bharosa Trust, performing informally to a film *mujra* in Naz Foundational International office, Lucknow, March 2007. (Author's photograph) 101
10. Publicity postcard for Honey's Dance Academy, UK, offering (a) choreography for Bollywood weddings, and (b) training for UK-based Bollywood wannabes. 118
11. Live Shows of Shiamak Davar's Victory Arts Foundation. (© The SHIAMAK Group) 126–127
12. Bhartiya Bargirls Union poster advertising a rally, (© BBU) 161
13. Rally of the Bhartiya Bargirls Union, (© BBU) 162
14. Varsha Kale giving a speech at Bhartiya Bargirls Union rally, (© BBU) 163

15. Bhartiya Bargirls Union publicity poster, 'Let us live too', (© BBU) 164
16. Advertisement in Balliya for a female dance troupe for wedding and other shows. Similar troupes of *kothi* performers are common in Balliya. (Author's photograph) 175
17. Professional *hijra* dancer, Simran. (Author's photograph) 186
18. Professional *hijra* dancer, Simran, performing at an *Urs* celebration in Rajasthan. (Author's photograph) 187
19. Female impersonators for *Binbaikacha Lavani* performance in Mumbai. (Author's photograph) 187

INTRODUCTION

INDIAN PERFORMING ARTS AND MODERNITY'S CULTURES OF EXCLUSION

Kamal Amrohi's 1971 film Pakeezah *tells the story of a courtesan, Sahib Jan, struggling to escape what she comes to see as a 'shameful' existence. The film starts with Sahib Jan's mother, Nargis, falling in love with a nobleman, Shahabuddin, whose father refuses to accept her. She flees in shame, and dies ten months later, leaving her newborn daughter, Sahib Jan. Sahib Jan grows up in the care of Nargis's elder sister, Nawab Jan.*

On a train journey a few years later, something happens that changes Sahib Jan's carefree life forever. While she is asleep, Salim, a nobleman and, as we later find out, the nephew of Sahib Jan's father Shahabuddin,[1] *comes into her compartment. As Sahib Jan turns in her sleep with the lurching of the train, one of her feet is left uncovered. Salim stares, transfixed with the beauty of her foot. He leaves a note for Sahib Jan tucked in between her toes:*

Excuse me, by chance I came into your compartment, and saw your feet. They are very beautiful. Please do not place them on the ground, lest they become dirty, yours, a fellow traveller.[2]

When Sahib Jan wakes in the morning and reads the note, the train has stopped at Suhagpur (literally, 'happy-state-of-marriage-sville'). Having glimpsed this new destination through the train windows, she is increasingly oppressed by and detached from her own courtesan existence and identity, whereby she must entertain but not marry men—and she reads the note again and again.

Sahib Jan is now living in her aunt's kotha *(salon), where she is a debutant (and virgin) courtesan. One night, she is taken on a boat by a client. The boat is attacked by elephants before the client is able to have sex with her, and she is washed up in a wilderness. Here, by coincidence, she comes across the camp of Salim, who is a forestry officer. She realises it is him when she finds in his possessions the feather he had taken from her book of poetry on the train. When he returns, they express their love for each other. But when he leaves her for the day to carry out his work, a search party from the* kotha *takes her back home.*

Sahib Jan later runs away following an attempted rape in the kotha *(her second lucky escape from sexual contact), and again, coincidentally meets Salim. He takes her to his family. Even though neither he nor his grandfather (Shahabuddin's father) know she is a courtesan, his grandfather refuses to allow a stray, unexplained woman to stay, saying it will disgrace the family. Salim leaves with her, and this is the moment she finds the courage to tell him that she is a courtesan, a* tawaif. *He accepts this, and they set off to marry. When the priest asks her name, Salim names her* Pakeezah, *'the pure one'. Just as they are about to get married however, she becomes overwhelmed by shame and runs away, returning to the* kotha.

She then receives a letter from Salim. Abandoned by her, he is marrying someone else, and he invites Sahib Jan to perform at his wedding. Giving what is to be her final performance, in anger and despair, she breaks a glass on the ground and dances on top of it, thus maiming the feet that Salim loved so much. She finally collapses in her aunt's arms, who, over the stunned silence of those present, confronts Sahib Jan's father and announces Sahib Jan to be his daughter. As Shahabuddin rushes to embrace and publicly recognise his daughter, the grandfather (who had previously refused to let Shahabuddin marry Sahib Jan's mother) shoots him, fatally wounding him. Shahabuddin's father is then compelled to accept his granddaughter, and his grandson's marriage to her. Shahabuddin's corpse is carried with Salim and Sahib Jan's wedding procession.

This exquisite film melodrama encapsulates the world of professional female performers in South Asia prior to modern reforms. With visceral clarity, it depicts how such performers fit, and do not fit, within South Asian patriarchy: their skill, art, allure and renown—yet their low status. However, the film is also didactic. It presents these conflicts as injustices and puts an end to them in a bloody, revolutionary and definitive manner. With Salim's love and acceptance of Sahib Jan, however, the solution presented is also compassionate.

In the film, modernity is the saviour. Salim, as a forestry officer, represents a professional new order, contrasting in attitudes to feudal patriarchs such as his father and grandfather. Significantly, a train—that unmistakable symbol of modernity in so many Hindi films—provides the space in which the new relationship and new values emerge. The dénouement confronts head-on the dual values of the feudal order in which married men enjoyed extra-marital relationships with women who could not themselves marry. These old values are stamped out by modernity's values—of fairness, justice and equality for all women.

In the real world, however, as this book describes, the end of the courtesan tradition has been less just, less compassionate, and less complete. Whereas modernity is presented in the film as the righteous judge and executioner, it has in reality exacerbated the very problems it sought to solve, and made the lives of many it sought to save infinitely worse. While courtesans such as Sahib Jan did not have an equal status to their patrons, they did have an important role in society and culture. They had the potential to gain wealth, esteem, skill, and—in significant ways—respect. Women from communities of professional female performers are nowadays typically spoken of only in terms of prostitution. They struggle not just for livelihood but for any identity other than that of 'problem', 'enemy of society' or, at best, victim. Whereas traditional courtesans occupied a liminal social status, lineages of female professional performers in twenty-first century India are excluded in an absolute sense. Those like Sahib Jan that achieved the 'salvation' of marriage and, through it, inclusion in the mainstream are few. A parallel world of transgender males performing as females has seen a comparable modern trajectory. Thus *Pakeezah* represents a deeply flawed vision, one that has come at a heavy social cost—indeed, a cost that continues to mount even today.

Pakeezah *and the paradigm of the traditional female public/erotic performer in South Asia*

At the core of contemporary zones of performing arts and the modern histories described in this book lie the conflicts that female public performers present to patriarchy, and modern India's responses to these conflicts.[3] As a performing art, dance is an embodied art. A dancer who performs in public or male space is on display and gives pleasure to the male or mixed audience through a living, bodily art form. However, under traditional forms of patriarchy, a woman must be controlled and owned by her father, her other male relatives and, eventually, her husband. Associating with or even being seen by men outside this circle can bring dishonour to her and her family. Dancing in public or for the entertainment of men is therefore incompatible with marriage and 'respectability'. *Pakeezah* plays out these boundaries, transgressions and contradictions throughout.[4]

The film shows Sahib Jan overwhelmed by shame and self-loathing. Yet the film also implies that she remains a virgin (showing two miraculous escapes from sexual contact). She is almost always wearing either red (the colour of the bride) or white (the colour of death, of widows, or of celibate devotees, *brahmacarinis*). Sahib Jan's virginity is a compromise for the mainstream audience who would be less likely to accept an 'impure' heroine. However, it also indicates that merely dancing for a male audience can be seen as dishonouring or defiling a woman. Salim's naming her *Pakeezah* also labours the point of her (sexual/inner) purity, which persists despite the fact that she dances. The film focuses on this central conflict of dance and respectability through an intense fetishisation of the courtesan's feet, which are the quintessence of her performing body. It is Sahib Jan's beautiful feet that the stranger falls in love with and it is between her toes that he leaves his message intimately lodged. Yet it is her dancing feet that mark her as a courtesan, destined to perform, and to become defiled. By placing her feet on the ground (i.e. dancing) she will live a life of disgrace and will not marry. When she shows Salim's letter to a friend, the friend tells her that the message was not for her:

> [when he saw you], you can't have had ankle bells [worn for dancing] tied to your feet. If your ankle bells had been tied to your feet then how could anyone have said that you shouldn't place [your feet] on the ground, that they would become dirty?

As Sahib Jan becomes increasingly alienated from and ashamed of her life as a courtesan and moves instead towards 'Suhagpur', her mode of performance becomes increasingly disembodied. *Inhin logon ne le liya dupatta mera* ('It is those people who have taken my dupatta'), the song she performs before finding the letter, is carefree and flirty and she dances with an innocent abandon.[5] The next song, *Thade rahio oh banke yaar re* ('Stay awhile, handsome friend') is much less light-hearted. In the song, she enacts an imaginary meeting with a lover who is present only in her mind. The song is never finished as a male audience member fires a shot part-way through. Later, she performs *Chalte chalte* ('While walking along') for the client who will take her out in the boat. Although the song is rhythmic and very danceable, she performs largely *abhinay*, expressive gestures with the upper half of the body while seated on the ground. This could be described as a partial dance and one that is embodied to a lesser degree. Later on during the song, she gets up and dances in a curtailed and restrained way, faltering at one point. In contrast to this, two other courtesans dance energetically throughout, highlighting her distance from the scene.

After meeting Salim face-to-face in the wilderness and realising her feelings are reciprocated, the possibilities of love and marriage become concrete. Sahib Jan has moved so far from her courtesan persona that she is now completely unable to perform. Once back in the *kotha*, the musicians play the lively music of *Inhin logon ne le liya dupatta mera*, but Sahib Jan neither sings nor dances. Instead she sits in a reverie, disembodied and detached from the present. She has become someone who would not wear ankle bells, who would not put her feet on the ground, and would thus remain undefiled. When she returns home after running away from Salim and marriage, she confides her feelings to her friend, seemingly resigning herself to her courtesan life in which she is a 'living corpse'—body and soul disembodied to the point of a form of death. The sense of death and disembodiment is made complete in the finale, *Aaj ham apni duaon ka asar dekhenge*, 'Today we shall see the outcome of our desires, the meaning of our dreams'. Half-way through the song, she smashes a glass lantern and dances on the broken glass, destroying her dancing feet, and with them her courtesan/performing/defiled body and persona.

Image 1: Sahib Jan performing *Inhin logon ne*. (DVD capture)

The film emphasises throughout the mutually exclusive nature of the lives of the courtesan on the one hand and the married woman on the other. Pointedly, when she reads the note left by Salim the train is at Suhagpur, 'Marriagesville', marking the start of her journey towards marriage and away from her dancing and courtesan self. Although she becomes reluctant and even incapable of dancing, the film implies that this psychological disembodiment is not enough to bridge the gulf between the courtesan and the married/marriageable woman. Sahib Jan thus flees in shame when Salim takes her to marry him. The film depicts Sahib Jan's final transition from courtesan to bride as a visceral form of disembodiment through the mutilation of her feet.[6] As she dances on broken glass, the white sheet she dances on becomes stained, an image that echoes the bloodied sheet of the wedding night that proves both the bride's virginity and her irreversible transition to a sexually active, married woman. Here the blood signifies and assures (due to injury) the physical end of the dancing body, and so the end of the courtesan. It is only this violent, ritualistic end of her life as a performer that enables Sahib Jan to make what was (and is) a heavily taboo transition from courtesan or dancing girl to married woman.[7]

This sequence is intensely melodramatic in its externalisation of emotion and conflict and its inscribing of social conflicts on the body. However, although extreme, the performance that enacts the transition from dancer to married woman is highly meaningful, since the archetypes of both dancer and married woman centre on the body. It is also salient in terms of the modern history of these performers, and the zones they now occupy. The courtesan is one of Hindi cinema's favourite figures not just because of the scope for costumes and music but, at a deeper level, because of the powerful conflicts of patriarchy, the female body and desire that she foregrounds—and courtesans are almost invariably accompanied by melodrama and histrionics.

Female public/erotic performers, patriarchy and transgression

Pakeezah is fiction. However, its depiction of the mutually exclusive zones of the female performer who performs in front of men and of the married woman is grounded in the pre-modern or un-reformed performing arts world in India.[8] For a woman to perform in front of men, particularly in a seductive manner, means that she cannot be married.[9] That a woman performs in front of men tends to mean that she will be seen erotically, and as sexually available, whether her performance is erotic or not. All 'traditional' female performers who perform in public or male space exist outside of (normal) marriage and patriarchal control, and can be divided into three categories:

Classical courtesans and other dancing girls: Like Sahib Jan, courtesans, and other dancing girls in North India, come from hereditary families of low caste wandering tribes. In addition to hereditary members, they also adopted girls or bought slave girls. Their ranks have also included women who 'fell' from marriage in some way or who were unable to marry: widows who left their husband's family, disgraced girls, etc.[10] These 'courtesan-type' performers live in communities that are in many ways matrilineal and separate from mainstream society. Once a girl starts to dance, she becomes unmarriageable, set out only for a life of dance.

Devadasis: *Devadasi*s are ritual in role, but also involved in musical culture in mainstream society. Rather than remaining unmarried like the courtesans or dancing girls, *devadasi*s are 'married' or dedicated to the deity of their resident temple. In practical terms, this sets them out for a life in which they may perform in front of men and have sexual relationships.[11] Because they will never be widowed—something seen as highly inauspicious in Hinduism—they are particularly auspicious, or 'always auspicious' (*Nityasumangali*), which is key to their role in temples.[12] In caste terms, *devadasi*s are of lower status than their patrons, but not of low or polluting classes.[13]

Transgender males or female impersonators: The third category that must be included with erotic 'female' performers is far less known or talked about. It consists of various overlapping types and communities of transvestite or transgender men who perform as women. They may be married to a woman, but because they are not (legally) married to a man, and because they have a male (or eunuch) body, they exist outside of the rules of shame, honour and patriarchal control. The most visible form of transgender performers in India are the eunuchs, who are ritual/auspicious in their role. Their performance is not seen in erotic terms (though they have been and are still very much active in sex work). There are also transvestite performers—boys or men who perform as women in theatrical traditions, from rural *Ramlila* to the urban Parsee theatre. These performers are not principally erotic, though may be seen homoerotically by a male audience.[14] They may or may not be effeminate in terms of gender and sexuality. The least visible group are transgender males known as *kothi*s, *zanana/janana* or *jankha* in North India, who undeniably constitute erotic 'female' performers (though not always in erotic roles) and have been—and still are in many ways—interchangeable with dancing girls. They are not just performing as females but identify in gender and sexual terms as females (being the 'passive' sexual partners of 'real' men). In many contexts their dance performance is erotic and seductive, and they are seen as sexually available by men in the audience.

The distinction between unmarried professional female courtesan or *devadasi* performers and married women has been made by several scholars based on historical or ethnographic sources.[15] Colonial sources also outline this differentiation, though usually in prejudicial terms. In Crooke's 1896 ethnography, for example, he says of the dancing girl/courtesan community known as *Gandharba*, 'Beautiful

Image 2: *Chalte chalte* from *Pakeezah*. (DVD capture)

Image 3: Sahib Jan's final dance, *Aaj hum apni duaon ka asar dekhenge*. (DVD capture)

girls or those who show from their childhood a taste for music are selected for prostitution and not allowed to marry in the caste. A meeting of the brotherhood is held before the girl comes to maturity, and it is settled that she is to be allowed to have intercourse with no one but a Hindu of high caste'.[16] Displaced or 'fallen' women and widows have also been appropriated into communities of courtesans, illustrating the easy interchangeability of categories of women outside of marriage. The term *randi* pejoratively means prostitute, but etymologically means 'widow'.[17] Many of the first commercial sex workers in Calcutta were Brahmin widows.[18] The only category of woman outside of marriage that is respectable and/or not inauspicious is that of the female renouncer or *Brahmacharini*. It is significant that a means of defending the *devadasi* institution has been to see it as a tradition involving pure 'nuns' which became corrupted.[19]

The erotic female performer fits into the framework of patriarchy. Women or effeminate men perform and are (in theory) sexually available for ('real') men in the audience. Men do not, in the traditional framework, perform erotically for women. Moreover, the dynamics of power and sexuality conflate with those of social status: the performers are low status in comparison to the audience, firstly through being female or effeminate, and secondly, through being lower caste, low caste or non-caste females (the case, variously, for *devadasi*s or courtesan-style dancing girls) or transgender men (who in their transgender, performing guise, are arguably not countable in mainstream or caste society).[20] For a high caste/status woman to perform in front of low caste/status men would be unthinkable.[21]

However, a situation in which women perform for men also creates conflicts and contradictions for patriarchy, and these female or transgender performers exist in liminal spaces, shaped and contained by patriarchy yet also transgressive of it.[22] In traditional mainstream society, as long as there is public, female performance, the existence of 'disreputable', sexually available women and/or transvestite or transgender men, who live outside marriage is necessitated. These women exist outside of the domestic sphere and, unlike domestic women, are in many cases highly educated and able to converse with men on an equal intellectual level. They are also economically independent from men, and have been the chief earners in their communities.

This system brings into intimate proximity not just men and women, but high status men and low status women or effeminate men.[23] For men to have relationships with courtesans and other dancing girls and enjoy erotic entertainment was acceptable in feudal society, in which marriage was not seen as the only preserve of sexual pleasure. However, in cases where a man actually fell in love with or wished to marry a courtesan, the public and domestic female roles became blurred. That it was a transgression is exhibited in the numerous cautionary tales for noblemen concerning courtesans.[24] In a twenty-first-century context, stories of men being ruined by bar dancers serve the same function.

At the heart of this transgressive zone is not just the matter of low status females' proximity to high status men. These women are also equipped with aesthetic and affective power through their arts of music, dance and poetry.[25] In this way, these women have power over men through their power over their emotions, and their position has always been problematic. The affective power of music and dance in South Asia is legendary and in classical music is extensively theorised. The root of the word *raga* (one of the melodic modes of Indian classical music) is to colour or impassion, and *raga* is, at its core, a system that focuses on emotion and affect, used for pleasure as well as spiritual meditation, devotion and healing.[26] However, other traditions of music and dance involve heightened aesthetic and affective dimensions too, including popular film songs. The affective power, status and value (social, economic and cultural) that female performers' skilled labour provides them have been sorely neglected in modern views that put the women on the level of prostitutes. Their role as performers, entertaining their audience of listeners or connoisseurs (*shauqeen* or *rasiks*), also differentiates the interactions they share with these audiences and clients compared to those offering sexual transaction.

The new order: mapping legitimate and illicit zones in Indian performing arts

As modernity, nationalism, and colonial and bourgeois morality began to sweep definitively across India in the nineteenth and early twentieth centuries, performing arts changed radically. A series of colonial policies and a nationwide 'purity' campaign known as anti-*nautch* (anti-'dance') targeted *devadasi*s and *nautch* girls from around the first part of the nineteenth century, stigmatising them and ultimately excluding them from reformed performing arts. This opened the way for the entry of upper class/upper caste women into performing arts, with a new sociological configuration that removed the transgressive dynamics of class and gender of the public/erotic traditional female performers.[27] Dancing girls (and many male court musicians) also lost patronage when the princely courts were abolished at independence. In a much less confrontational manner, female impersonators were sidelined from high status theatrical traditions and were increasingly presented as out of synch with modern aesthetics of 'realism' and therefore 'unmodern'. Although issues of sexuality were not discussed openly, female impersonators were also seen as 'unnatural'. Despite their beauty and appeal *as* women, they were not 'real' women.[28] Female impersonators were big stars in the early twentieth century but have no role in contemporary high status art forms. As with classical performing arts, and indeed the cinema industry, 'respectable' women were sought out as performers.

The new cultural terrain did not include 'disreputable' female performers or female impersonators, many of whom would have been transgender. What, then, happened to these professional women and male performers? What happened to the dimensions of culture that involved females performing in public or for men? Unlike in the fictional *Pakeezah*, the old order was not destroyed full stop. Rather, a new chapter of performing arts began and, in North India, the art of these communities was limited to realms low down in the cultural hierarchy. An underground, illicit, 'other' world of Indian performing arts began to form, unseen in media and official representations of Indian culture except in terms of 'prostitution' or 'problems'.[29] The late nineteenth and early twentieth century thus saw a new axis of social, economic, and cultural inclusion/exclusion added to the topography of Indian performing arts, and the trajectory of this inclusion/exclusion has continued into postcolonial and globalising India. This 'reform' of classical performing arts was a project of construction, of nation building. However, it was also a project of exclusion. This book as a whole highlights this illicit world of performing arts, its relationship to legitimate culture, and the socio-cultural space it occupies. Zones of exclusion extend to other areas of performing arts, but it is in the illicit areas that they are most stark.[30] Here I will briefly outline some of the broad contours of inclusion/exclusion in comparison to more familiar conceptualisations of performing arts and culture.

The legitimate and illicit zones of dance and music cut across categories of 'classical', 'folk' and 'popular', forming a distinctive contour to the performing arts map.[31] In terms of legitimate performing arts, the reformed classical traditions are the most prominent and the most fundamental. Now firmly in the hands of upper class, upper caste India, they are held up nationally and internationally as the pinnacle of Indian performing arts. Certain folk traditions have achieved fame and acclaim or at least a place in the official sphere of 'Indian culture'. Hindi cinema, film songs, and Bollywood dance have also joined this zone of legitimate, officially-sanctioned culture since the 1990s, representing a new order of middle class culture. In stark contrast with earlier disapproval of commercial films (let alone live, Bollywood dance), the closing ceremony of the 2006 Commonwealth Games in Sydney saw Bollywood dance performed by, among others, several film stars. Indian embassies now host Bollywood or Indian cinema events. Bollywood has become a form of 'soft power' for India and (officially-sanctioned) 'Indian culture' has been revamped and expanded.[32] Bollywood 'popular' dance now overlaps heavily in terms of sociology, status, and types of institutionalisation with 'classical' performing arts and, in many ways, has more in common with classical music and dance than it does with the illicit world. In fact, the growth of 'popular' culture and the use of the term to describe it, tends to falsely imply that this is the culture 'of the people' of India. Rather than embracing all, it in fact embraces and legitimises only some—those in the middle class realm—and does so in a modern, bourgeois framework as opposed to a feudal one.[33] In these terms, this 'popular' zone can

Image 4: 'A retrospective of the films of Shahrukh Khan' film festival booklet sponsored by The High Commission of India in Nairobi and the Ministry of External Affairs, New Delhi in 2006.

hardly be seen as standing in opposition to elite culture, and to describe it as 'low brow' or 'unserious' does not seem appropriate.[34]

The illicit dimensions of Indian performing arts cut across categories of classical, folk and popular just as radically as the legitimate ones. Certain communities of hereditary female dancers were, only a hundred years ago, central to classical performing arts, and many still perform genres such as *Kajri*, *Ghazal* or *Qawwali* that are a part of classical music. They also perform dance that has a *kathak* basis. Today's *tawaif* exhibit less virtuosity than classical performers, since it is not the focus of the performance, and they are less highly trained due to social and economic inability to access training. However, in terms of genre and core aspects of style, many are still very much linked to the classical traditions.[35] More widely, dancing girls and transgender *kothi* dancers are involved with what can be described as 'folk' repertoire, including dramatic forms such as *Ramlila* and *Nautanki*. However, in the last few decades, all female public dancers have been performing increasingly to Hindi film songs in a range of private or ticketed parties or shows and within the 'folk' dramas. Similarly, *mujra*, which is performed by many hereditary as well as transgender dancers, used to be a mainstream part of the elite, classical performing arts traditions. Now, however, it involves, in large part, dancing to Hindi film *mujras*, or to Hindi film songs more generally, and in some instances involves practices like sexually explicit or nude dancing. Nevertheless, many dance moves used by *mujra* dancers derive from the 'folk', 'classical' or 'light classical' traditions that they perform(ed) as well as dances in Hindi films (which themselves have drawn on classical and folk genres as well as global styles).

The term 'public culture' has been used to describe the cultures of mass-disseminated products of, in particular, late twentieth-century India that link radically different sectors of society and for which traditional elite/popular or high/low divides are not appropriate.[36] As Pinney writes, the term aims 'to capture … the mainstream authorized quality of much Indian public culture, and still leave room for the subaltern'.[37] In many ways the term is appropriate for much of the cultures of performing arts I describe—for example, the radically different sectors of society that all now dance (in very different contexts) to the same Bollywood songs. However, the term 'public culture' does not highlight that there are two parallel worlds, with the subaltern as extensive as the official, and that this structure is a result of processes of exclusion that were originally used to demarcate the legitimate world. Moreover, the processes of exclusion go back to the late colonial period and hence long pre-date the advent of cultures of mass-disseminated products. Also, the phenomena I describe occupy realms that extend into areas that are private, hidden, or not talked about, so the term 'public culture' seems at times inappropriate.[38] The term 'vernacular' culture can be useful in discussing the unofficial world of performing arts in India, since much of it is related to regional, 'low brow' forms such as *Nautanki*, *Tamasha*, *Lavani* and *Bidesia*, which increasingly include film music. 'Vernacular' culture can also encompass wedding shows and processions and bar dancing, the latter an urban vernacular tradition.[39] However, the illicit cultures I describe also represent direct links with the elite, non-vernacular traditions, for example *mujra*, or communities of court performers turned sex workers turned bar girls. Furthermore, they at times feature extremes of illicitness and exclusion, which the term 'vernacular' does not imply—though 'obscenity' and 'vulgarity' have always been an issue in modern India's dealing with vernacular culture.[40]

Through a focus on the axis of exclusion that began in late nineteenth-century India, this book introduces a new representation of Indian performing arts. This is not aimed at definitively categorising Indian performing arts over and above other models and formulations, or denying their relevance. Instead it makes visible both historical and current processes, boundaries and dimensions of performing arts that have hitherto remained hidden from or dismissed in official or public discourse and are only beginning to be taken seriously by academics. Importantly, it also links performing arts and 'culture' with profound social, socio-economic and development problems—something terms like 'vernacular' or 'public' do not do per se—and raises important questions of heritage, social justice and nationalism. The model presents the official and the illicit dimensions of India's performing arts as two sides of the same coin. However, as history progresses, there are signs that these parallels are meeting and interacting in new ways, and the model may be seen as more than a merely binary one. Before reflecting on these new changes, I explore in more detail the nature of the axis of inclusion/exclusion, and the role of the overlapping modern ideologies of liberalism, rights, progress and nationalism.

Colonial and postcolonial modernities, collateral damage and performing arts

One of the points I seek to highlight in this book is the continuing and, in many ways, progressive nature of the processes of exclusion. Hereditary female performers and transgender performers have become steadily more excluded since independence, increasingly unable to sustain a livelihood of performing and more and more reliant on sex work. In parallel, the embourgeoisement of performing arts continues, with the emergence of 'respectable' Bollywood dance marking a new watershed. Here, I examine some broad discursive and political features of modernity that span, in various forms, colonial and postcolonial India, and look at how they have played a role in the seemingly inexorable exclusion of female public/erotic performers that has accompanied the building of modern India.

Politically speaking, it is crucial that the birth of independent India represents a break from the colonial past and, indeed, an emancipation from it. However, as postcolonial scholars have explored, colonial history remains relevant in terms of the ways in which it has 'determined the configurations and power structures of the present, ... much of the world still lives in the violent disruptions of its wake, and ... the anti-colonial liberation movements remain the source and inspiration of its politics'.[41] Many postcolonial studies focus on relations between colonised countries and 'the West' in the form of reactions against colonialism, anti-colonialism, and independence movements; on the dominance or continued dominance of 'the West' over (ex-)colonial nations; and on other consequences of colonialism such as diaspora and transnational migration.[42] In the case of performing arts, however, the trajectory of inclusion/exclusion has been one of continuation from colonial to postcolonial times *within* India. Such continuities or inheritances are inevitable and extensive—though far from straightforward—features of postcolonial countries and the postcolonial world.[43] They are politically difficult, since they conflict with the notion of emancipation and, in the case of the legitimate versus illicit zones of performing arts, the process involves a self and other who are both Indian, rather than the 'us and them' of the West and the colonised subject.

The axis of inclusion/exclusion that has shaped Indian performing arts in late colonial and postcolonial India has been influenced by modernity on many levels. Fundamental, in this regard, has been the use of 'scientific' forms of knowledge that seek or use universal categories, a tendency that continues in form if not always in content in the contemporary world. I explore this in chapter one in relation to hereditary female performers. Hereditary female performers were categorised as prostitutes under colonial ethnography and censuses, and were subject to the same treatment as prostitutes in colonial policies relating to public health. A viewpoint emerged in late colonial times that '*a public/erotic female performer is a prostitute and therefore not a performer*'. Fed increasingly by purity campaigns, it became authoritative in describing these performers. Scientific, 'rational' ideas were also behind the move towards 'realism' that sidelined female impersonators, alongside more (albeit covert) homophobic ideas based on 'naturalness' (the sexuality of such performers was far too taboo to be directly attacked, or even perhaps considered, by nationalists).

The equation of female hereditary performers with prostitutes and not-performers has continued in postcolonial India. In contemporary sociological and development work, the term 'prostitute' or 'sex worker' is often used in regard to public/erotic female and transgender performers in a way that does not take account of performing arts as a significant form of skilled labour, or of historical identity. Both female hereditary performers and transgender performers have also been marginalised through their relative exclusion from bodies of knowledge (academic or mainstream/popular) dealing with performing arts and culture. At the same time they have been included in those dealing with sociology, development, 'prostitution' and India's 'problems'. Meanwhile, public/erotic performers have continued to be vilified by much of society, as seen in the case of the bar girls in twenty-first-century Mumbai.

However, this construction of public/erotic performers as not-performers has been underpinned and often accompanied by moves to 'save' them from 'indignity' or 'exploitation' and has justified countless campaigns or initiatives that have undermined their livelihood and socio-cultural identity. Open forms of demonization or intentional exclusion have arguably formed only the tip of the iceberg of marginalising pressures. Hereditary female performers and *kothi*s now form a large part of a vast economy of female and male sex work. It is difficult to see that this is the outcome that colonial reformers or modern day believers in social and cultural 'purity' would want, however hypocritical their stance may have been or may be. With transgender performers, initiatives to fight for rights and build identity have similarly led to reduced recognition as performers, as I introduce below and explore in chapter six. What has been remarkable is the continual elision of these performers' history, the uncritical repetition of categories and agendas and discourses born in the late colonial era, and a growing notion and socio-economic reality that *kothi* and female hereditary performers are irrelevant, backward, 'problems' of society and, at best, in need of 'help'.

To understand the long trajectory of exclusion of public/erotic performers requires a broader consideration of modernity—its power, its vision and its blindness—than an analysis only of colonial knowledge and categorisation, or indeed of direct class/caste/gender power relations. The changes in class and values, as well as in the discourse that has constructed and misconstrued female public/erotic performers as outside of 'Indian culture' and cultural identity, have also been interwoven with and facilitated by ideologies of progress, rights and nationalism in various manifestations and operating at various levels. In addition to 'scientific' classificatory knowledge, these ideologies form an arterial link of colonial and postcolonial modernity in India and worldwide, and indeed are part of the bedrock of liberal democracy. What Kaviraj terms the universal 'beneficence' and 'invincibility' of ideologies of 'rationalist modernity' have been central to the legitimising and authorising of initiatives that undermine the livelihood of public/erotic performers. They have also been central to processes of prioritisation and elision that have enabled history and contextual details to remain unimportant. The result has been an escalating and mutually reinforcing pattern of loss of identity as performers, loss of livelihood, loss of social and cultural place and status, and an increase in prostitution. Furthermore, these ideologies can be seen to engender new and far more absolute modes of belonging and not-belonging. Through the constant framing of initiatives and arguments in vilification of or even in support of these performers, their once liminal identity has been pushed into one of black-and-white exclusion. The immense, complex and sometimes contradictory power of these ideologies are fundamental to what have been unintended or undesired consequences of interventions concerning public/erotic female and *kothi* performers. Thus this book frames the modern history of hereditary female and transgender performers in terms of the 'collateral damage' of continuing trajectories of modernity, which have, in the context of specific class/caste/gender relations and historical and cultural changes in India, engendered extreme, progressive, self-perpetuating cycles of inclusion/exclusion and bifurcation.[44] I focus in this section on the role of discourses of 'progress', rights and nationalism in the processes of exclusion that have overwhelmingly characterised the modern history of these performers. I also explore other potentials or consequences of these ideologies that are emerging in neoliberal India of the twenty-first century.

Ideologies of 'progress', 'freedom' and 'rights' in the modern history of female public/erotic performers

The power and persuasiveness of the ideologies of 'progress', 'freedom and 'rights' can be located in their universalism. So too, however, can the potential for distortion, destruction and carnage.[45] These ideologies present human goods as universally achievable. However, as Gray writes, universal human goods conflict:

> For humans as for other animals there are species-wide goods and evils. Drawing up a list is not easy, but fortunately that is not necessary. As soon as we find a value that looks universal, we see that it clashes with other, equally universal values. Justice clashes with mercy, equality with excellence, personal autonomy with social cohesion. Freedom from arbitrary power is a great good—but so is the avoidance of anarchy. Moreover, goods may rest on evils: peace on conquest, high cultural achievement on gross inequalities. There is no natural harmony among the goods of human life.[46]

In practice, particularity and politics must be confronted and universal ideologies are, at best, ill equipped to deal with these.

A universal ideology, by definition, is one that is applicable to all. This means then that it has no viable or legitimate 'other', or cannot accommodate an 'other' that is reasonable, rational, lawful, or rightful. This leads to inconsistencies as projects and initiatives conceived in terms of the universal human benefit are applied to diverse reality. Colonialism and liberalism illustrate this in many ways. A democratic country exerting non-democratic rule over non-democratically-acquired colonies is a good example of this inconsistency.[47] In the case of India, circles were squared with arguments that, for example, Indians were not ready for democracy. However, conflicts were also resolved through reforms that forced the 'other' to conform, leaving the universal vision intact.[48] Essentially the same problems and paradoxes of dealing with the 'other' exist within contemporary human rights, a universal ideology of progress and rights with the same roots as liberalism. The human rights corpus 'seeks to foster diversity and difference but does so only under the rubric of Western political democracy. ... In other words, it says that diversity is good so long as it is exercised within the liberal paradigm, a construct that for the purposes of the corpus is not negotiable. The doors of difference appear open while in reality they are shut'.[49]

However, the change and reform that liberalism and human rights impose is not merely a need for conformity to the universal vision. An ideology that sees itself as applicable and beneficial to the whole of humankind, and as promising 'progress', goes deeper than this. It implicitly encompasses a moral imperative for its own propagation. Liberalism, therefore, actively justified empire.[50] The drive to 'progress' of human rights, similarly, has an imperative to reform.[51] This moral imperative justifying a right and need to reform and intervene is widely made manifest in terms of what Mutua calls the 'victim-savage-saviour' metaphor.[52] This is true of the post-Second World War human rights movement, much grassroots advocacy and also colonial liberalism. In a progressive, liberal-democratic society, freedom of choice and human rights must be upheld, so people may choose anything as long at it does not conflict with the rights and freedoms of others. However, choice is also limited by the fact that people may not choose—or it is seen as impossible for them to choose—to be 'backward' or to be 'exploited'. To be 'backward' or 'exploited' makes them by definition a victim (of some form of savagery), and therefore in need of saving. As the conflicting 'other' is framed as victim or savage, their agency and legitimacy is denied and, paradoxically, this can lead to social and legal moves to deny their rights.

This tautology is particularly clear in the case of the choices of those who are moral minorities, such as public/erotic dancers. The discourse which surrounded them in colonial times and which continues into twenty-first-century India has become locked almost entirely into a victim-savage-saviour construction in a variety of non-debates, as I explore in chapters one and five in particular. With the erotic dancers, it was and is seen or portrayed as impossible—when it is actually just impermissible according to the values of the hegemonic group—that they 'choose' to dance erotically for men who shower them with money and desire to sleep with them, or to have sex directly for money or, in colonial times, be unmarried while also performing for the erotic pleasure of men, and having sexual relationships with selected members of their clientele. Such a position can only be seen to represent 'false consciousness', to use the language of the universal ideology of Marxism. Hence, in the case of the bar girls, various rights-based groups supported the ban on the grounds that the girls were being exploited and were therefore unable to make 'free' choices and needed 'saving'. Liberal reformists took this same stance on *tawaif* and *devadasi*s in late colonial India. On the other hand, right wing groups also supported the ban on the grounds that the girls were malevolent homebreakers and therefore criminals/savages/enemies of society. In clashes between the universal 'human goods' of 'progress', 'rights' and 'choice', one party in practice assumes authority over another and imposes 'choice' on them, while justifying it in terms of the 'greater good', protecting their (universal) human rights, or protecting others from their 'savagery'. The tautological manipulation of agency that so easily takes place with arguments of 'choice', 'progress', 'backwardness' and 'victimhood' is compounded by the fact that socio-economic disparity creates another dimension of 'backwardness' for figures such as female or *kothi* public/erotic performers. Furthermore, their identity as 'victims' or 'problems' is compounded by the interventions (colonial, government, non-government) that seek to 'save' them.

These discourses and the complex and often confusing situations they engender may be critiqued by identifying false universality.[53] However, this is difficult in many ways. The grandeur and universality of these ideologies tend to make specificities of social, cultural and historical context appear small or irrelevant, when it is in fact these exact particularities that show the falseness of the universality and the play of power and politics. This has been the story of public/erotic performers, who are discussed incessantly in terms of 'exploitation', of 'dignity', of 'rights', of victimhood (with some variation for female or transgender performers). They are not, however, spoken of in terms of more straightforward narratives and histories of marginalisation, which would show the degree to which 'reform' and 'saving' them has led to their socio-economic decline.

Similarly, universal ideologies inhibit critique through their all-consuming positive rhetoric. Because in theory they support widely agreed universal 'human goods', they are highly persuasive and emotional. They need to be so if they are to claim the universality of a self-evident 'human good'.[54] In this sense, universal ideologies distort. They overvalue the agenda they frame, and delegitimize, deprioritise, disguise or deny what lies outside it. Right and wrong tend to be dichotomised and impassioned.[55] Framing an argument in the form of these ideologies can make it awkward to criticise because it can leave the critic in a position of appearing to support human evils—hence to support the bar girls or, earlier, *tawaif*, was akin to 'supporting exploitation and indignity to women'.[56] In representing a will to 'rise above' petty or individual self-interest of particular groups and to strive for a common good, universal ideologies can be used to further certain interests precisely through denying that this is what they are doing. Thus the rhetorical potency of these discourses also serves to devalue history and details of social and cultural context (for example, the differences between a *tawaif* or bar girl and a prostitute) and has been key to the combined exclusionary power of discourse, socio-economic status, cultural place and livelihood in the modern history of public/erotic performers.

Human rights are political and depend on forms of social contract and symbolic exchange.[57] However, they are used as 'moral trump cards', tend to 'dogmatism', and are presented as non-ideological.[58] As Mutua writes:

Over the last fifty years the international law of human rights has steadily achieved a moral plateau rarely associated with the law of nations. A diverse and eclectic assortment of individuals and entities now invoke human rights norms and the attendant phraseology with the intent of cloaking themselves and their causes in the paradigm's perceived power and righteousness. [...] the seduction of human rights discourse has been so great that it has, in fact, delayed the development of a critique of rights.[59]

A similar statement could be made about the modern history of female hereditary performers, which has continued to evade a proper critique in the public sphere, facilitated by its envelopment in the 'moral plateau' of universal ideology.

Modern universal ideologies, nationalism, and modes of belonging and not-belonging

Universal discourses, with their focus on ostensibly good things such as 'progress', 'protection' of the weak and vulnerable, and 'equality', are seductive in a rhetorically positive sense; but their power also emanates through negative, punitive channels. Unlike Christianity and many other religions, however, where the threat of punishment and damnation is explicit, with the modern universal ideologies, the promise is only of good. The punishment can therefore only exist by default, and is veiled or denied. By allowing no legitimate or rightful 'other', universal ideologies can aid hypocrisy and be destructive in ways that go beyond denial of particular interests or histories. As Butler writes, 'That individuals were easily killed under the Reign of Terror for the sake of "absolute freedom" is well-documented', and that 'Those who are dispossessed or remain radically unrepresented by the general will of the universal do not rise to the level of the recognizably human within its terms'.[60] In the quest to unify humanity as a whole, humanity becomes on an important level divided into those who are for the greater good and those who are defined as against it, either because they oppose particular agendas framed in these terms or because they 'choose' or persist in 'backwardness' or situations of 'exploitation'.[61]

The victim trope also places people in a position of being less than human, or 'violated human', though potentially restorable to the universal, human level by being 'saved'. In this sense, universals gain power not just from denying or hiding specific political interests or justifying change and reform, but through the ways that they configure and mobilise identities and group dynamics. They place people 'in' or 'out' in ways that are potentially at the extreme of humanity and de-humanity. The levels of demonisation, disempowerment, deletion, displacement and negation of public/erotic dancers that continues in contemporary India can be seen as related to their constant framing in these discourses.

Nationalism also creates problems and paradoxes of belonging that can take on absolute forms and that justify extreme violence and exclusion. The ways in which it does so closely parallel the effects of universal ideologies. In liberal, democratic nations, the two forces occur together since universal ideologies are used to represent secular value systems on which to found belonging and project the greatness of the nation. Nationalism is also an ideology founded on rights and ideas of progress. While universal ideologies involve the formation of groups 'with' them and 'against' them, they tend to outwardly deny this through their universalism. Nationalism, on the other hand, is explicitly about a given group: a nation.[62]

Ignatieff sees nationalism's group dynamics in terms of Freud's 'narcissism of minor differences', labelling nationalist discourse as 'projective and self-regarding': 'A nationalist, in other words, takes "minor differences"—indifferent in themselves—and transforms them into major differences. For this purpose, traditions are invented, a glorious past is gilded and refurbished for public consumption, and a people who might not have thought of themselves as a people at all suddenly begin to dream of themselves as a nation'.[63] In parallel with universal ideologies, 'the systematic overvaluation of the self results in systematic devaluation of strangers and outsiders'.[64]

However, groups are not defined only through the marking of differences to those external to the group. As Ignatieff continues, 'the aggression that is required to hold a group together is not only directed outward at another group, but directed inward at eliminating the differences that distinguish individual from group'.[65] Nationalism projects a sense that the nation not only chooses to belong together, but that its unity is right and natural on the grounds of, variously, shared culture, ethnicity, religion, territory, history, rights, ideology and so on. In practice, however, it is the project of nationalism to make everyone within the nation conform and make them one.[66] This parallels the imperative of universal ideologies to reform and change. National identity remains contested and can change, but the dichotomy of belonging/not-belonging that nationalism engenders persists, since parameters of acceptable difference are never limitless. To a certain extent and under certain nationalisms, what can be termed 'internal outsiders' may fight for legitimate space and rights. However, in brief, it can be said that identity politics produce the same tendencies of exclusion, rigidity and essentialisation as nationalism. This is because nationalism too is a form of identity politics, as I discuss in chapter six in relation to processes of sexualisation among *kothi* transgender performers.[67] I comment more on the potential for excluded performers to appropriate discourses of rights and identity below.

India's erotic dancers—female and transgender—are in precisely the position of 'internal outsider'. Part of the process by which India's 'glorious past [was and] is gilded and refurbished for public consumption' involved and involves the denial of the erotic dancers any legitimate role in present or even past Indian culture. The reason for this is that they clash with bourgeois morals and the middle class control of national identity through culture; they thus lie outside the parameters of acceptability for Indian nationalism. Their identity is not legitimate on the important level of the nation, and is undermined through legal and social projects to reform, restrict or 'save'. These include anti-*nautch*, the banning of dance in beer bars in 2005 Mumbai, and article 377 of the Indian Penal Code, which criminalised sex between people of the same sex and other forms of so-called 'unnatural sex' (instituted by the British in 1860, and only successfully challenged in 2009 in regards to sex between two people of the same sex). More commonly, these ideological forces have fuelled (ab)uses of a wider range of laws against erotic performers, which I explore in chapter one.

Because nationalism links everyone in the nation together as one, inclusion and exclusion at the national level tend towards the absolute as opposed to the contextual or the liminal. Before all Indians became one nation, the status and forms of belonging of erotic dancers varied in different places. In certain contexts they had close and intimate relations with elites and groups of higher status but, in other contexts or other ways, relationships were taboo. In certain contexts they were important and powerful, and in others, they were unwelcome and derided. However, in the modern nation state of India, there is no official, legitimate, licit or even, in some ways, legal space for erotic dancers. Where more feudal mindsets predominate, they sometimes just about survive. But they are increasingly dealt with by NGOs, framed as victims or one of society's social or criminal 'problems'.

Crucially, under nationalism, the intolerance towards those who do not fit the nation, who hence undermine it, becomes the interest and indeed the right of all those who are a part of the nation, echoing the way in which universal ideologies create a moral imperative to act to reform or 'save'. For example, while elites interacted with and had (non-marital) relationships with courtesans, this did not affect who they were. Under nationalism, it does. Even the smallest minority can potentially be a threat to the identity and integrity of the whole, especially if they are a 'disreputable', moral minority, and especially if they are in a position of cultural prominence that comes to characterise the identity of the nation. This has been the case with female hereditary performers and, to a lesser extent, transvestite or transgender performers.

In a sense it is puzzling to see why the drives that are supposed to 'save' or 'help' erotic performers have compounded their exclusion. However, this increase in exclusion to an absolute can be seen as tolerable within these framing discourses. With an identity of not-belonging, they are less of a threat to the identity of the nation; they are neatly categorised as problems or victims, in contrast to the proud, glorious or 'gilded' essence of the nation. Similarly, under Bauman's analysis of modernity's abhorrence of ambivalence, they can be seen as having been pushed into the more acceptable category of enemy rather than that of stranger.[68] As 'problems', they become an object for the moral imperative of liberal democracy, something that justifies its greatness; as enemies, they compound the strength and identity of the (legitimate) nation of 'friends'.[69] The inclusion of erotic performers as beneficiaries or targets of development work also builds an identity for them as 'problems' or victims, something that parallels the prostitution policy and social reforms of late colonial India. It is highly significant that in virtually all attempts to help the hereditary dancers, the idea of artistic and cultural rehabilitation is avoided, since this would make prominent a lifestyle and a history that is at present 'estranged' to, and impossible to legitimise within, the national narrative.[70] At the level of cultural identity, therefore, it is possible to see development and underdevelopment as mutually interactive.[71]

Key to these processes and problems of identity formation and the dynamics of belonging and not-belonging is the fact that nationalism, like universal ideologies, tends to elide historical and often contextual specificities. These details would reveal and critique much of the (concealed) politics of these processes. In the context of universals, specificities are by definition secondary or irrelevant and easily dismissed or not mentioned. With nationalism they are easily subsumed under essentialism and primordialism with the rhetoric of 'blood and belonging', to quote the title of Ignatieff's book (2001). As Renan said, 'Getting its history wrong is part of being a nation'".[72] This is compounded by the impassioning effect of the imperative of 'progress' or salvation that nationalism promises its people, with nationalism relying heavily on the trope of the victim to legitimise and engender support for its agendas.

Possibilities for and signs of change in post-liberalisation India

This book involves a critique of these discourses of rights and liberalism that have subsumed the modern history of public/erotic performers and constituted a key force in their exclusion. However, since the 1990s and the 2000s, these very discourses have begun to be appropriated by these performers in ways that have benefitted them. The bar girls' successful 2006 case in the Bombay High Court against the dance ban on the grounds of constitutional rights to livelihood and freedom from discrimination is an illuminating example, which I explore more fully in chapter five. Similarly, *kothi*s have become involved in the LGBT (lesbian, gay, bisexual and transgender) movement that has emerged in India since the 1990s, fighting for rights of belonging and recognition. The implications of this are rather more complex for *kothi*s and their place in society than for the bar girls, and there are dangers of essentialisation and also of conflict, as I discuss in chapter six. However, there is potential for inclusion too, though in a very different framework. Thus this is a development that must be carefully examined.

Although there is an inexorable continuity of these core ideological frameworks into contemporary India, the resulting historical trajectories are not necessarily inevitable. Indeed, the dynamism and progressive nature of these ideologies arguably makes change more likely. At some stage, continuity begins to constitute change, and there is potential for new things to happen. For example, the middle classes, having followed a long trajectory of liberal 'progress' in terms of women's rights and, more recently, sexual liberation, are now able to look upon erotic performers such as bar girls not just more sympathetically but also more empathetically. Indeed, the bar girls became something of a cause celebre. Thus, while they are still a small minority, activists and some middle class people are able to see the hypocrisy in the banning of bar girls while sexy Bollywood dance is allowed, as well as to look back on the courtesans with very different eyes from those of the British or the bourgeois nationalists of the nineteenth and early twentieth centuries. This was key to the judgement against the ban on dance in beer bars. Similarly, (small) parts of mainstream India are increasingly sensitised to homosexuality (though usually only in terms of elite and global gay/lesbian identities rather than traditional figures such as *kothi*s or *hijra*s), and there is potential for a reconsideration of the cultural role of female impersonators, including those who are transgender. Thus, there are signs that there is potential for change to the binary zones of legitimate versus illicit performing arts that have developed from the nineteenth century. The processes of inclusion/exclusion have become accelerated and consolidated since liberalisation; however, this period is also opening up real signs of possible change.

While researching and writing this book, I have become aware of the significant role that modern discourses have played in the marginalisation of public/erotic performers. I have become critical of them as a result. However, I have also increasingly realised the inevitability and potential—as well as the problems—of 'fighting fire with fire': the bar girls and other erotic performers fighting back and asserting their rights to belong, to work, to choose, to legitimise their lifestyle. Indeed, the history of rights and liberal discourse has been one of increasing appropriation by those who were denied such rights and of the growing impossibility of denying equal rights to these groups of people.[73] Thus, to quote the title of Bayly's recent book on Indian liberal thought, liberties may be 'recovered', whether by the colonised or by lower classes, blacks, women, LGBT people, sex workers, and so on. These groups may learn to speak back to former oppressors in the same language, indeed, often in a more sophisticated version of it, and thus become in certain ways included or equal. Given the above discussion, I am certainly not presenting these possibilities in a salvationist guise. However, rights are de facto the building blocks of the law, the state and the globalised world of liberal democracy. Rights therefore offer potential tools for groups and individuals to fight for themselves on their own terms, and there is a history of powerful precedents of such processes of appropriation.

These appropriations of rights and liberal discourses, and indeed, new sympathetic positions created through liberal social transformation, are very recent, arguably a result of India's liberalisation and globalisation. It is therefore impossible to comment on them here in anything but a speculative way. However, I highlight two particular approaches: labour, labour rights and livelihood, and heritage. In addition to the potential legal power of these approaches, at the discursive level they could temper the essentialising tendencies of identity politics grounded in sex and gender that are increasingly framing *kothi*s, as I discuss in chapter six. Similarly, they could form something of an antidote to and critique of the simple equation of female hereditary performers with prostitutes.

The notion of performing arts as labour is something that emerged powerfully in the bar girls' case. The history of female erotic/public performers has involved a negation of the value of their skilled labour, and a refusal to give it any social, economic or cultural value whatsoever, so subsumed was the debate with questions of the moral and universal good and society's 'reform' and 'progress'. While mainstream society still does not, broadly speaking, tolerate female public/erotic performers, it is crucial to separate these questions of morality and progress from the actual difference that a capacity and context within which to perform makes for these performers, in terms of socio-cultural place, status and belonging, and direct economic livelihood. The right to livelihood is a constitutional right in India. Moreover, notions of the value of labour are central to market economics, capitalism and class stratification and are well theorised in these fields. Radical discourses based on labour are of course also highly developed in Leftist politics.[74] Thus labour and livelihood offer important and sophisticated frameworks for discussing female hereditary or *kothi* performers.

Questions of heritage and ownership of culture are becoming increasingly pressing and politicised in the contemporary world. Intellectual property rights, intangible cultural heritage and indigenous or collective rights are all legal and political frameworks for apportioning culture's value in ways that aim to be just and to protect minorities in particular.[75] In these frameworks, culture is valued not just for its financial potential but also for its importance to identity and belonging—for an individual, a group, a minority or a nation. Questions of cultural ownership are often riddled with problems: who 'owns' culture, in what senses can it be owned, and how can it be sustained? Such considerations also tend to remain grounded in or limited by nation- or ethnicity-centric notions of culture, multiculturalism and identity politics and themselves construct histories and meanings that are far from neutral.[76] However, they nevertheless offer tools of legitimacy and agency that could potentially benefit India's hereditary female and *kothi* performers, as well as other marginalised performers. This would not be easy. In addition to the degree of stigma and denial surrounding these performers, further difficulty stems from the fact that the performance 'tradition' can be separated from the performers themselves. Indeed, in the case of classical music and dance in particular, these traditions are seen as having been 'saved' precisely in having been 'rescued' from 'disreputable' female or low status male performers. Thus the 'heritage' exists, but with very different culture bearers. However, campaigns of sensitisation and the use of these discourses of heritage could help construct these performers as a part of Indian culture with a legitimate claim in it, at least in terms of their identity and history.[77]

Recovering histories, valuing performing arts: the aims of this book

My own discovery of the illicit worlds of performing arts happened by accident in 2006. Researching a project on Bollywood dance, I followed up leads to bar girls in Mumbai. I then found myself in the loop of an underworld of Indian dance. From the dance bars I was led to communities of struggling contemporary courtesans, of court dancers turned sex workers, of males dancing *mujra* in female dress and seducing their male audience, and of a range of traditions such as wedding processions, dance shows, *Nautanki*, and *Lavani*, which involve female hereditary performers and/or *kothi*s/female impersonators, often interchangeably. I had been studying Indian performing arts, language and culture for thirteen years at that time, and was shocked that I had no knowledge of this extensive dimension of Indian culture. None of this world is visible in general accounts of 'Indian culture'. Over the course of my fieldwork, I witnessed remarkable talent and saw some deeply inspired dancing by female *mujra* and *kothi* performers. I also saw real desperation, exclusion, and a collapse in socio-cultural status, with lives and livelihoods made impossible or next to impossible. While there was energy, enthusiasm, talent and skill, there was only, at best, decreasing contexts within which to use them. Increasing stigma and hopelessness abounded. Writing this book thus has a strong ethical imperative. It aims to tell untold histories, to reveal unseen cultures, and to present a more accurate picture of the terrain of Indian performing arts. It also aims to give new perspectives on different phases of Indian modernity and concomitant questions of belonging and power—from the colonial, to the postcolonial, to the neoliberal-postcolonial. While the possibility of recovering liberties is a barely formulated notion for public/erotic female performers at present, this book aims to recover histories, or the knowledge of their lack, and analyse the processes of exclusion. Doing so will raise questions of culture, heritage and social justice in connection with these performers in India's past, present and future. Momentum is building rapidly in terms of research on female performers, on processes of exclusion in performing arts, and on 'low brow' cultures. This book aims to contribute towards the building of a critical mass on such topics that will make them more likely to be addressed in the mainstream by decision makers.[78]

My approach in this book is to seek to understand the present through looking back into history. My methods involve contemporary fieldwork and a descriptive, empirical approach. My understanding of these modern histories, however, has been particularly inspired by political, theoretical, philosophical and critical work on modernity, its ideological structures and its internal contradictions, and particularly that which focuses on liberalism, rights, progress, science, categorisation, nationalism, neoliberalism and belonging/not-belonging.[79] This study is, in its focus on discourse, centrally inspired by classic works by Foucault and Judith Butler.[80] However, it is also focused on the empirical reality of socio-economic exclusion of female hereditary and *kothi* performers in contemporary India. In this sense, it looks not just at discourse and history, but the 'materiality of discourse'.[81] The focus is, therefore, one that pertains to development, but with a poststructuralist and postcolonial approach that strongly interrogates development in terms of universal norms, standards, expertise and categories.[82]

This project is underpinned by a wealth of material on Indian performing arts and, as a whole, is grounded in an ethnomusicological approach, which seeks to understand social and political processes through music and dance. The approach affirms the integral and structural place of music and dance in lived human reality and identities and, crucially therefore, sees their value, power and substance.[83] It is allied particularly to 'applied ethnomusicology' and the emerging sub-discipline of 'development ethnomusicology'.[84] Here again it links with movements in (postmodern, poststructuralist and postcolonial) development studies that see specific histories and culture as key to understanding and addressing a range of development problems in ways that go beyond 'culturally sensitive development'.[85] While gender, sexuality and feminism do not form an overall frame for this book, these fields are of central importance to its content, in particular to the core problematic of the female performer, and to the study of *kothi* performers as female performers. This study is also of relevance to subaltern and postcolonial studies, and approaches from these disciplines are potentially useful in dealing with the material.[86]

This book begins with a historical overview of female hereditary courtesan-type performers. It examines the process of their stigmatisation and loss of livelihood in colonial India. It then turns to the repetition and continuation of this history in post-Independence India, looking at how such performers have been represented—or not represented—in academic and mainstream sources, and how laws (dating back to colonial India) are used/abused in ways that make a livelihood of performing almost impossible. The second chapter turns to a sociological examination of these hereditary female performers, looking at the tribes and communities they come from, examining questions of identity and social mobility. It then looks at various groups in present day India. Drawing largely from ethnographic sources, it briefly traces their history and considers their growing involvement in sexual transaction. The third chapter then introduces a less well-known dimension of Indian performing arts: transgender performers. It looks at their place in history through written sources and then examines the relationship of femininity and dance in this arena, drawing on ethnographic sources and theoretical approaches.

The second part of the book shifts to studies focusing on twenty-first-century performing arts culture, based largely on fieldwork. I look in more detail at the legitimate and excluded worlds in descriptive terms. However, I also explore the way in which, post-independence, the trajectory is not just a continuity or a repetition, but is a progression, a phase two. Paradoxically, because of this, it shows nascent signs of possible fundamental change. In chapter four I focus on the legitimate side of Indian performing arts. I look at the Bollywood dance revolution of post-1990s India and the Indian diaspora as a new watershed in the embourgeoisement of Indian performing arts. I parallel this to the earlier reform of Indian classical performing arts and drives for respectability in the Indian film industry. While there is no active link between the growth of Bollywood dance and the continuing exclusion of low status public/erotic 'traditional' female performers, I explore how this new level of sexual liberation in modern middle class India remains the other side of the coin of exclusion. I also describe how this causes a definitive shift, by which the illicit world may be judged in new terms, since it creates a terrain in which sexy performing arts by female performers may be legitimate. This is a crucial step in the story of the bar girls, which is the focus of chapter five. I look at the arguments used to ban the bar girls, the tautologies and gulfs in understanding among middle class India, as well as the new directions that this remarkable episode showed—in particular, the new readiness of some feminists to support such figures and the importance of a discourse of labour. Finally, in chapter six, I turn to the contemporary world of *kothi* dance, looking at contexts and genres of performance, changing patterns of livelihood, and the loss of socio-cultural space. I examine the involvement and role of NGOs and CBOs with *kothi* performers, looking at challenges and possibilities of advocacy, the fight for rights of belonging, and how this is transforming their socio-cultural space.

I then conclude with reflections on the role of labour, of heritage, and of the value of performing arts in a modern nation state. While the book critiques rights and liberalism, and analyses their role in over a hundred years of exclusion of public/erotic female performers, I reflect again on these ideologies in terms of their internal logic and their potential for conscious appropriation to provide new paradoxical twists to the patterns of inclusion/exclusion. This could shift the binary model into something new, which is interconnected in ways other than opposition and exclusion.

1

THE CREATION AND RECREATION OF INDIA'S ILLICIT ZONES OF PERFORMING ARTS

DYNAMICS OF EXCLUSION IN COLONIAL AND POSTCOLONIAL INDIA

In this chapter, I outline processes of exclusion of hereditary female performers that stretch from the first part of the nineteenth century through the twentieth and into the twenty-first. I first describe the colonial period, examining how initiatives, laws and campaigns identified female hereditary performers as prostitutes rather than performers, and attacked—sometimes directly—their livelihood. These reforms saw courtesans and dancing girls disappear from high profile and, in nationalist terms, legitimate, cultural life. Thus, by default, an arena of illicit performing arts was created, and an overarching axis of exclusion brought into being in the terrain of Indian performing arts.

I then turn to the post-independence period. Post-independence India has seen a continuation and, to some degree, acceleration of the deterioration in the status and livelihood of professional female performers. I focus on the means and mechanisms by which this has taken place, looking at knowledge, discourse and representations as well as policies and law. In the case of some communities of hereditary performers, the total transformation of the livelihood of women into a highly organised form of commercial sex work, with no involvement in dance, is something that has occurred only since independence. Similarly, the vernacular theatrical traditions have in many cases begun to break down as a viable livelihood for female hereditary performers only in the last few decades, involving increasing sexualisation of performance and more and more transactional sex. Large numbers of girls from hereditary performing communities, including those who had known only sex work as a livelihood, had become involved in the Mumbai dance bars since the 1980s. However, dancing in these bars was banned following a campaign approximating an 'anti-*nautch* II', and the girls lost their livelihoods. I examine these developments in more detail in later chapters. However, first I explore the core framework of exclusion of female hereditary performers.

Stigmatisation and the loss of status and livelihood of hereditary female performers in colonial India

Communities of female performers who existed outside the realm of marriage; performed in front of men or public audiences; and engaged in non-marital relationships have been a central part of Indian culture and performing arts for millennia. They have ranged from what can be described as courtesans, the most elite performers for which historical sources exist in abundance, to more general communities of *nautch* girls or *baijis*, who performed classical or local performing arts traditions in court contexts, to lower status 'street performers who entertain at festivals, and weddings' and who are associated with lower class clientele.[1] As Srinivasan writes, 'The Indian courtesan pervades pre-colonial art, literature, mythology, texts on rituals, polity, pleasure, and law books in the three major religions founded on Indian soil'. She terms these women 'keepers of culture'.[2] Courtesans also played a key role in public ritual and religious occasions, seasonal festivals, *melas*, marriages, and *urs* celebrations.[3] Patronage of these female performers continued through most of the colonial period by princely courts, where they performed in the courts themselves, as well as in temples and for some public occasions.[4] Lavish *nautch*es or 'dance performances' were held for British officials by Indian kings and nobility.[5] *Nautch*es were also used for high profile official occasions, such as the visit of the Prince of Wales in 1875, and that of his son in 1890.[6] Courtesans were also socially influential. Oldenburg quotes Sharar's mocking account of courtesan culture:

> ... It became fashionable for the noblemen to associate with some bazaar beauty, either for pleasure or for social distinction. A cultivated man like Hakim Mahdi, who later became Vazir [prime minister], owed his initial success to a courtesan named Piyaro, who advanced her own money to enable him to make an offering to the ruler on his first appointment as Governor of a Province of Avadh. These absurdities went so far that it is said that until a person had associated with a courtesan he was not a polished man.[7]

As major forms of patronage began to die out with the demise of courts, courtesans and dancing girls entered the new forms of public culture that emerged from the late nineteenth century and, in particular, the twentieth century. They retained a central part in culture until the 1930s. In her historical study of *tawaif*, Sachdeva describes how elite courtesans, trained in poetry and performing arts, were able to take advantage of what she terms technologies of 'print and self', and 'image, sound and self' to become celebrity performers and glamorous stars across North India from the late nineteenth century.[8] With cheap technologies of print and photographic reproduction, glamorous images of them and their *tazkiras* (collections of songs and poetry) could be circulated beyond their traditional elite audiences and patrons.[9] *Tawaif* also became popular subjects of orientalist operas and operettas, and European performers such as Ruth St Denis were influenced by their glamour and exoticism.[10] *Tawaifs* were also, as is well known, among the very first recorded artistes in India (with Gauhar Jan recorded in 1902). They continued to be high-profile artistes as gramophone culture gained pace.[11] At that stage there were no non-*tawaif* professional female singers and, equally importantly, *tawaifs* were the most sought after performers in courts, earning more than male performers.[12] Their place in the world of recorded music was a reflection of their high prestige as star artistes in courts and cities, and enabled them to reach out to new audiences in the early twentieth century, gaining a modern celebrity status connected with mass media.

Female performers also entered the new public culture via urban theatrical traditions. These included the Parsee Urdu Theatre, which was a high profile form of entertainment in late nineteenth- and early twentieth-century Bombay, before it was superseded by the cinema and the Marathi theatre.[13] Female performers, though presumably not the highest status courtesans, also entered vernacular theatrical traditions such as *Nautanki* for the first time, where previously only males had been used in female roles. Female professional performers entered the new cinema industry, where they were, in addition to Anglo-Indian and Jewish actresses, the biggest stars of the 1920s and 1930s.[14] High-class courtesans had initially shunned the cinema industry, considering it below them. However, dancing girls of the more common variety had been performing live at film screenings from the 1910s.[15] In the 1930s, the emergence of the talkies gave a renewed importance to courtesan actresses who were able to sing and speak with good Urdu diction.

The more elite courtesans and dancing girls thus continued to be at the centre of high profile cultural life in the early twentieth century, becoming celebrities in the modern sense with the advent of new media of dissemination and reproduction that vastly multiplied their audiences beyond the traditional elite. Gaisberg, who made the first commercial recordings of Indian artistes in 1902, described Gauhar Jan, one of the *tawaif* artistes he recorded, in his 1942 book *The music goes round*:

> Her flair for publicity is well illustrated by the feast she once provided for her cat when she produced a litter of kittens. This affair cost her 20,000 rupees. There were hundreds of guests, so naturally this feline function became the talk of the bazaars...[16]

However, by the mid-twentieth century, courtesan performers in India were nowhere to be seen in the emblematic national cultural forms of classical performing arts and the cinema, as I discuss in chapter two. Some former courtesans continued as performers in the (re)created classical arenas, but they joined mainstream society through marrying. No courtesans living in their traditional manner retained a role in classical performing arts or indeed the cinema after around the mid-twentieth century. Courtesans, *devadasis* and other erotic performers increasingly came to be seen as prostitutes rather than performers. In policy, law and also social campaigns, a combination of stigma and loss of livelihood dramatically changed the social status and place of these performers. Here I outline the creation of what became a mutually reinforcing nexus of exclusionary forces that has continued into postcolonial India.

Colonial knowledge, policy and laws

One of the main ways in which the identity of female performers was changed was through colonial ethnography and censuses. These classified female performers in rigid and also negative ways. In a drive to understand and hence better govern/control India, and within the paradigm of science and 'progress' that so strongly underpinned the British sense of their own right to rule, the colonial government undertook ethnographic studies and enumerations of peoples in the subcontinent. These studies are important sources of data but, at the same time, must be analysed in terms of the power their 'objective', 'scientific' knowledge came to have over Indian subjects.[17] Caste was transformed in terms of its rigidity and significance.[18] In the case of female performers (and also male performing groups), the processes of categorisation and the census reports also solidified formerly fluid categories:

> As social groups, the performing communities were flexible and included men and women of varying religious and caste affiliations. This ability to move across regions also meant difficulty in compiling clear classifications of these groups. Ethnographers were initially confused by their patterns of mobility and loose religious or social identities. However by the late 1860s ethnographic indexes and the census reports had become authoritative and wrote these flexible groups into rigid castes and religious categories as a process of social enumeration.[19]

At the same time, female performers were increasingly identified simply as prostitutes, a trend that the ethnographies themselves contributed to. Sachdeva reveals the emergence and growth of a caste of '*tawa'if*' in Awadh, which by 1891 came to be listed with 216 sub-castes. She argues that '*tawa'if* was not a term for a caste initially', but 'slowly transformed into a caste over the years', becoming amalgamated with other groups and communities of singing and dancing girls.[20] While the ethnographic studies included some reflection of different ranks and types of female performing communities, albeit categorising them under 'dancers and prostitutes', the census was cruder. As Sachdeva writes:

There had been distinctions between low ranking prostitutes and the *tawa'if* but there had also been overlaps. However, by the late nineteenth and early twentieth century, these distinctions had completely been erased by the census reports that made them all into a caste of prostitutes.[21]

The rigid and essentialised categorisation of the ethnographic studies and censuses thus erased 'the complexity within these groups and their histories'.[22] This is a process that has continued in various ways into twenty-first-century India.

Further solidification of the identification of courtesans and dancing girls with prostitutes came through measures targeted at the protection of British officers against venereal disease (VD). Since at least the late eighteenth century, lock hospitals had been used as a way of protecting British officers from VD by forcibly isolating sick prostitutes and treating them. These initiatives were turned into law with the passing of the Contagious Diseases Act (CDA) in England in 1864, and in India in 1868.[23] In 1864, the Cantonment Regulations were also passed, making the *lal bazaars* within cantonments that catered for British officers a form of legally regulated prostitution.[24] These Regulations also gave the Municipal Committees the right to relocate prostitutes. The Cantonment Regulations and the CDA included *tawaif* in the category of 'prostitutes'. As well as the damage to pride and status that came from being grouped together with common prostitutes, *tawaif* were also subjected to enforced examinations and treatment for VD.[25] The CDA and Cantonment Regulations also involved the relocation of courtesans to places outside of the city, greatly impacting their status in society.[26] By making the anti-VD measures law, the CDA also opened up the problem of abuse by policemen and others involved in law enforcement. This resulted in harassment and violence against female performers and prostitutes, which continues in postcolonial India through the use of laws relating to trafficking and obscenity, as I discuss below. Oldenburg interviewed an elderly *tawaif* in 1976, who 'told of incidents where women were abused, insulted, and beaten "by these coarse, low-caste policemen who took revenge on the women they coveted and lusted after but had neither the money nor the courage to visit"'.[27]

The CDA became an issue among British feminists in the late nineteenth century who staged protests against the violation of prostitutes' rights through enforced treatment. They also drew attention to the hypocrisy of placing all the responsibility for the spread of VD on the prostitutes rather than the men who visited them.[28] The CDA itself solidified and institutionalised the connection of even elite female performers with prostitutes. The fight for its repeal also reinforced the association of these performers with prostitutes, since misunderstandings of the special status of female performers existed on both sides of the CDA debate. Lord Robert, Commander-in-chief of the British Army in India in 1885, defended regulated prostitution in India, stating that:

prostitution is a trade amongst the natives and is practiced all over India; shame in a European sense does not attach to it. Mothers bring up their daughters to the vocations that they have followed themselves.

In a reply to this sweeping generalisation, Josephine Butler stated:

We know there is a recognised class of prostitutes in India, but they are a class apart. These *Nautch* girls and Temple girls are too well off to stoop to take the wretched four annas (less than an English four pence) the 'regulation price' which a British soldier is commanded to pay to the half starved slave who under military rules, ministers to his lust.[29]

Lord Robert's assertion that 'shame in a European sense does not attach to it' is in certain ways true in the case of the hereditary female performers. Yet his statement implies a moral degradation in comparison to Europeans rather than an alternative system of gender and social organisation—a lack of morality rather than a different kind of morality. It also fails to understand that elite female performers in particular have strong codes of dignity and etiquette, as noted by Josephine Butler. However, she simply identifies them as *elite* prostitutes, rather than seeing their extensive cultural and social roles. This inability to distinguish between different systems linking sexual and economic ties continues in contemporary development work, and itself regenerates the equation that a public/erotic performer is not a performer but a prostitute. It reinforces the notion that cultural and artistic status and skilled labour have no significance, further undermining social status and identity. While there were certainly distinctions between women living within and outside of marriage, colonial knowledge and later social purity campaigns made these distinctions more rigid, essentialised and morally polarised.

Another important paradigm that can be seen emerging regarding the CDA and the wider women's question is the rights-based arguments that structure players into victims, perpetrators and saviours.[30] In the case of the female performers and prostitutes, as Levine states, debates on the CDA and regulated prostitution show female performers and prostitutes were dichotomised into a position of 'victim' by missionaries, or 'dangerous outcaste' by colonial government.[31] This way of thinking is very much evident in the present day, and has had significant consequences in the approach of government and non-government organisations to dancers and prostitutes. These powerful universal ideologies and moral discourses tend to sweep away crucial details of the social, cultural and historical context of female performers, reinforcing crude dichotomies and inaccurate categories, which in turn affect their identity and livelihood. I discuss these matters in particular in the context of the bar girls.[32]

The CDA was repealed in England in 1886 and in India in 1888, but regulated prostitution continued till the late 1920s in cantonments.[33] However, new ideas were introduced into India and other colonies that, 'as indigenous reform movements, assumed a life of their own'.[34] Of key importance for female performers was the anti-*nautch* movement, discussed below.[35] These ideas of 'purity' still exist in postcolonial India, and formed a movement of considerable scale against dancing in bars from the early 2000s.

Another dimension of colonial policy and law in the stigmatisation of female professional performers is the 1871 Criminal Tribes Act (CTA), which marked a major new stage in the colonial government's strategy for dealing with criminality. Under this act, it was possible to declare an entire tribe as criminal. Members of Criminal Tribes thus notified could be forced to report regularly to officials, to have their homes inspected by police, to be restricted in their movements, to be resettled, or even to be placed in reformatory settlements, which the Salvation Army became involved with from the early twentieth century. The CTA was revised a number of times before its repeal after independence in 1952.[36] However, it was still possible to label a whole tribe to be criminal and the fundamental components of reporting, restriction, and settlement, remained—although not all communities were resettled, and not all members forced to report. On the repeal of the CTA following independence, all the affected communities became Denotified Tribes (DNTs). In present day India, all the female hereditary performers, including those lineages of elite courtesans, are DNTs. DNTs remain the most marginal category within Indian society.

The CTA targeted vagrant, itinerant, and nomadic or semi-nomadic tribes. Some were involved in criminal activities such as dacoity or petty thieving, though this was in many cases as a result of loss of livelihood due to modernising changes, as Radhakrishna argues in the case of the *Koravars* (2001). Some of these tribes were, however, only under suspicion because they were nomadic, semi-nomadic or 'gypsy' peoples, with the British unable to understand their role in local economy and society.[37] Among the itinerant and gypsy groups targeted were many performers and entertainers, including the hereditary female performers, some of whose menfolk were also involved in petty criminal activities, and some of whose menfolk were also performers.[38]

It is very difficult to ascertain the extent to which criminal notification affected communities of female performers or other itinerant performers. Research on DNTs is scant, and reflects the low profile of this group who never had a leader like Ambedkar to force their interests onto the national consciousness.[39] The most significant source on the effects of criminalisation on a performing community is Agrawal's work on the *Bedia*, which includes a focus on their history as a 'criminal tribe'.[40] The *Bedia* were only officially notified as a Criminal Tribe in 1913, but were referred to before that in the context of 'criminal' groups.[41] Agrawal cites sources from the colonial era as suggesting that the *Bedia* identity arose 'as a consequence of some of the erstwhile "criminal" tribes giving up both, their wandering lifestyle as well as engagement in criminal activities'. She sees an increased reliance on dancing and prostitution as a result of the *Bedia* becoming a settled community and as a means of escaping 'state persecution'.[42] She states:

> ...prostitution was considered far more legitimate than many other activities in which the members of these communities were alleged to be involved. Rather than forming the basis of their being notified as a criminal tribe, prostitution was a valid occupational identity many groups adopted in order to escape state persecution.[43]

There are no other studies that focus in this depth on entertainer communities and the important question of whether women performed or not, and who their patrons/paramours were. Most studies focus on the work of the male members of the group. Radhakrishna's book on *Koravars*, for example, states that, in addition to a number of occupations, principally cattle breeders, the *Koravars* 'were also acrobats, dancers, singers and fortune-tellers'.[44] Gandhi's study of DNTs in Andhra Pradesh provides information about the *Dommaras*, including their role as acrobats, dancers and singers, and clearly (although pejoratively) outlines their alignment with the paradigm of the traditional female public performer, glossing music/dance as 'prostitution':

> The treatment of Dommara women is very peculiar. From early infancy, they are trained in the mysteries of rope dancing and tumbling. Those who prove themselves adepts are reserved for prostitution and the rest are allowed for marriage.[45]

However, there is no information on how the livelihood and cultures of performing arts sustained by *Dommaras* were affected by criminal notification and settlement.[46] Another problem is that, in many cases, it is only certain subgroups or communities in particular areas that are involved in performance (this is the case with the *Doms*, for example).[47] It is still not possible to find comprehensive data from secondary sources on which communities were settled—information that would be of immense importance in terms of the history of female performers, and their livelihood and status. There is a need for much more substantial research on these topics in order to investigate the effects of criminalisation specifically on performers and performing arts, including on their status and livelihood, without conflating performing arts with prostitution. Criminalisation and settlement took place within the same period as the other colonial policies and laws that stigmatised female professional performers and placed them in rigid and inaccurate categories. It is potentially an extremely important factor in the dramatic loss of status of female performers during the late colonial period.

Anti-*nautch* and social reform

The anti-*nautch* campaign grew from the indigenising of reform and social purity movements started by British and other foreign reformers and missionaries initially around prostitution and matters of sexual morality. The campaign was a part of the larger movement to reform the status of women that gained critical mass in the late nineteenth century.[48] It was a movement against *devadasis* and courtesans in South India as well as North Indian courtesans and *nautch* girls. References to anti-*nautch* can be traced as far back as the first part of the nineteenth century, according to emerging research.[49] Existing sources trace the anti-*nautch* campaign to Madras in South India in 1892, perhaps suggesting a growth in momentum and scale at this time from much longer-term activities.[50] Pivar states that 'nearly all Indian reform associations had pledged support to the purity movement, including the antinautch and temperance agitation', and Sachdeva writes that, by 1898, out of 63 Indian reformist organisations, 'about 14 of them had passed resolutions to prohibit *nautches* or *nautch* parties as part of community weddings and celebrations such as Holi'.[51] In addition to upper caste Hindus, foreign Christian missionaries were also involved, and both aimed to stop *nautch* parties and the inclusion of '*nautch* girls' in high profile events by directly confronting those who were holding them.

Anti-*nautch* propaganda presented *nautch* as a 'social evil' and used vitriolic and alarmist material in its attempts to keep people away from what was seen as its degenerative influence. For example, the Madras Christian Literature Society, which had initiated the anti-*nautch* movement, had one pamphlet warning that attending *nautches* could lead to 'loss of wealth, bodily weakness, disease and harm to personal character'.[52] The drastic warnings of the dangers of *nautch* girls and *nautches* echo the cautionary tales of Mughal India. However, the cautionary tales differed from the anti-*nautch* propaganda in that they did not warn the Mughal *mirza* or 'gentleman' away from courtesans per se. A balanced amount of engaging with music, love and literature in the company of courtesans was positive and a part of being a gentleman, as Brown describes in her discussion of masculinity in the Mughal *mehfil*.[53] Rather, it was an excess of attachment to courtesans and to music and poetry that was emasculating. Here it is possible to see a clear move from a liminal social and cultural place in which courtesans were both central to and potentially transgressive of elite society, to one where they were seen as destructive and negative in a black-and-white sense.[54] In contemporary India, such warnings continue with stories of ruin at the hands of bar girls. Nationalism involves the imagining of all Indians as one group, with a shared identity—and hence small parts can affect the whole. Thus the behaviour and morality of courtesans and the old elites affected the identity of new middle classes, and engendered a need and a right to object that had not existed before.[55]

The anti-*nautch* campaign also affected the film industry directly in the 1920s. As Bhaumik writes:

> In the period following 1925, the industry came under increasing criticism from social workers and cultural critics for immorality. The hiring of dancing girls as actresses was seen

as dragging the brothel into the studio. A social worker's written statement to the ICC stated: "It is a fact that among cinema actresses there are a large number of dancing girls and common prostitutes. Some of these have not abandoned their former profession… I believe that it is owing to the fact that they continue as prostitutes that the industry is looked down on, and that some measure of control and inspection is necessary".[56]

The presence of such women was thought to bring disrepute to the industry, and inhibit 'respectable' women from working there.[57]

Overall, a critical mass of consensus that female performers were prostitutes and a danger to society was achieved, and it gradually became a solidified 'truth' in wider culture and literature. Chatterjee describes the image of prostitutes in Bengali texts of the nineteenth century, examining the novel *Swarnabai*, written in 1888 by Sri Nabakumar Datta.[58] This story clearly conflates courtesans and prostitutes, with the heroine first moving from child widow to prostitute, suffering the pain and indignities of venereal disease. She then learns music and dance and becomes a courtesan, but grows bitter and becomes addicted to alcohol. Then, 'unable to live on her own and thus exploited by young male servants', she again contracts venereal disease, and then tries to become a procuress. She becomes 'diseased in mind and body', horrified by what she has become. She is then 'saved' by a foreign missionary woman, is reformed, works as a maid, and later lives as an ascetic widow in Benares, where she dies.[59] Similar social reform themes against dancing girls were also played out in film narratives of the 'social' genre that emerged in the 1920s:

The social-problem film usually dealt with the problems of drink, gambling and promiscuity affecting the ideal Indian family, especially in times of economic hardship. … *Gunsundari* (Kohinoor, 1927) tackled the problems of an overworked husband and his housewifely spouse. Fed up with the daily drudgery of his life, the husband takes up with a dancing girl, forcing his wife to come out of her seclusion. Similar films made in this period include Royal Art Studio's *Gentleman Loafer* (1926) in which the dancing girl Gulab and her accomplice Durmad received 'just punishment' for destroying a family.[60]

Some important quarters resisted the anti-*nautch* campaign, and '*nautch*es continued to be held for English guests in princely courts till 1915'.[61] Many princely courts also continued to employ courtesans up until they were finally abolished after independence.[62] In private, courtesans still continued to be patronised by the elite of (former) royalty and landowners till well past independence. The Madras Devadasis Prevention of Dedication Act of 1947 effectively banned *devadasi*s in Madras, though they had stopped dancing, and in some cases temple worship, far earlier.[63] There was no such blanket, legal banning of 'secular' *nautch* girls in the North. However, the level of stigmatisation of *nautch* girls and courtesans meant that they were marginalised from the cinema industry and the classical traditions, leaving room for middle class, 'respectable' women to enter. They disappeared from legitimate and high status cultural traditions, and their arena became a low status, illicit one, increasingly so in the twentieth century following independence, and particularly since the 1980s and 1990s. *Nautch* girls and courtesans have in many ways also been written out of the history of classical performing arts and Indian film as I discuss below. These performers, previously central to culture and society, apparently ceased to exist.

Some *devadasi*s and courtesans 'ceased to be' through marrying and thus merging with 'respectable' society, a process which continues in contemporary India. This 'self-reform' is played out in many novels and films, as the prostitute/dancing girl is 'rescued' and either undergoes penance or manages to marry. This was indeed the aim of many reformers who wished to 'save' *devadasi*s, courtesans and prostitutes.[64] In real life, some courtesans were able to join the new classical traditions through marrying and leading 'respectable lives'.[65] A well-known example of this is Begum Akhtar, who stopped performing after marrying, and started again only after her husband died.[66] However, the majority of women from these communities continued in the traditional paradigm, and now probably number into the hundreds of thousands.[67]

The repetition and consolidation of history: Continued dynamics of exclusion of female erotic performers in postcolonial India

The 'evil' of *nautch* was not eliminated. Rather, it went underground, involving far more prostitution, less 'choice' and a lower status for the women involved. The 'death of the courtesan tradition' was the birth of the illicit realm of performing arts.[68] However, this new realm of illicit performing arts did not remain static in postcolonial India. Rather, the pressures that led to its formation in the late colonial period continued after independence and this illicit realm, as I describe in the following chapter, has continued to involve more sex work, less performing, an increasingly marginalised social status, and increasing social stigma. The 'monster' that was made by colonial modern India has continued to be made and remade in the postcolonial period, up to and including the campaign that saw tens of thousands of bar dancers in Mumbai lose their livelihood.

Here I look at how the exclusionary forces set up in the colonial period continue in postcolonial India. In the first section, I explore parallels of discourse in the colonial and postcolonial eras in relation to the marginalisation of erotic female performers. The view of courtesans and *devadasi*s as just 'prostitutes' was rooted in Victorian morality and (mis)understandings of Indian society and history. Here I explore how the equation, '*an erotic/public performer is a prostitute and therefore is not a performer*' continues to be (re)constructed in postcolonial India, shaping what is seen to be 'truth', what is sayable and what is unsayable, and acting as a self-fulfilling prophecy. While colonial knowledge has been critiqued for its inappropriate and fixed classifications, in postcolonial India, boundaries and rigidities created by categorisation and analysis and by demarcations of different fields and disciplines continue to affect the visibility and identity of female hereditary performers.[69] This is the case even with some critical academic work. I examine the ways in which female erotic performers continue to be constructed as not-performers, as prostitutes and as external to 'culture' in academic work and in work deriving from the broader public sphere or world of development. I examine journalistic discourse and public debate in more detail in chapter five in the context of the bar girls, where I also focus in more detail on discourses of 'rights' and 'freedom'.

In the second section, I turn to an examination of legal and practical restrictions on female hereditary performers in post-independence India. In colonial India, once they had been constructed as prostitutes, the female hereditary performers became subject to a range of laws and initiatives concerning prostitution. Similarly, in independent India, a number of laws, many of which were instituted in colonial times, are used to control prostitution, obscenity and trafficking. The (ab)use of these laws continues to make a livelihood of dancing and singing unviable for hereditary performers due to practical restrictions and stigmatisation. Hence, the law continues to be a part of the continuing vicious circle that names and treats public/erotic female performers as prostitutes and not-performers and results in their turning increasingly to prostitution.

Knowledge and representation of female erotic performers in literature on music, culture, and development

The deduction that 'an erotic/public performer is equal to a prostitute and therefore is not a performer', and its power to bring about a self-fulfilling prophecy has resulted in—and is in turn reinforced by—clear biases in the representation of these performers in academic and also more mainstream development-oriented and journalistic writing. Overall, erotic performers are with few exceptions discussed either under a rubric of performing arts and culture, or from a more development-oriented approach relating to questions such as prostitution and HIV/AIDS. Literature focusing on performing arts has typically either neglected these performers; or it has described them as a 'degenerate' chapter in the history of the great classical traditions; or it has studied them only in the context of the past. The present reality of these performers is generally discussed in the context of studies of prostitution and questions of 'development' rather than performing arts or 'culture'. In such studies, there is typically little knowledge or awareness of their present or past involvement in performing, or of the history that has seen them transformed into illicit performers or commercial sex workers.[70] Hence the equation remains and continues to self-reinforce, and there is scant work that critiques it through marrying the present existence and reality of erotic performers or sex workers from performing lineages with their centuries-long cultural role, their distinct sociology, and their modern history of exclusion. This arguably severely impedes their achievement of real forms of social justice. It also underpins present initiatives, campaigns and information in the public sphere that compound and continue their exclusion.

Critical scholarly work on courtesans and *devadasis* has emerged only since the 1980s. Srinivasan's ethnography of *devadasis* was completed in 1984, and her well-known article 'Reform and revival', examining the politics of exclusion of *devadasis*, in 1985. Substantial numbers of ethnographic and critical studies of or relating to *devadasis* have ensued, including critical examinations of their place within the history of South Indian traditions such as *Bharatanatyam* dance or Carnatic music, as well as in the context of gender.[71] More recently, Weidman's book on the (re)invention of Carnatic performing arts includes a chapter on female performers, and Soneji's monograph on *devadasis* represents a major publication, focusing on the present as well as the past of disenfranchised *devadasi* lineages.[72] However, there are still studies that see *devadasis* as an institution that became 'degraded', in particular by Muslim rule and Indian royal elites.[73] The idea of corrupted 'nuns' or, more simply, prostitutes still dominates the popular view of *devadasis*.

Academic work on courtesans in English also started at a similar time, with key work by Veena Talwar Oldenburg, Joep Bor, Peter Manuel and Jennifer Post.[74] Wider work on particular instruments, repertoire, and other aspects of North Indian classical music has also been crucial in writing these performers into history.[75] Work focusing on or relating to courtesans has continued to emerge in the late 1990s and 2000s.[76] In Hindi, Nagar's 1979 study on *tawaif* was groundbreaking, and continues to inform other work. However, it was only in 2008 that a book-length historical study on *tawaif* was completed, in the form of Shweta Sachdeva's PhD thesis. Although work on courtesans is gathering pace, they still remain largely written out of history or recorded as a 'degraded' chapter.[77] With North Indian courtesans, it is not only the desire to morally censor Indian music history that causes their exclusion, but also the desire to delete Muslims and Mughals from performing arts heritage. Courtesans are commonly seen to be a Muslim phenomenon, and are used to underpin the trope of the 'degeneration' of culture under Muslim/Mughal decadence.

Studies in English that focus on *tawaif* and other erotic performers as a part of contemporary India have taken even longer to emerge, pioneered in particular by Macisewski.[78] Articles by Oldenburg and Qureshi focus on courtesans in a more traditional yet marginalised guise in 1970s and 1980s Lucknow.[79] Nagar's 1979 study is also important, dealing with the problems of (formerly) elite courtesans in the decades following independence, including the raids of 1958. More recently, two books on *tawaif* in contemporary Lahore have been published.[80] Apart from a few very notable exceptions, it is also only into the twenty-first century that work dealing with female professional/hereditary performers beyond what are known to be (formerly) classical courtesans has emerged.[81] Mehrotra's 2006 biography of the *Nautanki* artiste Gulab Bai marked a new watershed in the study of female theatre performers, and Bhaumik's work on performers in the early Indian cinema industry also provides unprecedented information on dancing girls and courtesans, many emerging from the demise of court patronage in the 1910s–30s.[82] Work on contemporary South Indian hereditary female performers is even more recent. Jairazbhoy and Catlin's 2008 film *Music for a goddess* focuses on (low caste) *jogti*s dedicated to the goddess Yellama, who have active performing roles but are widely known for their involvement in prostitution. Soneji's monograph on (middle to upper caste) *devadasi*s marks a new level of study of these communities in contemporary India, and their enduring relationship with performing arts.[83]

This relative neglect or denial of the importance of female hereditary performers in the classical traditions and beyond reflects the late nineteenth-century construction of these women as prostitutes and not-performers, and their exclusion from the official establishment of classical performing arts.[84] Such performers are, for this reason, not on the radar of those wanting to study 'music'. Indian and Western scholars tend to be aesthetically and socio-economically elite, and hence have typically only encountered and been attracted to the classical or 'pure' folk traditions—or 'respectable' Bollywood—and not to traditions that are increasingly intermixed with transactional sex.[85] The methodology of studying Indian classical music through learning with a particular guru also tends to inhibit delving into the muddy waters of historical or gendered sociology, due to concerns of loyalty to the guru, or the need to enter their worldview.[86] Similarly, scholarly biographies or oral histories of female performers are sensitive and difficult. Qureshi's work on Begum Akhtar is an exception, as Akhtar did not attempt to hide her courtesan past.[87] Mehrotra's book on Gulab Bai is also remarkable in this context, though it is significant that Gulab Bai was a *Nautanki* rather than classical artiste.[88]

These long-standing biases are only beginning to be undone in academic work, where there is now a tangible sense of critical mass in scholarship on historical and even contemporary excluded female performers. In more mainstream work, however, the idea that courtesans and *devadasi*s are irrelevant to 'Indian culture', a 'degenerate' chapter of the great classical traditions, or a nostalgic part of India's courtly history now (safely) in the past is still an established 'truth'. Little has changed since the days of anti-*nautch*. Popular biographies of performers with *devadasi* backgrounds, including those that moved into the film world, do not generally mention their past. Similarly, popular biographies of performers of classical music and dance, as well as those of film actresses, gloss courtesan backgrounds. An autobiography of Malka Pukhraj, translated into English by Saleem

Kidwai, glosses her hereditary courtesan background and musical and literary training in terms of 'education' and 'a love of music and dance', which is presented as leading her into her profession.[89] Rare exceptions are a recent biography of M.S. Subbalakshmi in which her *devadasi* heritage is foregrounded in an entire chapter called 'Family, Caste and Gender'; and a book on the film star couple Nargis and Sunil Dutt, which tells the story of Nargis' famous courtesan mother Jaddan Bai.[90] A *devadasi* or courtesan lineage remains extremely problematic for contemporary classical performers and, generally is politely not mentioned. In the volume on classical dance in an 'Incredible India' series (published in association with the Department of Tourism, Ministry of Culture of the Indian government), there is no mention of *devadasi*s in relation to *Bharatanatyam* or of courtesans in relation to *Kathak*.[91] Similarly, in the volume *Regional Theatres*, there is an avoidance of any discussion of the sociology of female performers of *Nautanki*.[92] These matters are raised in the section on *Tamasha* and *Lavani*, to the degree that female artistes are said to have suffered from 'exploitation'. However, the non-marrying sociology of *Lavani* performers and their role as erotic performers is not mentioned.[93]

In films and literature, courtesans and *devadasi*s are typically presented as victims rather than professionals. Other forms of erotic dancers are found in Hindi films, namely cabaret dancers, vamps, and item girls. Here too, however, there is no representation of their sociological and cultural reality, and their importance lies in providing music and dance spectacle, pathos, and/or a moral compass to set the heroine against. The threat that their transgressive behaviour raises is always neutralised through the victimhood trope or other mechanisms and shows how enduringly problematic these erotic female dancers are for the popular imagination.[94] The coverage of bar girls in the press and their representation in films continues this kind of presentation, as I discuss in detail in chapter five. The extent to which erotic performers are seen as external to performing arts is attested to particularly strongly by the fact that a significant amount of work on courtesans and *devadasi*s as performers (as opposed to as 'prostitutes') has been done by scholars outside of performing arts disciplines. Srinivasan is based in Anthropology; Nair, Bhaumik and Sachdeva in History; Rege within Sociology and Women's Studies; L. Brown in Sociology; Soneji in Religious Studies; Mehrotra is an independent writer; Saeed a journalist; and Nagar an author and journalist.

In terms of daily reality, some communities of performers are now entirely engaged in sex work, and, for both female and transgender erotic performers, the overall trend has been one of increased reliance on a labour of sexual transaction rather than of performance. This has been especially so since the 1990s, as I discuss in chapter two and chapter six, in relation to female and transgender performers respectively. In this way, these increasingly disenfranchised performers or ex-performers are inevitably and also correctly considered in the context of studies of prostitution or HIV/AIDS. Several publications discuss dancing girls more or less briefly in studies of ancient, nineteenth-century, and contemporary prostitution.[95] Forbes' well-known book, *Women in Modern India*, also includes information on dancing girls and *tawaif* in the context of women and work.[96] A number of contemporary studies of such groups and prostitution also exist.[97]

This literature gives important information about the historical and everyday reality of the involvement of these communities in prostitution. However, the conflation of these performers with prostitutes is not problematised and this work therefore has contributed to or become a part of the larger construction of these performers as prostitutes and not-performers. While work on music and dance—when it avoids the 'degeneration of tradition' trope—is well aware of their cultural importance, the contemporary development-oriented work in particular has a limited understanding of these communities as performers. There is little awareness even of the fact that, before modern reforms, a female public performer could not be married, and that 'respectable' women could not perform. This knowledge, however, is crucial to understanding their transformation into prostitutes and their present development needs. It is only a limited number of scholars who combine in their work the cultural, sociological and historical aspects of communities of erotic performers with the present development issues of exclusion, poverty, or prostitution.[98]

The more development-oriented literature also suffers from a tendency toward rigid categorisations that reflect development as a vast, highly professionalised, globally-integrated system. As Kothari discusses, the skills of highly trained professionals who are able to work on development projects anywhere in the world are favoured over the kind of in-depth local knowledge that was more characteristic of colonial officers.[99] Categories and jargon have tended to become universalised, and history and local context less significant. The under-emphasis on history and context is also related to development work's core focus on universal rights, poverty or injustices, which represent apparently more compelling needs and issues than details of history and context; and also to more or less explicit normative ideas of modernisation or progress. Significant academic work exists that re-theorises development studies to move against this tide.[100] However, in terms of female erotic performers, in almost all cases I have seen in development work and in the media, the categories of 'prostitution', 'trafficking', 'sex work', and 'exploitation' tend to be used rigidly and sometimes polemically. There is strikingly little perceived need to critique the category of prostitution itself. In a situation where the construction of the erotic performer as prostitute has been so instrumental in their real exclusion from performing arts and in their involvement in prostitution, this is extremely problematic and parallels colonial knowledge exactly. I review in some detail selected parts of the literature on female erotic performers here, aiming to show the groundbreaking information they provide and, at the same time, the fundamental problems that still linger. It is especially important to address these problems because, unlike most work on music and dance, this body of work feeds into and also results from the actions of NGOs and other decision makers that have direct influence on the future of these communities.

Agrawal's 2008 monograph on the *Bedia* forms an unprecedentedly detailed study of a female hereditary performing community who, except for bar dancing, are now only involved in sex work. The book gives an immensely rich account of the current situation of family-based sex work and the implications this has for the whole kinship system. It constitutes a rare ethnography of a community that is not open to outsiders. Although it relies on an over-rigid use of the category of 'prostitution', the thorough nature of the analysis implicitly reveals in places certain problems with the conflation of performer with prostitute and the importance of more refined categorisation.

Agrawal states that elder generations of *Bedia* women were performers who had often long-term, concubine-style relationships with men. However, she identifies this as 'sex work/prostitution', 'akin to prostitution', or 'sex work of one kind or another' throughout.[101] She acknowledges that there are differences in these systems and the more modern forms of sex work:

> The nature of their engagement in this trade indeed differs from one region to another, within a region and interestingly, amongst different generations within a kin group as well. There are differences between urban and rural forms, between artistic and non-artistic commercial forms, as of course between relatively old and new forms that may sometimes be apparent even within a single context. Different forms involve different kinds of occupational demands, training, earnings, and relationships. The particular setting in which I have conducted my fieldwork consisted of women primarily engaged in commercial sex work but there were also a few belonging to the older generation who were involved in singing and dancing activities in their youth.[102]

However, she does not see these distinctions as of fundamental importance. Rather, she states that her aim is to explain the 'structural features of the community'—most significantly, the 'chaste wives and prostitute sisters' and the fact that women either do sex work or marry—rather than these differing kinds of 'sex work'.[103] Arguably, this is missing the crucial point: the understanding of the history of this community as performers is crucial to understanding the rationale of the 'structural features' of its social organisation of sex work. Agrawal writes of the *Bedia*:

> It is … truly unusual when a family's economy is primarily dependent upon the labor of unmarried daughters. Moreover, when we find that such a practice is accompanied by an institutionalized 'non-marriage' of daughters, the significance of such dependence is not difficult to assess. It is this condition of dependence on unmarried and not-to-be-married daughters that renders the *Bedia* family economy singular.[104]

However, as described in the introduction to this book, the mutually exclusive zones of the married woman on the one hand and, on the other, the female public/erotic performer (courtesan, *nautch* girl, *devadasi* and *kothi*), can be traced back centuries or millennia, and relate to the conflict of embodied, performing arts in a patriarchal society. Agrawal refers to *devadasi*s, but does not point out that the present dichotomy of 'chaste wives and prostitute sisters' is a modern continuation and variation on what is in fact an ancient paradigm. Agrawal addresses the question of how long the *Bedia* have been involved in prostitution, but conflates prostitution with being a dancing girl. This confuses in many ways the question of whether sex work in the *Bedia* is a 'tradition'. While *Bedia* performing and becoming concubines to upper caste men may be interepreted as a 'tradition' that can be traced back to at least the late nineteenth century, and in other cases much further back, the current system of sex work can not.[105] Furthermore, although the *Bedia* may not have been performers/prostitutes with indefinite historical depth, the paradigm of the female performer who does not marry is something that can be traced back to ancient times. In other words, the book makes clear distinctions between various forms of 'prostitution' on the one hand, and marriage on the other—a black and white distinction which is in many ways the legacy of the reform period.

The conflation of female public/erotic performers with prostitutes that is so ubiquitous in their representation since the late nineteenth century fails to take seriously the significance of music and dance performance as skilled labour and a crucial factor in socio-economic status and identity. Agrawal's detailed study of labour, economy and kinship in fact implicitly sheds light on the significance of this skilled labour. She explores how stable relationships of concubinage that *Bedia* women could once have formed with men are now not encouraged, since if a woman forms such a stable relationship, she leaves sex work and stops supporting her family.[106] Girls hence avoid doing this out of loyalty to, or fear of alienating, the natal family, which continues to own their labour due to their non-married status. However, in previous generations, women did form long-term or even permanent relationships with upper caste men. A crucial difference here is that previously, women who were performers could have long-term relationships but still support their family through continuing to perform. Or, in cases where the paramour refused to let the woman continue to perform, he would be expected to support the family, in addition to his own family. This is clearly shown in Mehrotra's 2006 biography of Gulab Bai, a *Bedia Nautanki* performer, and can be seen in other contemporary *Bhatu* performing communities, such as *Kolhati*, which I describe in chapter two. There is a clear conflict between marriage and the structures of a patriarchal society on the one hand, and a woman performing in public or being involved in sex work on the other. However, with sex work, the conflict is total, in that the labour itself is a sexual relation. With performance, the labour implies impurity or availability, but is still separate or separable from a sexual relation itself. In this way, the more a community is involved in sex work, the more difficult it becomes for women to have long-term relationships, since it conflicts with the family's control over labour, and there is no other form of labour to compensate. Furthermore, few men are willing to provide this level of compensation, due at least in part to the fact that to keep a performer was and still is prestigious for certain classes of men, whereas to keep a mistress or a prostitute is not, or is less so. Hence, sex work can be seen to increase because of the dynamics of labour and kinship, and not just due to the stigmatisation and loss of status, identity and livelihood that I focus on in much of this book. It is crucial to note that women—and *kothis*—who are performers are paid far more for sexual relations than those who offer just transactional sex because of the status that their skill in performance brings them. As the skilled labour of performing arts is significant to the social economy and has a calculable financial value, it is clearly not the same as 'prostitution' or 'sex work' in terms of labour and social status.

Agrawal's book categorises the *Bedia* as representing a form of patriarchy, again in somewhat rigid terms. Her research convincingly argues for the revision of previous interpretations of courtesans as matrilineal (in particular Oldenburg's well-known study of 1990) by taking into account the male members of the family.[107] Courtesans certainly traced their artistic identity in matrilineal terms, and they also owned their own establishments. But this is different from stating that their families were, in essence, matrilineal, or even a 'resistance' to patriarchy. Qureshi terms their social structure as 'loose matrilineality', and explores the balance of matriarchy/patriarchy in some detail.[108] To say, however, that the *Bedia* constitute a form of patriarchy is also an essentialisation, since the women are the main earners and, previously, the labour of some *Bedia* women involved the special artistic skills of singing, dancing or drama, which became an extra-familial lineage of social, economic and cultural importance. In-depth studies of *devadasi* kinship exist.[109] However, the same is not true of courtesans, and it is a topic that needs further research. Categorisations in terms of patriarchy or matriliny also need historicisation in order to take into account the disempowerment of these women. Loss of power occurred as a result of losing status as artistes and also, in many cases, losing ownership over the means of production in terms of ownership and control of their own establishments.[110]

The problems of the uncritiqued category of 'prostitution' and the dangers of a heavy reliance on (supposedly) universally applicable categories and theoretical terms in (albeit ethnographically grounded) literature can be seen when comparing this type of writing with work of a more narrative and descriptive type. The image of the *Bedia* and their history presented in Agrawal's monograph is very difficult to square with that of, for example, Mehrotra's biography of Gulab Bai.[111] Mehrotra's book explains in much more qualitative and contextual detail the kinds of relationships and the lifestyle Gulab Bai and other female members of the family had, including the roles of male family members. It is clear that the labour and the identity of *Bedia* women like Gulab Bai was fundamental to their social economy. According to Agrawal's analysis, however, it would be necessary to describe Gulab Bai as 'akin' to a prostitute. This is something that would be unacceptable to the culture Gulab Bai lived in, where women like her were, de facto, ranked as superior to and distinct from common prostitutes.[112] While there is little mention of the structural importance to the community of artistic skills and livelihood, Agrawal uses an image of a woman dancing on the front of this book, presenting this type of dancer as an iconic representation of a prostitute, thus compounding, rather than critiquing or historicising, the anti-*nautch* legacy. Again, this is common. A newspaper article on the Calcutta sex workers' collective Durbar used an image of a dancer or bar girl as an illustration.

SEX WORKERS' OFFER

Taxes to keep police at bay

Rakeeb Hossain
Kolkata, March 1

SEX WORKERS in Bengal want to talk business with the state government. We are willing to pay if you promise to keep the police away, they have said in a proposal they intend to present to the finance ministry next week.

The sex workers have worked out the arithmetic. The state exchequer will gain at least Rs 5.4 lakh a day or Rs 1.62 crore a month from the 60,000 sex workers who were willing to pay.

The payment will be recovered from the clients. "If their proposal is accepted, they will charge each of their clients Rs 5 extra," said Dr Smarajit Jana, chief adviser to the Durbar Mahila Samanwaya Committee (DMSC), which has over 60,000 of the state's nearly 80,000 sex workers as its members.

Dr Jana said that Rs 3 of the extra charge would go to the exchequer, while Re 1 would be "condom charge". The remaining Re 1 would go to the Self Regulatory Board which looks after their health and other problems.

On an average, a sex worker gets three clients a day.

"We are ready to pay to the government and in return we want the police atrocities on us to stop," said Gauri Das, president of the DMSC. "We want to be given the right to live and carry on with our trade peacefully."

Government officials said the proposal would fail as the sex 'industry' was illegal. Finance ministry officials said the Social Welfare Department will look into the proposal if it is sent to them. The department's principal secretary Sheikh Nurul Haque said: "It is not possible for the government to accept money from sex workers."

Illustration : JAYANTO

Image 5: Motif of a dancing girl used to illustrate an article about Calcutta sex workers with no traditional performing background.

Another important set of recent studies of the *Nat* hereditary performing community focuses on HIV/AIDS and development issues.[113] This work draws together health and development specialists with those who have local, ethnographic knowledge. It looks at current commercial sex work but states that it is essential to understand the cultural history of the sex workers in order to understand their present predicament, giving the examples of *devadasi*s in South India, and *Nat* in Rajasthan. These publications are unusual in locating the modern form of sex work in longer-term cultural forms and of combining development/sociology concerns with history, context and culture. Indeed, these publications constitute the most detailed information available on *Nat*. However, at the same time, there are some important elisions. The articles state the loss of patronage of *Nat* as having resulted in destitution and the recourse to sex work. However, the move to sex work has been far more specific, since as public/erotic dancers, *Nat* women were already practicing a form of labour that combined music and dance with eroticism and sexual availability (to specific, elite patrons), and they existed strictly outside of marriage. Thus a loss of artistic labour logically or naturally led to an increased reliance on sexual labour. Furthermore, although they cite many sources on *devadasi*s, including those with a critical and political focus, these articles do not mention the systematic stigmatisation of these performers by mainstream society from the nineteenth century.[114] Notwithstanding the importance of these articles in historicising the *Nat* and sex work in terms of lost artistic labour, they paradoxically slip into a conflation of performers with prostitutes through the term 'traditional sex work', a new category used in development work which further seals the image of a female hereditary dancer as a prostitute or sex worker—the legacy of anti-*nautch*.[115]

A source of information on communities of hereditary performers/sex workers that represents a collaboration of academic and government development organisations is *A report on trafficking in women and children in India 2002–2003*, by the Institute of Social Sciences, National Human Rights Commission, and UNIFEM.[116] This 443-page report is comprehensive in many ways, and the twenty-six chapters include one on 'Culturally sanctioned practices and trafficking', which discusses *devadasi*s and communities such as *Bedia* and *Nat*.[117] The report follows the familiar narrative of 'culturally sanctioned practices' that have 'degenerated', and in the case of *devadasi*s, upholds the myth that they were a 'purely religious institution' before 'degeneration' into 'a great social evil'.[118] Notwithstanding the moralistic language, the *devadasi* as a solely religious figure or 'nun' is something that has convincingly been shown to be false.[119] The report is also extremely selective in its sources. It cites many sources on *devadasi*s in particular, but omits those that critically study the politics of *devadasi* reform. Nair's article states, for example, 'As the *devadasi*s were symbolically and materially deprived of their resources, and consequently unable to practice their artistic skills, they were reduced to the status of proletarianised sex workers'.[120] The report does not cite any of the major sources on courtesans that tell so clearly of the loss of livelihood and prestige following campaigns by bourgeois society. It relies particularly on one source, Jogan Shankar's *Devadasi cult: A sociological analysis.*[121] The publication is at times clearly moralistic about the 'degeneration' of the *devadasi* institution and courtesans in North India and emphasises the role played in this by Mughals, Muslim rulers and Indian elites. For example, in a paragraph on 'alien rule' in North India quoted in the report, it is stated that Aurangzeb ordered singing and dancing girls to marry or leave his kingdom:[122]

> An anarchical period followed the death of Aurangzeb and lasted up to the advent of British rule in India. This period became notorious because the standard of morality among the princes and public men sank to the lowest level. Their sensuality affected their court and through them it reached the general populace. As a result of this, there was enormous increase in prostitution. These women were called for dancing at wedding feasts or other private entertainments. Dancing and prostitution had become inseparable in India since the earliest period.[123]

Sen and Nair's report, on top of this thin and clearly biased 'analysis' of 'culturally sanctioned practices', employs a number of powerful universal terms and buzzwords with little attention to exactness. Firstly, the report includes *devadasi*s and courtesans under the category of 'trafficking'. This term implicates force into this form of labour whereas, most typically, erotic female performers were born into such roles.[124] While being born into any profession represents a lack of 'choice', the term 'trafficking' makes a blanket conflation of hereditary female performers with girls deceived, kidnapped and sold into sometimes bonded sexual labour that is grossly inaccurate. Similarly, the report states that *tawaif* and other 'castes' of performers have become 'victims of CSE [commercial sexual exploitation]'.[125] These labels of CSE or 'trafficking' are extremely powerful, and, like human rights discourse in general, can be used to trump or end debates.[126] In terms of the moral outrage and the crude categorisations that glaze over crucial facts of history, sociology, labour and culture, this report represents a close parallel to information from the late colonial period. However, with its academic-style referencing and use of contemporary 'development' categories such as 'prostitution', 'trafficking', and 'CSE', it exudes an air of authority, neutrality, and ethical soundness.

Practical and legal restrictions on dancing girls and mujra in post-independence India

The anti-*nautch* campaign resulted in legislation in certain areas that prohibited the dedication of girls to temples in order to become *devadasi*s. However, there was no legislation against secular courtesans, *nautch* girls, or *mujra* that banned them or made them illegal per se. Rather, it was the stigmatisation and boycott of the performances of *nautch* girls that caused irreparable damage to their status and place in society and to their livelihood. Since independence, there have been no nation-wide social reform campaigns comparable to anti-*nautch*, and there have not, on the whole, been any outright bans deriving from new legislation. In other words, *mujra* or *kotha*s are not banned outright, but rather, restricted, controlled, shut down or made economically unviable. The case of the dance bars in Mumbai, which I discuss separately in chapter five, is unusual in the history of North India in that it constituted an actual ban made by the amendment of an existing law.[127] Hence, in a similar manner to the late colonial era, the key driving force of the practical and legal restriction of these performers continues to be stigma, which in turn fuels a vicious circle. The stigma of these performers drives the (more or less tenuous) local application of a variety of pre-existing laws to raid premises, to arrest women working there, or to shut down premises. Similarly, the legal restriction of these performers drives their stigmatisation, as they continue to be denied a viable space to carry out their livelihood as artistes, and clients are put off by police raids which mark their premises as illicit or illegal.

A thorough investigation into the legal issues that have affected female hereditary performers in post-independence India would constitute an important piece of work in itself and is certainly beyond the scope of this study. However, in overview, it can be stated that it is laws that pertain to prostitution and trafficking; obscenity and nuisance; and the licensing of musical performance or commercial premises that are key to the ability or inability of female entertainers to carry out their business. There has been a mixture, variously, of lack of clarity in many of the laws; lack of education, knowledge of rights and self-organisation on the part of female performers; social stigma; and downright abuse by police. These factors have left female hereditary performers vulnerable to raids and harassment, the closing down of their establishments, making their livelihood as performers impossible, which has invariably pushed them closer towards sex work.

The Indian Penal Code (IPC) of 1860 includes various clauses that relate to trafficking. Article 376 of the Bonded Labour System (Abolition) Act, 'explicitly forbids the purchase and sale of human beings, forced labour and all forms of bonded labour'.[128] There are also prohibitions against 'the trafficking and sale of minors' (articles 372, 373, 354, and 359–68).[129] Trafficking is also prohibited in India's constitution.[130] Following India's signing of the 1950 UN trafficking convention, the Suppression of Immoral Traffic in Women and Girls Act (SITA) was passed in India in 1956. SITA was amended in 1986 to the Immoral Traffic in Persons Prevention Act (ITPPA, normally referred to as PITA).[131] Neither of these laws 'prohibits prostitution per se, but both target commercialized vice and forbid soliciting'.[132] Both SITA and PITA are easy to use against female performers, since with female performers assumed to be prostitutes, it is possible to make allegations of trafficking, which can then lead to raids and cases. A particular problem for female performers is that a career in dancing and the beginning of sexual relations with patrons has traditionally started at puberty, rather than above the legal age of consent of sixteen.[133] Hence, there can be allegations of 'minors forced into prostitution'. I knew a bar girl whose daughters sometimes danced with her. Although there was no sex involved, this could be enough to ignite accusations of the 'trafficking of minors'. Gargi mentions that SITA forced sex workers and *nautch* girls to leave their professions, leading many to *Nautanki*.[134] Allegations of trafficking (which were not substantiated) were key to bringing in the dance bar ban in Maharashtra though, as stated, the dance bar ban itself was a result of new legislation rather than the use of SITA or PITA (which are only able to target incidents or bars one by one). Compared to SITA, PITA includes a greater number of punishable conditions—for example running brothels—which has given it greater scope for the protection of victims, but also for abuse by police. The introduction of PITA has in this respect played an important role in the increase in raids on the establishments of female performers since the 1990s and the increased restriction of their livelihood. For example, it is possible to declare a *mujra* establishment to be a 'brothel' and therefore to close it down under PITA, as well as bring particular charges of soliciting against individual females working there.[135]

Prohibitions against indecency and obscenity found in the Indian Penal Code (IPC), dating from 1860, are also commonly used against female performers, as are local laws. Sections 292–294 of the IPC deal with obscenity. Section 292 deals with obscene books etc., section 293 with the sale of obscene objects to a young person, and section 294 with obscene acts and songs. Section 294 reads,

> Whoever, to the annoyance of others, does any obscene act in any public place, or sings, recites or utters any obscene song, ballad or words, in or near any public place, shall be punished with imprisonment of either description for a term which may extend to three months, or with fine, or with both.[136]

The Dramatic Performance Act of 1876 cites section 294 of the IPC (as well as section 124A, which deals with sedition). However, this act also enabled colonial and later, postcolonial authorities more scope in censoring performances taking place within places of 'public amusement'.[137] There are also similar prohibitions in local laws. For example, section 110B of the Bombay Police Act (1951) reads:

> Behaving indecently in public: No person shall wilfully and indecently expose his person in any street or public place or within sight of, and in such manner as to be seen from any street or public place, whether from within any house or building or not, or use indecent language or behave indecently or riotously, or in a disorderly manner in a street or place of public resort or in any office station or station house.

Section 33 deals with 'regulation of traffic' and 'presentation of order in public place, etc.', and includes many sub-clauses relevant to performers and the licensing of performances. Part (wa), inserted in 1953, deals with matters of morality and decency:

(i) licensing or controlling [in the interest of public order decency or morality or in the interest of the general public with such exceptions as may be specified, the musical, dancing, mimetic or theatrical or other performances for public amusement, including melas and tamashas;

(ii) regulating in the interest of public order, decency or morality or in the interest of the general public, the employment of artists and the conduct of the artists and the audience at such performances;

(iii) prior scrutiny of such performances [and of the scripts in respect thereof, if any, and granting of suitability certificate therefore subject to conditions, if any, ...]

(iv) regulating the hours during which and the places at which such performances may be given.

It is section 33 of this Act that was amended by the government of Maharashtra in 2005 specifically to ban dancing in the dance bars.

The Indian Penal Code and the local obscenity or nuisance laws can be used by any member of the public to complain of having been 'offended' or 'annoyed' by a public performance. This can initiate a police raid followed by a First Incidence Report (FIR), which can lead to cases against performers and the closure of premises. It is difficult for the police to win cases against obscenity, as Mazzarella discusses in the context of the bar girls.[138] However, these laws are used to harass and make livelihood extremely difficult. The nuisance laws are more commonly used to actually close down premises, with neighbours able to complain about noise pollution or people coming and going. It is likely that it was under nuisance if not obscenity laws that the long-standing *kotha*s in some cities in North India were closed down around 1958.[139] It is sometimes cited that *mujra* has been 'banned' or made 'illegal' in these and, more recently, other places. However, I am not aware of any actual legislation that has made it so. *Mujra* exists legally in parts of Bihar, Uttar Pradesh, Delhi, Maharashtra and other states, and many performers have licenses. Constitutionally, it would have been difficult to ban *mujra* just in the cities and not other parts of the states but, without organised forms of protest, it perhaps could have happened.[140] It may have been that, for example, people living near the *kotha*s filed complaints or a Public Interest Litigation (PIL) and initiated the closing down of those premises. Though it would have been possible for the *tawaif*s to fight back, they may have been hindered by lack of knowledge of laws and rights, lack of organisation, or intimidation. It is possible that some did fight back but did so only in smalls groups, or were not successful. Similarly, I have heard reports of 'bans' on 'dance parties' at *mela*s in Uttar Pradesh in the last five or ten years, but again, it is more likely that dance performances are not being held because police raids and harassment (on the grounds of complaints against obscenity) are rendering them impossible. A group of *Brijwasi* performers I met in Safedabad in the outskirts of Lucknow said they had had to move from the city centre, having been accused of *ang pradarshan* ('body show'), implying that they had been closed down by a legal process relating to complaints against obscenity. With increasingly dense living conditions in cities, the potential for complaints from neighbours has increased, fuelling these processes. For example, tall tower blocks now overlook Fores Road in Mumbai, greatly increasing the potential for neighbours to complain of nuisance or of having been offended by the activities of the area, or even of having seen girls soliciting, thus invoking PITA.[141] A proper understanding of these issues would require the examination of numerous cases across India, and would constitute a valuable and substantial study in itself. Dancing girls have had elite and powerful customers, and there will certainly have been lawyers who have fought cases for *kotha* owners and *mujra* dancers over the years. Such a study would almost certainly shed further light on the story of the demise of *tawaif* in the twentieth century.

Prohibitions against obscenity in the IPC or local laws have been made against women ranging from film actresses to *Lavni* performers, bar girls, *mujra* dancers and prostitutes. It is interesting to note that in section 33, part (wa) of the Bombay Police Act, performances include *mela*s and *tamasha*s. There are exemptions in the Indian Penal Code for 'tradition', particularly in the sense of 'religious tradition' (these laws were instituted by the British in the context of non-interference in Indian custom).[142] The trope of 'tradition' is still used to defend against obscenity.[143] However, 'traditional' performances can still be curtailed or restricted on the grounds of obscenity, public nuisance, or charges of soliciting or trafficking. Furthermore, what is 'traditional' is of course highly political, and much of the late nineteenth end early twentieth century was spent in changing the definition of the classical traditions, denying their formerly erotic nature, and declaring the courtesan and *devadasi* traditions 'degraded'.[144] Following anti-*nautch*, *mujra* in particular has been seen, almost by definition, as obscene, and the performers as dissolute and basically prostitutes. Hence, charges of obscenity are easily made and raids are initiated on performances that are without a doubt less 'obscene' (in terms of revealing flesh and of gestures and expressions) than many average film songs.

Needless to say, it is possible for police to arrange complainants, or cite fake phone calls of complaints in order to raid or arrest on charges of obscenity or nuisance to neighbours and so on. This happened in the case of the bar girls.[145] Similarly, police can raid premises citing violation of SITA or PITA, accusing the owner of commercially benefiting from the prostitution of those working there, of running a brothel, or of having trafficked the workers. Studies on prostitution invariably report a high level of police abuse, including physical violence, rape and demands for money. The female performers, prostitutes and *kothi* performers I spoke to all complained of police raids, which in addition to harassing them also turned customers away and made the establishment appear criminal and disreputable, thus harming business. In this way, it is very easy for the business of dancers to be made unviable through raids and arrests that can be made on the basis of a complainant, even if a case is unsuccessful. Closing down premises does take more legal process, but again, is possible or relatively easy if those concerned are not informed of their rights, unable to organise themselves, and have less powerful resources than those who seek to close them down or evict them. Establishments are most commonly closed under nuisance laws or PITA, rather than obscenity laws.

Systems of performance licensing exist in India that regulate or give permission to perform for commercial purposes, or in public. The laws vary from state to state, but may come under the Shop and Commercial Establishment Act or alternatively those laws relating to the licensing of entertainment or amusement. These include The Dramatic Performances Act (1876) and (in Maharashtra) Rules for Licensing and Controlling Places of Public Amusement (other than Cinemas) and Performances for Public Amusement including Melas and Tamashas (1960). Different rules come into play for performing to recorded or amplified music.[146] However, as *mujra* involves acoustic instruments and singing, a license is strictly speaking not necessary. *Mujra* has in many places been performed in what are private residences rather than commercial establishments. Without entrance fees, fixed rates, or even any compulsory payment, licenses are not necessary. Performers receive a *bagsheesh*, an (auspicious) 'tip' or 'reward', rather than a payment. In this sense, it is legal to perform in one's own home, to 'guests', and to receive 'gifts' of money or other items.[147] However, neighbours may complain of disturbance or annoyance (at guests coming and going), which can enable the police to raid and shut down premises. Accusations under SITA and PITA can also be made. Under PITA, it is particularly risky for landlords if the establishment is declared a 'brothel'. This, in turn, inhibits their willingness to rent to *mujra* performers.[148] In many cases, *mujra* performers obtain licenses in order to protect them from police raids and to assert that what they are doing is licensed performing (and not prostitution).[149] Varsha Kale reported that some *kotha* owners in Fores Road in Mumbai (which are private rather than commercial residences) took her advice to apply for performance licences in order to give themselves some protection against police raids. This was only around 2007, prior to which they had performed without licenses.[150] Some performers, however, have held licenses long before this. Agrawal reproduces in an appendix to her study of the *Bedia* a license held by a *Bedia* woman, dated 1968. It states, 'It is certified that this establishment meant for *public entertainment (dancing and singing)* is registered under the Rajasthan shop and commercial establishment regulation, 1958 on 11 September 1968'.[151]

The snowballing process of the identification of female performers as prostitutes, along with restrictions on livelihood, raids, harassment, and hence reliance on sex rather than performance, has continued throughout the twentieth century. There have, however, been some attempts to counteract these trends, the most significant of which is the support of *Lavani* and *Tamasha* by the Maharashtra government after being banned for some time in the 1940s.[152] *Nautanki* and some of its artistes have received some support and recognition from the government, though certainly too little and too late.[153] There have been independent initiatives to support *Deredar tawaif*.[154] I discuss these matters further in chapter two.

In addition to morally-driven laws on obscenity, prostitution and trafficking, female performers are also affected by laws regarding women working at night. Commercial or government infrastructure and construction projects have been behind the closure of performance premises, too. Furthermore, entertainment taxes have apparently dealt a heavy blow to a number of popular forms of public performance in North India, as Mehrotra reports in her biography of the famous *Nautanki* artiste, Gulab Bai (a member of the *Bedia* community).[155] Gulab Bai successfully campaigned for the lifting of crippling entertainment taxes in the 1980s, but *Nautanki* was by this time no longer 'self-sustaining'.[156] The rise of the mass media, DJs and more recently, middle class dance troupes, have also affected the dwindling livelihood of traditional performers.

Conclusions

For female hereditary performers, postcolonial modernity has represented an overwhelming continuity and entrenchment of colonial and early bourgeois-nationalist modernity. The equation that 'a female hereditary performer is a prostitute and therefore not a performer' has become increasingly cemented and now forms the almost entirely unquestioned basis of the manner in which these communities are treated in contemporary India. It evades critique even in much academic work, especially due to the disciplinary separation of studies of 'culture' and 'performing 'arts' versus those of development or sociology. The identity, status and livelihood of female performers have all been undermined to the point where their categorisation as prostitutes has for many become a reality, and an increasingly present threat for others. Not all loss of livelihood had been directly due to stigma, since court performers (male and female) lost livelihood at independence. However, stigma has certainly inhibited them from transferring their skills into the reformed classical performing arts, or into other kinds of performing arts.

My focus in this chapter has been on knowledge, discourse and laws. However, it is important to emphasise that these developments have also been taking place at the level of the nation alongside conceptions of universal human good and progress. Hence the forms of not-belonging that have been engendered are particularly profound in nature and particularly black-and-white, as I discuss in the introduction to this book. The reform period of late colonial India, the laws that are (ab)used in connection with female hereditary performers, and also much contemporary development work all exist in the framework of progress or rational modernity. Thus female hereditary performers have been identified not just as prostitutes, but increasingly as 'backward', as 'problems', as 'exploited', or as 'victims'. Excluded from the conception of universal human good, they 'do not rise to the level of the recognizably human';[157] neither do they rise to the level of proper, productive belonging in the nation.[158] This is further reinforced by empirical socio-economic change—as the middle classes have strengthened, hereditary performers have become increasingly distant and 'backward' from mainstream and 'modern' society and its norms.

The delegitimisation of hereditary female performers has been further compounded by the powerful processes of embourgeoisement that took place within classical performing arts and, to a lesser extent, the film industry from the 1930s. It continues in globalised India in the arena of Bollywood dance. This I turn to in chapter four. However, first I explore further the illicit world of Indian dance, looking at the modern history of female hereditary performers in more detail, and the transgender dimension of female public/erotic dance.

2

FEMALE HEREDITARY PERFORMERS IN POST-INDEPENDENCE INDIA

COMMUNITIES, HISTORIES AND LIVELIHOODS

In the previous chapter, I described the broad history of exclusion of hereditary female performers, looking at knowledge, policy, law and social campaigns from the nineteenth century to the twentieth and twenty-first centuries. In this chapter, I focus on the communities of female hereditary performers themselves, and on ways in which they have adapted and changed in the face of the forces that have been brought to bear on them. Drawing on evidence from colonial ethnographies as well as from contemporary fieldwork, I begin by outlining the structure of female hereditary performers as one of interrelated networks of tribes and communities that stretch across North India. I identify female hereditary performers as an entire sub-stratum of performers consisting of varying statuses, including but extending far beyond known communities of classical *tawaif*. Although what I am presenting constitutes a preliminary study of very under-researched areas, it reveals much concerning the social mobility of these groups, changing patterns of labour and identity, and reactions to stigma. It also hints at a range of ways in which the terrain of Indian performing arts has shifted sociologically in response to the contours of legitimacy and exclusion that began to be engendered from the nineteenth century.

I then turn to the post-independence history of selected communities of female public/erotic performer. While it is well known that female hereditary performers were stigmatised in colonial and bourgeois nationalist India, it is not well known that this exclusion continues in post-independence India. Drawing on contemporary fieldwork and other sources, I show that it is after independence that some communities of female performers became involved in sex work rather than performing arts (the work in dance bars that emerged from the 1980s in Mumbai and the Gulf is an exception). For those that continued to be performers after independence, it is since the 1990s in particular that life has apparently become most difficult, with a livelihood from performing almost impossible, especially after the closure of the dance bars in Mumbai in 2005. During this time, vernacular traditions such as *Nautanki* and *Tamasha/Lavani* have also, in many cases, involved more sexualised performance and/or more harassment for performers, and a more illicit status. Many performers have become more reliant on sexual transaction, with the older systems of long-term concubinage breaking down.

Tribes and communities: the social organisation of hereditary female performers

The majority of erotic and/or public female performers of North India belong to what can be described as a set of interrelated tribes or communities that extend into Pakistan, Bangladesh and Nepal.[1] Although compelling, research on this topic is still preliminary, and in the case of colonial sources, problematic. Female performing and sex work communities have different names and statuses from area to area, but it seems they can for the most part be identified by the term '*Bhatu*'. *Bhatu*, however, is a broad category and includes groups with other occupations, too. As Agrawal writes, it 'encompasses many apparent divisions among the erstwhile nomadic communities'.[2] *Bhatu* is not given as a caste/community/tribe name. I was first informed about this word from the Bhartiya (Indian) Bargirls Union (BBU), since bar girls are from a wide range of performing *Bhatu* groups. The BBU leader, Varsha Kale, told me that she had been trying to find out about the caste/community background of bar girls, and had, after much resistance due to the secrecy of these communities, gained some knowledge of the existence of the groups *Nat*, *Deredar* and *Bedia*. She hence started to ask bar girls if they were one of these. A bar girl advised her that it was better to ask 'Are you *Bhatu*?' and then if they said they were, to ask 'which *Bhatu* are you?'. I have since heard members of these communities state that 'yes, we are all *Bhatu*', and that they are linked to each other as such. Shyam Lacchiya, a member of the *Nat* community whose niece was a bar girl, and who had worked for the union and spoken to many bar girls about their communities, also corroborated the existence of *Bhatu* as an overarching community of these groups.

In her ethnography of a *Bedia* community in Madhya Pradhesh, Agrawal argues that different *Bhatu* groups can be seen as 'kindred communities'.[3] Drawing on detailed evidence of marriage connections between the *Bedia* with other *Bhatu* groups, she states that *Bhatu* 'can be treated as "endogamous" in that members belonging to many different segments intermarry', and that *Bedia*s 'are more like a subdivision of a larger social entity that can be treated as a "caste"'.[4] It is difficult to see *Bhatu* as an endogamous caste since large numbers of women who belong to these groups, in which women perform and/or do sex work, do not marry and have children by men outside the *Bhatu* group—traditionally upper-caste patrons, and more recently the general public. I hence continue to describe *Bhatu* and individual *Bhatu* groups as 'tribes', 'communities' or 'groups' rather than castes (although *Bhatu* such as *Nat* or *Kanjar* are in practice often referred to as castes). However, Agrawal's evidence of the 'kindred' nature of different *Bhatu* groups is highly persuasive.[5] In modern India and in colonial ethnographies, classification of these groups can be confusing, with inconsistent patterns of interrelations and different names in different places for what appear to be the same groups. All these groups belong to what were formerly nomadic or semi-nomadic 'gypsy' tribes who were criminalised by the British from 1871. Agrawal understands the shifting nature of their identities as a reaction to the stigma of criminalisation: 'the fragmentation and multiplication of identities served as a useful political device'.[6] In addition, it appears that social mobility has driven identifications and dis-identifications in recent or longer-term history, as I argue in more detail below.

A factor that provides strong evidence of *Bhatu* commonality and common origin, and indeed of the different female public/erotic dancing groups, is the existence of a common language, similar enough for groups who live in disparate parts of North India to understand each other. Shyam described how he was able to communicate with bar girls from different *Bhatu* communities through this language. These groups are not open to outsiders, and this secret language is a particular marker of this (it is forbidden to teach it to outsiders).[7]

In terms of the *Bhatu* communities in which women perform and/or do sex work, there are common rituals and social practices. These groups follow the traditional paradigm of the female dancer, in which a female who enters into the dance—and now in many cases prostitution—line does not marry.[8] These groups also share the ritual of *nath utarna*, the 'taking off of the nose ring', when a girl has sexual relations with a client/patron for the first time. For those communities now involved only in sex work, *nath utarna* involves a client paying a particularly high price for sex with a virgin girl. This is one of the practices most frowned on by progressive mainstream society, which sees it simply as the sale of a girl and her virginity. For those in the older patterns of patronage, there is expectation of longer-term relations and financial commitments. *Nath utarna* is described as *shaadi* or 'marriage' by many hereditary performers now.[9] These communities also take bride price for the girls who do marry, something that again tends to be interpreted by mainstream society as the 'exploitation' of females.

I was given the following non-exhaustive list of communities of girls dancing in bars via the BBU (compiled by Shyam Lacchiya): *Nat*, *Kolhati*, *Deredar*, *Gand-*

harva, Bedia, Kanjar, Kanjarbhat, Doli, Sansi, Chari, Sakhlighar, Kalandar, Jaagari, Kilbila/Chilbila, Kalbe, Gwar, Garara, Kuchabanda, Bhat, Patharvat, (*Bazigar*). All these groups are *Bhatu*, and all have at least some subgroups where girls perform and/or do sex work. However, it is important to note that performing and sex work is the profession of these groups to a significantly varying degree, and may only be the work of particular subgroups.[10] I also met a group in the outskirts of Lucknow known as *Brijbasi* who were public/erotic performers and involved in sex work. Although not apparently dancing in bars, they do seem to constitute another *Bhatu* group in which the girls dance and/or do sex work. Most of these groups can be found in colonial ethnographies of North India. I make a tentative attempt here to trace to some degree the history of these groups through an examination of colonial sources and contemporary ethnographic evidence. These colonial sources illustrate the *Bhatu* structure of interrelated 'kindred communities' and, significantly, the overlap and interconnection of groups with radically different social status and identity in today's India. This itself sheds light on the list of bar girl *Bhatu* groups with their greatly varying involvement in what are seen as the 'disreputable' professions of female public performance and sex work. In addition to showing the relation of these hereditary female performing groups to those with occupations unrelated to performing arts, it also shows previous overlaps in male and female performing groups now seen to constitute very different categories. Thus this history suggests a high degree of social mobility among performing groups. I draw selectively (in the interests of space) from Carnegie, *Notes on the races, tribes and castes inhabiting the province of Avadh* (1868); Risley, *The tribes and castes of Bengal. Ethnographic glossary* (1891); Sherring, *Hindu tribes and castes as represented in Benares* (1872); Enthoven, *The tribes and castes of the Bombay Presidency* (1920); and Crooke, *Tribes and castes of the North-Western Provinces and Oudh*, Volumes I-IV (1896). I focus particularly on *Nat, Bedia, Kanjar, Gandharva* [*Deredar*][11] and *Kolhati*, discussing these groups in more detail from contemporary sources in the second part of this chapter. I have underlined groups mentioned in these ethnographies that are included in the above list of *Bhatu* bar girl performers, and also *Brijbasi*.

Historical interconnections of contemporary female performer/sex worker communities and other *Bhatu* groups

As in contemporary India, the colonial ethnographies illustrate a consistency of inconsistent connections between *Bhatu* female performer groups in and across geographical regions. Carnegie's ethnography on Avadh includes a section on 'The *Nats, Bazigars, Kanjars* etc'.[12] He states that *Nats* are known as *Bazigars* ('players') in Persian, and include seven subgroups that all intermarry: *Chari, Athbhya, Bensa,*

Parbatti, Kalkur, Dorkeni and *Gangwar* [*Gwar*?].[13] He states that the *Nats* in Avadh have seven subdivisions, including *Brijbasi* and *Bareah* [*Bedia*?].[14] Although he links *Nats* and *Kanjars* in the main entry, he says that the *Nats* in Avadh, from whom he gained information, claimed they were entirely distinct from *Kanjars*.[15]

Risley's ethnography on Bengal describes *Bedia* as 'the generic name of a number of vagrant gipsy-like groups, of whom it is difficult to say whether they can properly be described as castes'.[16] He describes seven groups as *Bedia*, one of which is '*Bazigar, Kabutari, Bhanumati, Dorabaz*, acrobats and conjurors, probably closely akin to the *Nats* and *Kanjars* of Hindustan', and states that the women are the chief performers.[17] He also states that *Brajabasi* are 'a synonym for *Bedia*' (whereas Carnegie includes them as a subgroup of *Nat*).[18] He describes '*Nar, Nat, Nartak, Natak*' as 'a dancing and musician caste of Eastern Bengal'.

Sherring's ethnography of Benares lists '*Nat, Kanjar, Madari, Chai*, and *Badhak*' under 'Gipsies, jugglers, rope-dancers, snake-charmers, thimble-riggers, and robbers' in a chapter on 'Aboriginal tribes and inferior castes'.[19] He states that *Nats* have seven occupational clans involved in various forms of dance and entertainment as well as '*Kshatriya*' ('warrior').[20] He lists the *Nats* in Oudh as having eight subdivisions, two of which are *Bhatu* and *Brijbasi*.[21] The *Kanjar*, he does not describe as entertainers.[22] Sherring also mentions *Bhats*, and links them to *Badi* in one of three branches of the group.[23] The *Badi* exist in the contemporary Indian Himalaya and western Nepal. In the former, they perform as reputable (but low status) husband–wife pairs.[24] In the latter, the women perform erotically for men.[25]

Enthoven, in the section 'Wandering and predatory tribes of the Bombay presidency', includes *Garodi Mang*, and states 'The *Bhat* or *Khanjar* dacoits of Northern India are said to have been originally a branch of this tribe'.[26] Under *Kolhati*, he writes 'Their women are prostitutes; but are not the same women more generally known as *Kolatnis*, the common dancing women of the Dekhan'.[27] The entry on *Bhat* states, 'These are the *Khanjars* of Gondwana, and the *Sausis* or *Sausiyas* [*Sansis*] of Northern India'.[28] *Nat* he lists separately under 'The tribes and castes of Kattywar'. In contemporary India I have heard Rajasthani *Nat* state that *Kolhatis* are *Nats*—they just have a different name in Maharashtra. This may be why *Nat* are listed separately as 'itinerant rope-dancers, jugglers, actors and the like' in this ethnography.[29]

Crooke's ethnography of North-Western Provinces and Oudh [Avadh] is the most detailed of these sources and provides the most information on the historical equivalence or interrelatedness of many of today's *Bhatu* performing groups. The *Bedia* he describes as 'a caste of vagrants found in various parts of the Province. They are very closely allied if not identical with the *Sansi, Kanjar, Habura, Bhantu*, etc'.[30] He states that the Census returns give a total of 250 sections of Hindu *Bedia* subcastes, and twelve Mohammedan. These include 'caste' names 'common to them and similar vagrant prostitute tribes, such as *Brijbasi*, *Dhanuk*, *Gandharb*, *Gidhmar* ("kite killers"), *Jangali*, *Kuchbandhiya*, *Kapariya*, *Karnataki*, *Nat*, *Paturiya*, *Rajnat*, and *Tawaif*. He mentions the *Badi*, *Hurkiya*, *Darzi*, and *Dholi* under an entry on *Dom*, citing them as one of four classes of *Dom*, 'beggars and vagrant musicians of the hills'. While Sherring links *Badi* to *Bhat*, Crooke links them to *Nat*, stating, 'The *Badi* is the village musician; in the plains he is considered to be a *Nat*'.[31] He does not specify if women perform in any of these *Dom*-related groups. Under the section on *Kanjar*, Crooke clearly links many of today's known *Bhatu* groups, stating 'There can be little doubt that the *Kanjars* are a branch of the great nomadic race which includes the *Sansiya*, *Habura*, *Beriya*, *Bhatu* and more distant kindred, such as the *Nat*, *Banjara*, *Baheliya*'.[32] He lists twelve divisions of *Kanjar*, six of them being *Kuchbandiya*, *Nat*, *Beria*, *Sansiya*, *Dom*, *Bhatu*. '*Kabutarwala* or *Brajbasi*, who are really rope-dancing *Nats*' are mentioned within sub-castes of *Kanjar*.[33]

In a lengthy article on *Nat*, Crooke states, '[T]hey appear to be identical, at least in occupation, with the *Kolhatis* of Bombay, who are also known as *Dombari* ...'.[34] He cites another source connecting the *Kolhatis* with 'the great *Sansya* family of robbers'.[35] He later states, after considering more sources, 'There seems, then, very little doubt that under the general name *Nat* are included various tribes; some of whom are closely allied to the vagrant, criminal races, like the *Sansyas*, *Beriyas*, and *Haburas*'.[36] He lists ten main subcastes of Hindu *Nat*, including *Brijwasi*; *Gual* [*Gwar*?] 'cowherds'; and *Sapera*.[37] Further, he provides lists of *Nat* in different districts and their subcastes, which include many of the contemporary *Bhatu* groups.[38] Later, *Badi* are mentioned as a sub-caste of *Nat*.[39]

Kinds and classes of performer

These ethnographies show that groups whose women perform have connections with the following other groups: those in which the men also perform; those where only the men perform; and those in which women and men perform in husband–wife pairs (apparently the only configuration that enables women to perform in public and be married and to be, in this sense, 'respectable'). This is highly significant in terms of the contemporary female performer/sex worker groups, which are seen simply as 'castes' of 'prostitutes' whose men who do not work (they are 'pimps'/'layabouts').[40] In modern India, communities of male performers are typically distinguished from the groups in which women perform.[41] For example, Muslim musicians form separate communities from the female performers whom they teach and accompany. Saeed describes how the *Kanjar* and their *Mirasi* accompanists and teachers are like 'oil and water', with clear distinctions between the two and no intermarriage.[42] These ethnographies, however, suggest that such divisions may not have been so fundamental in the past. Risley describes *Nat* men as performers: the boys are dancers known as *Bhagtiyas* (often counted as a separate group) and grow up to become musicians who 'attend on dancing girls (*Bai*)'.[43] He states that the women do not perform in public.

Sherring does not mention explicitly that women are involved in the six entertainment-related occupational subgroups of *Nat* (snake-exhibitors, bear-exhibitors, jugglers, dancers, rope-dancers and monkey-exhibitors). Neither does he mention that they are involved in 'prostitution'. However, he states that arts are passed 'father to son', implying that women did not perform, or did not perform specifically for male (erotic) pleasure in these *Nat* groups.[44] *Ramjana*/*Ramjani*, on the other hand, are listed as a group whose women are involved in prostitution. Risley also states that *Ramjana*/*Ramjani* men are performers who instruct singing and dancing girls as well as undertaking other occupations.[45] He states that *Gaunharin* are dancing women, and this group also play *sarangi* and *tabla* (presumably referring to the men, since women playing these instruments is unheard of prior to modern reforms, and still extremely rare).[46]

In an entry on *Gandharba*, Crooke describes them as 'a caste of singers and prostitutes' and mentions that the men perform too, playing *tabla* and *sarangi*—something which is not the case with contemporary *Gandharb*.[47]

Looking back to the *Ain-i-Akbari* (the chronicles from the court of Akbar, 1556–1605), '*Kanjari*' are described as a group in which both men and women perform: 'The men of this class play the *pakhawaj*, the *rabab* and the *tabla*, while the women sing and dance. His Majesty calls them *Kanchanis*'.[48] As Brown writes, '[b]y the reign of Aurangzeb ... the *kanchani*, reigned supreme as the principal courtesans of Mughal society'.[49]

Contemporary evidence also supports far more flexible or varied configurations of male and female performers within individual and related groups than is generally assumed. In a *Nat* community from Rajasthan, the men as well as women used to perform until patronage ended after independence (more on this below). In Servan-Schreiber's work on itinerant performers in the Bhojpuri region, *Nat* are described as performing in male-female pairs (presumably like *Badi* in the Indian Himalaya), and it is not suggested that the females' role is an erotic one.[50]

Today's female performer/sex worker communities are linked in colonial ethnographies with other groups who have a range of occupations. Carnegie links *Nat* and *Kanjar* to *Bazigar* and also *Banjara*.[51] *Bazigar* are listed as musicians in the *Ain-i-Akbari*, but are not generally known as a community whose women perform or do sex work in India today (although there were some *Bazigar* girls dancing in bars). *Banjara* women are also not known to perform. Sherring links *Bhat* to *Badi*, and Crooke links *Badi* to *Nat* via subgroups of *Dom*. *Bhat* are known as genealogists and their women are not known to perform—it is apparently a particular subgroup (or an anomaly?) of *Bhat* whose girls are dancing in bars. *Badi*, as stated, perform in reputable husband–wife pairs in the Indian Himalaya and as erotic performers in western Nepal. *Dom* are not generally known as a group whose women perform or do 'prostitution', but I have heard of males and females who are involved in performing, and girls who dance may join *Nat*.[52] In Brown's study of Mughal court musicians, *Domnis* were said to perform mainly for females, 'but were permitted to enter public male space on liminal occasions such as wedding celebrations'.[53] She states they performed 'sexual roles', becoming courtesans, from the eighteenth century.[54]

Furthermore, occupations that go beyond performing are found in communities of what are today female performer/prostitute groups in which the men do not work. In addition to six kinds of entertainers, Sherring also lists *Kshatriya* as an occupational clan of *Nat*.[55] *Kshatriya* literally means 'warrior'.[56] In contemporary Rajasthan, a *Nat* man recounted being told that his forefathers had been warriors for their patrons, and how he himself used to hunt for Rajput patrons, supporting this reference to *Nat* as warriors. Sherring does not mention the *Kanjar* in Benares to be entertainers, but lists them as makers of 'ropes and reed matting', of cotton and hemp, and also brushes.[57] Crooke lists many sub-categories of *Nat*, not all of whom are performers and not all of whose women perform or do 'prostitution'.[58] Crooke also states that the *Bedia* carry out 'all the usual gypsy trades' but 'have no talent for music'.[59]

Servan-Schreiber's more recent work on *Nat* also supports this involvement of female performer/sex worker groups in wider occupations. She describes that they had many occupations besides dancing, and that *Nat*s 'lost many of their erstwhile opportunities' over the twentieth century, but does not give any more detail.[60] The *Bedia* studied by Agrawal state that they used to be *Bhat*s, or genealogists, or cite descent from *Banjara*. Historical documents provide some support to these claims, and these *Bedia* communities still intermarry with certain low status genealogist groups, who, however, do not identify themselves as *Bhat*.[61]

An interesting entry in Enthoven's ethnography describes the linkage of the 'reputable' performing group *Kalawant* (probably originally an occupational group rather than a 'caste') with 'disreputable' female performing groups. In Chapter IV of 'The Castes of Bombay and its Neighbourhood' Enthoven lists *Kalawant* as consisting of five branches—*Patra*, *Ramjani*, *Ghikari*, *Ranganli* and *Kanchan* [*Kanjar*]—and says 'these subcastes intermarry, and follow the same profession of singing, dancing, and prostitution'.[62] *Kalawant* have come to be recognised as elite male classical musicians whose women do not perform and would not be seen today as in any way linked with groups such as *Kanchan* or *Ramjani*, whose women are performers for men.[63] However, the listing in Mughal sources of *Kanjari*/*Kanchan* as a group whose women and men performed, and whose women were the most prestigious courtesans of Mughal society, suggests that this linking is not entirely implausible.[64]

Also interesting is the way in which groups such as *Nat*, which include low status acrobats or wandering performers, can be directly or indirectly linked with groups that are known to have been high status '*tawaif*'. In an entry on *tawaif*, Crooke describes them as 'The caste of dancing-girls and prostitutes'.[65] He divides *tawaif* roughly into a Hindu branch (*Patar*, *Patur*, *Paturiya*) and a Muslim branch (*Kanchan*), the latter identified by Brown as the main courtesans in Aurangzeb's court.[66] *Kanchan* are believed to be the same as *Kanjar*, who are widely linked to *Nat*, *Bedia* and *Sansi*. Crooke then states that 'the term *tawaif* includes a number of distinct classes', and cites '*Gandharap*, *Kanchan*, *Kashmiri*, *Paturiya*, and *Ramjani*' among the Hindu branch. He also lists:

the *Hurukiya* ...; the *Kabutari*, who is usually classed with the *Nats* and is so-called because she has the flirting ways of a pigeon (*kabutar*)'; the *Mangta* or "beggars"; the *Mirasi*, who is a *Dom* singer; the *Miskar* or *Mirshikar* ...; and the *Naik* .... In addition to these is the *Gaunharin* ...; the *Brajbasi* ...; and the *Negpatar*.[67]

In this way, '*tawaif*' are linked to *Nat*s and to *Brijbasi*. Oral history tells that *Nat*, *Bedia*, *Kanjar*, *Kolhati* (but probably not *Sansi*) have all in the past been *tawaif* or *Baiji*s, employed in courts or doing *mujra* in *kotha*s.[68] This suggests that nomadic and itinerant performing groups, and *tawaif* attached to particular *kotha*s in urban areas, are all connected in terms of tribe/community. They are also connected to female court performers, such as *Nat* women in Rajasthan (more on *Nat* communities below). As with the different configurations of male and female performers and their different kinds of occupation, this suggests a high degree of social mobility among these groups, in which the negotiation or emergence of status plays out according to varying historical and geographical contexts within and between different kinds of performers, rather than according to fundamentally different groups.[69]

Occupation, genealogy, identity and social mobility

One explanation for the often overlapping or contradictory connections of many of the performing groups can be found in the occupational as well as the hereditary elements of community identities and names. As Crooke states in relation to *Nat*:

Nat (Sanskrit *nata*, 'a dancer') a tribe of so-called gypsy dancers, acrobats, and prostitutes who are found scattered all over the Province. The problem of the origin and ethnological affinities of the *Nats* is perhaps the most perplexing within the whole range of the ethnography of Northern India, and the enquiries, of which the result is given here, leave its solution almost as uncertain as ever. The real fact seems to be that the name *Nat* is an occupational term which includes a number of different clans who have been grouped together merely on account of their common occupation of dancing, prostitution, and performance of various primitive industries.[70]

In this sense, any group may be known as *Nat* on assuming, for whatever reasons, these occupations.[71] However, at the same time, there is evidence of *Nat* who were involved in occupations other than performing arts, as well as high status performing arts, or non-erotic performance by females. Occupational groups may also augment their ranks by going beyond genealogical connections. Sachdeva's work shows that communities of *tawaif* adopted or bought slave girls, and that new lineages could be established if a prostitute became trained in music and dance and established herself as a *tawaif* (2008).[72]

The consequence of what was or has become a particularly negative, occupationally-driven identity is that mobility is only possible if a person exits the particular occupation and the particular group. Thus many lineages of *tawaif* and other groups of female public performers have come to an end as women have ceased to perform, perhaps managing to marry and join mainstream society; or have been able to get their daughters married instead of putting them into the dance—and now sex work—line. With the female dancer holding such a stigmatised position, in particular by the late nineteenth century, groups could most visibly negotiate upward mobility if the women stopped performing. Many individual women have moved out of these professions, and continue (or attempt) to do so, as I discuss below. It appears that, prior to the late nineteenth century, more groups contained both men and women who performed publicly than now. Some groups whose women have stopped performing (or never did so) negotiated a reputable identity. Those whose women did perform and continued to perform have been utterly defined by this. The identity of the female hereditary performer groups is now so stigmatised that people of these communities who have any contact with mainstream society almost invariably hide their family background. They take upper caste surnames which, for the children of the earning women, are the names of their fathers, or false names. In this way, individuals or small groups from these communities are constantly morphing into or masquerading as upper castes, with members of new generations managing to get educated and work and most crucially (in the case of females), marry. They are hence no longer counted among the 'original' community. In this way, although many individuals move into other occupations and identities, the groups' occupation is so rigidly defined and so stigmatised, that the groups themselves are stuck in an identity and practice of sex work. Because the groups are low status, and those who move up deny contact with them, a 'creamy layer' is constantly being skimmed off—arguably driving downward mobility in the 'original' community. This vicious circle of stigmatised identity has also made dance unviable, and put more and more women into sex work instead. It is difficult to imagine how groups such as *Nat* or *Bedia* could now negotiate a more positive group identity and a more mainstream occupation while keeping the same name in the manner that other groups whose women were once public/erotic performers have apparently done in the past.

Female hereditary performing communities in contemporary India

While all female erotic/public performers in India in the late nineteenth century and today can be identified as *Bhatu* and as interrelated, they should not be assumed to have rigid lineages with identities and occupations that go back neatly in time. An awareness of tribe, community, occupation and mobility is essential for exploring more nuanced histories for these groups and for understanding dynamics of exclusion. An analysis of the workings of stigma, discourses of 'culture', and ideologies of nationalism, 'progress' and 'backwardness' is also needed.

In this section, I turn to a more detailed focus on contemporary India and provide some glimpses of the circumstances of female *Bhatu* performers in terms of different communities and their histories. This includes contexts of performance; changes in performing and sexual labour; and changes in livelihood and status. I provide brief accounts of *Nat*, *Bedia*, *Kanjar*, *Kolhati* and *Deredar* based on my own fieldwork and/or secondary sources in order to illustrate a range of *Bhatu* female performer groups.[73] All these stories illustrate a loss of performing livelihood through loss of patronage, and increasing difficulty in carrying out work due to police raids, stigma, and the ban on dance bars from 2005.[74]

Nat

Nat are a large tribe or community spread across northern India and into Pakistan (and probably into Bangladesh). Like other *Bhatu* communities, *Nat* were historically nomadic or semi-nomadic. Most are now settled but some are still semi-nomadic, with one *Nat* woman I met in Calcutta saying that they sometimes migrate between Pakistan and India for dance and sex work. Although most, if not all, *Bhatu* now have a home village, they still migrate long distances for work—whether to Mumbai to perform in dance bars, or to the Gulf. *Nat*, like *Bedia*, are now becoming known for 'community-based sex work' or 'traditional sex work', terms which tend to essentialise and conceal history. Many *Nat* communities, for example in Rajasthan, are indeed now involved in brothel-based commercial sex work on trucking routes, having all but given up dancing.[75] There are *Nat* girls in *kotha*s in Mumbai, but at least some of these function more as brothels, where girls only dance if clients particularly request it. There are *Nat* communities, however, that are still predominantly made up of performers.[76] Here, I discuss two specific communities of *Nat*, one in Uttar Pradesh, the other in Rajasthan.

Sultanpur, Uttar Pradesh: In Sultanpur District, there is a collection of villages where *Nat* performers are settled. It is likely that these villages date from around the time of independence. I made brief visits to one village in October 2008, and one in January 2010. The communities were remarkably open, considering I did

Image 6: Eighty-five year-old *Nat* former court performer with his disused *sarangi.* Tonk, Rajasthan, 2010. (Author's photograph)

not have a direct contact. On both occasions I came with a local person of the *Thakur* community (the traditional *jajmans* or patrons of these performers) and another male (*kothi*) friend. In the first village, they avoided telling me which community they were from, saying that 'matters of caste were not important'. I spoke to two women, who explained that they perform locally in weddings during the marriage season, and used to then travel to Mumbai during the rest of the year and perform in the bars when they were still open. In the room where we talked there was space for performing plus some instruments that looked as though they were still in use. The women said they were also engaged in farming (*kheti*).

The people of the other village were also quite open, though understandably suspicious of us. They said that they (and all the surrounding villages) were *Nat*, and I was able to speak to two elder women who were retired performers. One, who was about fifty-five years old was happy to talk about old times, and said she used to

Image 7: Eighty-five year-old *Nat* former court performer shows his shield, used for hunting for Rajput patrons. Tonk, Rajasthan, 2010. (Author's photograph)

dance for '*rais log*', local landowners or *zamindars*. She spoke perfect Urdu and had knowledge of classical *ragas*, which is not the norm for women in this area. As with most *Bhatu* performers, she said that the current environment or *mauhal* was bad. Whereas she used to be called '*tawaif*' or '*Baiji*', earned good money and was treated with respect, she reported that they are now called *randi* or 'whore'. They had started performing for lower castes from around fifteen years ago. She said they are now getting their daughters out of this line and getting them married instead.

In this village, they said that, unlike the first village I visited, all their girls were married. They denied that any were still dancing, though said there were still a few girls from the village living in Mumbai. However, there were no young girls present at all, and one of the young men admitted to one of my friends that his sister had in fact been dancing in Mumbai dance bars (though apparently girls from this village did not perform anywhere else). One young married woman talked quite openly about her mother, who performed *mujra* in Mumbai, and about the problems of being a dancer now. Her aunt, for example, who was also present, had been left alone after her long-term client/patron left her, and she was then too old to perform.

The local people I went with said that girls from this collection of *Nat* villages who still work locally are not doing brothel-based sex work, or even sex work alone, but continue to perform and make liaisons with audience members. The girls in Mumbai who had been dancing in bars may have been involved in sex work as there were few opportunities for bar girls following the ban in 2005 and many did go into (or back into) sex work. The second village was made up of well-constructed, concrete '*pakke*' houses, probably made possible by wealth that had come from money earned in dance bars. This community were clearly living in a precarious way in social terms. The young man who had admitted his sister was in Mumbai said that his wife did not know about the community—she knew they were performers in the past, but did not understand in what sense. He also said it was difficult for them to study in school because they got teased and bullied. As with most people from these communities, rather than using their own surname, they call themselves Thakur—the surname of the traditional patrons and hence the fathers of many of them.

Tonk, Rajasthan: In contrast to the villages in Sultanpur where girls were still actively dancing, *Nat* communities in Rajasthan and Madhya Pradesh, are not known to be dancing in their local areas. Most are instead doing brothel-based sex work along trucking routes.[77] This has become a highly organised community-based business, like that of the *Bedia* that Agrawal describes.[78] While *Nat* and *Bedia* are generally known simply as 'sex workers', or even 'traditional sex workers', this move to sex work has, in the case of this community, only happened in the last forty years. I visited the *Nat* villages with Shyam Lacchiya, a member of the community who I had met through the BBU in Mumbai. My visit was again brief, but I was able to gain a preliminary history of this group from interviews with people from a range of ages. I also used information from Shyam and other members of his family in Mumbai, including his niece called Pinky. She grew up in Rajasthan and entered *dhandha* (sex work—literally, 'business') but later escaped, came to Mumbai, and became one of the earliest bar girls in the late 1980s.

I met a number of old people in this community, the eldest of whom was an eighty-five year-old man (see images 6 and 7). He told me that both women and men had been performers for Rajputs, in princely courts. This was very interesting, given that the image of this community in contemporary India is one in which men pimp out their sisters. I also learned that communities existed in which men were performers and women courtesans, though, as discussed above, I later found further evidence of this configuration in the colonial ethnographies. The women had been referred to as '*Baiji*' by their patrons, a term for courtesans. Men used to play various instruments including *tabla*, harmonium, *sarangi*, *dholak* and *bansuri*. The men and women were also skilled at tightrope walking and other gymnastic feats, as well as what was described as 'drama'. The elder men I talked to clearly knew *rag* music, and had some instruments. The eighty-five-year-old was unwell and bedridden with a broken leg when I met him. However, he became highly animated as he talked of the past in clear Urdu (which people of this area would not normally know), also speaking the local Marwari language with his grandson who accompanied me. He sang some of the traditional songs they used to sing in praise of the Rajputs in an extremely powerful and projecting pre-microphone voice. He also had a broken *sarangi* and an old drum hanging by his bed. He told of how he used to go hunting for his patrons, demonstrating with an old spear and shield. He boasted of how he used to be a wrestler, and would drink five litres of milk in the morning and five litres in the evening. He also told how, before his father's time, they used to fight for the Rajputs.

This community of *Nat* used to be mobile performers with no fixed home. They would travel with their luggage on horseback, performing in certain courts for a period of time. Some of the women became concubines of particular Rajputs, staying long term in a particular place. They talked of having been treated with respect, and of having been rewarded well by their patrons with gifts of land, silver, jewellery, or foodstuffs such as grain, sugar, or *ghi*. The eighty-five-year-old told of the places he had visited: Kanpur, Lucknow, Faraqabad, Meerut, Saranpat.

When India gained independence, these princely courts were abolished. The Rajputs were able to continue their lifestyle for some time after independence, but it started to die out during the 60s and 70s. They were settled in villages by the government, claiming, with regret, that in the days of Rajput patronage they had not used or kept track of the gifts of land and other things they had been given by their patrons, and had lost them. People would come to their villages looking for dance and sex and then, from the 70s and 80s, people started to come just for sex. Sex work became gradually institutionalised in a brothel-based system. The men thus lost their livelihood whereas the women became sex workers rather than courtesans or *Baijis*. It was during this time that they began to have sex with men of lower castes, as opposed to only with the Rajputs. A forty-four-year-old woman I met (born in 1966) said she had never seen a livelihood of dance, and had done only sex work. The *Nat*, like *Bedia*, keep the system of 'chaste wives and prostitute sisters' described by Agrawal, whereby those who marry do not do sex work and vice versa (2008). However, this system, rather than being one of modern 'community-based sex work', follows exactly the same pattern as the previous generations who were court performers, whereby if a girl began to dance, she could never marry; marriage and performing remained mutually exclusive zones.[79]

Some *Nat* women were also performing *mujra* in various cities across Northern India. A *Nat* bar girl told me how her elder sister, probably born around 1950 and now retired, used to perform *mujra* in Meerut. I was told that in Jaipur *mujra* was 'banned' in the mid-1980s, contributing to the community's problems. I was informed that *Nat* are still doing *mujra* in Rajasthan (Indaur, Ujjain, Jabalpur), Uttar Pradesh (Saharanpur, Barabanki, Buland, Harpud, Benaras, Sultanpur, Ghajhapur, Faizabad, Paradiha, and Dahema), and West Bengal (Bahubazaar in Calcutta, and Rampur).[80]

From the late 1980s and 1990s, girls began to go to Mumbai to dance in beer bars, which enabled many to get out of brothel-based sex work and earn very good money. Approximately half the *Nat* community are now living in Mumbai. The ban on dance in beer bars in 2005 has meant that many are doing sex work in Mumbai or struggling with the meagre income of waiter service. Others have returned to their villages, and to sex work. The community are not extremely poor, earning reasonably well from sex work. They do not earn enough, though, to be able to get daughters married and out of the line they are in; or the community are apparently too invested in *dhandha* to get out. Bar girls in Mumbai were getting their children educated and managing to avoid putting daughters into the line but, following the ban, this trend has been reversed. Although not extremely poor, their social exclusion is extreme, and it is very difficult for children to study well in school due to teasing. Sex work (and dance) is also a difficult livelihood from the point of view of raids under PITA, as I have discussed in the previous chapter.

In comparing the histories of *Nat* in Rajasthan and in Sultanpur, it is evident that those in Rajasthan have suffered a far more radical loss of traditional socio-cultural space. The Rajasthani *Nat* were attached to the Rajputs and princely courts. When these were abolished, the *jajmani* patronage was cut abruptly. Those in Sultanpur were attached to the local Thakurs or landowners who did not lose their wealth and position in this way. Thus these performers continued far longer in the *jajmani* relationship, and only began performing for and having sexual relationships with lower castes approximately fifteen years ago. In addition, due to extended drought, *Nat* in Rajasthan have not been able to gain a livelihood from farming the land they have, unlike those in Sultanpur.[81]

Bedia

The *Bedia* exist across North India and have, since at least the late nineteenth and early twentieth century, been involved in performing. This includes performing in *Nautanki*, as well as singing and dancing for upper caste patrons and *kotha*-based *mujra*.[82] However, their history is apparently not so tied up with performing as *Nat* or *Kanjar* (though this may be due to *Nat* in particular being an occupational category rather than strictly one based on genealogy). *Bedia* are now heavily involved in sex work, and community, brothel-based systems, similar to those of *Nat* communities, exist in Rajasthan and Madhya Pradesh.[83] The image of this group is increasingly one of 'community-based sex workers' or 'traditional sex workers', as opposed to one of *Nautanki* artistes and *Baiji*s.

Bedia women are still involved in *Nautanki*. However, because *Nautanki* has become increasingly eroticised, many artistes choose to get their daughters married and into mainstream society. Mehrotra describes the period since the 1990s in particular as involving eroticisation, with *Nautanki* performance often being used as a vehicle to attract customers for transactional sex.[84] There are also communities of *Bedia* that are still involved to some degree in *mujra*, or at least still reside in *mujra* establishments where they have licenses to perform. This is the case, for example, in Congress House in Mumbai (which includes *Bedia* and *Deredar*); in Calcutta, where many of the '*Agrawalis*' are *Bedia*;[85] and in GP Road in Delhi.[86] It is clear that in the course of only a few generations there has been an overall move towards increased reliance on sexual labour and, in particular, transactional sex. Anand Sharma, who runs a sex-workers group in Delhi linked with Calcutta's sex-work collective Durbar Mahila Samanwaya Committee (DMSC) and has published a book about sex workers (2001), stated that the level of sex work versus dancing started to increase from the 1980s.[87] Around this time, people organising weddings began to call DJs rather than traditional female entertainers such as *Bedia*. However, there are broader social, economic, and cultural factors involved in the rise of sex work. It was around the same time that women started to have relationships or transactional sex with the general public as opposed to upper caste *jajmani* patrons or audience members. *Bedia* women in a very down-at-heel *kotha* I visited on GP Road in Delhi in 2007 said that their livelihood had become far more difficult since the mid or late 1990s. Police raids had increased, involving harassment of customers and violence against the women themselves. They did not know what had initiated this change but suggested the Mumbai bars as one factor—police would demand large amounts of money (Rs 10–100,000) from girls who were looking to regain 'entry' into the Delhi *kotha*s after returning from dancing in Mumbai bars.[88]

Bedia girls, including those in Congress House, were also heavily involved in dancing in Mumbai's beer bars from the late 1980s till the ban in 2005. Women in many *Bedia* communities are apparently still skilled dancers, though it is not clear how often those involved in brothel-based sex work dance, if at all; or whether they perform when they get the chance in beer bars, or privately arranged '*mujras*', which can involve explicitly erotic or even nude dancing and also sex. *Bedia* women in Delhi are involved in an organisation that works specifically for sex workers' rights, linked to DMSC.[89] In Calcutta itself, however, the '*Agrawali*' *Bedia* women do not embrace an identity of commercial sex workers, and choose not to include themselves in DMSC.

Kanjar

Kanjar are found in North India, Pakistan and possibly Bangladesh, and the community in Lahore is the subject of two ethnographically-based books by Saeed and

Brown.[90] As both books show, *Kanjar* girls in Lahore are from a classical courtesan lineage, with the tradition of *mujra* still alive, though increasingly run down.[91] The system of concubinage is also visible, but with increased instability for *Kanjar* women; as their livelihood of performance and economic independence reduces, they become more reliant on earning money directly from sexual relationships or encounters with men. These books describe the phenomenon of girls going to the Gulf as dancers and concubines, and sometimes for the sale of their virginity (*nath utarna*). The practice of going to the Gulf has existed for several decades, and is a progression from the far older practice of migration and nomadism of these groups. Girls from other *Bhatu* groups such as *Nat* or *Deredar* also go to the Gulf, mostly via Mumbai, and this has involved charges of 'trafficking' against the communities, as I discuss in chapter five. I am aware that *Kanjar* are involved in performing in Rajasthan from Neuman, Chaudhuri and Kothari's publication, which includes a brief description and a picture of *Kanjar* (female) dancers.[92] *Kanjar* are also involved in 'community-based sex work' in Rajasthan and probably other areas of North India, where performing has entirely ceased to be a livelihood.[93]

Kolhati[94]

Kolhati are found in Maharashtra and are said to be *Nat* (known as *Kolhati* only in this part of India). They are the principal female performers of *Lavani*, which is an (erotic) song and dance genre performed within *Tamasha* and contexts known as *Sangeet Baree*.[95] *Kolhati* women have also been involved in performing *mujra*. *Tamasha* and *Lavani* have had a history of struggles for legitimacy including Victorian disapproval, legal objections on 'obscenity' grounds, and a general decrying of 'vulgarity'. These have continued during the twentieth century and into the twenty-first.[96] In the 1940s, *Tamasha* was banned by Bombay State due to the obscene nature of *Lavani* lyrics.[97] *Tamasha* has also undergone a certain amount of 'cleansing' and *Lavani*, in the form of *Sangeet Barees*, has been relegated to a lower status than the dramatic parts of *Tamasha*. Yet *Lavani* has not been eliminated from official culture as, for example, *mujra* has. Despite a complex and chequered history, *Lavani* and *Tamasha* have been supported by the state government and promoted as 'Maharashtrian culture' with a great deal of pride (though there has been less focus on *Sangeet Barees*).[98] Furthermore, *Kolhati* women have not been excluded from *Lavani* and *Tamasha* like *tawaif* or *devadasis* have from the classical traditions. Neither has there been a process of embourgeoisement of these traditions—rather, a bourgeois Marathi theatre modelled on Victorian theatre emerged in addition to, and not entirely at the cost of, *Tamasha* and *Lavani*.[99]

Tamasha and *Lavani* have continued to receive enough state promotion and approval to make them cultural traditions of standing (despite criticism and disapproval) and a viable livelihood. In recent years, about 150 *Tamasha* theatres have been built in Maharashtra, including rooms where song and dance performances (*Lavani* and also film songs) can take place (*baithaks*). *Lavani* and *Tamasha*, despite their problems with conservative parts of the government and general public, have received vastly more support and status than *Nautanki*, the 'folk' theatre of Uttar Pradesh which, since the 1980s and 1990s in particular, has become run-down, disreputable, and, like *mujra* and 'shows', relies on increasingly eroticised performance by female and *kothi* artistes.[100] Despite interest in *Nautanki* from the arts establishment, there has not been nearly enough done to subsidise it in the way the government of Maharashtra has supported *Tamasha* and *Lavani*.[101] It is notable that *Kolhati* are possibly the only *Bhatu* female performers who were, out of choice, not dancing in Mumbai's beer bars. This was because they saw bar dancing as 'vulgar', and to dance in bars would represent a drop in status for them (whereas for most other *Bhatu* it was distinctly higher status with better remuneration).

However, although *Kolhati* women maintain an identity as performers as well as a (difficult and liminal yet) genuine place in the socio-cultural fabric of Maharashtra, the trends of other *Bhatu* performers can be discerned in their experiences. There is an increasing reliance on sexual as opposed to artistic labour, although there is not yet the level of sex work seen with *Nat* and *Bedia*.[102] There are also increasing amounts of harassment and teasing of performers, as well as increasing difficulties in maintaining a performing livelihood. This is to be connected with a representation that eroticises and subordinates the *Lavani* dancer, as well as broader socio-economic trends, which I discuss below.

The descriptions given by *Kolhati* performers of their lives are similar in many ways to the accounts of female *Nautanki* artistes before the 1980s given by Mehrotra in her biography of Gulab Bai.[103] There is still scope for some female performers to achieve fame and considerable fortune, and for most performers to make a viable living. However, there are many factors to be balanced. *Kolhati* performers earn money directly from performing, in the form of a share of the profits (from ticket sales and tips) of the particular *Tamasha* party to which they belong.[104] They may also receive gifts from admirers, such as gold jewellery, or longer-term financial support from men with whom they establish sexual relations, known as *kaja*.[105] These were often life-long relationships in the case of *Tamasha* performers born before about 1970. In almost all circumstances, the *kaja* are married men, and the relationship with the *Kolhati* performer is extra-marital. Dancers face difficult decisions concerning these relationships, since they do not have any kind of legal basis, unlike marriage, which can protect a woman against abandonment (and *Kolhati* girls, once they start performing, cannot marry). Some *kaja* insist that the dancer give up performing and be a full-time 'mistress'. For this, the dancer needs to be assured there is enough income to support herself and usually a large extended family. However, there is a real anxiety in these situations that, having given up dancing in her prime and missed the chance of earning through performing or of attracting a possibly more prestigious and wealthy paramour (as her fame as a dancer increases), the man may not be true to his commitment, or may have relationships with other dancers. This is happening increasingly. While the most successful women perform into their elder years, for more average dancers, good careers generally end with youth.[106]

Younger performers are involved in increasingly short-term relationships with *kaja*. However, the government theatre system limits this trend to some degree. At the theatres, performers are not normally allowed to go outside the complex, where there are living quarters for the performers as well as the theatre for *Tamasha* and rooms for *baithaks*. In recent years, however, an informal and also illegal system appears to be working where girls are given *chutti* (literally 'holiday') whereby they can go out for the night with a man. These liaisons require substantial setting up on the part of the man, and may turn into a longer-term relationship. If a man likes a particular girl, he will arrange a '*baithak*', or performance in a small private room (where her accompanists and other dancers are present). He will also send her gifts. After arranging such *baithaks* at least four or five times, he may negotiate with the Party leader to take the girl on a *chutti*, which the Party leader discusses with the girl. If the girl and Party leader are agreed, the theatre owner is informed. The client will then ask to book a number of '*baithaks*' (the prices are fixed at the theatre), which is the agreed sum for the liaison with the girl. Half of this sum is kept by the theatre owner. The other half goes to the *Tamasha* Party as a whole, from which the girl in question will get her usual share.[107]

Although the women gain economically from sexual relationships with *kaja*, it is important to understand that their ability to establish such relationships, in particular prestigious ones, depends on their status as performers—and, of course, their youth and beauty. For men, it is prestigious or desirable to keep a *Kolhati* performer precisely because she is a performer. The money from tips and from the shorter-term *chutti* liaisons is shared out among the whole *Tamasha* Party, including accompanists, since they all contribute to her artistic status and ability to perform.[108] The value of skilled, artistic labour and the status and power it brings can be illustrated very simply by comparing the costs of a liaison with a *Tamasha* performer and one with a commercial sex worker. At an NGO in Pune that works with female sex workers and *Tamasha* performers—called the John Paul's Slum Development Project (JPSDP)—I was told that brothel workers were paid about Rs 60; and girls working in lodges about Rs 500. *Tamasha* performers, on the other hand, would get upwards of Rs 5,000 and would not be available so directly for sexual transaction.[109]

This difference between commercial sex workers and performers is well understood by both *Tamasha* artistes and commercial sex workers. When I visited JPSDP

Image 8: John Paul's Slum Development Project, Dr Khan, author and other staff discussion with commercial sex workers, Pune, 2010. (Author's photograph)

in Pune, Maharashtra, Varsha Kale, the BBU leader, and I were invited to address a meeting of sex workers. Varsha asked them what the differences were between them and *Tamasha* performers. They mentioned the fact that *Tamasha* dancers do not need to solicit, whereas they do. They also mentioned differences in the ways that they interact with their clients. They said that *Tamasha* dancers get respect, whereas they do not (though *Tamasha* dancers also report diminishing respect nowadays, but their status is still different to that of brothel or lodge-based sex workers). The issue of remuneration came up directly when one sex worker told of how she had once gone to watch *Tamasha*, and was dancing along to the show in her seat. The man sitting behind asked her to go with him to his hotel. He paid her Rs 2,000 for sex—way beyond the rates that she was used to—which she interpreted as being because he thought she was a dancer. Another important point that the group of sex workers raised was that they suffered much more violence and abuse from police and *gundas* ('louts' or professional criminals) than *Tamasha* artistes. The theatre-based system can be seen as protecting *Kolhati* women from the levels of violence suffered by sex workers (as well as female and *kothi* performers working in *kotha*s, shows, or *Nautanki*, etc.). The sex workers also explained that the *Tamasha* artistes do not mix with other sex workers, and do not have meetings with them. In this respect they are like many other female public/erotic performers, such as the *Agrawalis* in Calcutta, and the bar girls. *Kolhati* performers are still sufficiently well established for this distinction to be clear. One of the first things that Dr Khan from JPSDP told me when I interviewed her about their work with *Kolhati* women was, 'First of all, a *Kolhati* woman, who is in *Tamasha*, who dances, she will never consider herself a sex worker, she will never think this …'. Consequently, it took her a very long time to get the performers to open up to the understanding that they are high risk in terms of HIV and other sexually transmitted infections and to take advantage of the help and facilities available for their health needs. Not all NGOs or individuals are able to work this sensitively, and performers are likely to be labelled as sex workers, which they deeply dislike.

Although the position of *Kolhati* performers is clearly far more prestigious than most other *Bhatu* performers, some of whom are now simply brothel-based sex workers, these performers explain that the scene has become unpleasant ('*mauhal kharab ho gaya*'). Like the *Nat* I met in Sultanpur, elder performers explained that, although it is possible to earn money as an artiste, things have become increasingly unsavoury—there is not the respect for their art there used to be and there is more harassment by audience members, with people asking 'when will you come on *chutti*?' and so on. There are also continuing problems with complaints on the grounds of obscenity. On the whole, like *Deredar* performers, these women now seek to get their daughters married rather than having to lead an insecure, difficult and increasingly disreputable life as performers. This is only possible if they are able to achieve enough financial security for the extended family to get by without the earnings of a new dancer. Many more girls are getting married now. A performer in her forties reported that in previous generations, it was only a minority of girls who married, whereas now it is the majority.

This change in the working context is seen as having started at least fifteen years ago—the same timescale for a marked downturn in livelihood and status as that reported by many other groups (including the *kothi* performers, as I describe in chapter six). Government support of *Tamasha* and the provision of theatres is vital in the maintenance of the *Kolhati* identity and livelihood as one of performer rather than sex worker. Yet, this is still not enough. These trends can be attributed to increasing demand, availability of money and the social acceptability for short-term recreational sex with multiple partners that is a part of socio-economic change since the 1990s. Rather than being the preserve of the elite, who kept them as life-long mistresses, *Kolhati* performers, like the bar girls, are now in reach of a significant sector of the general public. The general public have less understanding of the status and norms of *Kolhati* women and less pressure and ability to honour relationships.[110] *Kolhati* performers are also certainly affected by the blanket association of such traditional female public/erotic performers with prostitution that became instituted with *anti-nautch*. Yet more specifically, Rege (writing in 1995) describes a process by which *Lavani* performers were sexualised and subordinated in Marathi films through, for example, being represented as 'hot chillies' or 'red chillies' (*lavangee mirchi*) who are tamed by the (upper caste) hero. Under pressure from theatre owners, *Kolhati* women would have to dance film *Lavani*s with provocative dance steps added, thus sexualising their image in representation and real live performance. Rege writes of a situation where *Lavani* was almost dead, with its revival 'next to impossible and the alternative spaces for *Lavani* performers ... almost non-existent'.[111] The short overview I present here falls far short of a proper update on the trajectory of *Lavani* in the rapid socio-economic and cultural changes that globalisation has brought since Rege's article was published in 1995. However, from my fieldwork in 2011, *Lavani*, in contexts across Maharashtra, did not seem to be 'finished' to the extent that *Nautanki* or *mujra* for the most part is. It is a flourishing business, though there is an increasing pressure for sexualised performance and the sexual labour of the female *Kolhati* performers.

Deredar

Deredar, who are said to be the same as *Gandharva* (except Muslim rather than Hindu), are found in Uttar Pradesh and Bihar, and have also migrated to Mumbai and presumably other cities. They include some high profile and well-researched communities of elite courtesans in places such as Lucknow, Benares and Muzaffarpur. *Deredar* apparently ensured an elite status for themselves in the late nineteenth century, asserting that they were '*Deredar tawaif*', and distinguishing themselves from prostitutes or cheaper dancing girls.[112] They are thus identified and identify themselves as classical *tawaif*, distinguishing themselves from other *Bhatu* female performers (and may not even say they are *Bhatu*). However, as discussed above, many kinds of *Bhatu* were in fact *tawaif* or *Baiji*s.

The marginalisation of *tawaif* has been discussed in chapter one, referencing much literature that specifically discusses *Deredar*. The process involved intertwining forces of stigmatisation (naming them as 'prostitutes'), alienation from classical music, distance from prestigious teachers, loss of skilled labour, loss of artistic livelihood, and raids and restrictions. Qureshi writes how courtesans had been driven from city centres in civic cleansing drives from 1856. However, as she continues, 'The final blow came when both reform objectives [of eliminating courtesans and promoting classical performing arts as a respectable, national tradition] resulted in police raids ordered by the Central government that closed down all musical salons by 1958. This happened almost concurrently with the abolition of landholding rights, thereby effectively eliminating the economic base for feudal patronage'.[113]

More recently, ethnographically-based studies by Maciszewski have emerged that look at the contemporary pressures on those *Deredar tawaif* who continued as performers, instead of marrying or retiring. They focus on the intense exclusionary forces on *tawaif* from the 1990s onwards, and the struggle to maintain an existence as artistes even in what is a distinctly lower position in the cultural hierarchy than that which they occupied before the reforms of the first part of the twentieth century. These publications introduce a new view of *tawaif*, firmly raising questions of socio-economic exclusion, as well as of justice and heritage.[114]

I visited *tawaif* in Muzaffarpur in March and April 2007, and also met *Deredar* families in Mumbai in 2007 and 2008, initially in connection with the bar girls, since girls from these communities were very much involved in bar dancing in Mumbai. The account from Muzaffarpur told of harassment and increased raids by police and an increasing difficulty in existing as a performer. Although Maciszewski documents long-term pressures on *tawaif* in Muzaffarpur and decline in their livelihood and social status, in my meetings with them, they identified the degradation in the *mauhal* or atmosphere as having happened particularly since 1997 and definitely not before 1992. They cited police raids, which put customers off visiting their *kotha*s since they were afraid of shame and possibly arrest. They also said that increasingly people came just asking for sex, with no interest or appreciation of their art. An elder *tawaif* spoke angrily of how the *tawaif* area was described as the 'red light district'. Audiences also demanded more film song repertoire, and interest in classical genres was diminishing. The *tawaif* were still well versed in the local repertoire of *chaiti*, *kajri*, *ghazal* and, in some cases, *qawwali*.

The increase in raids in Muzaffarpur has been connected with allegations that *kotha*s are a hotbed for criminality. This is a common and clichéd representation that has also been levied against dance bars, as I discuss in chapter five. Stories of *kotha*s and *tawaif* as nexuses of crime had been generated by a local journalist (who was later informed of the history and cultural role of *tawaif* by Varsha Kale and myself, and began subsequently to publish articles defending their identity as artistes). A local NGO, funded by Care International, was also contributing to the consolidation of the identity of the local *tawaif* as sex workers. Unlike the JPSDP project in Pune, and despite working with *tawaif*, they did not know of the differences between *tawaifs* and sex workers in terms of livelihood, history, culture or self image. The raids in Muzaffarpur were also linked to increased police power granted by PITA against 'trafficking'.[115] *Tawaif* in Muzaffarpur have travelled to the Gulf, and have also been heavily involved in dancing in bars in Mumbai, with some permanently settled there.[116] These activities are easily branded as 'trafficking', as I discuss in chapter five in the context of bar girls. I met some *tawaif* who had decided of their own volition to visit the Gulf, had a successful six months or so there, and come back. However, at the same time, I heard of male and female members of the *Deredar* community in Mumbai who are involved in not-entirely voluntary transfer of *Deredar* or impoverished girls for sex work/*mujra* in the Gulf, as well as the (non-forcible) arrangement of engagements for such girls for commission, i.e. pimping. This is the case with all these communities. Even for girls who go willingly, it can be extremely dangerous, with several bar girls and/or *tawaif* having been killed in the Gulf.[117]

An unusual feature of the *tawaif* community in Muzaffarpur has been the existence of projects involving artistic rehabilitation. Guria, an NGO based in Benares, works with sex workers and also provides support to marginalised performers. In conjunction with the ethnomusicologist and performer Amelia Maciszewski, they organised performances aimed at providing an arena for *tawaif* to showcase their art, and to thereby help build their image as performers.[118] A similar project was undertaken by a group in Muzaffarpur with local *tawaif* when I was there in 2007, following the visit by Varsha Kale. This was covered by the local press, with the above-mentioned journalist supporting the venture and the presentation of *tawaif* as artistes as opposed to sex workers. Such artistic rehabilitation projects are very rare amongst *Bhatu*, with most NGOs concerned more with health care or gender conditions.[119] It is also notably absent in virtually all government projects, who similarly do not distinguish the cultural role or history of different kinds of 'prostitutes'. However, it is only artistic rehabilitation that actually targets the cause of social exclusion and vulnerability to sex work—the loss of livelihood and status. To successfully raise status, standards and livelihood within these genres, artistic rehabilitation would need to involve large-scale programmes and large-scale funding and the creation of infrastructure. The funding of *Tamasha* by the Maharashtra government, though intended to promote 'culture' rather than 'development', has done far more for the development needs of *Kolhati* women, through pre-emption, than much of the gender/sexuality/rights/HIV/AIDS-based government or NGO intervention. The latter too often serve to consolidate the identity of these performers as sex workers whilst doing nothing to provide a long term viable livelihood and social identity. Indeed, cultural exclusion has led to socio-economic exclusion. At the moment, because of the identity of and attitudes towards these performers, such initiatives are unthinkable on a broad, let alone governmental, scale. When I joined members of the DNT commission in a discussion of communities like *Nat* and *Bedia*, where 'entire villages' were involved in sex work, I commented that for most *Bhatu* bar girls, dancing in bars had been 'rehabilitation from sex work'. This comment, which was factually correct, was somewhat brushed off and the conversation changed.[120]

Conclusions

In this chapter, I have given a preliminary view of the social organisation of North India's hereditary female performers, discussing sociological patterns, traditions and rituals as well as questions of genealogy, occupation, identity and mobility, particularly in the context of the stigmatisation of such performers. I have also presented accounts of several communities based on fieldwork (my own and the work of other scholars). These show the clear trajectory of the undermining of a livelihood and identity of performing, and increasing reliance on sex work and/or sexualised performance. This is allied with falling respect and esteem, and increasing harassment.

This chapter has covered a large amount of terrain in a way that has been necessarily cursory. More research on these communities is urgent—in particular research based on oral histories—if former status and livelihoods are to be recovered, and a fairer image and identity for these communities built. Archival research is also imperative to uncovering the longer histories of these communities, and to engendering a more accurate understanding of the ways in which they have contributed to Indian culture over the centuries.

The depth of stigma and the rigidity of definition of these groups is particularly worrying, especially given the significant social mobility that has clearly been negotiated in the past. This was caused in no small part by the processes of census, categorisation and enumeration begun by the British in India, and now a feature of modern India, and states worldwide.

3

TRANSGENDER EROTIC PERFORMERS IN SOUTH ASIA

In this chapter, I introduce another dimension of traditional female public/erotic performers: men or boys who perform as females. Indeed, this is another articulation of the illicit world of Indian dance, and has suffered comparable or parallel forces of exclusion to that of the female hereditary performers. Female impersonation is a widespread and traditionally culturally acceptable practice in South Asia. According to what is openly said, boys dancing or performing as girls are female in performing role only. Indeed, this is true in many cases and, in some traditions, in all cases. However, out of the totality of boys/men performing as females in drama and dance across South Asia, a significant proportion see themselves as females in terms of gender and sexuality and are known commonly in North India as *kothi*.[1] The term *kothi* has gained some controversy, and appears to have become much more current since the 1990s, when it became a politicised identity. However, it certainly pre-dates this time, and effeminate male performers can be traced back far further into South Asian history.[2] Performing arts and dance have traditionally been one of the most common occupations for *kothi*s. In many traditions in which *kothi*s dance as females, their performance is erotic, and they perform as alternatives to or alongside female hereditary dancers. In some cases they are equivalent to females, in some cases preferred. Even with roles that are not explicitly erotic or seductive, or with dancers who are transvestite rather than transgender, these performers allow for a 'different kind of femininity'—one with homoerotic potential, as Hansen describes in her study of female impersonators.[3] Although not all cross-dressed male performers are *kothi*, *kothi*s perform commonly in *Ramlila*, in wedding shows, in wedding processions, in *Nautanki*, and in all-male forms of *Lavani*, as well as many other genres.

Traditionally, *kothi*s occupy a liminal and opaque place in South Asia, with a public identity that is not differentiated from boys/men. As an 'invisible' sexual minority, unlike the *hijras*, people generally do not know about them and those that do would not talk openly about them in mainstream society. The British criminalised same-sex sexual relations in 1861 under section 377 of the Indian Penal Code, which outlawed sex 'against the order of nature'. The prohibition of consensual same-sex relations under this law was declared unconstitutional in 2009. This came about as a result of a case initiated by the Naz Foundation in 2001, which linked back to and continued moves begun in 1991.[4] Unlike prostitution and *nautch*, there was no open attack on same-sex relations in early nationalist India, presumably because it was too taboo a subject to discuss. As 'homosexuality' has been debated more openly in Indian in recent decades, it has widely been claimed not to be a part of 'Indian culture'. Thus, *kothis* have been shrouded in opacity, invisibility or denial for much of their modern history. However, while this continues, they have, like other males who have sex with males (MSMs), gained visibility due to the crisis of AIDS and the world of activism and health intervention that has grown in response to it. They have also gained visibility due to the spread of LGBT politics from the West.[5]

Kothis are most commonly discussed within frameworks of gender, sexuality, marginality, violence, prostitution, rights, identity and HIV/AIDS, and an increasing body of information is available on them in connection with these issues.[6] In parallel to female performers, these discourses often place *kothis* in the context of 'problems', victimhood, and needs-based struggles and political agendas. While such a focus is in some form or other absolutely imperative given the current challenges, it has built up a somewhat limited view of the socio-cultural space and significance of *kothis*, and has the potential to essentialise them and thus to affect their identity and image, as I discuss in chapter six. Research on *kothis* is beginning to broaden out.[7] However, no studies in this body of literature include a real focus on the role of *kothis* as performers.[8] This is despite the fact that, historically, *kothis* have formed an important sector of India's female public performers, and performing has been their major livelihood until recently, when reliance on sexual transaction has taken over in many areas. While most literature discusses *kothis* squarely as MSMs, I would argue that they are—in terms of livelihood, cultural role and patterns of exclusion—as close to female hereditary/public performers as they are to *hijras* or other MSMs. As stated in the introduction to this book, public female dance is an arena that reveals many inconsistencies and 'cracks' that belie the limits of the dimorphic gender system, one that is produced by patriarchy and its hierarchical gender binaries. Public female dance supports the system, yet is also deeply transgressive of it. An exploration of the arena of public female dance through the lens of *kothi* performers represents an illuminating angle on many aspects of gender, transgendering, and performing arts, in India and beyond.

While the literature revolving around gender, sexuality, identity and present needs and problems does not discuss *kothi*s as performers, sources on performing arts do not discuss *kothi* performers because (legitimate) performing arts have marginalised such female impersonators, as they have female hereditary performers.[9] Transgender 'female' performers are thus almost entirely invisible on literature on performing arts.[10] A focus on performance is a crucial dimension to understanding *kothi*s or effeminate males and their modern history. As with female erotic performers, looking at labour, livelihood and identity relating to performing arts is essential to understanding the social, cultural and economic place the majority of *kothi*s have occupied in Indian society, and to understanding the ways in which this liminality is breaking down and changing into far more absolute forms of exclusion and also confrontation. It is also a key, and so far neglected, aspect of placing them firmly within 'Indian culture', history and heritage.

In this chapter, I introduce *kothi*s as female and erotic performers historically and in the present day. I start by locating erotic *kothi* performers within India's transgenders and sexual minorities. I compare them with and distinguish them from the more visible and well-known *hijra*s and gays/bisexuals in terms of gender, sexuality, performing role, ritual status and class. I then discuss historical sources relating to erotic male performers in India, illustrating that, as with the female erotic performers, they have deep roots in the past. The chapter then focuses on *kothi* performers in the context of gender and performance and explores dance as a traditional (liminal) space for *kothi*s, drawing on theoretical as well as ethnographic material. I compare *kothi*s with female performers, as opposed to *hijra*s, and interpret female hereditary performers as, in many senses, also 'transgender'. I focus on issues of marginalisation and political discourse on sexuality and rights, as well as practical livelihood and life in chapter six. Both these chapters aim to broaden and enrich the discourse on *kothi*s to one that includes them within Indian performing arts and culture.

MSM transgenders and sexual minorities in South Asia

Although the divisions overlap in practice, MSM transgenders and sexual minorities in South Asia can broadly be divided into *hijra*s, who are highly visible and well known; *kothi*s, who are not identified or visible as a group and are known about only in certain circles; and gays and bisexuals in a more Western sense.

Transgenders in the form of *hijra*s or 'eunuchs' are a highly visible part of India for Indians and foreign visitors. They have been the subject of book-length ethnographic studies.[11] Their official role in Indian society is ritual/auspicious, relating in particular to reproduction, something that is rooted in their inter-sex status. They are powerful, but at the same time extremely low status.[12] People give them money to perform *badhai* or blessings at the birth of a (male) child.[13] Giving money to a *hijra* who is begging results in an auspicious blessing. However, *hijra*s also have the power to curse, so people may give them money to avoid this. The third major occupation of *hijra*s is sex work, performing some kind of 'female', 'passive' role in sex with men. This is not a socially or ritually sanctioned role, and *hijra*s are generally thought of and profess to be asexual. It is only since around the early 2000s that *hijra*s have begun to be open to HIV/AIDS interventions in Delhi, for example, even though communities have been hit extremely hard by the disease.[14]

When someone joins the *hijra*s, they effectively leave mainstream society and many of its norms, such as marriage. They are taken on by a guru, becoming their *chela* or 'disciple', and become subject to the rules of the *hijra* community/household. Some *hijra*s undergo the emasculation ritual, *nirvana*, where the penis and testicles are cut off.[15] After this they are known in many parts of India as *nirvan*, or 'reborn'.[16] On becoming *nirvan*, a *hijra* achieves a higher status in the community, and, for example, a higher proportion of earnings from performing *badhai* than the non-emasculated *hijra*s, known as *akhwa hijra*s. Those born as hermaphrodites also make up a minority of the *hijra* community.

*Kothi*s are, in a sense, linked to *hijra*s, since a male is first a *kothi* before becoming a *hijra*, and many *kothi*s do indeed make this leap.[17] *Kothi*s are also linked to the *hijra*s through a largely shared secret language known as *Farsi*. Indeed, I was informed by many *kothi*s that the word '*kothi*' comes from this language and means 'neophyte', someone not yet initiated to the *hijra* community. In other words, a *kothi* is something you are, whereas a *hijra* is something you become. Being a *kothi* is fundamentally about being feminine, which includes being anally penetrated by a man; commonly some involvement in performing arts as a female; and other feminine/feminising behaviour such as doing housework or being a beautician.

Unlike *hijra*s, *kothi*s are not defined as a group in any consistent or visible way. They may be cross-dressed some of the time, but not necessarily. While the *hijra*s are extremely low status and outcaste, a *kothi* need not be. The social organisation of *kothi*s is also nebulous, as I discuss in chapter six.[18] Whereas the *hijra*s are ritual/auspicious performers, *kothi*s are usually erotic performers, or more generally non-ritual performers (though some roles they, and non-transgender boys, play are religious, such as Sita in *Ramlila*). These differences are represented in the figure below. Since the 1990s and the 2000s in particular, the *hijra*s have become far more open, and there is a blurring of *hijra*s and *kothi*s to a degree that represents marked change. I explore this in chapter six too.

Another crucial factor in the structuring of India's (male) sexual minorities is class. *Hijra*s and *kothi*s are from the lower socio-economic strata, with *hijra*s in particular seen as being extremely low by many *kothi*s. Men from the upper socio-economic strata who are homoerotically inclined generally identify themselves as gay or bisexual. For a high status man to take on a feminised identity, especially publicly, would traditionally invite ridicule and, in theory, the high status men are the 'active', 'real men' in sexual encounters or relationships with the feminine *kothi*s. These men are known by *hijra*s and *kothi*s as *giriya*s or *panthis*—again, words from the *hijra* language. A *kothi* would, therefore, tend not to identify as a 'homosexual' man. As one *kothi* working for an HIV/AIDS Community Based Organisation (CBO) put it, 'you can put me in the category of gays, but I see myself as a kind of female'.

*Hijra*s	*Kothi*s
Ritual/auspicious in status	No ritual status
Extremely low status	Not low status per se
Renouncers of the householder's life; a form of cult	Exist mainly in mainstream society, but also (to a greater or lesser degree and largely secretly or in a manner 'unseen') outside of it
Ritual, non-erotic performers; officially asexual	Erotic performers
Visible	Invisible/opaque
Organised into a tightly coherent (across the whole of India) hierarchical community with explicit and strict rules, from which people can be excluded if they break them	Organised into nebulous, localised communities and networks with norms rather than rules, and no means of officially excluding people who do not adhere to these norms

Erotic feminine male performers in historical sources

Vanita and Kidwai's volume *Same Sex Love in India* (2000) has been groundbreaking in writing same-sex love back into two millennia of Indian history and culture, retrieving many references from bowdlerised translations. It reveals that transgender or effeminate erotic male dancers have been a part of performing arts culture in India for millennia. Although 'homosexuality' in today's India is commonly blamed on either the Muslims or the West, as Vanita writes, erotic cross-dressed male performers are very much a part of India's pre-Islamic past:

> Given the widespread popular assumption in modern India that boy prostitution, eunuchs and even anal sex appeared only following the advent of Islam, it is important to note that in pre-Islamic texts, men and boy prostitutes and dancers who service men are represented in descriptive, nonjudgmental terms, as normally present in court and in daily life, evidence of the affluence and splendour of urban culture.[19]

Here, I draw on selected translations of primary historical sources in order to give a glimpse of effeminate, erotic male performers in history, and to highlight many striking similarities with contemporary *kothi*s.

The ancient Tamil epic, *Shilappadikaram*, dated probably from the early Christian era, clearly references erotic boy entertainers. Vanita writes, quoting from Danielou's translation:

> In the *Shilappadikaram* a king called Nurruvar Kannar whose kingdom is in the Gangetic plain sends as tribute to the Chera king Shenguttuvan a large number of gifts including animals, jugglers, musicians, dancing girls and 'one thousand brilliantly dressed *kanjuka*, boy prostitutes with long carefully burnished hair'. These boys are described as 'fine-spoken'.[20]

A text from the medieval Persio-Urdu tradition tells of the Sufi saint Jamshed Rajgiri, 'Akhi', being swept away by a group of Hindu boys dancing in female dress on *Holi*, with others from the city following suit. The story depicts devotion as intense and passionate love and the abandonment of asceticism or orthodoxy, which is typical of both Sufism and devotional Hinduism:

> ... Akhi Rajgiri was sitting alone in his world of spiritual delight, absorbed in contemplating the scintillating beauty of ultimate reality. Suddenly a large band of handsome Hindu youths came wandering through his courtyard. They were decked out in jewels and sporting the alluring clothing of brides. They were singing and dancing, teasing each other and playing with each other. They were all singing melodies of longing and passion, dancing with all manner of delicate and beguiling gestures, languorous winks through half-closed eyes, and beseeching nods. They came bobbing along the road from the city, as if they were the bridesmaids of passion set to rout the self-control of ascetic discipline.
>
> On laying his eyes upon these waves of passionate love, Akhi Rajgiri let slip the reins of self-control that he had once imagined to be in his command. He was gripped by a state of blissful unselfconsciousness. He rose up intoxicated by the onslaught of desire, and joined their joyful band dancing among them with total abandon, spreading ecstasy and reciting poems of love. Three days and nights passed while Akhi Rajgiri stayed with these young men, engrossed in tasting love and falling into trances.
>
> At this point, the whole city fell into disarray and confusion. All the people from Kanauj and the surrounding towns poured out of their homes and gathered at that place to catch a glimpse of the beauty of Akhi Rajgiri's sainthood. Each one who saw him dancing and singing with the youths was struck by the sight, and tearing his clothes would rush to join that gathering that pointed the way to real love.[21]

Although this story should perhaps be read as much as a myth of religious mysticism and passion as a record of contemporary practices, such teasing, flirting and seductive troupes of *kothi* performers are something I have seen in twenty-first-century Lucknow. However, in Lucknow, such groups only roam around at night, and far less openly than the boys in this historical source. *Kothi*s dance on *Holi* in contemporary North India but this too happens at night. As is well known, much devotional Hinduism involves the transgendering of male devotees, with the human soul seen as female, and its longing for union with the divine presented in terms of the sexual love and passion of a lover for the beloved.[22] This may support cross-dressed performances in certain manifestations of Krishna-worship in particular. For example, in *Raslila* (the enactment and dancing of scenes from Krishna's life), the milkmaids are typically performed by males, commonly *kothi*s. However, the restriction of females, especially in religious dramas (since any females who performed would necessarily be 'disreputable'), is also a reason for the all-male cast. All-male casts have traditionally been the norm with *Ramlila* too, and Ram worship and the Ramayana do not have the tradition of feminising devotees or eroticising worship that the Krishna *Bhakti* has. Sufism also involves transgender subject positions in many of its strands, with devotees taking on a female persona and devotion to the divine expressed in metaphors of love.[23] The feminine voice addressing a male beloved is consequently common in much Persian and Urdu poetry, and similarly may have supported cross-dressed performance. In *rekhti* poetry, the male poet writes in the feminine voice of love for a female beloved; and in *mehfils* where such poetry was recited, there were instances of cross dressing.[24] This can be seen as connected with *kothi* performers.[25] However, modern day *kothi*s operate in a strongly female-male, heterosexualised framework, as I explore below.

One of the most detailed accounts of organised troupes of cross-dressed dancers, whose purpose was to entertain, seduce and beguile male audiences, is found in the *Muraqqa i Dehli*, by Dargah Quli Khan, which records observations of Delhi dating from 1738 to 1741.[26] The detail suggests that some were equivalent to courtesans, providing musical and literary entertainment, witty conversation and eroticism and sexual liaisons for those who liked the male body rather than, or in addition to, the female one.[27] I quote excerpts from Kidwai's translation at some length. Describing the sights of the two main markets, Quli Khan writes:

> Young good-looking men danced everywhere and created great excitement. ... Young men and pubescent boys are at the fringes of the crowds. Whenever one lifts one's eyes, the gaze glides over the beauty of a moon-faced one and if one extends one's arm it seems to become entangled in some young man's tresses.[28]

He describes a troupe of performing boys:

> Taqi is the head of a troupe of boys who mime, dance and perform conjuring tricks. He is a favorite of the king and has access to his private chambers. The great nobles desire to know him and treat him with great respect. ... Like flowers of many colours, young men are always present in his gardenlike home. In that verdant meadow there are beautiful dark boys blooming like tender flowers. [...] His dwelling is like a vision of fairyland and his establishment would be the envy of a house of wonders. Dainty waists sway like the petals of a flower and tresses are envied by the scented hyacinth. The slender, well-proportioned beauties capture hearts with their graceful strutting, and the dark-eyed send out messages with their

looks. Wherever there is a boy who is unhappy with the male garb, Taqi's eyes spot him and wherever he sees a soft and tender boy, the gardens envy his discovery. He is the master and patron of all sorts of catamites because they know that he has carried this art to new heights. He is the leader of all the eunuchs and they feel proud to be his disciples. In short he is the leader of the eunuchs and a patron of pimps.

[...]

Sultana is a twelve-year old dark-complexioned youth. When he dances his gestures and movements are enchanting, and when he sings, he charms the universe and drives his listeners crazy. He is young but musically very skilled. He is just a bud but can match any flower in full bloom and even though he is only the flame of a candle, he can claim equality with the sun. His admirers can never have enough of his singing and those who want to gaze at him forever are embarrassed at the misfortune of the limits of their vision.[29]

This description of erotic male performers chimes closely with many of my observations of *kothi* performers in contemporary India—their seductiveness, charm, grace, femininity, and joy in performing. Contemporary *kothis* share many of the characteristics Quli Khan describes: they identify each other by an effeminate gait or air (unhappiness 'with the male garb'); the performers have troupes, with leaders; and many men are bewitched and seduced by them. However, today's *kothi* performers are not accepted nearly so openly as a part of the colour and richness of cultural life. Instead they exist at a lower socio-economic and cultural level, with very few places in which they can be seen in a feminine guise during the day.[30]

An account from the first few decades of the twentieth century describes male dancers known as *Bhands*, who came to Lucknow from Delhi and wore a feminised version of male clothes. They introduced in their performances:

... a young boy who wears his hair long like a woman and dances with such animation and vivacity that his activities arouse the spectators... in these performances, a handsome adolescent boy with long hair in the chignon style, wearing gaudy-coloured male clothes and with bells on his ankles, dances and sings.[31]

The description of the long-haired boy wearing 'gaudy-coloured male clothes' and dancing with 'such animation and vivacity' describes almost exactly a troupe of performers I saw by chance dancing on the street during a festival in Pune. There were several feminine male dancers with long hair dressed in brightly coloured kurta pyjama, dancing in a way that was at once feminine but, in its vigour and muscularity, had a kind of 'masculinity'.

Such sources as these represent open descriptions and indeed celebrations of erotic male, effeminate performers within elite entertainment as well as religious cultures of Sufism and devotional Hinduism. They show the level of acceptance and status the performers held in society. In colonial sources from the nineteenth century, there is very little mention of male dancers, and certainly no description of them in such admiring, erotic terms. Walker quotes a passage from 1851, which depicts cross-dressed male dancers in a humorous guise:

Conceive, if you can, the unholy spectacle of two reverend-looking grey-beards, ... dancing opposite each other dressed in women's attire; the flimsiest too, with light veils on their heads, and little bells jingling from their ankles, ogling, smirking, and displaying the juvenile playfulness of '—limmer lads and lassies—'.[32]

Groups of buffoon-type male dancers, sometimes cross-dressed, can be found in earlier sources too. Cross-dressed male dancers are also mentioned in the context of Hindu festivals such as *Holi*, or the religious drama *Raslila*. Again, however, they are not described in alluring, erotic terms. In her exploration of the history of *kathak* and the *Kathak* community, Walker mentions a travelogue from 1813, the earliest to cite performers called *kathak*s:

Thomas Duer Broughton briefly described the fondness of Hindus for 'exhibitions of dancing boys' during the spring festival of Holi. The boys, he explained 'are called *Kuthiks*; and are, as well as their attendant musicians, always Brahmans. Their dress is nearly the same as that of the Nach girls; but their dancing and singing is generally much better'.[33]

As I describe in chapter six, *kothi*s have become invisible in legitimate culture in modern times, and female impersonators are found only in regional/vernacular theatre, having disappeared from high-profile, urban traditions. An excerpt from Malka Pukhraj's biography, written around the end of the twentieth century, contrasts strongly with the passages quoted above, especially those from before the eighteenth century. It describes memories from the princely court of pre-independence Jammu and Kashmir and gives a somewhat disapproving account of a maharaja who brought with him a troupe, not of female performers, but what are described as *hijra*s.[34] It is clear from this description that this was not looked on well, and the maharaja himself is described as strange or deviant:

He was dark, weedy as a twig, tall as a pole and with no hair growing on his face. He was young, but his face had wrinkles instead of hair on it. There were also dark marks on his cheeks. On his head was a turban, which looked as if it was made up of rope. He wore a brocade achkan and, on his stick-like legs a churidar pajama, and gold embroidered shoes.

Following him were twenty or twenty-five *hijras*. They wore expensive peshwazes and were loaded with jewellery and they followed the Maharaja with their mincing gait. This was the Maharaja of Alwar. He and his staff sat down on the chairs. Scornful, sarcastic smiles appeared on the faces of the other maharajas. [...] [T]he Maharaja of Alwar [...] gestured to his *hijra*s who, after blessing him a few times, began to sing. Within five minutes other maharajas began to leave. Our Maharaja, being a good host, stayed for fifteen minutes and then left, saying he had to go to bed. [...]

Till then I had only seen *hijra*s when one or two badly dressed ones appeared with a dholak round their neck at the birth of a boy. They would accept a few rupees, bless the child and leave. But these *hijras*! Bedecked in gold and dressed in silver embroidered peshwazes, they had enough airs and graces to beat any woman hollow. Their faces were those of men but they behaved like women. Their voices were off-key. They danced to thumris and dadras, which they sang in their grating voices.[35]

Kothi*s, femininity, dance and eroticism*

The vast majority of *kothi*s are drawn to (female) dance. A large proportion are actually involved as professional or semi-professional performers, and others just dance at gatherings such as the drop-in sessions of the various CBOs that work on HIV/AIDS and other MSM issues. *Kothi*s form an important sector of India's professional performers, with many thousands of them operating in networks in North India alone. Here I analyse this important but largely invisible or unacknowledged portion of India's 'female' dancers, examining the dynamics of this tradition or traditional practice in terms of gender, sexuality, dance and the body.

Judith Butler's well-known work theorises gender in terms of performativity and performance. She states:

> Gender ought not to be constructed as a stable identity or locus of agency from which various acts follow; rather, gender is an identity tenuously constituted in time, instituted in an exterior space through a *stylized repetition of acts*. The effect of gender is produced through the stylization of the body and, hence, must be understood as the mundane way in which bodily gestures, movements, and styles of various kinds constitute the illusion of an abiding gendered self.[36]

Rather than being something that exists as a fundamental truth and is a pre-existing human 'role' or essence that is or should be 'acted out', gender is something that is performed. Its continuous performance makes it a constant fact of social life, immanent in the body. Butler refutes the distinction that gender is 'cultural' while sex is 'biological': 'Gender is not to culture as sex is to nature; gender is also the discursive/cultural means by which "sexed nature" or "a natural sex" is produced and established as "prediscursive", prior to culture, a politically neutral surface on which culture acts'.[37] Dance, as an embodied, highly stylised, and strongly affective performing art has the potential to be a particularly gendered, and hence gendering, arena. In the context of the dynamics of gender, gendered space, dance, eroticism and the body in South Asia, it is a medium by which the maleness rooted in the male body can be transcended, and the body can become female. As I discuss further below, *kothi*s are categorised as transgender according to thinking that roots gender in sex. However, if gender can be seen as independent of sex (and I would argue that it can), it is more accurate to describe them as a type of female and, in certain (liminal) spaces, *kothi*s are indeed equivalent to females.

The performers: Dance, embodiment, and performing femininity

*Kothi*s 'perform' femininity in a number of ways: dancing female dances, wearing female clothes and makeup, shaping their eyebrows, applying henna, doing housework, adopting the feminine mode of speech, calling each other sisters/mothers/

daughters, adopting a swaying walk, a particular tone of voice, training as beauticians, and so on. Dance, however, can be seen as a particularly powerful part of gender performance—an arena par excellence for the constitution of gender—and hence something that *kothi*s are drawn to, appreciate and respect. Although all acts are stylised in terms of gender and contribute to the constitution of the gendered body, the performing art of dance exists purely to be seen; it displays the moving body as something in itself rather than as a means to an end, as is the case with housework, for example. Desmond, in her study of tourism, theorises this role of 'bodies on display' stating, 'I have been struck by how ubiquitous are the ways that bodies function implicitly as the final authenticators of identity categories. In numerous realms of thought, and not just the obvious ones, bodies are the epistemological equivalent of "the buck stops here"'. [38] Dance, similarly, can be seen as an activity that, for *kothi*s and their audiences, makes them feel and appear feminine in a way that is 'natural' and bodily. Through dance and its performance to audiences, this femininity becomes a privileged social fact, though only in the liminal public and/or male spaces in which it takes place.[39]

In addition to being offered as display, dance is also stylised over and above mundane acts and, in the case of the dance traditions *kothi*s perform, the style is consummately feminine. Furthermore, in the typical repertoire performed by *kothi*s, the dancer is firmly placed not just in an ordinary female role, but an exaggerated and/or iconic one, and usually in the highly emotionalised context of erotic love. This is true of songs/dances by female characters in Indian films and also in the theatrical traditions such as *Ramlila*, *Raslila*, and also *Nautanki*, where characters have a traditional/epic and religious iconicity. *Kothi*s also perform romantic/erotic dance songs within these theatrical traditions, sometimes during scene changes. In film songs, the performer is not just playing the film heroine, vamp, courtesan, item girl—epitomes of femininity—they are also indexing the film star (who plays these particular roles). They do so through imitating their style and expressions, thereby adding another layer of feminine iconicity to the performance.[40] In this way, *kothi*s perform and embody particularly potent and highly gendered forms of femininity in terms of iconicity and also emotion.

When I have watched *kothi*s dance to individual film songs (rather than in theatrical roles), style/stylisation is intimately linked to emotion and feminine personae through the technique of *abhinay* (the acting out or miming of lyrics or sentiment in dance). *Abhinay* is common in many forms of South Asian dance, and is always emphasised in performances by *kothi*s. While all dance moves potentially involve stylisations of gender, with *abhinay*, the female subject's specific words and emotions (themselves heightened through poetic expression) are enacted in stylised and hyper-feminine forms. Generally, the *kothi*s I have seen performing in CBOs centre their dance style on *abhinay*, expressing the words, meaning and emotions of the female character, and thereby focusing on embodying the subjectivity of the song. They use *abhinay* to identify with and become the character in their emotional state, and to display this persona to those watching. In the middle class world of Bollywood dance, in contrast, although *abhinay* is involved, there is much more focus on non-*abhinay* dance moves and on dance as fitness. It is also significant to note that *kothi*s perform largely improvised dance and *abhinay*, reflecting informal training but also a high degree of spontaneous embodiment and identification. In contrast, the new Bollywood dance scene involves memorised routines, often in groups.

Butler's work understands embodiment and the body as central to gender since they are necessarily and by definition involved in performance. Her study looks at the signifying of the body, the stylisation of the body, and the way the body acts. Connell's more somatic and sociological approach to gender emphasises 'the activity, literally the agency, of bodies in social processes'.[41] He focuses on the social constitution of gender as a 'body-reflexive practice', looking at how the feelings, sensations and physicality of the body are involved in the ways in which gender is played out and constituted (though not determined).[42] He defines gender as follows:

> Gender is a way in which social practice is ordered. In gender processes, the everyday conduct of life is organized in relation to a reproductive arena, defined by the bodily structures and processes of human reproduction. This arena includes sexual arousal and intercourse, childbirth and infant care, bodily sex difference and similarity. ... Gender is a social practice that constantly refers to bodies and what bodies do. ...[43]

In the gender norms that have existed in India, as discussed in the introduction, a female body that performs in male space, or a male body that becomes female through performing as female in male space, tends to be seen erotically. Much of the dance that *kothi*s perform is erotic. This may be explicitly so in particular contexts but in general tends to focus on romantic/erotic love and female characters. *Kothi* performance, because it is generally targeted *at* a (male) audience (rather than just performed *before* an audience) is also often actively seductive as well as erotic, with desire sought and incited. The attraction of female dance comes not just from appearing feminine, but actually being in a position where it is possible to attract male attention and male lovers—to feel feminine and to be feminine in terms of the dynamics of bodily desire. This is also heightened by the emotional potency and, in certain ways, the additional feminising dynamics of music, song and dance, which I discuss more below. In this way, it is possible to see how female (and, in particular, erotic) dance constitutes femininity through its embodied, highly stylised and displayed nature, as well as through its relationship to the 'reproductive arena' of sexuality, emotion, passion and the dynamics of bodily desire between performers and audience. In this sense, dance can be described as a privileged space for performing gender—a place in which gender is constituted in a way that is particularly visceral, emotional, passionate and, potentially, strongly felt and 'real'.

The overwhelming majority of *kothi*s are attracted to dance and find it a 'natural' medium in which to be feminine and express their 'true' femininity. To be a good dancer also brings prestige and respect in the *kothi* community, since it makes the individual more feminine. In this way, it is prized as a skill as much, or even more than, feminine beauty. As an observer, I too found that it was when *kothi*s were dancing that they seemed most feminine, with a skill, grace and passion that seemed rooted in a core femininity and female subjectivity, and a sense of the 'true', inner feminine self. Through moving the body in this hyper-feminine, emotionally deeply-invested and often seductive manner, the femininity becomes physical—it is rooted in the body, and hence appears to be as 'natural' as if the body itself were female. All the *kothi*s I met were clearly effeminate and, before I knew about the concept of the *kothi*, I had automatically assumed several to be 'gay'. However, seeing them dance was something quite different. I met a professional *kothi* dancer from Lucknow who was slightly balding, had something of a paunch, was in his late thirties or forties, not particularly 'pretty' or 'feminine', and was wearing an old kurta-pyjama at the time. However, as soon as he performed a few movements of *abhinay*, there was an astonishing transformation into an accomplished, graceful, courtesan-type figure. *Kothi* dancers are well aware of this power of dance. An effeminate *Sikh* man in his fifties with a beard and turban who had performed extensively when he was younger said that it was only when you were really accomplished as a dancer that people would see you purely as a female.[44] In this sense, dance and movement have the potential to overwhelm even clear physical markers of the male sex such as beards or baldness. Many *kothi*s boasted to me that when they danced in female clothes, no one could tell they were male. Several also stated that when seduced audience members got close enough to realise, they did not care. In addition to the fact that they were by then so aroused, in terms of the politics of penetration, a man who is 'passive' is feminine; and, through the gendering power of dance too, the *kothi* performer is equivalent to, if not actually, a female.

Kothi performance can be seen as highly transgressive, since it involves male-to-male eroticism. However, the equivalence to a female is so close that it is, at the same time, very conformist. Comparisons can be made between *kothi* performers and Butler's description of drag and performativity in performance.[45] Drag, like *kothi* performance, belies the artifice of gender. As Butler writes, 'In imitating gender, drag implicitly reveals the imitative structure of gender itself—as well as its contingency'.[46] But with *kothi*s, the emphasis is rather more on the naturalness of gender performance, or an artifice that is 'real' and 'natural', particularly in the context of (liminal) social place. Irony has a role in *kothi* performance, as I discuss below, but there is a stronger emphasis on sincere and close identification and equivalence with (biologically) female performers from the point of view of both performers and audiences. Seeing *kothi* performers as transgressive and, in particular, as out of place appears to be a predominantly modern phenomenon, emerging from the influence of Western ideas of gender, homophobia, and sex-gender frameworks.

While everyone is (largely unconsciously) performing gender, for *kothi*s, who have a male body but are female, their performance goes against social norms and they therefore have to try harder to be feminine. They must create an illusion that goes further than the general illusion of gender. Comparing the *kothi*s I saw with (biologically) female dancers, the *kothi*s displayed a level of enthusiasm and energy in performance (even those who did not dance well) that I did not see with the female dancers. Unlike some female performers, I never saw *kothi*s dancing half-heartedly. The female performers' lack of enthusiasm relates in part to their lack of status and opportunity as dancers, and a sense of depression and hopelessness in these communities as a whole. However, in many ways, the *kothi*s too are becoming increasingly involved in sex work and are, in many cases, unable to survive from dance alone (as I discuss in chapter six). This, however, has not translated into any kind of lack of enthusiasm or sense of pointlessness about dance. Here, although they are in so many ways equivalent to each other in terms of their social role as (erotic) female performers, it is possible to see how the meaning, value and purpose of dance for *kothi*s has some key differences from hereditary female dancers.[47] For *kothi*s, who are male in body, it is through doing rather than being that they are female—and so dance has a particularly profound importance. Because their body is seen as male, it is not enough just to be, or to perform average or mundane femininity; or to simply show flesh (the crucial parts of which are of course padding). Rather, they have to do: to move, to perform (or outperform). They then become female, and indeed, more female than most women. While I have witnessed bar girls in Singapore simply strutting around the stage, tossing their hair and swinging their hips (more showing off their bodies than dancing), *kothi*s almost never underperform when they dance. Their energy and relish for dance makes many of them extremely good 'natural' (typically untrained) dancers. The enthusiasm is also visible with *kothi*s that are not particularly good dancers. I remember one drop-in session at Bharosa Trust in Lucknow at which *kothi*s were dancing to film songs together or one after the other. One *kothi* danced with such energy and abandonment that other *kothi*s started joking and whispering, '*isko current lag gaya*' ('s/he's plugged into an electric current').

As I have mentioned, the power of dance as a medium and platform for seduction is important for most *kothi* dancers, at least at some stage in their life. However, dance is also something they do amongst themselves or for someone such as myself, who wishes to watch and appreciate them. Many *kothi*s were keen to show me their dancing, something female dancers would not do unless we were very close acquaintances or a proper occasion had been arranged, including payment. For the female performers, then, dancing was strictly a professional activity. After they had performed for me at Bharosa, one *kothi* commented with enthusiasm that I'd now seen them in a 'new form' (*naya rup*). In Balliya, we were discussing dance with one *kothi* who suddenly got up and started dancing to a film song playing from another room. Cross-dressed and with long hair, she looked very feminine even before she started to dance—but as she danced to a short excerpt of this song, myself and the other *kothi*s agreed how very like Madhuri she was, in an innocent, 'sweet sixteen' way. She obviously had a real desire to show herself in this fashion to such an appreciative audience.

Among *kothi*s, it is very common to be attracted to, in particular, female dance from early childhood. One *kothi* from Mumbai stated that, although she started dancing professionally as a female from the age of fifteen or sixteen, 'before that feelings are there. I'm feeling like a girl, I'm a girl, I'm not a boy. I'm feeling like that since childhood. I'm playing with girls. I dance with girls'.[48] When a *kothi*

Image 9: Divya Sagar, staff member at Bharosa Trust, performing informally to a film *mujra* in Naz Foundational International office, Lucknow, March 2007. (Author's photograph)

starts to perform in public, feelings are shown, acted out, and given a platform. The feelings become a form of witnessed 'truth' and are validated as a social (performative) truth. Again, returning to the role of 'bodies on display', it is clear that, at a personal level, dance is very important for *kothis* as a way of being 'naturally' female. A proportionally higher number of *kothis* are naturally drawn to or involved in dance than are girls and women, even though increasing numbers are now dancing in India. Dancing for *kothis* has rewards that do not exist for biological females and they tend to bring a particular passion to it. The effects on the *kothi* community of the shrinking spaces for dance performance and the rise in sex work should be considered in this context. Sex work can be seen as an activity that is on a par with dance in terms of its potential to make femininity visceral, empassioned and 'real', and to constitute a livelihood. There are other visceral ways in which *kothis* appear to channel their passion to be feminine and to identify with women that are difficult to see as positive. Beyond extremely conservative ideas of what it means to be a wife or girlfriend, which independent women find challenging, many *kothis* actually desire violence or abuse from male partners because it makes them feel female.[49] One *kothi* told me that there are even some who wish to be raped. I questioned whether this was possible, given that rape is, by definition, something that happens against one's will. S/he said, 'no, they say that they are not satisfied until they are screaming and desperate for the man to stop'. I discuss such issues of social spaces in which to be feminine/female in more detail in chapter six.

The art: gendering dance and performance

Dance and music can themselves be seen as potentially feminising in terms of emotion and aesthetics and also with respect to the dynamics of performers, audiences, status and power.[50] Brown discusses the emotional power of music specifically in terms of gender and eroticism. She refers to Islamic cultures—specifically Mughal India—in which there is particular restriction on music due to its known emotional power. However, what she says is highly revealing in terms of the contemporary context of erotic, *kothi* dance, where the dynamics of status, gender, eroticism and the emotional power of music interweave:

> Music has always been highly controversial in Islamic cultures. It is no accident that those who played the roles of courtesans and catamites in the Mughal Empire were often musicians and dancers. Because the emotional power of music was considered raw and uncontrolled, music was deemed, like love, to have the potential to rob a man of his self-control and virtue. It was believed to possess the same, subversive erotic power as the beloved. Because of its potentially destabilising feminine power, music *itself* threatened the *mirza*'s [the elite, Mughal man's] masculinity.[51]
>
> [...]

Professional male dancers in Indo-Muslim culture were stereotyped as objects of erotic desire. Other than in the Sufi assembly—often as exception to the rules—for a man to dance was to indicate his receptivity to erotic attention, a passive erotic behaviour that was unacceptable for a *mirza*. Erotic objectification was clearly a risk appropriate to the status of the professional musician, but definitely not to the patron. It seems that the social distance mandated in the British Library *Mirzanama* between patron and musician was also designed to avoid transgressions of the *mirza*'s masculine sexuality. It is difficult to avoid the conclusion that the Mughal elite viewed the act of singing in public, or even excessive love of music, as somehow feminising.[52]

Interestingly, dance appears more unsuitable than singing for high status men, perhaps because, in an immediate and visual sense, it is more embodied and hence (potentially) more eroticising. Brown quotes from the British Library *Mirzanama*:

[A mirza] should under no circumstances indulge himself in singing, but leave this rather to the professional musicians. Singing can lead to dancing, and that necessarily to other disgraceful and ignominious actions.[53]

Despite hundreds of years of history, the role of music and dance as impassioning, and performers as objects of desire—and hence low status and feminine—still very much exists. Although dance has gained a new status and respectability in India during the twentieth century, it is often still seen as an unsuitable occupation for men, as well as women. While for women it is parallels with the figure of the dancing girl or *nachnewali* that implies prostitution, for men, the associations are less explicit, but involve notions of status and masculinity. *Kothi*s are always lower class men. The effeminate upper class Sikh man I mentioned above was given a lot of trouble from his family because of his acting and performing as a female dancer, since it identified him as low status or low class. Upper class/caste men who are homoerotically inclined do not identify themselves as *kothi* but as gay, and are not professional erotic performers in these traditional contexts. Gay or effeminate men are fairly numerous in the new world of Bollywood dance, and indeed in the classical world. However, they perform as men in a rather more unisex role, and certainly do not cross-dress. Given that classical performing arts are now largely gender neutral and entirely middle class, male dancers (whether gay/effeminate/straight) avoid associations with the kinds of male dancers Brown describes in Mughal India. Similarly, the middle class institutionalisation of Bollywood dance and its high degree of gender-neutral roles makes it safe for male as well as female dancers, as I describe in chapter four. A number of *kothi*s commented explicitly on the feminine or feminising potential of dance. One said to me that when s/he had put on female clothes, s/he suddenly found s/he was able to dance. Another *kothi* based in Delhi told me how s/he was trained as a *kathak* dancer, and also used to dance at *Ramlila*s and in shows in and around Delhi. S/he had lots of female clothes at home plus jewellery and makeup that s/he wore to perform, and his/her parents were quite happy, and indeed proud, of his/her dancing (they were a lower class family—a middle class family would not have accepted this). However, after someone maliciously told his/her parents that s/he had sex with boys, the parents, who had had no idea this was the case, were furious. His/her mother burned the clothes, smashed the jewellery and makeup, and forbid him/her to dance—not just female dance, but all dance, saying 'dance is making you feminine'. While this *kothi* did not see dance as making him/her feminine (this, rather, was his/her nature), s/he stated that 'dance itself is feminine'.[54]

It is also possible to see this feminising and eroticising character of dance and dancers in terms of the politics of the gaze—the fact that a performer possesses, indeed must possess, what Mulvey has termed 'to-be-looked-at-ness'. Being on display, in a specifically framed performing space, and performing in a way that is specialised and highly stylised, encourages the male gaze. As Mulvey states in her well-known piece:

> In a world ordered by sexual imbalance, pleasure in looking has been split between active/male and passive/female. The determining male gaze projects its phantasy onto the female figure which is styled accordingly. In their traditionally exhibitionist role women are simultaneously looked at and displayed with their appearance coded for strong visual and erotic impact so that they can be said to connote to-be-looked-at-ness. Women displayed as sexual objects is the leit-motif of erotic spectacle: from pin-ups to strip-tease, from Ziegfried to Busby Berkeley, she holds the look, plays to and signifies male desire.[55]

While Mulvey's discussion is based in a Western (cinematic) context and draws on Western psychoanalytical theory, it ties in very much with the reasons why the Mughal gentleman should not perform, especially not dance; why (homo)erotic performers are feminised/female; and indeed, the principles of *purdah* and of marriage, ownership and control of movement of a woman that restrict her to-be-looked-at-ness to her husband and other safe 'audiences'. It is interesting to note that, in the style in which *kothi*s and girls perform in bars and shows, and indeed the *mujra* style, the performer invites the (male) gaze, often with intense eye contact. This turns the performer into much more than a passive recipient of the male gaze, in that she can actively and selectively seduce members of the audience. This is one way in which she uses her art and body to wield power over the audience, to control men's emotions and desires, and to hold court, as Qureshi has powerfully described.[56] This also translates into greater status and earning power, as I describe in chapter six in relation to *kothi*s and in chapters one and two in relation to female hereditary performers. In this sense, these performers (female and *kothi*) can be seen to constitute a kind of ultra-femininity. However, at the same time, this makes their femininity transgressive and 'unfeminine'.

Female erotic performers as transgender

In pre-modern South Asia, to have females performing in male or public space represented the workings of patriarchy in the sense that men ranked above and dominated women and feminised men; and their (extra-marital) sexual and entertainment interests were legitimised whereas those of women were not. Yet at the same time, this is a situation in which men could be vulnerable to seduction by performers with the power of sexual charm and charisma as well as the affective and performative power of music and dance. The female performers thus hold power over men and the arena is transgressive and dangerous, as is illustrated by the cautionary tales Brown describes from Mughal India, the current debates surrounding bar girls, and indeed, the entire project of middle class reform and appropriation of performing arts.[57] The conflicts of public female performance and patriarchy and gender, however, run deeper. The system of patriarchy that 'protects' the honour of women by restricting them in male or public space necessarily requires or produces females who cannot have honour, either through their being 'disreputable' or through being male (in body). The system of patriarchy that requires women to marry and become the property of men necessarily produces females who cannot marry, as well as cross-dressed males and homoeroticism. The logic of patriarchy and a binary gender system can be seen to exceed itself to produce an arena where gender cannot be binary and the control of men over women is threatened, and thus the system becomes its own subversion. Arguably, the more powerful patriarchy and binary gender rules are, the more powerful this subversion becomes. This arena reveals particularly clearly that gender is a construction of power rather than of nature.

I began this chapter by describing *kothi*s as 'transgender' and comparing them to *hijra*s, the community of transgenders in India that people are most familiar with. I have also described how *kothi*s are female or feminine, in terms of how and what they perform, and of course, in terms of their role as passive partners in sex with men. However, it is in many ways accurate to say that *kothi*s are akin to female erotic performers more than to females per se.[58] In comparing *kothi*s and female erotic performers, it becomes clear how the latter too can be described as 'transgender'. As Brown states with reference to courtesans in her study of performers and gender in Mughal India, 'As highly accomplished women who made their living dancing in the male world, the transgression of their feminine identity bodily manifest in the unfettered sexual entertainment they offered, they were something both less and more than "women"'.[59] In terms of the stylised hyper-femininity of their performance, and the ability not just to be receptive to male erotic attention but to invite it, outside of marriage, both female hereditary performers and *kothi*s are 'more' than women, but at the same time, less than or transgressive of female norms. They are both accurately described as 'transgender'.

In mundane spaces, gender can be seen as an approximation, and by no means consistent. For example, some women are more feminine than others, and some women are less feminine than some men. In the zone of female performance in public/male space, what Connell terms the 'relationality' of gender still drives identification.[60] Yet because it cannot find containment and closure in this transgressive and conflicting arena, the relational logic necessarily extends deep into non-normative gender areas. The identifications and narratives of performers become particularly complex, contorted or contradictory—in some ways conformist, and in some ways ironic.

In many ways, female performers, since they have a female rather than a male body, have to deal with the norms of patriarchy and their transgressive position more than *kothi*s. Hence, female hereditary performers and bar girls tend to lie about their backgrounds and reel out tragic stories to customers of how they were 'driven to dance'. *Kothi*s, on the other hand, can embrace dance in a less constrained way. However, their status as 'both less and more than "women"' can be seen in other aspects of their relationship with dance. *Kothi*s are generally passionate about dance and, as I have discussed, the identification is intense and sincere and underpins this dimension of performing arts. However, they are also capable of performing with single or multi-layered irony. They can do so with any style of song/dance—traditional or modern, racy or modest. The coy modesty of Hindi film heroines, even when performing quite sexy songs, may be the object of considerable irony and humour by 'dancing boys' who, while profoundly identifying with the heroines, are also aware that they are 'not quite' the characters they are performing. Their performances can mix on the one hand utter grace and naturalness in the dance and its various shades of feminine wiles and seduction, with irony and teasing on the other. In addition to mocking and parodying gender, they also satirise sexual morality in their performances with particular brazenness, being in many ways even further from patriarchal control than the courtesans and bar girls. I remember one *kothi* performing a film *mujra* that begins with a dramatic, *alap*-style, slow introduction, '*Tehzeeb, sharaafat, admiyat*' ('Culture, decency, humanity'). S/he wore trousers, with an off-the-shoulder bra top, a long wig with hair cast over one shoulder. S/he began the song stationary holding a transparent veil around her/his whole face and body, which s/he let fall at the word *sharaafat* ('decency'), blatantly sending up notions of honour.[61]

In other ways, however, *kothi* performers can actually be seen as more akin to the mainstream image of courtesans than female hereditary performers are. Female hereditary performers are brought up with a certain professionalism in treating male clients. They are aware of the rules of their society from a young age and are trained not to fall in love or rely on men (although, of course, some do transgress these norms and fall in love). *Kothi*s, on the other hand, grow up in families where people get married, yet they are unable to get married as a woman to a man. Instead they have to live life as men and husbands to women. They rarely find true love or a life partner and see themselves as used by men; generally, they are destined to remain on their own. Even those who have a life partner cannot get (publicly) married and display their love to the world. There is a sense of sadness and melancholia in the community and a powerful identification with the hyperbole of unrequited love, romance and tragedy of the (film) courtesan, and the image of longing for the love of a man and marriage that she can never have.

Traditionally, these transgressive zones are contained within liminal realms of society. In chapter six, I question further what happens to *kothi*s as the livelihood and performance space of dance that is such a key part of this liminality is eroded; and what happens as their presence becomes less opaque, and legitimate social space is sought through advocacy and identity politics. As I discuss, this leads to circles being squared in new ways, and new zones of conflict and danger.

Conclusions

In this chapter, I have shown that erotic male performers have deep roots in Indian culture, with clear resonances between historical depictions and present day *kothi* performing culture. There are also, however, significant differences between the past and the present, relating especially to the increasingly underground and illicit space of *kothi*s in contemporary India. While *kothi*s are categorised increasingly as MSMs, I link them in this chapter with female performers, exploring dance, performing and femininity. Looking at *kothi*s as female public/erotic dancers sheds unique light on the socio-cultural space they occupy. However, it is also highly illustrative of the roles and spaces that female hereditary performers occupy. It shows how public/erotic dance by female or *kothi* performers is part of one domain, structured by, as well as transgressive of, patriarchal power structures. The parallels in the marginalisation of *kothi*s and female hereditary performers are also strong. I explore these in more detail in chapter six when I look at the changing socio-cultural space of *kothi* performers, the role of NGOs and CBOs, and global discourses of 'homosexuality'.

4

THE BOLLYWOOD DANCE REVOLUTION AND THE EMBOURGEOISEMENT OF INDIAN PERFORMING ARTS

As I describe in the introduction to this book, under traditional paradigms, a woman who performed in public or in front of men tended to be seen in erotic terms, as sexually available, and as low status. The role of such a performer was mutually exclusive with that of a life of marriage and respectability. However, from the first few decades of the twentieth century—amid radical shifts in paradigms of performance, class, and gender—upper class/upper caste women began to enter classical performing arts and the film industry. Classical performing arts have now become a middle class preserve, an important form of cultural capital, and a respectable career for women. The cinema industry too, although carrying a more ambiguous status, has been broadly-speaking middle class since the mid-twentieth century, and is certainly not an arena in which only low status, 'disreputable' women can work. Since the 1990s, a new arena of live, Bollywood dance has swept middle class India, and girls from good families dance live in often tight and sometimes skimpy costumes to film songs, as amateurs, semi-professionals or professionals—and this in no way adversely affects their reputation.

In this chapter, I focus on the axis of inclusion/exclusion that became a feature of modern Indian performing arts. The embourgeoisement of performing arts and the exclusion of, in particular, female erotic performers, have been two sides of the same coin. The reformed classical traditions and the gentrification of the cinema industry have relied upon and directly driven the exclusion of low status hereditary female performers and the delegitimisation of their arts. This, together with the colonial policies and purity campaigns described in chapter one, created the illicit worlds of performing arts. The Bollywood dance scene, too, has been made possible by its separation from the illicit worlds thus established. I begin by outlining the reform of classical performing arts. I then look in overview at the transformation of the film industry into a broadly middle class zone, as well as the role of film texts in changing the meanings and associations of dance.[1] I then focus on Bollywood dance, outlining the culture, ideology and manifestations of this new zone of performing arts.

I examine the Bollywood dance revolution in terms of a continuity or culmination of long-term processes of embourgeoisement of performing arts, following increasing respectability created within reformed classical performing arts and/or the early film industry in the 1920s and 1930s. These include institutionalisation, the development of stylistic canons, a de-gendering of performing roles, and discourses of nationalism, spirituality, technology/training, 'quality' of performance, and other criteria of 'distinction'.[2] This continuity also involves the embodiment of socio-economic and ideological change that parallels and extends that of the earlier phase of reform. By the late nineteenth and early twentieth centuries, under British rule and the climate of increased global connectivity, ideas of liberalism, rights and nationalism had become established in India along with a bourgeois middle class. In the 1990s, global connectivity increased exponentially into what is now termed 'globalisation', with India's economic liberalisation and the spread of neoliberal reforms to more countries across the world. Middle class Indian life included foreign TV shows, shopping malls, trendy restaurants and increased travel. This created links between the Indian middle classes and first world non-resident Indians (NRIs). Processes of mutual identification grew, as did the compatibility of 'Indianness' with Westerness, where before the two had been presented as oppositional.[3] In the world of film, music and entertainment, these changes led to a process of 'Bollywoodisation', which the Bollywood dance craze is very much a part of. Top-end Hindi films were increasingly oriented in style and production standards to the highly lucrative NRI markets in the US, UK and Australia in particular. The cinema and its paraphernalia, glossed by the term 'Bollywood', became a trendy celebration of 'Indian culture' in middle class India and the diaspora.[4] *Bhangra*, which became popular in the UK from the 1980s, has also played an important role in this process of legitimising Bollywood and Indian popular culture, and has in many ways helped facilitate the spread of Bollywood dance, in particular in the UK.[5]

However, although the Bollywood dance revolution represents a continuation and extension of processes of embourgeoisement and liberalisation of culture and national identity, there are features that mark it out as a new watershed, or a fruition of earlier processes. With its celebration of the body and its embracing of sexiness, the new Bollywood dance scene breaks one of the most important legitimising factors of reformed classical performing arts: the de-eroticisation of performance. This legitimate sexiness reflects the adoption of Western, hegemonic norms in India via globalisation through international dance styles and the internationalisation of Indian identity.[6] However, it can also be interpreted in terms of middle class India gaining a critical mass of self-sufficient identity and cultural production so there is no longer any danger of confusion with 'disreputable', low status performers—thus resulting in a sensuality and liberation of the body not possible before. New models of gender, class and performance have been able to emerge because the performers that embodied or embody the older paradigms are out of sight, forgotten, made un-threatening, and excluded from 'respectable' India, as I have described in the first three chapters of this book.

At these levels, the Bollywood dance revolution represents not just continuity, but culmination. However, at the same time, it can be seen as involving something that can be described more definitively as change. The comprehensive exclusion of disreputable, 'traditional' female performers has enabled a liberation of middle class performed sexuality. However, this very distance or unrecognisability of what has been excluded enables, potentially, its reinclusion, though under new parameters. Thus, the legitimacy of sexy Bollywood dance (on and off screen) makes it impossible for some middle classes to decry bar dancers and push them (back) into illegitimacy and illegality, as I explore in the next chapter. Continuity has apparently led to change and transformation. Thus in this chapter, and in the one that follows, I explore contemporary processes in terms of continuity and consolidation of inclusion/exclusion, but also identify glimpses of new turns that could link the two zones of Indian performing arts in new ways.

Classical performing arts

The transformation of classical performing arts from a feudal arena involving low status performers and high status patrons to a bourgeois system of upper class–upper caste performers and audience and public/state institutions has received a substantial amount of scholarly attention.[7] I outline in brief the key developments that enabled this to take place. These developments have set up patterns and precedents that are continued or paralleled in the establishing of Bollywood performing arts as a respectable, middle class zone nearly a century later.

One of the most fundamental factors that established classical performing arts a respectable, middle class zone has been the exclusion of hereditary, 'disreputable' female performers.[8] In the same way that the zones of the married woman and the dancing girl are mutually exclusive, it was impossible for bourgeois performing arts to involve the mixing of 'respectable' and 'non-respectable' women, since this would leave the status of the 'respectable' women ambiguous. It was only *after* the exclusion of courtesans in around the 1930s that a place for 'respectable' women started to be pioneered.[9] The processes of stigmatisation of hereditary female performers had begun from the early part of the nineteenth century, yet apparently gained critical mass in the last quarter, as I overview in chapter one.

It was not just a matter of excluding the courtesans and *devadasi*s themselves from the new classical performing arts, but also of removing vestiges of them and the erotic culture of female entertainer and male patron that were embodied in aspects of style. While in the early days, an upper caste woman risked being mistaken for a courtesan or *devadasi* just by appearing on stage, to actually perform and interact with the audience in the manner of a *devadasi* or courtesan is something that could evoke these figures long after they had been eliminated as performers. Performing arts were hence de-eroticised in terms of performance practice and in terms of song texts.[10] While the classical courtesans and *devadasi*s used to sing, dance, and perform *abhinay* (the seated interpretation of lyrics while singing), music and dance were separated in the new classical traditions, disembodying the one from the other.[11] Aspects of performance style such as eye contact were eliminated, so female performers would dance or sing to an audience rather than for a particular patron.[12] In North India, performing arts became largely gender neutral through these changes in style, repertoire and performance practice.[13] In this way, the gender gulf—and of course the status gulf—that was such a key part of the eroticism of performing arts under the feudal-style system, was removed. Classical performing arts as erotic entertainment for patrons or direct seduction of audience members was also obscured and transformed through the paradigm of religious devotion, with the interpretation of erotic texts in terms of the love of Radha and Krishna.

Also crucial to the respectability of classical performing arts has been their institutionalisation, creating respectable and high-status middle class contexts for teaching, learning and performance. Narayan Bhatkhande and Vishnu Digambar Paluskar set up teaching institutions with the help of wealthy individuals. These institutions began to give classical performing arts the status of 'modern education', and emphasised a more literate, Sanskritic and *shastrik* basis for Hindustani music.[14] This contributed to a larger discourse of Muslim hereditary performers and in particular *tawaifs* as having degraded classical music into vulgar entertainment.[15] Bhatkhande had refused to meet *tawaifs* who 'would not help in the systematization of music, his primary aim in life'.[16] Institutionalisation, systematisation and canonisation thus all intertwined, with processes of 'distinction'. Thus classical performing arts were set on 'purer' or 'higher' levels on the basis of intellectual, textual, religious and aesthetic criteria.

These developments interlinked with discourses of nationalism, with classical performing arts reinvented in the context of national identity and national pride, thus, the state has been a key patron of classical performing arts from the twentieth century. The processes of 'sanitisation' and 'purification' represented the classic nationalist narrative of the rescue of the 'golden age' of a people. The classical performing arts traditions became Indian Classical Performing Arts in discourse, in their networks of institutions, and also, very importantly, in the All India Performing Arts conferences that Bhatkhande began in 1916. *Tawaif* were, in the early days, explicitly excluded from these middle class institutions. They were also 'banished' from All India Radio, one of the most important modern patrons for classical music, with the then Broadcasting Minister B.V. Keskar declaring in 1954 that they would not hire any woman 'whose private life is a public scandal'.[17]

Indian/Hindi films and the film industry

As the first full-length Indian silent film was made in 1913 (*Raja Harishchandra* by Dadasaheb Phalke), a whole new performing arts context opened up, and with it the need for performers. As Bhaumik writes, the cinema 'grew as a disreputable bazaar institution through most of its early years', only gradually becoming appropriated by the bourgeoisie from the 1920s and 1930s, with 'respectable' male and female performers entering the industry.[18] Also significant to the respectability of the film industry and the larger trajectory of performing arts have been the films themselves.[19] Films are one of the most powerful means of representing not just society, but also dance and its place in society. Cinema has had an immense influence on the growing respectability of dance for elite and middle class females and, in the 1990s, can be seen to dovetail into the Bollywood dance revolution that was taking place outside of films.

Off-screen: female performers

A key aspect of the film industry's attempt to gain respectability was to employ reputable female artistes. However, reputable women were inhibited from entering the industry when courtesans, *nautch* girls and low status male artistes were working there. While in classical performing arts, female hereditary performers had been excluded several decades prior to the entry of middle class performers, in the film industry, there was an overlap of several decades. The gradual move to middle class actresses was negotiated in a number of ways.[20] Jewish or Anglo-Indian actresses provided something of a compromise, and more wealthy studios were able to improve their image by using these actresses, or at least high-class courtesans, rather than more common female entertainers.[21] The attraction of 'reputable' female performers was also encouraged by the influx to studios in the 1920s of middle class male workers (as opposed to traditional, low status, male performers), including writers, poets, directors and technicians.[22] The industry was directly urged to improve itself and become a place where respectable women could work. Studios were critiqued for not providing suitable working environments for respectable women, and social workers targeted 'prostitution' in the industry. Technology and technological prowess also became important discourses of respectability in studios.[23] 'Quality' of acting was linked to the class of performer, encouraging women from 'good' families to join the industry.[24]

The industry also worked to change its image through self-representation. Films were produced about the industry itself that showed it to be a reputable place, including interviews with film stars describing their working conditions and other actresses they worked with in positive terms.[25] The emerging star system was key to building prestige, showing female performers as glamorous and beautiful on-screen; and off-screen, as rich and modern. The cinema was then able to gain real moral capital from the presence of women.[26]

During the 1930s, the middle classes established a firm hold on the film industry (although the coming of sound in the early 1930s initially boosted professional female performers and male actors from the world of the stage because it enhanced the importance of music).[27] The intensified nationalist climate added to discourses of the undesirability of courtesan performers and drew films far closer to themes of social reform. The coming of sound also enabled the cinema to develop genres that were closer to middle class sensibilities and enhanced modes of representation for attracting women from respectable backgrounds. By independence, the taboo on performing in the cinema had broken down, and non-courtesan and non-Anglo-Indian actresses became the norm, with those from courtesan backgrounds hiding this fact.[28] However, being a heroine was certainly not a choice for a girl from a 'good' family.[29] It is notable, though certainly not discussed in the press, that many actresses playing heroines have come from unconventional backgrounds, for example single parent mothers, or unmarried mothers.[30] Similarly, while girls from lower middle class families were junior artistes and earned good incomes, it was not until the late 1990s or 2000s that such positions would not lower the social capital of a girl or her family, or raise eyebrows. A taboo on heroines acting after marriage also existed, which has only begun to be eroded from the late 1990s. However, despite remaining problematic for heroines and other female performers, the industry can be described as having become broadly middle class or at least mainstream. It has changed markedly since the days when only traditional, low status male and female performers, or at best Anglo-Indians, could act.[31]

In addition to these processes of exclusion and the building of the industry as a middle class institution, another interesting parallel in the gentrification of classical performing arts and the film industry can be found in how the fundamental conflict of performing arts for women has been negotiated through forms of disembodiment. In classical performing arts, women stopped dancing and singing together. Singing therefore became (relatively) disembodied, and dance became devoid of the immediacy of the performer's own voice and the expressive and affective power of singing and lyrics. In the film industry, playback singing became the norm by the late 1930s, a technique that also splits voice and body. Songs are not sung by the same actress that performs them on screen, and thus the power of visual, bodily performance, and vocal affective and expressive performance (actually itself embodied, but not so clearly as dance) are thus split. In other words, playback singing, although emerging for clear pragmatic and technical reasons, can also be seen as facilitating the negotiation of respectability through disembodiment.[32]

On-screen: female characters and dance in Hindi films till the 1990s

In the 1910s, the majority of films were foreign made, and emphasised action, thrills, excitement and adventure. As Indian production of feature films began in 1913, the mythological became important. Historicals became increasingly common after 1925, and were usually Rajput romances, which presented the heroine in erotic guise, including dances. Also immensely popular were stunt films, Indian versions of which emerged in the 1920s, and involved the erotic presentation of the heroine.[33] Historicals and stunt films continued through the 1920s and 1930s. However, key to the embourgeoisement of Indian cinema was the development of the social film in the 1920s, and more definitively during the 1930s. The social was the middle class film par excellence, and represented the emergence of a form of 'highbrow' cinema. The social film placed emphasis on the contemporary world and critique, rather than the retelling of old tales. This genre relied less on performative modes of address, which was greatly facilitated by the coming of the talkies in the early 1930s. Thus, the social embodied a move to more intellectual and realist themes and styles as well as a greater modernity, all intertwined with notions of class. The development of the social film can therefore be seen to parallel the re-creation of classical performing arts as systematised, codified and literate, rather than mere 'frivolous' or 'vulgar' entertainment. The social enabled the representation of many topics relevant to the industry, such as moral stories about dancing girls. It also enabled the industry to represent itself and thus to directly construct itself within a respectable, bourgeois world through self-reflexive films, including those about female performers.[34]

The early talkies saw an increase in dancing. However, as the middle class hold on the cinema grew during the 1930s, this became counteracted by discourses that connected unsuitable sexuality in films with dance and (Muslim) courtesan actresses. A Hindu ethnoscape thus became core to the respectability of films, and dance a target.[35] Songs and dance were seen as lowering the moral tone. Dance, particularly live dance shows at silent films, was singled out as frivolous and in conflict with realism. Live dance shows died out completely as the talkies emerged and it became possible to present music and dance together on-screen. However, hierarchies of culture that were well underway by this time made certain kinds of dance acceptable. For example, a critic 'prescribed "the idealism of Uday Shankar's dance" that depicted "inner and deeper values"' in a piece on the 'desired form of dance in cinema'.[36] '*Shastric*' music and romance was also acceptable.[37] However, live dancing at silent film shows was also something that was targeted within these issues of moral/class 'distinction', and became disapproved of. Live dance shows also died out as the talkies emerged and it became possible to present music and dance together on-screen.

A 'restrained' style emerged as ideal for the Hindi film heroine, something that has continued well into post-independence cinema. The desire for dance and erotic entertainment continued, however, and thus two strategies emerged, echoing earlier practices in part. The first involved heroines who do not dance, or who dance in '*shastric*' ways, for example the classically-trained stars such as Vijayantimala. This 'pure' heroine was often set against 'bad' female leads, sometimes the courtesan, or a more modern vamp. By the late 1960s, the vamp emerged as a regular counterpart to the 'pure' heroine, a character who would dance with abandon. As Pinto states, 'She fell, she smoked, she drank, she danced, she snuggled, she smuggled, she died'.[38] As Pinto has pointed out, the vamp provided not just the erotic entertainment that the heroine could not, but also a moral polar opposite of the heroine, crucial to structuring the heroine's own purity as well as other moral aspects of the film.[39] This moral splitting of the female roles and stars (because performers who acted as vamps did not generally act as heroines) became a classic part of Hindi *masala* cinema until around the mid-1990s.

Gradually, however, the pull of an erotic female star was such that heroines themselves danced, in ways that are clearly sexy as opposed to the respectable, 'restrained', '*shastric*' dances of the early dancing heroines. By the 1980s, all heroines danced, with actresses like Hema Malini and, in particular, Sridevi and then Madhuri Dixit, pushing the boundaries (for this context) of erotic display. The vamp still existed, but other strategies were now necessary to mark the fact that, although the heroine danced, she was still pure and good. This involved a range of excuses and compelling circumstances (*majboori*) that made the heroine's performance noble. Clear examples of this are *Jab tak hai jaan* in *Sholay* (1975) where the heroine is forced to dance by the villain in order to save her sweetheart's life. Such devices protect the heroine and protect the audience from seeing themselves as illicit voyeurs. They also preserve the morality of Hindi films, though sometimes only tenuously. Similarly, having song and dance numbers as staged performances, perhaps for the pleasure of the villain or lascivious onlookers, disavows the audience's erotic gaze.[40] This has changed significantly in films from the late 1990s, and reacted explosively with wider global, social and cultural trends, as I discuss below.

Playback has also helped heroines sing and dance yet retain their 'purity'. As argued by Neepa Majumdar, the playback singers' voice becomes embodied by the on-screen artiste.[41] But in the sense of sexual morality and respectability, we can see how the actress and film character is 'envoiced' by the singer and given an 'untainted soul' by the pure disembodied voice of the playback singer. This is especially powerful in the case of Lata Mangeshkar.

The Bollywood dance revolution: new horizons of dance in middle class India

Beyond the classical arena and select elite theatrical traditions, performing in public remained at best ambiguous for women, and still evoked the paradigm of the 'disreputable' traditional performer described in the introduction. From the 1990s, however, Bollywood dance became popular in Indian diaspora communities in the developed world and in India itself. Middle class girls now perform what are often sexy numbers in public in sometimes skimpy costumes, without being seen as disreputable or equivalent to prostitutes, but rather, as normal and trendy. Being able to dance in fact enhances a socially accepted kind of attractiveness and desirability for girls related to globally hegemonic ideas that originated in the West about the body, fitness, health, confidence and performance. Indeed, many Bollywood dancers are married and include those performing professionally or as keen amateurs as well as housewives dancing for fun and exercise—something impossible within the traditional paradigm of female performers in male/public space. Many families would still not let their daughters follow a career even in classical singing or dance, let alone Bollywood. But the net is rapidly widening, with burgeoning numbers of middle classes enjoying dance carefree. This acceptance of Bollywood dance in middle class circles is also seeing a far wider range of girls keen to dance in the industry itself, as well as the now vast arena of shows found beyond the cinema.

Here, I examine the emergence of Bollywood dance as a new, legitimate zone of national culture—a genre in the real world as opposed to just in or for movies. Key to the phenomenon are paradigms of respectability set up by the classical performing arts establishment and the film industry over the twentieth century; the development of respectable middle class institutions for teaching and learning and contexts for performance; and discourses of distinction and 'higher purpose'. Precedents have also entered India internationally, with a leading role played by non-resident Indians (NRIs) and global media in bringing fashions in dance and fitness and new ideas of the body from countries such as the USA and UK. At the same time, films themselves have been crucial in pushing the boundaries of respectability of dance, with increasingly sexy or sensual dance in real life performing arts culture legitimised by the more liberal filmic representations of dance. Another critical factor has been Bollywood dance becoming a profession that pays in quantities that most middle classes would aspire to. The Bollywood dance revolution is a continuation of the embourgeoisement of performing arts and of middle class India's growth and power, including the exclusion of 'disreputable' female performers. Yet it reflects a new chapter, one associated with post-liberalisation India, the Indian diaspora, changes in media, and the globalisation and commercialisation of late capitalism. In terms of the ways in which it affects opinions about figures such as bar girls or courtesans, it possibly represents real change to the contours of inclusion/exclusion in Indian performing arts, as I explore more in the next chapter.

Films, media and the changing status of dance from the 1990s

The processes of liberalisation that began in 1991 caused radical changes to India's media that have altered the place of dance in society. With the entry of commercial cable television, the number of available channels grew from one (the state run *Doordarshan*) to many, including music channels such as MTV and Channel [V]. The scope for visual consumption of music dramatically increased. This in turn enabled the effective marketing of music, leading to a dramatic rise in the com-

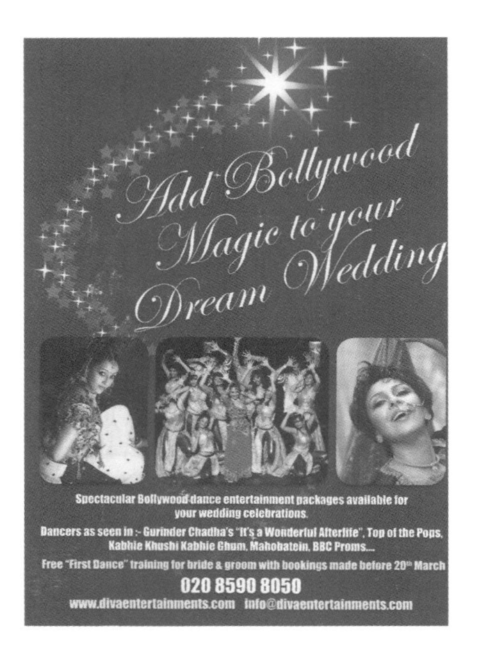

Images 10a and b: Publicity postcard for Honey's Dance Academy, UK, offering (a) choreography for Bollywood weddings, and (b) training for UK-based Bollywood wannabes.

mercial value of film songs. As Harish Dayani, then vice-president of marketing at HMV, stated, '[with the advent of commercial television] the marketing of music actually started in a professional manner, if I may use the word, whereby you take part of the film and use that to promote your music', and that 'the marketing of music took I would say some amount of lead in terms of not only promoting the music but thereby also promoting and creating the awareness for the film'.[42] The advent of a widespread visual medium for the consumption of music also directly enhanced the importance of dance in films, and indeed in popular music across the world. In this new audio-visual media world, dance is too important to be restricted to the vamp and/or contrived situations. In a film like *Kal Ho Na Ho* (Karan Johar, 2003) for instance, there are three big dance numbers, 'Pretty woman', 'It's the time to disco', and '*Mahi ve*'. The 1990s thus marked a new stage in the growth of dance in terms of its prominence and scope.[43] One of the most significant changes was the demise of the vamp by the 1990s and, by the 2000s, the freedom for the heroine to dance in an unrestrained way, without having to have narrative justification through ploys such as 'noble sacrifice' or *majboori*, as described by Kasbekar.[44] This unproblematic coding of dance in films has impacted attitudes to dance in the wider world, and the inclusion of big dance numbers has also fed the Bollywood dance craze, as I describe below.

The effects of visual media on the prominence of dance in popular culture and on its socio-cultural value and legitimacy can also be seen in the mushrooming of dance shows on television. Again, this trend has existed not just in India but across the world. In India, television in the 1980s and early 1990s featured a number of singing talent contests and quiz shows such as *Sa Re Ga Ma* and *Meri Awaaz Suno*, some of which still continue. However, since the late 1990s and 2000s, it is dance programmes that have taken over, and they are taking the country by storm. Some of these shows are fun-oriented, with celebrities learning to dance (e.g. *Nach Balliye* or *Jhalak Dikhhla Jaa*, India's version of *Strictly Come Dancing*).[45] They also include high-pressure instructional talent competitions along the lines of X-Factor, for example *Dance India Dance*, where contestants have to learn and perform many styles; and choreographer Saroj Khan's show *Nachle Ve with Saroj Khan*. These shows present Bollywood dance as an activity and entertainment that is not only fun, but is endorsed by celebrities and other glamorous and successful people (or those who aspire to be so), and hence anything but down at heel. The production standards of these shows are high, and hence Bollywood dance is shown to belong firmly in affluent India. It is presented as hard work, and an activity to be taken seriously and respected.[46]

The commercialisation and globalisation of the media has affected dance in other ways, too. In the early 1990s, a new generation of choreographers started to introduce a different kind of physique to dance sequences in Hindi films by using non-union chorus dancers. Union dancers typically had a plump physique and the way they danced did not emphasise athleticism. The choreographers Farah Khan and Ahmed Khan brought in dancers who conformed to international standards of a slim, young, sexy, attractive body. They also brought new standards of professionalism to Hindi film chorus dancing, reflecting those that already existed from circuits of live shows. Justine, one of these non-union dancers, explained:

> ...in shoots you can, you know, still get away with ... false steps whereas at a show you can't. And Farah and Ahmed wanted the same performance level [as in shows], they wanted a certain standard of performance and a certain look and a certain body type. They didn't want to have plump dancers. [The union dancers] used to be plump and not good dancers. So they wanted good dancers with good bodies not necessarily tall or anything but just fit and those who didn't look like they were mothers of two kids or much older. ... They wanted a young look, a youthful, fresh look, and they took dancers from outside and got into big trouble.[47]

This change with regards to chorus dancers foreshadows the film *Dil To Pagal Hai* (Yash Chopra, 1997) and its lycra-clad bodies, which gave critical mass to the Bollywood dance revolution. The Cine Dancers Union fought back against the use of non-union dancers, negotiating a percentage of the non-union dancers' pay to go to the union. This lasted till around 1998, when they were able to stop the use of non-union dancers, with only a few exceptions.[48] However, the use of outside dancers introduced Western, hegemonic standards of beauty, fitness and slimness into the industry, and the accompanying aesthetic of the body as representing desirable fitness and health—a new discourse that has been crucial to the legitimising of the physicality and sexiness of Bollywood dance. These non-union dancers largely eventually joined the union by making cards themselves.[49] Gradually, the 'traditional', plump, non-athletic union dancer has become a thing of the past. During this time, heroines also became slimmer, and heroes began to exhibit a gymed-up look—and both had to be excellent dancers. Heroines also began to be taken from the ranks of models and, conversely, film stars have become increasingly involved in advertising. In this way, the convergence of visual media, globalisation, commercialisation, and dance has played a key role in the radical change to ideas about the body as well as dance's prominence in films and society.

Institutionalisation: centres of teaching and learning

One of the key factors in the establishment of Bollywood dance as a legitimate, respectable and mass cultural form has been its institutionalisation into professional, reputable, business-based establishments of teaching and learning. These institutions also embody ideologies and values that negotiate legitimacy and respectability for Bollywood dance. I discuss these separately below.

There has been a select number of dance schools pre-dating the 1990s.[50] However, the most important dance school in light of the Bollywood dance revolution is, without a doubt, Shiamak Davar's Institute of Performing Arts (SDIPA). SDIPA, which in 2006 had some 25,000 students across India as well as branches or classes in Canada, Australia and the UK, dwarfs other institutes. It grew from the humble origins of a jazz dance class of just seven students, set up by Shiamak Davar in Bombay in 1985.[51] SDIPA grew to a limited extent from 1985. However, it was following the explosive and timely collaboration of Davar and Yash Chopra for the film *Dil To Pagal Hai* (1997) that SDIPA began to grow exponentially and the whole Bollywood dance revolution took off. The process has thus involved at core the symbiotic relationship of a filmic representation of society and real life performing arts.

International standards and ideas of dance, the body and desirability had entered the film industry in the early 1990s, as described above. In *Dil To Pagal Hai*, these powerful new trends were made the centre of a film, with a story of a love triangle involving three jazz dancers. The film exhibited a new look of lycra-clad bodies—slim, fit and relaxed in their sexuality—loft-style living spaces, and a strongly jazz-based dance style.[52] The film was a massive hit. While Shiamak's choreography and the ethos of his dance style are what made the film, the film also very much made SDIPA, as Shiamak readily admits.[53] It was only with the level of publicity gained by the film—including a national award for Shiamak Davar—that SDIPA moved from being a phenomenon largely of elite, Westernised Bombaites (Shiamak himself is Parsee) to one that had spread to major cities across India and involved India's new (mostly upper-) middle classes en-masse. The Bollywood dance craze gained critical mass, and shows no signs of abating. Dance classes and institutes, as well as performance contexts, have mushroomed in both India and the diaspora, and SDIPA continues to feed into the film industry, with Shiamak one of the most selective and prestigious choreographers.

SDIPA, as a middle class environment for teaching and learning, forms the backbone of respectability for Bollywood dance. SDIPA, and the many other dance institutes that now exist, can be seen to parallel the early twentieth century reinvention of classical performing arts with the birth of modern music schools, and also the development of 'respectable' studios in the film industry. However, whereas the core institutions for classical performing arts are state owned, the Bollywood dance institutes are private companies. This reflects the very much corporate and commercial identity of Bollywood dance as well as India's post-1990s national and international identity. The middle class pioneers of classical performing arts learned from low status male performers and, in the case of *Bharatanatyam*, directly from *devadasi*s. In the case of the film industry, they overlapped considerably with, or worked with, professional female hereditary performers. Bollywood dance institutes, however, are generally run by those who have trained entirely in middle class private institutes in India or abroad—Shiamak himself studied at Pineapple Studios in London. These include those who are trained in classical performing arts or other institutes, and increasing numbers of SDIPA-trained dancers. SDIPA itself generally trains its own instructors, and has an extensive in-house system of promotion in terms of performing, teaching, and/or administration.[54] At most, Bollywood performers or choreographers may be self-taught (for example, Ganesh Hegde, who learned through imitation and performing in competitions throughout school). I have not heard of any *mujra* dancers or bar girls being involved in such institutes. There is no active exclusion of such dancers; rather, they exist in different worlds. In terms of style, too, the hereditary performers and bar girls are very different from the institute-trained dancers. Bollywood dance institutions are enclosed in a middle class world of modern training and administrative models. Running a dance school involves business and management skills, as well as skills in teaching classes in the standardised manner that has become the norm. One dance school I visited had been set up by an ex-student of SDIPA who had gained an MBA in the UK—an epitome of the new world of Bollywood dance.

These institutes have also created safe, respectable contexts for amateur performance, with in-house shows and events for their students. One I visited in Jalandhar, in the Punjab, had regular functions, including a Shakira night. Many people with no aspirations to perform publicly or professionally—and for whom it would be unthinkable to go somewhere like a nightclub—are able to enjoy internal dance and party events. There are even ladies-only classes in some institutes. Performing at all, however, is still problematic or even off-bounds for some students. As one teacher with her own institute in Delhi stated, 'Some people are learning [dance] for learning's sake, some people are not learning it for performance sake, they don't want to go on stage, but they can be very good, they may not be shy, but they are not supposed to go on to the stage, it's like that'.[55] Institutes like SDIPA, however, do have professional troupes and train vast numbers of dancers who perform in public. These dancers tend to have an attitude to dancing that is more like that found in the West than in traditional India. Indeed, these institutes have helped to establish Bollywood dance in India and internationally as a style alongside salsa and *bhangra*. By doing so, Bollywood dance is placed in a middle class context of health, fitness and attractiveness as opposed to the older ideas of shame and sexual availability that once surrounded dance. Institutes in the UK offer Bollywood as one style among many. Similarly, many institutes in India now offer a range of international styles such as salsa, ballroom, or even belly dance.

The ideologies and values of the new Bollywood dance

A description of Bollywood dance style is beyond the scope of this book.[56] However, in the context of this discussion, what is particularly interesting is that, unlike classical performing arts, it is neither restrained nor de-eroticised. Although less erotic than some dance sequences in films, Bollywood dance is still openly sexy in the sense that it is a highly embodied, vigorous, ostentatious, unashamed celebration of the body. It involves in some contexts skimpy costumes (often worn on top of a body suit) and/or body-hugging lycra. The establishment of a middle class zone of teaching and learning institutes and contexts for performance has been crucial in legitimising this dance form, as has been the growth of the mass visual media and its representation of Bollywood dance. Here, however, I look more closely at the discourses, ideologies and values embraced and advocated by the institutions, practitioners and media, and how they are working to legitimise this new form of dance. These groups are keen to keep it from falling into older paradigms, or being seen as 'cheap' or 'vulgar'—a charge that has been much levied against song sequences in films.

A key aspect of the new Bollywood dance led by the dance institutions is that it is imbued with a sense of spirituality and higher purpose. This strongly parallels the reinvention of classical dance, where the spiritual aspects were greatly emphasised. In classical dance this was a way of downplaying the erotic or giving it new meaning (so that love and eroticism were portrayed as devotional, not earthly, and certainly not as relating to the seduction of audiences). However, with the Bollywood institutions, spirituality tends to be very closely woven with ideas of personal development and mental and physical health, so rather than a strict Hindu (or Sufi) devotional ideology, as in classical performing arts, there is also a global and even new age philosophy. This mind/body spirituality and well-being is crucial for Bollywood dance's ability to celebrate the body and physicality, and is an element of dance that classical performing arts and film dances have shied away from. The mind/body spirituality and emphasis on fitness also enables the Bollywood dance world to wholeheartedly endorse fun and enjoyment without being superficial, illicit or 'cheap'.

These values are to be seen clearly at SDIPA. While Shiamak Davar himself is born Parsee, he strongly follows an open spirituality and belief in god, which he relates closely to his work in dancing and teaching:

> ... I believe only in spirituality, ... I believe there's one god, I don't believe in any caste, creed or racial discrimination, I don't believe in any of that, I believe that my prayer is service and to be selfless and to contribute because the gift that's given to me it's not mine, it's his, we're just his instruments, ... so we can't claim ownership of something that's not ours. We're very grateful to have been given the gift, so that's... why I start work. Like, you see these crutches out there, I'm going to choreograph a song with my dancers on them and do a song, a modern piece on that. So that's the way I'm thinking now. ... there's nothing more important than *seva*, what we call service. ...[57]

The sense of selflessness and service to god (*seva*) is a central concept in Hinduism. This concept can also be seen in the emphasis in many institutions on teaching and helping (even extending to charitable work and the waiving of fees in the case of SDIPA, as discussed below). I asked a long-standing SDIPA member, who has performed and taught for SDIPA in Vancouver, whether dance is now seen as a 'perfectly respectable' activity. She replied that the money a dancer can earn has made it a serious living, but she also stressed the importance of teaching:

> Oh for sure. Maybe not perfectly but … I think more than anything [it is] intriguing to people that 'oh you dance for a living, how can that be, do you make enough money?', I'm like 'you know I make a lot more money than you can ever imagine a dancer would make', and what I keep correcting everybody is that I am a teacher first, I'm a dancer second, because our shows are just like Shiamak says icing on the cake, our most important thing is like to [teach].[58]

SDIPA is far more than just a place to learn dance—it's a place for spiritual, mental and physical development through fitness, creative movement, and the gaining of confidence. SDIPA classes I visited had a tangible atmosphere of earnest, focused and sincere absorption. I commented on this atmosphere and the positive attitude of the institute members to Shiamak, and he replied:

> We pray, we have something called inner dance movement where I teach them yoga practice and movement to still your mind. So we do that. I don't advertise it too much because then people think it's a fad, so I quietly do it. [59]

All SDIPA classes begin with a non-denominational prayer.[60] The philosophy of dance as a way of gaining inner peace and strength forms the basis of wider interventions run by SDIPA's charitable arm, Victory Arts Foundation (VAF).[61] VAF teaches underprivileged children to dance, and the general therapeutic value of dance is something that Davar aims to spread to all he is involved with. He stated:

> In fact now we have kids who come who are problem children at school, alcoholics, juvenile delinquents, people from jails, drug addicts, but today they're all so reformed through dance as therapy … HIV affected or infected kids at risk, children at risk, we also teach … physically mentally challenged, visually impaired, as therapy, and people find it's a very healing place, so even today, they're not going to become dancers, you know, here out of a thousand people maybe one or twenty five or fifty will become, but the rest is a healing, it's a healing centre, you know, because people find a lot of joy, a lot of faith in themselves and self worth which people don't get nowadays because too much suffering everywhere. So this is a place where they meet people, they, you know, they connect.[62]

The ideal of spiritual selflessness also comes across strongly in the inclusiveness of Bollywood dance—the drive to spread the benefits and enjoyment of dance to everyone (even the sick, old, poor and handicapped), without anyone being excluded. Many dance institutes clearly exhibit their 'all ages' policy. In addition to interventions with underprivileged kids, Shiamak Davar waives fees for a number of students. This inclusiveness is also found in the manifestation of Bollywood dance in the middle class family with the wedding *sangeet* performances I discuss below.

While there is a sense of inclusiveness and acceptance of all, there is also great emphasis on fitness and physical health at SDIPA. The phrase 'fit bodies' is to be heard repeatedly from SDIPA staff and Shiamak himself.[63] A new physique of fit, toned bodies featured in films from the early 1990s, and the 1997 collaboration of Shiamak Davar with Yash Chopra in *Dil To Pagal Hai* put a definitive seal on it. This period also saw general health and fitness consciousness appear in India, with a now fast-growing weight-loss industry targeting India's affluent middle classes that the dance institutes are very much a part of. The style of Bollywood dance taught in institutes is intensely aerobic and athletic, emphasising fit, toned bodies. Many gyms also teach Bollywood dance as a form of aerobics. In classical dance, although there is need for immense strength, stamina and skill, the body need not necessarily be slim or thin and the body's strength or athleticism itself is not foregrounded as it is in the new Bollywood dance. The style of dancing to film songs that is performed by bar girls, *mujra* dancers and *kothi*s also involves great skill and strength. However, there is emphasis on a more spontaneous, 'natural' expression and embodiment of emotion—an *abhinay*-based style—rather than the execution of particular moves in sequences. While the new Bollywood dance is choreographed and involves repetition of moves or sequences in patterns of two or four, *kothi*s and bar girls improvise and their dancing is not based on this kind of formal bodily or spatial symmetry. The body is a focus of eroticism rather than an overt display of strength, athleticism, speed and energy. This makes the new Bollywood dance style more androgynous, and indeed, it often involves identical or near-identical moves for male and female performers. This in itself underplays eroticism, while maintaining an intense physicality and celebration of the body. In this way, the body in middle class Bollywood dance is presented in terms of health, fitness, energy, physicality and sexiness rather than eroticism and seduction.

SDIPA is not unique in its philosophy of spirituality, personal growth and mind-body balance through dance. The Sparkling Pearlz Institute of Fine Dances and Grooming, set up in Jalandhar (a medium-sized city in the Punjab) in 2004, strongly espouses similar values. The owner of the institute, Gaggun Bedi, who has been passionate about dance since he was a child, stated again and again the benefits of dance in the context of twenty-first-century living: how dance helps people to open up, lose inhibitions, and get outside of themselves and their egos. He explained the rationale of naming his institute Sparkling Pearlz in these terms:

> Pearl is the name of my grandmother. But what do you mean by pearls, sparkling pearls? Sparkling pearl is a shining pearl. ... where do you find pearls from? ... Inside the shell, you have to break the shell, and then only the pearl comes out and then you clean it and then you put it up in the showcase and then it gets sold off in the market, the more it shines, the

Cricket Club of India & Rotaract Club of H.R.
Presents

Images 11a (top left), 11b (bottom left), 11c (top) and 11d (bottom): Live Shows of Shiamak Davar's Victory Arts Foundation. (© The SHIAMAK Group)

more it goes out, the higher its price. So we people are the same, we have shells around ourselves, we are ourselves a pearl, we have shells around ourselves, we are not ready to break them, we are not ready to realise our shine. ... Can't we go inside ourselves, because the inner world is larger than the outer world? ... to have control inside yourself you have the biggest success ... to traverse inside your world. ... So that is what dancing helps with ... my passion is to make people realise.[64]

This ideology clearly combines ideas of personal development and the individual with those of success, something squarely rooted in modern, Western discourse, increasingly intensified in the neoliberal era.

The institute runs classes for a variety of people, including children. The day I visited there were a number of ladies' classes consisting largely of housewives, many of whom attend classes several times a week. Like SDIPA, the institute had a real buzz and people were on a high. In this case though, since the students were amateurs, there was less seriousness and hard work, and more focus on the joy, release and therapeutic benefits of dance. I asked one student, who had been learning for a year, what her family thought of her going to the dance class. She said she had no problem from them:

Because, dancing is not all about, dancing, you know, it improves you on many spheres, you know it brings a new self confidence, you become more open to society, you get the confidence to talk, to carry yourself, and it makes you feel much better ... it eliminates the stress factor, the main thing. You know everyone is modern you see now. Stress is an uninvited guest. Even if you don't want it it will be there. ... So, just to cope with work factor and your daily life just to reduce stress, dancing I think is the best workout that you can have. ... I feel absolutely great to be here. Because, you know, Gaggun sir, he is not only an instructor, ... he is so connected with spirituality ... he just raises your energy levels ... he just boosts up your confidence level, makes you feel more positive that you can do it, just go ahead.[65]

Another student had been learning for three years and, when I asked about her interest in dance, said, 'I was suffering from bored housewife syndrome', which received laughs from the whole group and was repeated by a number of the women. Similar to many others, she was forty-five, with grown-up children, enough money to have servants take care of housework, and not enough to do. She was first attracted to the institute for weight loss rather than dance per se:

I saw an advertisement, there were some weight loss programmes combined with dancing, so that attracted me. I used to go to the gym before, but I didn't lose much. And it was so monotonous, ... weight training and all.[66]

She was inspired to became a public relations officer for the institute and motivated many other mature and older women to join.[67] When I asked generally about their involvement with the institute, many students eagerly volunteered how much weight they had lost. As one said, 'Thanks to him we all are here, and we go back happy. I must have lost 10 kilos'.[68] Another stated:

I lost 4 kgs in three months. And everybody says I look younger [one of the group agrees, saying 'she looks younger']. I look happier and it shows on your face and it's been just three months, and I want to thank you [addressing Gaggun].[69]

This student, a family friend of Gaggun's, had initially been against his idea to open a dance institute, seeing it as 'unconventional', particularly since he comes from a highly successful, business family. She used to be told off by her family as a young girl for dancing even informally at the weddings of friends and family.

Several students explained that they had been taking anti-depressants but had come off them since joining the institute. A young woman, probably in her early thirties, came to see Gaggun to inquire about joining the class after a friend had recommended it to her. She said she had been 'passing through a very difficult time' and looked tired and downcast. She later told us that her husband had passed away in an accident a year ago. As she came out of the class the change in her was remarkable. Her face looked like a cloud had lifted, and her energy and tone of voice had gained a lightness and spark. She told me, now smiling, that it was the first time in a whole year she'd felt happy and that she thought she could start to come off her anti-depressants now. This moving story demonstrates the immensely powerful positive potential of dance. The institutes carefully hone this potential in their response to the ills of affluent modern living that India's new middle classes are suffering from. In this way, they are involved in much more than 'just' dance, and the participants' fun and enjoyment gains legitimacy from very real therapeutic benefits.

While there is a strong emphasis on the joyful, healing and uplifting aspects of dance at all institutions, there is also a strong emphasis on professionalism and hard work. That professional dancing is a tough profession requiring industry, talent and large amounts of energy is a fact. However, in the world of Bollywood dance, this idea is frequently espoused, thereby helping to justify dance as a profession of substance and seriousness and hence worthy of middle class attention and time. In SDIPA, this sense of professionalism and hard work is used explicitly to distinguish SDIPA performers from the old-school industry dancers, who, it is claimed, perform carelessly and make mistakes.[70] However, in a deeper sense, this discourse answers a long history of dance as the occupation of low status individuals, and moreover of female performers as 'just prostitutes' rather than artistes and professionals, which spread from the nineteenth century. It follows paradigms set up by the reform and appropriation of classical performing arts by the middle classes as well as strategies used to distinguish middle class from traditional performers in the early film industry outlined above. These discourses of hard work and seriousness also present dance as an activity that goes beyond therapeutic personal development and constitutes a route to professional success, with fame as the ultimate aspiration.[71] This ideology is clearly connected to global ideas of stardom that have come from the spread of the mass media. It is also highly evident in the TV dance competitions described above. Bollywood dance, in its more professionally-oriented institutes like SDIPA, as well as in TV shows and other competitions, embodies middle class socio-economic aspiration in reality as well as in ideology, since Bollywood dancing can lead into lucrative careers. This clearly marks it aside from classical performing arts, which have not been emphasised as a career route in this way, and in which professional 'success' looks quite different.

Bollywood dance institutes have a need to distinguish themselves from the vulgar image of dancing often associated with Hindi films. Some instructors do so by explaining that they do not teach things in a vulgar way, and strongly criticise the films and pop videos. The leader of one institute stated that they did not teach chest moves, and only limited *jhatkas* (hip movements).[72] Justine, who now has her own institute, reported parents asking her 'And I hope you are ... not going to be teaching our kids how to dance to *jhatkas* and *matkas*'. Many parents wanted their children to learn dance, but not necessarily Bollywood dance.[73] At the same time, some of the more traditionally seductive moves are being re-signified in terms of holistic attitudes to fitness and less stigmatised notions of sexuality. For example, another instructor said that vulgarity depends on how the moves are done, and that people take time to get used to them and realise they are just a way of making the body supple and expressive.[74] As mentioned above, these institutes are broadly middle class zones, and so effectively segregated in terms of extreme class difference. In some cases, they are also segregated in terms of gender. In Mumbai, an instructor explained that belly dancing was women-only, and they never let men see the class.[75]

Far from dancers being society's lowest of the low, in these institutes, people dance in order to gain confidence, grow as people and become successful and healthy in mind and body. This is true whether they are amateurs there for fun, weight loss or de-stressing, or people with serious aspirations to the world of professional dance. Shresthova describes a professional SDIPA dancer as exemplifying the epitome of the new look, confidence, professionalism, and health of this world of Bollywood dance:

She walks down the street with her head held high. She does not hesitate or waiver. Her hip-hugging sweatpants and form-fitting t-shirt accentuate her figure. She is lean, toned, and confident. Her long hair is pulled back in a high ponytail. In her sneakers, she looks ready to move. She could strike a dance pose or sprint at any instant. Her poise and confidence cut a stark contrast to the dusty hustle-bustle of Bombay's Matunga street market around her. She stops and surveys her surroundings with purpose. She has a reason to be here. She flips open her mobile phone and sends a quick text message. Then she sets out again with renewed urgency. As she pushes forward to cross the congested street, heads turn in admiration. Her name is Aneesha and she is a lead dancer and instructor at the Shiamak Davar's Institute for the Performing Arts (SDIPA). She grew up in Bombay and has already danced in many SDIPA productions. She has appeared in all the Hindi films choreographed by Shiamak Davar dancing beside the heroes and heroines. As a recognizable featured dancer, she is something of a demi-heroine herself.[76]

Bollywood dance is also increasingly legitimised through having become an accepted part of 'Indian culture'. Nationalist discourses of identity are explicit in the diaspora in which Indians form minorities. In India itself they are more implicit, and the fact that Bollywood dance has become legitimate 'Indian culture' is perhaps an effect more than a cause of its institutionalisation, ideologies, new contexts and so on. Bollywood and Bollywood dance are increasingly used to proudly represent India.

Contexts of professional performance

Previously, the only context for 'Bollywood dance'—although it wasn't identified as such—was in the films themselves. Now, a range of contexts that cater for amateurs and professionals have emerged for Bollywood dance reflecting its new legitimacy as well as endowing it with further validity in something of an upward spiral. It has now become a living performing art. Perhaps most dramatic is the embracing of Bollywood dance by official India with the performances at the closing ceremony of the Commonwealth Games in Australia in 2006. These were choreographed by Shiamak Davar and performed by his dancers as well as Bollywood stars such as Aishwarya Rai. An official and internationally high-profile event like this was a real watershed for Bollywood dance, and of course Bollywood in general. This official approval of Bollywood is doubtless connected to the culture of Bollywood and Bollywood dance among NRIs. Bollywood dance has been used to represent Indian culture for some time at Diwali celebrations etc., and gained a real visibility and status through the Andrew Lloyd Weber musical *Bombay Dreams* in 2002, as well as the Bollywood theme at the famous London department store Selfridges in the same year.[77] Another important stage in mainstreaming Bollywood music and dance was Danny Boyle's *Slumdog Millionaire* in 2008 and the 2009 Bollywood Prom in the UK. As is well known, the first world NRIs have been leading the new generation of Bollywood with their first world status and ticket buying power for some time. Similarly, the Bollywood dance craze is very much a phenomenon involving the synergy of India, NRIs, globalisation and liberalisation.

The Commonwealth Games performance can be seen as a particularly important example of a widespread phenomenon of shows. At the top end are the international star shows that tour important NRI regions, and involve big budget, spectacular performances at venues such as the O2 or Wembley Arena in London. These involve stars, playback singers, choreographers and their troupes of dancers (largely consisting of industry dancers). Performances as part of various award ceremonies—involving big name choreographers from the industry—have also provided significant showcases for Bollywood dance.

Below the level of the big star shows and award ceremonies are circuits of 'corporate shows', which opened up from the late 1990s.[78] These involve groups associated with dance institutes (including SDIPA) or alternatively freelancing performers who perform on their own or together. Some of these performers dance, or have danced, for the film industry, whereas others will have learned from institutes or are self-taught. These corporate shows may mark any kind of corporate occasion, for example an opening event or a Diwali show. Dancers may also be hired to dance for the launch of a nightclub, or as a part of a fashion show.[79] Groups may also put on their own public shows for the purposes of earning a living and providing entertainment. SDIPA has its own shows, for example, which involve Shiamak and his dancers performing around India and internationally in big NRI areas. Other private dance troupes also have their own shows, but generally on a less lavish level.

Professional troupes are also hired to perform at private parties of any kind, whether a wedding, an engagement party or a birthday. It could be said that these new Bollywood dance troupes are taking over contexts where previously traditional dancers (or sometimes just a DJ) would have been hired.

Bollywood dance as livelihood and career

Bollywood dance as a cultural phenomenon in middle class, globalised India is grounded in the fact that it is now a considerable industry. It is, in this way, crucially different from classical dance, which functions more through government institutions than the private/commercial and corporate sector and is a product of India's first bourgeoisie rather than the new middle classes of post-liberalisation India. With the dance schools, the film industry, the wedding *sangeet*s, and all the shows at which dance is performed, dance is much more than just viable in terms of a career. With its combination of respectability and decency; its association with fame, fortune, desirability and a chic globalised image; as well as high earnings for professional dancers and particularly, teachers and choreographers, Bollywood dance is a career with rapidly mounting socio-economic status.

The figure typically given to me between 2006 and 2008 for earnings of dancers in the industry is Rs 30–40,000 per month, which is an extremely good salary. At that time, in the industry, dancers were able to earn from Rs 1,500 to up to Rs 3,500 per day dancing for films, depending on the film budget, the choreographer, and the beauty and talent of the dancer themselves. In addition to this, industry dancers perform in the international star shows, which involve choreographers who bring troupes of dancers with them. They were able to earn Rs 8,000 per show. However, dancers do not work daily, so, for example, they may work twenty days in a month, and if they earn Rs 1,500 per day, it would come to Rs 30,000 for that month. Work can be irregular, and can include long gaps, and it is also gruelling, involving rehearsals, performances and a lot of travel to location shoots as well as tours for shows. Union dancers can work with any choreographer, though most choreographers have at least a core group of their own dancers. Ganesh Hegde works only with his own dancers, whom he pays above normal rates for exclusivity, in order to ensure standards of work and familiarity with his repertoire and style.[80]

Membership of the Cine Dancers Association requires an audition and a one-off fee, which in 2006 was Rs 100,000. The union limits its numbers, and hence is not always open to new members. Rs 100,000 is a very considerable sum of money for people from poor families. However, the earnings of a union dancer are such that, if they are able to get in, they can fairly quickly pay off this outlay. Union dancers are on the whole said to be from modest backgrounds, and are often supporting many family members with their earnings. Choreographer Ganesh Hegde stated that, given the extremely gruelling schedules of industry dancing, and the problems of often late travel to and from rehearsals, let alone foreign tours, it is not something people (especially girls) from elite backgrounds with a range of choices would do.[81] As stated above, apart from a brief phase in the early 1990s, choreographers are not generally allowed to take on non-union dancers. There are some exceptions—for example Shiamak Davar has negotiated the use of his own dancers rather than union dancers, since he is not principally a film industry choreographer. Another significant exception is the foreign girls now dancing in Hindi films.[82]

Non-union dancers who freelance outside the industry—performing in the circuits of shows, events, advertisements and music videos—earn, on average, a similar sum of Rs 30–40,000 per month. They are paid more for their performances, but get less regular work than union/industry dancers. Four dancers may earn anything from Rs 5,000 to Rs 15,000 for a show (so Rs 1,250–3,750 each).

These kinds of earnings are especially considerable given that most dancers are very young. Gaysil, a freelance dancer in Mumbai, explained that when she just got out of college, a summer job might have paid Rs 2,000 per month. It is possible, however, for her to earn this sum for just one show, plus a few days of rehearsal.[83] Justine, an Anglo-Indian who danced in the industry in the 1990s and now runs her own dance school, commented similarly on students getting into dance: 'A lot of people in Bombay could do it because they are students its good money, its better than working in an office for 3,000 and 4,000 a month. And if you have the talent why not'.[84] It is easy to see why young people who start dancing for fun get into professional dancing when opportunities arise. This was the case with many dancers I talked to, from the top choreographer Ganesh Hegde, who started dancing in school, to highly successful dancers such as Gaysil and Justine. Gaysil moved into professional dancing because it was her particular passion (her initial training was in ballet), while Justine was spotted at a party by choreographer Ahmed Khan.

Justine was a trained *Bharatanatyam* dancer but, like many, enjoyed film dancing and other contemporary global styles and found it easy to pick up.[85]

SDIPA provides its own structure of professional dance engagements and a salary scale for talented members. Good dancers gradually get promoted up the salary scale and become involved in teaching as well as performing in Shiamak Davar's shows (in India and abroad); others might take on administrative jobs within the institute. Virtually the entire institute is run by dancers, promoted from the inside.[86] In this way, it provides an ultimately safe and respectable environment not just for learning, but also for becoming a professional dancer—whether as a teacher or a performer.

While dancing in the industry or in the circuits of shows can give dancers very good money, the career of a performer is limited, tailing off from about the age of thirty. A lifelong career and potentially far more money can be made from setting up a dance school or institute, and also from choreography. Working as a choreographer for films is extremely competitive but, with experience, good union dancers do have opportunities to work as assistant choreographers, for which they can earn Rs 4–5,000 per day. The choreographers themselves can earn from Rs 50–100,000 per song, with some taking up to Rs 800,000 per song.[87] Some dancers also get into directing or other behind-the-scenes aspects of film-making, having built up contacts within the industry. With the burgeoning wedding *sangeet* scene, there is immense scope for high earnings among teachers and choreographers outside of the industry, with owners of successful dance schools and/or those choreographing for weddings, able to earn monthly salaries of *lacs* (hundreds of thousands of rupees). Shiamak Davar, who has by far the biggest dance institute certainly earns in *crores* (tens of millions). Hence, this new arena of Bollywood dance offers to those who can combine talent, experience and, crucially, organisational and business skills, extremely lucrative careers. It is also worth mentioning that, in addition to the dancers themselves, the wider industrial infrastructure of Bollywood dance involves personnel such as agents, coordinators and events companies, all of which offer careers.

In terms of respectability, things have clearly changed since the 1990s and the 2000s, and the money is certainly a part of this. When I asked about the image of dancers, one long-standing union dancer stated simply that 'times have changed', and that 'everyone wants money'. While before, women dancing in the industry were viewed rather ambiguously, a great many families would now have no problem with it. Justine commented that '... People have become more open to it. I am telling you ten years ago if my mum said to somebody of her generation that her daughter was dancing for Bollywood films they would turn their nose up. Now we say that it's ok'.[88] She described how a local newspaper had interviewed her after appearing in the film *Rangeela* (1995, Ram Gopal Varma) and had reported that, 'she is a dancer and yet she is happy doing it', implying that this was surprising, or that 'she shouldn't be happy' doing this job. She had given the interview very positively, and had discussed life as a dancer with pros and cons 'like any job has'. While at that stage there was still some stigma attached to being a Bollywood dancer, now, as she stated:

> a lot of people come to me of a certain strata in life, those people who need to make a living, who need to run their homes, who are sort of middle class families, and they want to be dancers. They come to me and say we want to dance with Ganesh Hegde, for a movie. They can't afford to make [union] dancer cards but they want to learn all that dance. They think it's amazing that I dance with Ganesh Hedge so they look up to me.
>
> [The new generation] think its cool. And some of my older students, I have students which are 30, 40, 50—the mothers, they also think it's quite impressive that I have been to Bombay and danced with the stars and done shows. They are also okay now. ... Now it's all ok. Five to ten years ago, even five years ago it was just starting.[89]

Justine stated that, previously, for a girl to aspire just to be a chorus dancer or remain a 'struggler' in the industry was a 'complete no no'.[90] Attitudes have evidently changed markedly. Kalpana described having had, along with her sister, a lot of trouble from some of their family around two decades earlier: 'we had a lot of major problems [learning dance], my relatives, my father's relatives, they used to call us *nautch* girls, they said "are you going to become *nautch* girls"'.[91] Their mother, however, was extremely determined. Coming from a princely family herself, she had watched dance performances (from within the women's quarters) and clearly been mesmerised by dance and decided that, while she herself had no chance of dancing, her daughters would be dancers.

While there is an increasing recognition of Bollywood dancers as skilled, hard-working, and decent professionals (in addition to being glamorous and talented) there are still factors that need to be considered in terms of female dancers performing live to an audience, corporate or other. Gaysil stated that she will only dance on stage and will not let anyone else come on stage, and this she negotiates with the booking.[92] This clearly distinguishes her from dancers who will go amongst the audience, such as foreign dancers and, according to popular perception, bar girls.[93] Another significant point is costumes: Bollywood dance involves skimpy outfits, which may be acceptable when on screen but not when live. Justine explained that for shows they always wore a body suit under the skimpy costume (which also made quick costume changes easy, since privacy wasn't required). This crucial point that the flesh on display is not actual flesh but just the semblance of it, is also cited in discussions of Helen and her enduring charm and respectability, despite her vamp roles.[94]

Wedding choreography: Bollywood dance, romance and the middle class family

One of the most important contexts for the new Bollywood dance craze is wedding *sangeets*. The *sangeet* (literally, 'music') used to be a female-only gathering in which close female friends and family sang auspicious traditional songs for the bride. Since the late 1980s, they have gradually transformed into vast, choreographed Bollywood events, increasingly imitating the big wedding song and dance scenes of Hindi films, which are themselves an imitation, elaboration and idealisation of real life weddings. As with the growth of Bollywood dance generally, the synergy between song sequences in films and real life performing arts drive the popularity of Bollywood wedding *sangeets*.[95]

Kalpana Bhushan, a classically trained dancer who runs a school with her sister and works extensively in wedding choreography, reported that the opening up of the Indian wedding *sangeet* to the whole family rather than just female members began in Calcutta in the 1970s. However, it was then still based on a traditional repertoire. Kalpana and her sister moved to Delhi in the 1980s and arranged choreographed *sangeets* that she described as 'very sublime ... nothing very extravagant ... very classically based, very soft and very nice, very traditional minded'.[96] These involved traditional songs and classical choreography, primarily for women, though male family members were also encouraged to participate. As this fashion gathered pace, choreographers in Delhi increasingly branched out, and by the late 1980s were starting to use Bollywood music and non-classical or non-folk choreography. *Sangeets* also emerged in NRI circles around this time.[97] The Bollywood wedding *sangeet* craze later spread to other cities in India—for example, in Jalandhar in the Punjab, wedding choreography has been a big business only since 2004.[98]

The Bollywood *sangeet* has grown into a choreographed show of about twenty minutes performed by many family members as well as friends. Film songs are chosen to create a storyline, medleys, and/or parodies of film songs. As Kalpana explained, the story could start with the birth of the girl, perhaps with the mother or aunt lip-syncing and dancing or acting to *Mere ghar ayi ek nanhi pari* ('A tiny fairy has come into my house') from the film *Kabhi Kabhie* (1976, Yash Chopra); or it might involve the mother looking ahead to the girl's marriage, with the song *Gudiya rani, bitiya rani, parion ki nagri se ek din raaj kumar ji aenge, mehlon men le jaen* ('Little doll, little princess, one day a prince will come from fairyland and take you to his palace') from the film *Lamhe* (1991, Yash Chopra). Film songs are used to enact the girl's life right up to the romance with the bridegroom, for which there are endless choices of songs.[99]

The storyline structure has been used since the 1990s. By then, the movies were supplying enough suitable songs to piece a narrative together, and the synergy of films and real life in this arena came to critical mass. As Kalpana commented:

> Films copy us, and life copies films and films copy us. So it was so intermingled that the more [*sangeet* choreography] was happening the more films were also providing, the more films were providing songs the more *sangeet*s were happening, so it was a full circle. Then people started really concentrating on *sangeets*....[100]

Bollywood *sangeet*s and the craze in general also require big dance numbers. Again, in a process of 'reel' and real life synergy, most twenty-first-century Indian movies provide at least one big song and dance number that can be performed in shows or *sangeet*s.

In planning a wedding *sangeet*, the choreographer meets the family and friends and gets to know the kind of people they are and what style of music would be appropriate—whether to include some traditional songs, traditional-style film songs, or to go for some Western numbers—and to ascertain how racy and daring the family are prepared to be in this enactment of love, romance and relationships in front of the extended family. In each family, there will of course be different dramatis personae, but the trend has been for more and more people to dance, and now, as Kalpana put it, 'everybody's dancing, anyone and everybody'.[101] In particular, more and more mothers and even grandmothers are wanting to dance. This trend has arisen from imitating films, where mothers are seen singing or dancing in wedding numbers (in a manner suitable to their age of course). Examples of this include *Kal Ho Na Ho* (Karan Johar, 2003), where the mother sings a verse *Chanda meri chanda* in '*Mahi ve*'; or *Dilwale Dulhania Le Jaenge* (Aditya Chopra, 1995), where the parents of the bride nostalgically remember their own love during the song and dance at the engagement party of their daughter. The bride and groom generally perform at the new *sangeet*s, but in some cases they will not. In particular, it may be considered inappropriate for the bride to dance—as Kalpana states, some people have the attitude that their 'daughter's going to get married, she can't go onto the stage and dance like this'.[102] This clearly demonstrates the shadow of the paradigm of the traditional female entertainer and is true whether the dance is classical or Bollywood. Interestingly, some such parents will let their daughters go to a disco and dance, but not dance on stage. This shows clearly that this attitude is particularly about dancing on display and for the pleasure of an audience, as opposed to that which is just for fun.

These wedding *sangeet*s are taken very seriously and, as is very much typical of this new middle class cultural arena, people are determined to put on a really good show. There is a strong element of ostentation and competitiveness in terms of lavishness (with rapidly inflating budgets and spectacle in the show), as well as skill in performing. Preparing for the *sangeet* may take some months. In addition to the choice of songs and creation of the medley/storyline, any parodied songs are re-recorded by professional singers with lyrics that are apt and witty for the family characters and relationships in question. Everyone taking part then has to learn the dances in classes provided by the choreographer, as well as practice independently. These *sangeet*s cost Rs 1–200,000 or more in Delhi and are performed in front of all the guests, which number into the thousands for these kinds of weddings.[103]

The transformation of the *sangeet* from a private, all-female gathering to a lavish, ostentatious show to over 1000 guests reveals a radical change in the meaning and function of the performance. The events are no longer all female, and female family members perform in front of male and female guests. The focus is largely on lavish entertainment and the showing off of talent and wealth. This represents the merging of the all female, private *sangeet*, and the public celebrations that involved (and still do involve in many areas) dancing girls or *kothi* dancers performing for male or mixed audiences. This could only take place with the replacement of traditional low status performers with middle class ones: family, friends or professional dancers. Without low status dancing girls present, and with all women and men a part of the same networks of bourgeois conjugality and friendship, there is less need for segregation. However, this merging of the traditional segregated zones has also occurred through the imitation and referencing of films and the gaining of legitimacy through imitating film models. The Bollywood *sangeet*s show most strongly, perhaps, the level of legitimacy that Bollywood and dancing have gained, with dancing and skits established at the core of the most important family events.

Bollywood dance performances and Bollywood medleys/parodies on storylines are also used for other occasions, though perhaps not so lavishly. Examples of this include engagement parties, where the girl's friends get together and put on a show; or birthday parties, where family again may represent their child's history through film scenes, characters, songs and dances; or name-giving (*namkaran*) parties for a child. Dance has become a key part of the enjoyment and entertainment at family gatherings: 'everybody's dancing nowadays, the enjoyment is: dance, thanks to Bollywood again, enjoyment has, the synonym is dancing [sic]'.[104] Dance is so mainstream that going to a disco is now an acceptable thing for the middle classes to do. Discos play a lot of Bollywood music, with an entire genre of remixes catering for this. Whereas before, if a girl went to a disco she would be seen as loose, now girls from 'good families' may go to the disco for their eighteenth birthday celebration. Bollywood dance is also becoming established in schools in big cities, with functions involving professional choreographers.[105] This circuit gets youngsters into dance and, as stated above, many classes cater to kids.[106]

Conclusions

The Bollywood dance revolution has a strong ethos of inclusivity, with dance classes reaching out to the poor and disadvantaged, the young and old, and mothers and grandmothers being rallied into performing in weddings. There is a sense from the dance classes, the television shows and the wedding *sangeets* that nowadays 'everyone' dances. This is further emphasised in public and also academic discourses of 'popular culture', where Bollywood is now acceptable where it had not been before. However, as I describe in this book, there are large swathes of people dancing to Bollywood songs that are far from acceptable to mainstream middle class India, and that are not included in what is generally referred to as 'popular culture' or indeed 'Bollywood'.[107] Thus ideas of Bollywood dance as popular culture that embraces 'the people' are not accurate.[108] The different fortunes of the legitimate versus the excluded worlds are extremely stark. In the legitimate world of Bollywood dance, the economy and livelihood of dance is flourishing, more and more people are getting involved, and there is a thriving confidence and wellbeing among professional dancers as well as vast numbers of amateurs who take part for a range of keep-fit or therapeutic purposes. However, as I explore in the other chapters of this book, in the excluded world, livelihoods are shrinking, female and *kothi* performers have dramatically lost status, place and respect, and they suffer increasing amounts of harassment and violence. The destitution and sense of depression is impossible to miss.[109]

It is important to note again that the Bollywood dance craze, unlike the reformed classical performing arts or the film industry, has not involved any direct attacks on female hereditary performers, and the ideal of inclusiveness is sincere. However, the craze has only been made possible by the almost complete separation of 'disreputable' dancers from middle class life. By the 1990s, not only were traditional performers excluded from and hence invisible in the iconic, national arenas of performing arts, they were socio-economically so distant from the new middle classes of big urban centres to be more myth and legend than reality. The middle classes have become so distant from manifestations of the feudal past that they are able to engage with abandon and freedom in a form of dance that is not highbrow in the classical sense. In fact it is fun, sexy and very much embodied—breaking or radically rewriting many of the core paradigms of dance and respectability found in classical performing arts and the film industry. Key to much of the Bollywood dance revolution has been the spread of the idea among a large proportion of upper and, to a significant extent, lower middle class girls that there is no answer to the question 'why not dance?'. In this sense, the Bollywood dance revolution represents the liberation of the middle class, with discourses of 'freeing yourself' through dance abounding. With the emergence of an enclosed middle class zone, dance can be safe, or safe enough.[110]

An exploration of the trajectory of embourgeoisement of performing arts is crucial to understanding the illicit world because it is the 'other' of the legitimate world, and the two have mutually created or depended on each other at various levels. Moreover, with the continuity of the trajectory of inclusion/exclusion, the two sides of the coin have become more cemented, more defined, and clearer in their separateness. However, this has paradoxically led to new potentials for identification. In particular, the openly sexy nature of middle class Bollywood dance, while structured very differently from the seductiveness and erotic nature of the illicit world, provides the potential for people in the middle classes to look on bar girls or courtesans in very different ways than they did previously. This has been crucial to the nascent legitimacy and glamour that the bar girls gained from an albeit small, liberal, globalised portion of the middle class. It was crucial to the support they received when the state banned them and to their ultimate victory against the ban, at least in the High Court. Indeed, not only has the world of Bollywood dance not played any role in actively excluding these performers, there is actually a high level of sympathy for the bar girls within the realms of the film industry and middle class dancers in Mumbai. Shiamak Davar himself was taken by the bar girl union leader Varsha Kale to see a *mujra* by some hereditary *tawaif* performers who were also bar girls, and promised to support them by choreographing a song for them.[111]

Here, we can see the continuity of the axis of inclusion/exclusion leading to a preliminary possibility of change—of a twist developing in the binary included/excluded topography of performing arts. The legitimate world has required the exclusion that created the illicit world, yet it is now generating moves that may integrate it and provide it with legitimacy. This is ironic, hypocritical even, when viewed in its full historical trajectory, though certainly not in terms of the involvement of individuals in the Bollywood dance scene. Indeed, it is a pattern often found when looking at the ways in which rights and legitimacy have spread. I explore these matters of continuity, consolidation and change in the following chapters in the context of Mumbai's dance bars and also by looking at the world of *kothi* performers, where the rise of LGBT rights is offering them a new form of legitimacy, though in highly problematic ways and, crucially, not yet as artistes.

5

MUMBAI DANCE BARS, ANTI-*NAUTCH* II, AND NEW POSSIBILITIES

The twentieth century has seen a precipitous decline in the social and cultural status of hereditary female performers, with heavy moral stigmatisation, loss of patronage due to the demise of the princely courts, a decline in the esteem of their arts, police harassment, and continued hostility from mainstream society. However, the exception to this trend was the emergence of dance bars in Mumbai, which began to make their mark on the city in the 1980s, with twenty-four dance bars by 1985–6. The emergence of dance bars was related to a new government policy of supporting liquor sales (on which it collected taxes), granting licences for music and dance in 'permit rooms' to encourage the consumption of alcohol by guests.[1] It also related to the growth of a wealthy, Maharashtrian vernacular (i.e. non-Anglophone) (lower) middle class.[2] Over the next decade, dance bars increased to around 210, and then, in the decade 1995–2005, mushroomed to an estimated 1,300.[3] Girls from dancing communities from across North India converged on these bars, and are estimated to have formed the vast majority of the 75,000 bar girls.[4] Girls earned good money dancing in these bars. Some became rich, and a small number became exceedingly rich.[5] Bar girls became seen as icons of glamour and beauty, and objects of intense desire, fascination, and fantasy for this vernacular Maharashtrian middle class as well as for other sectors of society. With the bar girls, the 'common man' could feel like a *nawab*, flirting and showering money on beautiful dancers in glittering dresses.[6] Dance bars represented a game of love, seduction, youth, glamour and beauty—the old configuration of wine, women and music, but this time to Bollywood music rather than *thumris*, *ghazal* or *kathak*. It was, as with the courtesans and *nautch* girls, a dangerous and transgressive game, clearly distinguished from the middle class Bollywood dance craze. The dance bars represented a power and visibility that was unprecedented in erotic performing arts since the exclusion of courtesans and *nautch* girls in the early to mid-twentieth century. Like the *tawaif* of the early twentieth century, bar girls were becoming 'celebrity entertainers'—though for a middle class rather than an elite sector of society—and female seductive performance was starting to regain something of a legitimacy.[7]

However, by late 1998, as Agnes reports, 'something went wrong'.[8] The initial problems related to a breakdown in consensus between government, police and bar owners on license fees and also *haftas* or bribes for police.[9] The government had been making good money from bars with a 20 per cent tax on liquor sales plus entertainment license fees. However, in late 1998, the annual entertainment license fee was increased 300 per cent. At around the same time, '19 bars were raided in one night'.[10] In 1999, the 'Fight for the Rights of Bar Owners Association' (FRBOA) formed. The FRBOA attempted to cooperate with police to ensure that rules were followed and raids did not happen. This failed, principally because the police gained more from bar owners not following the rules and thus having to pay bribes.[11] The government changed in 1999 from the BJP and Sena alliance to that of the Congress Party and National Congress Party (NCP). The FRBOA attempted to work with the new government, 'greasing palms' of politicians to negotiate legal late opening hours so that what had become vast bribes would not have to be paid to police.[12] This failed, and 'the government decided to increase the police protection charges from Rs 25 to Rs 1500 per day per dance floor', subsequently reduced to Rs 500 after the FRBOA held rallies and approached courts.[13] Moral pressure on dance bars also increased. A committee was formed in 2002 to create recommendations or rules for dance bars in order to avoid 'obscenity' or 'vulgarity'. However, its recommendations were not followed up.[14] From 2004, a dramatic increase in raids began after an alleged incident between an NCP security guard and a bar worker. Fifty-two bars were raided in February 2004; sixty-two in March.[15] The FRBOA accused the government of political motivation in carrying out the raids, and approached the courts, eventually filing a Writ Petition in the Bombay High Court against 'constant police harassment'.[16] During this time, the government continued to issue entertainment licenses.

It was in this context, on 20 August 2004, that the Bhartiya (Indian) Bargirls Union (BBU) emerged with a vast rally.[17] Their aim at this time was to fight police harassment in the form of raids on bars and girls being arrested and abused by policemen.[18] Although the problems bars faced had initially related to politics, police, licenses and bribes, the campaign against bars became focused on moral issues of exploitation of women through vulgarity and obscenity, and damage to society.[19] In 2004 the government started accusing bar owners of trafficking in minors, and Prerana, an NGO that works against trafficking, also stated that bars were a nexus of trafficking and prostitution.[20] The trafficking agenda had great importance at the time, since India was dangerously close to being declared by the United States a Tier 3 country with regards to trafficking. This would have resulted in sanctions.[21] The term thus carried not only moral force, but also financial and political clout, and was crucial to the money, time and energy available to governmental and non-governmental organisations for the campaign against the bar girls. R.R. Patil, one of the leaders of the NCP and, at the time of the ban, Deputy Chief Minister and Home Minister of Maharashtra, wanted to ban the bars. The debacle thus moved into another phase, with a focus on the bar girls themselves.

Fear, disapproval and the exclusion of public/erotic female performers has been fundamental to India's definition as a modern nation in culture and morality. Although the growth of the vernacular Maharashtrian middle classes in the context of globalisation created the core clientele for bars, this group also represented a socially conservative force, linked in certain ways to the politics of the Hindu right wing or Hindutva. This group tends to be against anything that threatens middle class (Hindu) family life, including moral threats, security threats (terrorism from Muslims and Muslim nations) and outsiders taking jobs from Maharashtrians.[22] The ban, therefore, constituted a populist move on the part of the government to play into the socially conservative faction of Maharashtrian middle classes. The Bill to amend the law banning dancing in bars was passed unanimously in Parliament, which Agnes cites as unusual, and no doubt related to its heady moralism.[23] The populist nationalist morality of the ban was also reflected in the fact that it came into force on 15 August 2005, India's Independence Day.

Although framed in certain specificities of the time, the campaign against the bar girls and the dance ban represented a continuation of the history of exclusion of these hereditary performing communities from a livelihood and identity of dance. Essentially the same rights-based arguments for protecting women from 'indignity' and 'exploitation', and of protecting Indian culture and society from ruin, were used. The specific history, social organisation and cultural roles of these performers were elided, as they have been throughout the twentieth century. Although exclusionary pressures on public/erotic female performers (including *kothis*) have been continuous through postcolonial India, the scale of this episode marks it out as something large enough to be termed 'anti-*nautch* II', a parallel of the anti-'dance' campaign of the late nineteenth and early twentieth centuries occurring in globalising India.

However, the episode had other dimensions that made it more than just the re-exclusion of these performers following their rise to a high profile part of Indian culture. Changes in class, culture and morality meant that the conservative middle classes were strong and there was widespread condemnation of the bar girls and support of the ban. However, socio-economic change had also resulted in the emergence of middle classes (typically relatively elite and Anglophone) with far less conservative ideas of 'Indian culture' or morality, as I began to explore in the previous chapter in the context of Bollywood dance, with forms of sexy or sensual dance gaining real legitimacy.

Furthermore, civil rights awareness and activism had emerged that extended even to groups such as the bar girls. The bar girls received moral and legal forms of support and a lot of sympathetic coverage, particularly in the English language press. Moreover, via the BBU and other activists and lawyers, questions of labour and livelihood were opened up, and debates about 'exploitation' and 'indignity' did not entirely dominate. Thus the anti-ban lobby, including the bar girls themselves, appropriated discourses of rights and shifted the debate into some new areas. Key to these remarkable developments was the fact that the government was trying to and eventually succeeded in instituting a legal ban on dancing (unlike anti-*nautch*, which was principally a social campaign). This allowed for a legal challenge to the ban, with the bar girls supported by legal experts, and the ban subjected to intense scrutiny. The Bombay High Court ruled the ban to be unconstitutional on 12 April 2006. This represented a victory unprecedented in the modern history of public/erotic performers. However, the ban remained in force after a stay was granted to the State of Maharashtra. The State of Maharashtra also appealed against the ruling. After many delays and adjournments, the hearing of the case in Supreme Court was completed in May 2013, and the judgment was due in July 2013. Thus as this book went to press, the outcome of this landmark case was still in the balance.

The bar girls affair forms a particularly interesting chapter in the history of public/erotic female performers in India. The repetition and continuation of history is striking. Just as striking is the fact that there was no sense of déjà vu. However, significant new currents in class, culture, morality and civil rights are also visible. As stated in the previous chapter, these new currents have emerged from the same bourgeois, nationalist, liberal/neoliberal trajectory, but have continued so far along on it that they represent change as much as they do continuity, consolidation or culmination. In this chapter, I look in particular at how discourses of justice, fairness, morality and progress have acted both socially and legally in connection with the bar girls. I analyse this episode as one more in a history of exclusion—evidence of the umbilical link of postcolonial modernity to late colonial class hegemony, culture and morality. I then look at the new currents that have emerged. I focus on the role of the different players, in particular, the media, the BBU, and the law. In addition to being an important phase in the history of public/erotic female performers, the case of the bar girls reveals new shifts in socio-economic configuration and middle class cultures of India, as well as new perspectives on Indian modernity, its problems and its potentials.

*The continuation and repetition of history: The dance bar ban as anti-*nautch *II*

Exploitation of women and the ruin of society and culture

The campaign to ban dancing in bars essentially focused on the same two arguments as anti-*nautch*: the girls were victims of exploitation and/or they were evil forces bringing about the destruction of good people.[24] In terms of the dance bars, essentially the same arguments as anti-*nautch* are expressed in a paid-for advertisement by the pro-ban lobby, published in *Mid Day* on 13 May 2005, which attempted to rally support for the campaign. Entitled 'Sweety v/s Savitri', the subtitles read, 'Should dance bars be banned or not? Is it a fight between bar owners and R.R. Patil? Or a fight between bar culture and Indian culture?'. The article pits the (Westernised and) seductive bar girl 'Sweety' against the idealised (Hindu) wife Savitri, and 'corrupt' Westernised culture against 'pure' Indian (Hindu) culture.[25] The article challenges those who support dance bars to ask, 'Why are they supporting dance bar owners and the vulgar culture that goes with it, instead of families that are ruined because of it?'. The piece also expresses compassion for the bar girls, but calculates—literally—that although 'our sympathies are with them', the harm they do is effectively ten times more than the harm they will suffer: if each bar girl has ten customers, she therefore wrongs ten wives (the calculation assumes all the customers married), and if there are 75,000 bar girls, then there are 750,000 wronged wives. The article includes a highlighted box, asking 'Why should dance bars be banned?', which lists a number of reasons, mostly based on the idea that the bar girls are exploited, degraded, and in some way 'forced' or 'compelled' to dance:

- It is the biggest atrocity against women, making them dance seductively, compelling them to make suggestive gestures, and exploiting their sex appeal to make money (even if they resist prostitution).
- It is greatest lie to say that bar girl loves it. It is like saying that teenage girl loves prostitution and women love being beaten up or abused.
- It is sex shows by dance girls and vulgar money show by visitors.
- Because many of these bars indirectly promote prostitution, though the method differs. [...]
- It debases the person and creates urge and desire that generally a wife cannot fulfil, thus worsening the situation.
- It is an addiction that ruins mans family and home. When thousands and lakhs are spent in bars, what is left for home?
- In such homes kids grow up in wrong influences. In some cases causes for crimes.

The article concludes, 'Finally the issue boils down to this. Either you are for women sexploitation or for women liberation. Please standup and be counted'.

Another advertisement, issued by the Maharashtra State Commission for Women in the *Indian Express* on 22 August 2005, gives a similar pro-ban view.

Issued seven days after the ban came into force, the advert was responding to those tempted to feel pity for the bar girls or critical of the government's actions following stories in the news of the plight of unemployed bar girls. Entitled 'The bar girls issue—the exploitation behind the tinsel and the makeup', the article states:

The past few days have seen several sob stories being purveyed in the media about the broken lives and the desperation of the bar girls facing unemployment after being used to a lifestyle of earning twenty thousand rupees a month.[26] These bleeding heart stories have ignored some basic societal issues.

- What about the untold stories of families ruined by this multi-crore industry when men spend their earnings on liquor and sex in these joints? ... The tears of the women left at home, who suffer abuse from alcoholic husbands, the children whose lives are ruined by a parent sucked into alcoholism and moral ruin have no news value. But their agony is also as real as the story of the bargirls looking for new jobs.
  [...]
- Artistes can stage performances in theatres and earn a living with the dignity of such a profession. But those who want to commodify women's bodies would rather have women dance in a bar as 'objects of lust' for men. This is against women's status and dignity. CEDAW (the international conventional on eliminating all forms of discrimination against women) to which India is a signatory, binds us to prevent the commodification of women's bodies.
  [...]
- The Maharashtra State Commission for Women does not want women to be driven to this 'profession' of dancing in bars. Instead women should be provided opportunities to work with dignity and earn a decent livelihood.

Again, there is a tension between presenting the girls as people who are harming society and ruining lives (for whom pity is out of the question), and on the other hand, as themselves victims of exploitation. As with 'Sweety vs. Savitri', it states that girls do not choose to dance, but are 'driven' to do so. This article directly implies that the girls are not artistes, they are simply 'commodified women's bodies' (the Marxist–feminist view) and, for them, dance is not something that can be called a profession.

These two direct statements of the pro-ban lobby can be compared with writings that targeted courtesans and *devadasi*s around a century earlier. For example, in 1894, a *nautch* girl is described as:

a hideous woman ... hell is in her eyes. In her breast is a vast ocean of poison. Round her comely waist dwell the furies of hell. Her hands are brandishing unseen daggers ever ready to strike unwary or wilful victims that fall in her way. Her blandishments are India's ruin. Alas! Her smile is in India's death.[27]

The language is that of fire and brimstone Christian morality whereas the pro-ban lobby appealed more to 'rational' rights and (Hindu) family values. However, the sense of the *nautch* girl or bar girl as evil and destructive, not just to men, but to India or 'Indian culture' is the same.

The more sympathetic presentation of the bar girls as victims, as exploited, and as forced to dance also has its parallel and predecessor in anti-*nautch* (and indeed in the wider debates on women's issues), and can be seen in Mutthulakshmi Reddy's statements in 'The *devadasi* question', written in 1930:

> I have been feeling all along and feeling most acutely too that it was a great piece of injustice, a great wrong, a violation of human rights, a practice highly revolting to our sense of morality and to our higher nature to countenance, and to tolerate young innocent girls to be trained in the name of religion to lead an immoral life, to lead a life of promiscuity, a life leading to the disease of the mind and the body.[28]

Although the view is ostensibly sympathetic to *devadasis* as victims, a more accusatory undertone can be sensed, since *devadasis*, although forced into their position, were, once they embarked on it, leading 'an immoral life ... a life of promiscuity, a life leading to the disease of the mind and the body'. The idea that the *devadasi* or *nautch* girl is evil and has 'mysterious' power over helpless men is present in both the bar girls case and anti-*nautch*. Reddy mentions people 'who have been addicted to the custom and who take their stand behind religion'.[29] The term 'addiction' was also used in reference to customers of the bar girls. For example, a press article reports a father describing how his son was saved by the dance bar ban after nearly ruining the family: '"his addiction grew on him and I was on the brink of insolvency. Then came the ban and everything changed", Shah says with a grateful glint in his eyes. "After the ban, he has mended his ways and is leading a normal life"'.[30]

The anti-*nautch* campaign essentially used appeals to rights and 'liberation' of women as well as to the need to protect 'morality' and 'Indian culture', as did the pro-ban lobby in the case of the bar girls. At the time of the anti-*nautch* campaign, the overt conflation of women, nation, honour and culture with discourses of purity, status and nationalism was rather more readily accepted than in twenty-first-century Mumbai. Hence, while the 'immorality' of the *nautch* girl or *devadasi* was directly confronted, sometimes with very fiery language, during anti-*nautch*, in the case of the bar girls, the expression of sexual morality was generally rather more muted. It was claimed by some key players, there was no moral stand against the girls at all, just concerns about 'trafficking', harm to the girls, and/or harm to the wronged wives.[31] This reflects a very different balance of attitudes towards sex in late twentieth and early twenty-first-century India compared to the days of anti-*nautch*. There were many vociferous objections to moral policing and hypocrisy in the debates over the dance bar ban, with issues over liquor licensing compounding these.[32] Whereas anti-*nautch* was a social campaign against moral wrongs, the heavier emphasis in the dance bar ban on violations of human rights also reflected the fact that the ban involved amending a law and there was thus a legal dimension to the campaign. However, as I discuss below, both moral and human-rights based arguments, resting on absolutes and universals, served many of the same purposes, and the victimhood trope loomed large in both, although with different configurations.

Liberalism, human rights, victimhood and dogs chasing their tails

When looking at these two campaigns, I was struck by the extent to which history was repeating itself. Girls from the same (north Indian) communities that had been under attack by anti-*nautch* from the late nineteenth century were being targeted by essentially the same arguments again in twenty-first-century Mumbai. Yet what struck me more was that this glaring parallel was not being reported in the press, and did not form any part of the debates on the bar girls. The BBU told all journalists, as they had told me, of the hereditary performing background of the vast majority of the girls, and the lawyers representing the BBU were also well aware of it.[33] There was a large amount of sympathy for the bar girls, in particular in the English language press. But their specific history and sociology, which was so relevant to the how and why of their circumstances, was not reported.[34] The debates by the pro-ban lobby focused on issues of prostitution, exploitation, choice/free will/helplessness and trafficking, and those of the anti-ban lobby were largely monopolised by these same topics. The positions can be summarised as follows:

Pro-ban: a) The girls were social evils, prostitutes who were making easy money while ruining homes and society, and so should be stopped; b) the girls were helpless, trafficked, prostitutes; they were exploited and needed to be saved.

Anti-ban: The bar girls have no choice but to dance, they are not prostitutes, and they are not making easy money; they are victims of society/family breakdown, and to lose their jobs would make them (more) destitute.

These issues were discussed endlessly and resulted in some daring and witty investigative journalism. For example, in one piece, a journalist went undercover in order to find out whether or not the girls were prostitutes. He reports, describing his experience in a bar:

> I have eyes only for the pretty girl in blue. I beckon her, spray out some notes, and that sparks off a duet that I guess usually plays out at dance bars. More the money I shower, harder the girl dances. I try to grab Sunayna's hand, she shies away. I tell her she's very sexy, she blushes and dances some more. I tell her I'd like us to meet after hours, she only smiles mysteriously. Encouraged, I dance with her. … I quietly slip a post-it into Sunayna's hands. It has my cell number. She winks, and promises to call. We leave Deepa with great hope. I'm still waiting for my phone to ring.[35]

Three girls at other bars similarly shun him, and the article challenges the view of bargirls as prostitutes, carrying the title and headline 'They did not sleep with me, Mr Patil. Four bargirls turn down correspondent Anil Thakraney. Still think dance bars are a front for prostitution, Mr Home Minister?'. In another article, *Mid Day*, reporter Swati Ali went undercover, dancing in two bars over two nights in order to find out the truth about being a bar girl. When she sits next to a man on a sofa in order to hear him, she reports, a girl tells her off, saying 'You are not here to get physical with your customer. You have to only dance for him'.[36] Another advises her, after a customer sends her a note asking if she'll stay the night with him, '"who sleeps with these men? Just say yes and let him spend some more money on you". She tells me that after work, the girls all leave in taxis provided by the bar, and nobody dare touch them'.[37] Her experience leaves her with 'unadulterated admiration' for the bar girls.

However, a brief consideration of the specific sociological background of the bar girls makes it clear that these debates on prostitution, and the other 'headline issues' of 'free choice' and 'exploitation' miss some fundamental considerations:

a) The bar girls were overwhelmingly from hereditary performing backgrounds, so dancing was neither free choice, nor coercion in the sense of 'trafficking', but a family trade, the *khandani pesha*. With some communities having turned almost entirely to a system of family sex work, dancing in bars was in fact for many girls a rehabilitation from sex work.
b) As public/erotic female performers, these communities have an alternative system to mainstream society whereby girls who dance do not marry and those who marry do not dance. Thus, normative questions of 'choice' or 'force' are no more relevant to their occupation as erotic performers than they are to the system of more or less compulsory marriage for mainstream society. Rather than being destitute or abandoned by husbands, their society is matrilineal in many ways—they do not marry, and their fathers are often unknown to them or not significant to the family unit.
c) The bar girls and other erotic/public female performers are not accurately described as prostitutes (as long as they are able to perform). At the same time, however, they operate outside the bounds of mainstream honour and respectability. They look for longer term, advantageous relationships with men which, in the case of the bar girls, depend on flirting, seduction and tips. They do not undertake transactional 'per shot' sex work when they are earning well from dance, and classify themselves as different and superior to prostitutes. Outright prostitution in these communities has historically resulted from a loss of performing livelihood and identity, rather than being concomitant with it.[38]
d) Such performers have been fundamental to large swathes of 'Indian culture', up until the early or mid-twentieth century, before 'respectable' women were able to be professional performers.

Without their social and historical context, the key debates were seriously compromised. Despite a clear repetition of history, the link with the past, and indeed, the cycles of stigmatisation and exclusion which this campaign was in fact repeating and continuing, were not mentioned, and history continued.

Crucial matters concerning the specific history and sociology of the bar girls were rendered unsayable, irrelevant or foreclosed (even by those sympathetic to them). The reasons for this are partly grounded in the anti-*nautch* legacy and the broader social reform upon which Indian nationalism was founded. These movements set the terms of the debate over these kinds of dancers. The pro-ban lobby continued these arguments, and the anti-ban lobby responded on these terms. Yet the problems with the bar girls' debates also stem from the characteristics of modern knowledge and ideology. The blanket category of 'prostitution' is inappropriate when applied to hereditary performers, whether they are *devadasi*s and courtesans in the nineteenth century or bar girls in the twenty-first. Colonial modernity rigidly classified them as prostitutes, as discussed in chapter one, because of a lack of understanding, but also because of the drive to categorise everything 'scientifically'. The contemporary world has continued to rely on categorisation to produce authoritative knowledge with universal application, and terms such as 'prostitution', 'sex work' and 'trafficking' have been globalised by the arenas of development and human rights (with international development increasingly connecting professionals that transcend specific place and region).[39] So authoritative are these terms that it was almost inevitable that the anti-ban lobby should also use them as a basis for its arguments. Thus, even though they were far off the mark, they constituted the terms of the debate, and the finer details of history and of social or cultural context were elided.

However, the terms of the debate related not just to categorisation and authoritative knowledge but to the discourse of human rights and notions such as 'dignity', 'freedom' and 'choice', including their violations in the form of 'exploitation' or 'trafficking'. Although the set of rights that people are automatically deemed to have has changed in significant ways between colonial and postcolonial times, in terms of basic principles and structures, these discourses represent a powerful link between the two eras. Thus the pro-ban lobby repeated in essence the arguments of the anti-*nautch* campaign, not just because its categories still stood (having been defined in part by anti-*nautch*), but because the deeper structures within notions of justice, injustice, humanity and inhumanity did, too. These ideologies are universal, as are the aforementioned categories of knowledge, and hence potentially render other matters secondary. The arguments are particularly compelling because they deal with these core notions of justice, humanity and the universal human good, and are hence highly emotional or emotionalising, as I discuss in the introduction. Because they claim to stand for a universal and axiomatic 'good', they place anyone who opposes them in a position that tends to dehumanise them. For this reason, once raised, they require answering, or those accused stand the risk of, for example, appearing to be indifferent to, or even worse, pro-'exploitation'.[40] Hence, the terms of the debate, as rooted in the discourse of universal human rights, was almost compulsive; once the argument started using these emotionalising 'moral trump cards', it would seem natural and necessary to answer with other trumps rather than challenge fundamental categories and discuss history and social context.[41]

The domination of the debate by arguments concerning fundamental rights also led to its compromise. As discussed in the introduction, the discourse of human rights tends to divide people into victims, perpetrators and saviours. Saviours have a moral mandate to act in the interests of victims. Within the progressive and liberatory discourse of universal human rights, if something is (deemed to be) exploitative, people cannot wish for it if they are in their right minds. In terms of the pro-ban lobby, there was an insistence that girls were exploited and were forced or compelled to dance, despite the existence of a trade union of 7,800 bar girls fighting to be able to work. I questioned Praveen Patkar from Prerana, an NGO that works on prostitution and trafficking, who played a particularly central role in the dance ban, on the fact that the bar girls appeared so clearly to be choosing to dance:

> A hundred Percent of the members of a slave community come and say that we are here by choice. What do you derive from that statement? ... So on what indicators do you decide [if it is really their choice]? It is not correct to go by the statements of the slaves because slaves don't have the right to express their real desires. By the fact that they are slaves their ability to express their true interests is fractured and limited. ... As a learned person, as a civilized person, that is what I believe. I am not an opportunist or a politician who would say 'Alright, since eighty percent of them are saying that they are there by choice now the matter is over'. See I have not learnt democracy that way. I have learned democracy in a very classical way, as a value phenomenon and not merely electoral calculation. ... In the same way, if the slave community comes and says, even if hundred percent of them say that [they are there by choice], as a civilized person I don't immediately come to the conclusion that that is true. It is my responsibility to create conditions whereby they are able to speak freely and openly and then I will take ... their statement. Otherwise, I [would be] using that kind of their weakness in order to justify my failures as a civil society person.[42]

Ironically, arguments professing to liberate the bar girls results in 'sectioning' their free will, concluding they are not free enough to have free will.[43]

The pro-ban lobby rested on two principal arguments: that the girls were social evils (perpetrators) and that they were also victims of exploitation. These arguments appear contradictory. Yet the ways in which such rights-based arguments remove the agency of both perpetrators and victims mean that such arguments are in fact not in conflict but lead to the same conclusions (the removal of the bar girls) under, essentially, the same logic.[44] The neutralising of the bar girls or *nautch* girls by positioning them as victims, shows how the discourse of rights and dignity serves, in practical terms, the same purpose as demonising them, and has the advantage of appearing to be modern, rational, unconcerned with 'morality', and in the interests of the 'victims'. It could be said that the discourse of rights is the 'good cop' to the 'bad cop' that declares the girls to be home-breakers and social evils.

That the pro-ban lobby used these 'liberatory' arguments against the expressed wishes of the bar girls is unsurprising, and can be construed as a hypocritical or manipulative use of discourses of rights, in the same way that America's 'liberation' of Iraq in the name of 'freedom' has been widely deemed hypocritical. It can also be seen as a convenient way of universalising and thus legitimising what are in fact partial moral stances—a dislike of the culture of (extra-marital) eroticism and sex that the bar girls were involved with. However, what is more noteworthy is that many of the anti-bar statements leant on the victimhood trope, marginalising and blunting the bar girls' agency. In a sense, therefore, these statements were inadvertently acting as the 'good cop' of the pro-ban lobby, eliding social and historical context, as well as some of the fundamental questions of the 'how' and 'why' of the situation. The girls were victims in a very direct way, in the sense that they would face destitution or prostitution if they lost their jobs, and it was indeed necessary to put this across. However, the anti-ban lobby also emphasised again and again that the girls had 'no choice' but to dance and that they were victims of life/society. Hence much of the anti-ban lobby, like the pro-ban lobby and anti-*nautch*, refused to accept that the bar girls may conceivably choose to dance, want to dance, or enjoy doing what they do in any way that is not, effectively, a form of 'false consciousness' or helplessness. This stance reveals the omnipresent or default nature of discourses of rights and victimhood, and also their compelling nature, in that apparently only fire is strong enough to fight fire. Yet it also reveals their ability to compromise agendas severely through distraction and confusion.

An article in the *Times of India* on 29 April 2005 (i.e., in the run up to the ban) is one of many that illustrate these problems. The article aims at fair coverage by presenting 'for' and 'against' points of view. Called 'Women vs Women: The bar that divides us', it reports on the fact that women's groups are split on the matter of bar dancers. The pro-ban opinion is given by Priti Patkar of Prerana, and begins in a way that denies moral policing and asserts concern for the girls: 'We support the ban on dance bars because it will curb the trafficking and exploitation of thousands of girls and not because we believe that dance bars are a corrupting influence on the youth. …' The anti-ban position is given by Mariam Dhawale, state secretary of the All Indian Democratic Women's Association (AIDWA):

> In a situation in which there is large-scale poverty, unemployment, an acute agricultural crisis and the closing down of industries, shutting down of dance bars is just going to throw thousands of more girls out of jobs. These girls are not dancing in bars of their own free will—it's because the government has been unable to provide them with jobs.

This situation has arisen due to a wider crisis of economic policies. … Women do domestic work or scavenging just as they dance in bars because it helps them survive. …
This is not a morality issue at all.[45]

Dhawale's stance highlights the important issue of livelihood, which I discuss in more detail below. However, it bases the legitimacy of the bar girls' need for support on their having 'no choice' but to dance due to generalised poverty and economic problems.[46]

However, the focus on victimhood engendered by the human rights-based agenda goes beyond an undermining of bar girls' agency, or indeed, clarity of analysis and information, and can come dangerously close to sensationalism. A set of six articles by Sonia Faleiro, 'The dying of the evening stars: The lives of Mumbai's bar girls', foreground the victimhood and tragedy of bar girls vividly with stories of courage in adversity ranging from their entry into the profession to the problems they face after the ban.[47] One bar girl, Vaishali Haldankar, a singer not a dancer and not from a hereditary performer background, who was the focus of the fifth article in Faleiro's series and a number of other articles in the press, had suffered almost unimaginable difficulties and abuse, including having been raped by her own son.[48] Vaishali later published her autobiography in Marathi, *Barbala* ('Bar-girl', 2010), which contained lurid stories of her life of abuse, sex work, and music, and was a huge success. Faleiro's book on bar girls, *Beautiful thing: Inside the secret world of Bombay's dance bars* (2010), which deals with the lives of two bar girls and is seen as an authoritative account of bar girls, also enters into a frame of sensationalism. Details of the main protagonist Lila's bitter relationship with her mother, an ongoing tortured affair with a bar owner, and even the bar owner's remedies for chronic constipation are described in vivid detail. Moreover, the author is clearly distant from these lives—a mixture of compassionate, curious, cool, composed, and amused by the antics of the protagonists (though becoming more emotionally involved in the destitution that hits them after the ban).

While I do not deny the truth of any details published about the lives of particular bar girls or things they have said to journalists, I question whether this is representative of bar girls in general. There is a tendency on the part of authors or publishers to focus on girls from particularly dysfunctional and unhappy families in extremely close and intimate quarters in these 'real lives' accounts, which makes for painful reading in places.[49] There are bar girls who, for the most part, lead positive and stable relationships with their families—even among those who were inducted into family-based sex work from their early teens, though this is difficult to fathom within normative frameworks of middle class society. The focus also tends to be on larger-than-life bar girls, who lead engagingly crazy and chaotic lives. However, some bar girls are shy and some are serious and focused professionals. These books do provide information about bar dancers, the nature of the work, its pressures and also the effect of the ban.[50] However, there is a sense in which it has become acceptable, normal and representative to provide such coverage of bar girls and their tragic or messily hedonistic or materialistic lives. Such a portrayal of the middle classes would be seen as very dark and cynical indeed, even though there is no shortage of dysfunctionality, despair, chaos, hedonism and embarrassing details there.

There is certainly a thirst from mainstream society to see bar girls in these terms. However, the focus on victimhood and sensationalism has also been driven by the bar girls themselves, who reeled out many clichéd or shocking stories of helplessness and victimhood. These can translate effectively into enhanced generosity from men or sympathy from journalists and mainstream society, not to mention payments for stories or interviews. The story of how they became a bar dancer is almost invariably framed in family tragedy and victimhood rather than a hereditary profession. They are well aware of the moral laws of mainstream society and know that telling the truth would alienate most customers. Hence, there were many stories of bar girls as abandoned women, abused by husbands or fathers and struggling alone.[51] An example of the classic abandoned female 'victim' bar girl is Monalisa in Suketa Mehta's *Bombay: Maximum City*.[52] In addition to her portrayal as the object of immense erotic fascination, she was framed with a sense of pity, as the abandonment by her father meant that she ended up as a bar dancer. However, the BBU informed me that this bar girl was from a community of *Chari* hereditary female performers in Gujarat. Mehta's portrayal of bars, and other aspects of Bombay, brings unique and previously unpublished dimensions and images of this city to mainstream view. However, whatever pain and difficulties existed in Monalisa's life, the sense of being 'driven to dance' out of *majboori* (compulsion) reflects the culture and discourse of such dancers, rather than sociological reality.

In this way, the bar girls were surrounded from both inside and out by the 'victim' trope, as it was used by the pro-ban lobby, the anti-ban lobby, and the bar girls themselves. The reasons for this can be found in the stigma attached to hereditary female performers, with the girls unwilling or unable to reveal their background. However, the reasons also lie in the compelling nature of the human rights framework of the debate, which meant that journalists did not investigate details of the background and history of the bar girls, even when told about them. The universal discourses of liberation, saving, freedom and choice were endlessly repeated. Their qualities of universality, pre-eminent rationality and 'rightness' consumed the debate like a vortex and made different positions extremely difficult to trace to a given group and their particular interests (more so even than the directly moral arguments). The attention and sympathy raised by the press did serve an important purpose despite these problems, in part because it helped fuel the more productive and grounded questions of labour and livelihood, which I explore below. But to a large degree, the core arguments served to (often unconsciously) stultify and strangle debate.

On another level, the need to either demonise or disempower the bar girls by making them victims can be understood as a reaction to their very formidable power, presence and agency—their very lack of victimhood. They had become, once more, after many decades, 'celebrity performers'.[53] They were on the face of contemporary Indian culture and had become an accepted and legitimate part of Mumbai's identity.[54] However, this was of course a threat to the very construction of India and Indian culture that the original exclusion of public/erotic female performers had created, and which has been continued and expanded in India under neoliberalism. As Mazzarella writes, 'the dance bars were both a symptom of [the] globalizing moment and an intolerable irritant to its ruling ideology'. They had spread to many locations around the world, including the Gulf countries, Singapore, Malaysia, the US and London and, 'as far as global Brand India was concerned, they were disastrously "off message"'.[55] Hence, for these reasons of (inter)national identity and middle class hegemony, another anti-*nautch* campaign was necessary and expedient.[56] As 'victims' or 'problems' the bar girls were devoid of legitimate agency and were less threatening. As discussed in the introduction, being (once again) made into people with no place, they could more easily belong through not-belonging, through constituting the 'other' of modernity and a target for 'progress', 'saving' and 'reform'. Portraying the girls as prostitutes rather than as performers also made them less threatening, since they could more easily be bracketed into categories of those who have 'no choice' and are in need of 'saving'. Most importantly, it also meant that they could not exist in the realm of high profile performing arts that connects in such an immediate way to nation and identity. As Agnes questions, 'Is it [the bar girl's] earning capacity, the legitimacy awarded to her profession, and the higher status she enjoys in comparison to a sex worker that invite the fury from the middle class Maharashtrian moralists?'[57] To explore questions of dignity, choice and exploitation effectively and fairly would require considering a much broader social, cultural, political and historical context, which would bring to light some very uncomfortable yet foundational aspects of modern India. These questions also required exploration through concrete attention to livelihood and working conditions, which was a central success of the BBU and other activists and lawyers, as I discuss below.

Following the ban, a very small proportion of bar girls were able to get work singing in bars, and a small proportion went to the Gulf to work in dance bars there. Around half became engaged in 'waitressing', which is a front for prostitution. Establishments called 'Restaurants and bars' (i.e. with liquor licenses but not entertainment licenses) employ sometimes twenty or thirty female 'waitresses' serving in a room of about as many men, wearing in some cases skimpy clothes, sitting next to men and talking with them (in contrast to dance bars, where audience members were not allowed to touch or sit next to the dancers). Nearby, 'Lodging and boarding houses' have mushroomed, where 'waitresses' go for sex with men from the 'Restaurant and bars'. Girls also operate directly from lodges. The occupation of the remaining proportion of bar girls is unknown, but it is thought that many are involved in forms of sex work on the street ('floating sex workers'), in brothels, or back in the village; others are doing menial jobs or other work back in their home villages.[58]

The pro-ban lobby had claimed bars were a nexus of 'trafficking'. This term, encompassing some of the most extreme human suffering and injustice of the subcontinent, carries with it an immense emotional and moral force. It also constituted a political pressure, since the US was threatening sanctions on India for failing to control trafficking. The ban managed to make redundant 75,000 girls who were earning decent wages and sending their children to school—and was heralded as a victory against trafficking. Rather than saving the girls from exploitation, the ban put many of the girls into or back into prostitution. For many girls from hereditary performing communities such as *Nat*, where performing arts had ceased to be a livelihood since the aftermath of independence, dancing in bars had been a form of rehabilitation from sex work, and a livelihood that offered more choices for the next generation.[59] There are forms of prostitution in Mumbai that indisputably consist of exploitation, with girls kidnapped or trafficked through deception and literally forced to do sex work. These, however, were not targeted. When the ban was challenged in the High Court, no evidence of trafficking, or even prostitution, was found in connection to bars, as I discuss below.

Socio-economic disparity and gulfs in understanding

The strengthening of the Marathi-speaking middle classes since the late twentieth century has been a critical factor in sustaining the illicit economy of dance bars and, ultimately, generating enough political capital to bring about the dance bar ban. This largely conservative sector of society has almost identical views on bar girls as late nineteenth-century reformers had on *devadasi*s and courtesans, and morality and questions of 'exploitation' and 'prostitution' were able to dominate debate. However, it could be argued that the economic development that bolstered this sector of society also supported misunderstandings and non-debates on the bar girls. Beyond the all-consuming discourses of rights and freedom, it is possible to see the bar girls trapped in forms of alienation and marginalisation deriving from the social and cultural politics of contemporary India. As is now well known, disparities of wealth in India have risen dramatically since economic liberalisation began in 1991, with the Indian middle classes now living in a world that is increasingly distant from the 42 per cent of the population who live off less than $1.25 per day.[60] This immense gulf is another reason why, even when there is a will to make things fairer and better for the 'have nots', this may be impaired by a total unawareness of some basic realities. One English language journalist of elite background based in Mumbai, for example, reporting on the bar girls, was extremely sympathetic to their plight and told me they suffered from 'addictions': they chewed tobacco to help counter exhaustion as they had to dance all night. Chewing *paan* is actually a normal part of lower class life in much of north and northeast India and Bangladesh; yet this too was interpreted in terms of the omnipresent victim story. In contemporary Mumbai, it is next to impossible for people with the with the kinds of socio-economic backgrounds that most, especially English language, journalists come from, to understand how this kind of dancer can be anything but helpless, desperate, lacking choice, or a prostitute (since anti-*nautch* so definitively conflated female hereditary performers with prostitutes). Thus, although journalists were told again and again that the girls were from traditional dancing communities by the bar girls' union leader in interviews, these details of social organisation and history were hardly ever explored and thus the obvious route to defend the bar girls was to state their helplessness.

There is a sense, particularly in parts of the English language press, that the only India that is relevant is that of shopping malls, multiplexes, credit cards, nightclubs, and luxury consumer goods, so powerful are the globalised middle classes in defining India.[61] The enlarged middle classes, who grow up on *The Bold and the Beautiful* and are eager to see India on the level of first world countries, have little sense of or interest in the 'other' India, except when they see it as a problem or, in certain circumstances, a tourist attraction. In a strong critique of the new middle classes in India, Pavan Varma asserts that the poor have lost their place in India's collective identity post economic reforms.[62] He quotes an 'ideologue of the new school of thought from the editorial page of a national newspaper':

> We should all get this clear, that a country of the size and importance of India has no choice but to clamber to its new tryst with destiny inside shiny buildings of chrome and glass at the free market. There is no mileage in looking wistfully at quaint mud huts rushing by the car windows because they, and their ilk, cannot meet our burgeoning needs, and if truth be told, never have.[63]

In a sense, the bar girls have been grouped together as general 'unfortunates' of India by the pro- and anti-ban lobbies. The terms 'illiterate', 'backward',[64] 'uneducated' and 'impoverished' came up again and again in both sides of the debate, and also in the High Court judgement. More specific details were generally not delved into. The lack of engagement with the social and historical facts of the bar girls by the press, even when informed of them, is a symptom of the growing marginalisation of such groups from dominant society due to economic and social disparity. However, this omission is itself part of the cause of marginalisation, since understanding the history of these communities and their role in Indian cultural heritage would necessitate seeing them as a part of India, of including them, and even of questioning their previous treatment by society.

New directions: The bar girls debacle as an unprecedented chapter in the history of public/erotic female performers in India

Middle class culture and morality

Changes to class configuration provided the strength to mobilise political will towards a dance ban in bars. In other ways it caused a further layer of confusion about who the bar girls were in social, cultural and historical terms. However, the same rapid economic development that brought about the socio-economic and cultural change that acted against the bar girls, also brought about changes in class and culture that have been crucial to their success, providing an opportunity that the *devadasi*s and *tawaif*s of the late nineteenth and early twentieth century did not have. The same kinds of middle classes who are separated by a gulf of social, economic and cultural reality from the bar girls are also those who are potentially most sympathetic to them and, despite a certain amount of confusion, they have been fundamental to the immensely successful ways in which the ban has been contested. Since the 1990s, a very significant sector of the middle class has started to learn Bollywood dance, as described in chapter four. Many also go to bars and discos in mixed groups. Increasing numbers drink and smoke (cigarettes and also joints), have pre-marital sexual relationships, do not necessarily have objections to casual sex, and are more and more open to gayness. People in this kind of milieu are less and less willing to see people judged or regulated on narrow ideas of 'morality' and 'Indian culture'. In these ways, what were previously elite modes of behaviour and attitudes have become more widespread. Such people still form a minority of the middle classes; for example, 87 per cent were in favour of the ban in a *Times of India*–TNS survey published 20 April 2006.[65] However, they are a significant minority. Indeed, this socially and culturally liberal outlook is common among English language journalists in particular, and the assertion of 'freedom' and 'choice' and objection to 'moral policing' gained considerable coverage, at times poking fun at the 'ruin of Indian culture and society' arguments of the pro-ban lobby, making them sound outdated, unfashionable and absurd. Writer and poet Jerry Pinto, for example, while admitting his life would change little as he is not a frequenter of bars, stated '... they are being closed down for all the wrong reasons. They are being closed because they "tear the fabric of Maharashtrian culture"'. He points out that this destruction of culture is apparently not endangered by either corruption or unsustainable exploitation of the environment. He continues:

> I wonder what the next step will be. Perhaps it will be the eating of non-vegetarian food. (All that meat heats the blood and leads to sex). Perhaps it will be the singing of Antakshari

at college picnics. (All that singing heats the blood and leads to sex). Perhaps it will be the sari. (All those exposed midriffs heat the blood and lead to sex).[66]

He concludes on the counterproductive nature of such bans.

Many celebrities also expressed views against bans and moral policing. The hypocrisy of allowing sexy dances in films and shows but not allowing fully clothed girls to dance in bars was raised by people in the film industry, such as Bollywood actress and director Soni Razdan.[67] The issue was also raised by Mayank Shekhar, a writer on movies, in an article titled 'Ban Bollywood now!' He also raises questions about the wishes and freedom to choose of the clientele of the dance bars:

> What about the loss of a source of legal leisure that was perceived as part of pop-culture of a city for years. How simple was it for the state to snatch it away in seconds, while no one raised a middle finger. Clearly no one, but no one, saw it as an infringement on a freedom, or openly discussed it as one. ... Everybody, including the Press has moved on. And I think peoples or cultures that can do away with their liberties so easily and so soon, never deserve any in the first place.[68]

Another article, entitled 'Do Mumbai's bar girls corrupt morals?', presented 'for and against' views. In it, ad filmmaker Prahlad Kakkar is quoted as saying 'Who has given the government the right to decide how we should lead our lives? That's the key issue here. Whether I sleep with my wife or my secretary is no one's business but my own'.[69]

Labour rights and new feminists: The Bhartiya Bargirls Union (BBU), women's groups and the press

While the discourse of rights has been (conveniently) used in a manner that has inhibited some of the most significant social, historical and cultural aspects of this case from surfacing, rights have also developed into broader arenas. These developments include civil and labour rights for even the most stigmatised sectors of society, with activists willing to support them, lawyers willing to represent them and a press willing to cover the stories sympathetically.[70] These rights are potentially easier to ground in empirical facts than are those relating to 'free will' versus 'false consciousness'. A crucial development in this broadening of rights and access to rights has been changes in feminism which have seen figures such as prostitutes and bar girls included among those women whose interests and rights should be protected (as opposed to being viewed as fundamentally in conflict with the 'true' or 'right' interests of women).[71] Women's groups remain deeply divided on this issue, as the aforementioned press story about 'the bar that divides us' shows. However, that there is a division at all, as opposed to a unanimous voice against such women, dates only from the 1990s, and marks the vigorously contested dance bar ban as something different from anti-*nautch*. A new generation of 'feminist' activists, some from the more elite and liberal middle classes but many from 'alternative' sectors of non-Anglophone backgrounds, thus emerged in support of the bar girls and, crucially, they have had enough sympathy within the press for their views and activities to be covered. These developments of class, and these ideas of justice and citizenship, both emerged, in part, as a result of globalisation—with globalisation bringing about a growth in wealth as well as the spread and development of ideology and attitudes across larger sectors of the population.

The BBU is very much a part of and a new watershed in this movement. The trade union was set up in 2004 on the initiative of Varsha Kale, an activist from a middle class Marathi background. She also launched her own political party, the Womanist Party of India (WPI), on 31 March 2003, and works for women from a variety of poor and marginalised backgrounds. The BBU clearly asserted that bar dancing was a job. It thus began to pull debates away from slippery and inevitably subjective ideas of 'exploitation', morality/immorality, social harm and social freedom onto more specific questions of labour and livelihood. The BBU had around 7,800 paid-up members at the time of the ban. The union stopped taking or renewing membership when the ban came into force, itself a compelling statement of the 'choice' to work on the part of bar girls. This point was made even more strongly by mass rallies and a number of bar girls talking articulately to the press. With the BBU, there was an official body through which it was possible to contact bar girls and tap into their views, something which is otherwise difficult. This was the route I followed, as did many journalists. The BBU represented an absolutely unprecedented mass mobilisation of public/erotic female performers. The *devadasis* had hardly been able to fight the anti-*nautch* campaign and the banning of their office, especially because the menfolk of their communities became vigorously involved in outlawing the institution within the politics of anti-Brahminism.[72] In the north, *tawaif* had established *sabhas* or 'associations' that promoted a new and respectable image for themselves that distinguished them from prostitutes, responding to nationalist discourse and the stigmatising pressures that had made them a 'caste' of prostitutes.[73] However, nothing on the scale of the BBU took place, partly because of the sheer number and concentration of bar girls in a single city, which, with modern communications, was something that had no parallel with the *devadasi*s, *tawaif*s, and *nautch* girls of the late nineteenth and early twentieth centuries.

In addition to fighting against the ban, the BBU focused on the labour rights of bar girls in the form of proposed standards for working conditions. These would ensure the girls were paid fairly by stipulating the proportion of tips they could keep for themselves and also ensure their safety and dignity through dress codes and rules of conduct between bar girls and customers. It sought to educate bar girls about their rights and to establish bar dancing as a recognised profession (independent of sex work) that did not involve trafficking or prostitution. In short, the BBU fought for proper regulation of bar dancing. They also campaigned for government rehabilitation of bar girls following the ban.[74] The BBU avoided tropes of victimhood and questions of 'exploitation', focusing instead on labour conditions and livelihood. The BBU also made public a lot of information about the bar girls and their backgrounds, countering many myths.[75]

Image 12: Bhartiya Bargirls Union poster advertising a rally, © BBU.

Image 13: Rally of the Bhartiya Bargirls Union, © BBU.

The formation of the BBU put the bar girls on the agenda of women's groups in and around Mumbai.[76] Flavia Agnes was a director of Majlis, a centre for rights discourse that grew from the women's movement of the 1980s, and which became a key player in the bar girls case.[77] Varsha Kale asked Agnes to represent the bar girls against police harassment. There were many crucial links in the chain of activists and lawyers, all of whom were prepared to support the bar girls in the context of fighting for the rights of women and vulnerable people. Forum Against Oppression of Women (FAOW), Aawaz-e-Nishan, Women's Action and Research Group, Akshara and Women's Centre formed one group that petitioned against the state of Maharashtra in the High Court case. The Sanmitra Trust and Ekta Self Help Group formed another, petitioning the state as well as the police and various government organisations regarding HIV/AIDS and other health consequences of the ban. FAOW and the Research Centre for Women's Studies (RCWS) at SNDT Women's University in Mumbai, in collaboration with a number of the above groups as well as several others, undertook the most extensive piece of formal, sociological research about the bar girls, 'Working women in Mumbai bars: Truths behind the controversy. Results from survey among 500 women dancers across 50 bars'.[78] This piece of work drew up a list of sixteen myths about the bar girls, including: bars were a nexus of trafficking; 75 per cent of bar dancers were Bangladeshis (and hence not rightfully working in India and/or a 'security threat'); minor girls dance in bars; thousands of homes are ruined because of bars; girls are forced into sex work; young men become corrupted because of the bars. The same partnership of RCWS and FAOW produced another publication nine months after the ban in December 2006, 'After the ban: Women working in dance bars'. The findings of these reports were picked up by the press and reported, and the government was challenged for hypocrisy and making tenuous or untrue claims.[79]

The question of labour that was raised by the BBU was also covered in the press. The bar girls' labour was investigated from the point of view of whether it was prostitution and whether it was genuine work.[80] Although such journalists supported the bar girls because they 'had no choice' but to dance, they emphasised that the bar girls were working hard and legitimately and, following the BBU, they distinguished bar dancing from prostitution. The press also independently investi-

Image 14: Varsha Kale giving a speech at Bhartiya Bargirls Union rally, © BBU.

Image 15: Bhartiya Bargirls Union publicity poster, 'Let us live too', © BBU.

gated the results of the aftermath of the ban, looking at changing forms of labour and livelihood, concentrating particularly on the fact that the ban had resulted in more girls engaging in transactional sex work (which was significant, since the ban professed to act against prostitution and trafficking). Although the trope of victimhood was often used in a manner that represented bar girls as general unfortunates—with no details of the specific history and social organisation of the majority of them who were from hereditary performing/sex work communities—these articles also spoke directly to questions of labour.

The BBU also lobbied for the attention and support of wider women's groups. They contacted the National Commission for Women in New Delhi in May 2005;

met Sonia Gandhi; and met the well-known Bengali writer and activist Mahasweta Devi, who has been a particularly strong supporter of denotified tribes such as *Bedia, Gandharva* and *Dhanavat*, which most bar girls hail from. Devi donated royalties from three of her books to the rehabilitation of bar girls from West Bengal.[81]

Legal scrutiny and the role of constitutional rights

In this chapter and in this book as a whole, I cite the ideological and socio-economic agents of 'progress' and modernity of twentieth-century India as central forces or facilitators in the exclusion of hereditary female performers. However, by the time of the Mumbai dance bar ban, these very currents also present some new opportunities for these groups. This is manifest particularly clearly in the High Court victory for the bar girls, and the way in which the case was discussed in the judgement. One of the most important differences between anti-*nautch* and the Mumbai dance bar ban was the fact that the former consisted almost entirely of a social campaign—a process of stigmatisation and boycotting of patronage and then exclusion from legitimate and official culture—whereas the latter implemented an actual ban by amending a law.[82] This ban brought into play constitutional rights, lawyers and meticulous attention to legal details. In challenging the ban, petitions were presented on various grounds, all of which the court was duty-bound to consider. In many ways the judgement reflected changed attitudes and social factors, as I explore below. It also illustrated a level of rigour and level-headedness in dealing with the rights in question that was missing in much of the public debate.[83]

The ban was constituted by the following amendments to section 33 of the Bombay Police Act (I omit details of penalties for contravening the ban):

> 33A ... 'holding of a performance of dance, of any kind or type, in any eating house, permit room or beer bar is prohibited' ...
>
> 33B 'Subject to the other provisions of this Act, or any other law for the time being in force, nothing in section 33A shall apply to the holding of a dance performance in a drama theatre, cinema theatre and auditorium; or sports club or gymkhana, where entry is restricted to its members only, or a three starred or above hotel or in any other establishment or class of establishments, which, having regard to (a) the tourism policy of the Central or State Government for promoting the tourism activities in the State; or (b) cultural activities, the State Government may, by special or general order, specify in this behalf'.[84]

Petitions were lodged by The Indian Hotel and Restaurants Association, the BBU, a collection of women's groups, a collection of groups involved in HIV/AIDS and health work, two individual bar owners, the Fight for Rights Bar Owners Association, and a single bar owner. These petitions variously challenged the state of Maharashtra on a number of legal matters from their different perspectives concerning the ban, including on several fundamental constitutional rights. Challenges relating to discrimination on grounds of religion, race, caste, sex or place of birth (article 15) and the right to life and livelihood (article 21) were unsuccessful. Challenges on the grounds that the ban violated aspects of article 19(1)(a), the right to freedom of speech and expression, were also unsuccessful. However, the ban was struck down on the grounds that it violated 19(1)(g), the right to practise a profession, or to carry on any occupation, trade or business. It was also struck down because 'the exemption [given to certain categories of hotels as well as clubs] is not concurrent with the aims and objectives of the statute and hence it is arbitrary and violates Article 14 of the Constitution of India (the clause pertaining to equality and non-discrimination)'.[85]

The judgement consists of a 256-page document exploring, within a legal framework, dance as expression and as livelihood. It also considers dance in the context of questions of vulgarity, obscenity and exploitation. A number of points are particularly interesting in comparing this judgement with anti-*nautch*. Through a social campaign, anti-*nautch* stigmatised female hereditary performers, engendered a massive boycott of their performances, and positioned them outside of 'culture'. It was able to succeed because there was sufficient social consensus, and because voices of resistance were either not numerous enough or not well enough organised or represented. In the case of the bar girls, there is an identical attempt to position them as outside of 'Indian culture', as something other than performers, and their dance as vulgar/obscene. However, in contemporary Mumbai this is far more difficult, and the recourse to a ban in itself reflects an agenda that is, socially, only tenuously supported. In the days of anti-*nautch*, according to bourgeois morality, all public female performers were 'disreputable' since they could not marry. However, the campaign to ban the bar girls took place well after the reform of performing arts, which resulted in an entire legitimate zone of performing arts in which 'reputable', married or marrying women perform. This zone has even extended to Bollywood, particularly since the 1990s. In other words, there was no longer the assumption that a female dancer is the same as a prostitute. Therefore, it became necessary to distinguish between different kinds of dance (the State tried to claim that dances in exempted establishments were 'culture' as they were linked with Indian or Western classical dance). It was also necessary to distinguish between different establishments.[86] This led to the ban being struck down because it was discriminatory. The judgement states:

> The distinction sought to be made by the State based on the class of the establishments and the kind of persons who frequent the establishments or those who own them cannot be supported by law or by our constitutional philosophy. The financial capacity of an individual to pay or his social status is repugnant to what the founding fathers believed when they enacted Article 14 and enshrined the immortal words, that the State shall not discriminate. The law for application of a license both for place of public entertainment and or

performance makes no such distinction. All who apply must meet the same tests. The classification has been upheld on the ground of the distinct type of the dance performed in the prohibited establishments.[87]

If the dances, therefore, which are permitted in the exempted establishments are also permitted in the banned establishments then, considering the stand of the State, they would not be derogatory to women and or amount to exploitation of women and are unlikely to deprave or corrupt public morals. By using the expression western classical or Indian classical in the affidavit is of no consequence, as the Act and the rules recognize no such distinction. All applicants for a performance licence have to meet the same requirements and are subject to the same restrictions. We are, therefore, unable to understand as to why non-vulgar and non-obscene dances cannot also be permitted in the prohibited establishments as they are still entitled to obtain a performance licence. If women can work other than as dancers and that does not amount to exploitation, then how is it that it becomes exploitation, when women dance to earn their livelihood. There is not material to justify the basis for a conclusion, that there is exploitation. If the test is now applied as to whether the classification has a nexus with the object, we are clearly of the opinion that there is no nexus whatsoever with the object. Treating establishments entitled to a performance license differently, even though they constitute two different classes, would be discriminatory as also arbitrary, considering the object of the Act. Section 33A and consequently section 33B have, therefore, to be held to be void being violative of Article 14 of the Constitution of India.[88]

In the days of anti-*nautch*, dance could not be, by mainstream standards, a legitimate or respectable profession for women because it was deemed to be 'prostitution'. However, this was not the case in Mumbai in 2005, since large numbers of middle class women danced professionally, whether this be in the classical or Bollywood arenas. The judgement concluded that dance could not be seen to be something inherently harmful and so *res extra commercium* ('a thing outside commerce') and it was hence a legitimate profession, trade or occupation:

... it is submitted that dancing by itself or because dancing is performed by young girls cannot be inherently pernicious nor invariably or inherently pernicious. Merely because there may be some instance of prosecution of bar dancers and establishments having license where dances are performed by itself cannot result in the activity being declared as activity which is res extra commercium. In the earlier part of the judgement we have adverted to the fact that dancing as a form of art and expression has been known to our civilisation from times immemorial. It is reflected in our cultural activities, carved out in stones and is a source of a large number of books. The dance and sculptures many a times are erotic or bordering on the erotic. Dance, therefore, by itself per se, cannot be said to be an activity which would be res extra commercium. The petitioners have produced voluminous documents to show that dancing was common both to religious and secular activities.[89]

Dancing as we have noted earlier is one of the earliest forms of human expression and recognised by the Apex Court as a fundamental right. If it is sought to be contended that a particular form of dance performed by a particular class of dancers is immoral or obscene that by itself cannot be a test to hold that the activity is res extra commercium. It can never be inherently pernicious or invariably or inevitably pernicious. If the notions of the State as to dancing are to be accepted, we would have reached a stage where skimpy dressing and belly gyrations which today is the Bollywood norm for dance, will have to be banned as inherently or invariably pernicious. We think as a nation we have outgrown that, considering our past approach to dancing, whether displayed as sculpture on monuments or in its real form. Dancing of any type if it becomes obscene or immoral, can be prohibited or restricted. Dancing however would continue to be a part of the fundamental right of expression, occupation or profession protected by our Constitution.[90]

This statement cites ancient expressions of erotic dance as well as Bollywood in support of the assertion that even erotic dance and bar dancing is a legitimate occupation. The anti-ban lobby also used arguments based on 'Indian traditions' to legitimise bar dancing, as Mazzarella points out.[91] However, this 'tradition' itself has been formed through the exclusion of low status and 'disreputable' performers by middle class India. Ironically, it was the colonial and bourgeois nationalists who at first stigmatised female professional dance traditions and who now, on the grounds of the 'respectability' of the reformed traditions they instituted and appropriated over the twentieth century, are declaring bar dancing to be legitimate and 'traditional'. The other side of the irony is that the loss of labour and legitimacy suffered under anti-*nautch* was itself a cause of the increasingly illicit nature of the performing arts of hereditary female performers and their reliance on sex work. The report asserts that times have changed and certain attitudes have been 'outgrown', and indeed they have—but the extraordinary ironies and injustices involved in this 'outgrowing' remain unseen. In this context it is particularly clear that it is the middle classes, the hegemonic group, who define what culture is. In this case, the embourgeoisement of performing arts worked in the bar girls' favour, with the extension of respectable dance to Bollywood significant. Although partly for the wrong reasons, there is a sense of justice for the hereditary female performers in terms of their history. Additionally, it is highly significant that legitimate performing arts in India are now being held up in a way that supports the illicit world; this is an unprecedented meeting of these two zones.

The court declared that the ban constituted a restriction on the trade and profession of the bar girls, but not a prohibition. The question then was whether the restriction was reasonable or whether it curtailed a fundamental right; and whether there was a nexus between the restriction and the object of the ban. A major problem that emerged for the pro-ban lobby was that it was only dancing that was banned, so singing continued to be allowed in bars, and girls continued to work as waitresses. In twenty-first-century India, unlike the days of anti-*nautch*, there is an extensive workforce of women working in the public domain. Hence, as with distinguishing between types of establishments, banning only dance became arbitrary. However, a ban on dance, singing, waitressing and other occupations in which women might potentially be exploited or performing in 'obscene' or 'vulgar' ways would include fashion models and film actresses, as well as any woman working in the public domain, and would therefore be impossible. The pro-ban lobby was, as the saying goes, stuck between a rock and a hard place. Society had 'moved on'. The court examined the various objects of the ban and, because dancing was singled out as the culprit, declared them to be unconnected to the ban itself.

The ban was also declared out of tune with its objects for other reasons. The ban was claimed to curb prostitution in bars, but there was no evidence that bars were overwhelmingly places of prostitution.[92] Regarding the charge that dances in bars were obscene and vulgar, it was stated that pre-existing laws and rules exist to control these problems.[93] It was also stated that there was no evidence that public disorder was created purely from dancing.[94] The court similarly concluded that the ban against dance did not serve to restrict trafficking, undermining the State's claims that the girls were illiterate, poor, desperate, and lured into working in bars:

> No explanation is given as to why it amounts to trafficking only for dancers and not other forms of work by the women, like waitress, singers and other jobs. The State did not conduct any study in support of the argument that there were elements of trafficking. Though the State has launched various prosecutions, no material has been brought on record from those cases that the women working in the bars were forced or lured into working in the bars and there was no voluntariness and that they were sent back to their villages or homes or from where they have been lured on their complaints or complaints of N.G.O.s or concerned citizens.[95]

The court also objected to the ban as a means to stop bad practices on the grounds that the government had not proven that the problems could not be dealt with under existing laws, or that other measures had been tried first. For example, the committee formed in 2002 had made recommendations to improve conditions in dance bars (regarding, for example, the dress code of girls and practices of tipping) but these had not been followed up. The judgement states, 'If the State had placed material to show that they had taken all reasonable steps and inspite of that the activities continued, it would have been open to the Court to consider the argument in a different context'.[96]

Conclusions

The defeat of the government in this case came as a surprise to all concerned. The government appealed the ruling in the Supreme Court, and despite various delays, the hearing of the case was completed in 2013 and the judgment was due in July 2013. At the time this book went to press, the judgment had not been announced. However, it is possible to comment on the consequences of the two possible basic outcomes in this case, which promises to be one of the most significant events in the modern history of female hereditary performers. If the Supreme Court upholds the judgement of the High Court, the zone of illicit performing arts that bars constitute will gain a far stronger legitimacy, and dance in bars is likely to become an increasingly regulated occupation, with help from the BBU and other groups. The appeal of dance bars will increase with this legitimacy, and they may well become places where middle class youngsters hang out, especially given the level of publicity they received during the campaign to ban them. Given the trajectory of middle class involvement in performing arts, it may be that middle class girls would gradually start dancing in bars, in the same way that the film industry has opened up to middle class women over the decades, to the point where even dancing in the chorus in films or in live Bollywood shows is a reasonably respectable living. I met a Bollywood dancer in Singapore who said he used to go to Indian dance bars there to watch the girls dance and to learn new moves. In Singapore, where law and order is far tighter than in India, these dance bars, though hardly establishments for all the family, are nevertheless much less illicit than in India. He told me how a female dancer he was talking to there had said that she danced for the film industry in Mumbai, but had come to dance in Singapore during a quiet period in her work in Mumbai. The money in Singapore was good (roughly equivalent to earnings in the Indian film industry) and it was not too sleazy.[97] If the judgement is upheld, it is possible that dance bars in Mumbai could become similarly safe and mainstream.

Thus if the Supreme Court revokes the ban, it could transform the fortunes and the legitimacy of the communities of hereditary female performers, as well as the smaller number of *kothi*s who danced in bars in Mumbai (I explore this in the next chapter). This would link the illicit and legitimate zones of performing arts in new ways, breaking down the binary system to some degree, again opening up the mobility for India's disenfranchised traditional female performers and, if bars became more mainstream, actually increasing it. However, an increased legitimacy and more stable livelihood could result in the middle classes entering dance bars, and possibly, as in the past, the exclusion of the 'disreputable' performers; or perhaps not, this time. While it is unthinkable in Mumbai right now that girls from 'good families' could dance in bars, several other comparably insurmountable taboos have been overcome in the past, and the example from Singapore is strongly illustrative of what could happen if bars were even just a bit safer and more reputable. However, if the ban is supported in the Supreme Court, for the time being, the legitimate and illicit worlds will remain as they are. The only avenues for performing for hereditary female artistes will be very down-at-heel ones, and more and more of them will be absorbed (back) into prostitution.

6

THE CONTEMPORARY WORLD OF *KOTHI* PERFORMERS

CHANGING PATTERNS OF LIVELIHOOD AND SOCIO-CULTURAL SPACE[1]

The historical sources presented in chapter two show that erotic effeminate performers had been an acceptable or even celebrated part of elite culture up until at least the mid-eighteenth century, although they were clearly not as numerous or prestigious as courtesans or *devadasi*s. By the early twentieth century, male erotic performers are either not visible at all in elite culture or are disapproved of or seen as out of place.[2] Certain female impersonators gained national acclaim in the early twentieth century within the Parsee theatre and also existed as star performers in the Marathi and Gujarati theatres.[3] It is highly probable that some or many of these performers were *kothi*. However, they were not lauded for their eroticism in the manner of the historical texts, and it appears that they were taken ostensibly as female impersonators and not themselves as effeminate or transgender.[4] In time, they, too, became marginalised from these traditions.

The disappearance of *kothi* performers from elite or high profile culture fits in with the known homophobia, censorship and marginalisation of non-heteronormative identities and sexualities that emerged from nineteenth-century discourses of science and 'deviance' instituted in India by the British and vigorously continued by India as a modern nation.[5] As Vanita states, 'at most times and places in pre-nineteenth-century India, love between women and between men, even when disapproved of, was not actively persecuted'.[6] Certainly, the marginalisation of male erotic or cross-dressed performers has not happened via explicit campaigns such as those that targeted courtesans and *devadasi*s. This would inevitably have involved naming what was supposed not to exist.[7] In terms of high status traditions, Adarkar's work on women in Marathi urban theatre, and Hansen's on Parsee, Gujarati and Marathi urban theatres show that female impersonators became increasingly marginalised from the late nineteenth to the early twentieth century in the context of discourses of realism and modernity and the entry of female performers.[8] This occurred within narratives of reform and modernisation, in which there was a growing sense that female impersonators represented a 'backward' and also awkward aspect of Indian performing arts (an idea that is still very much alive today). In terms of respectability and status, the entry of female performers from 'good' backgrounds was essential for all performing arts and cinema at this time.[9] Pani, too, describes the disappearance of female impersonators from theatrical traditions across India, as they have been rendered increasingly unfashionable and obsolete as female performers have replaced them.[10] Little is known about the processes of marginalisation of female impersonators and/or erotic male performers from elite performing arts from the eighteenth century onwards, with only sparse references to male erotic or cross-dressed performers. It would take a substantial project to explore this in detail. It is also difficult at times to distinguish between erotic male performers, likely to be *kothi*, and female impersonators, who may or may not be, and who could also belong to hereditary communities of performers.

In terms of post-independence, official representations of 'Indian culture', such performers are now largely invisible. Apart from social taboo, *kothi* performers are now a lower class and in many cases an illicit phenomenon, at best a feature of increasingly down at heel and eroticised vernacular traditions. As stated in chapter three, this has resulted in virtually no research on such performers, or on perspectives of gender, sexuality and eroticism relating to male performers. Rather, the overwhelming discourse on *kothi*s revolves around issues of gender, sexuality, health, violence, prostitution, identity and advocacy, divorced from performing arts and culture.[11] In terms of the public sphere, *kothi*s are not distinguished from *hijra*s, and I found that few urban, middle class Indians knew or admitted they existed as erotic performers. Films openly (or almost openly) exploring middle class, urban, international-style gay identities have emerged in Bollywood since the late 2000s.[12] However, the lower class, small-town, non-Anglophone *kothi* is not visible as a character or as a performer.[13] The world of *kothi* performers is now a marginal arena of lower class India, existing well below or invisibly within the radar of 'Indian culture'.

In this chapter, I examine the practical reality for *kothi* performers in contemporary India and the social and cultural space they occupy in terms of the contexts in which they perform, their professional organisation, their livelihood and their exclusion. Historical processes of marginalisation from elite culture are traceable only in broad strokes. However, in terms of contemporary *kothi* performers, I present ethnographic data charting the last several decades that shows a clear course of loss of both livehood and identity as performers in even these non-elite contexts, and a rise in sex work as well as violence and harassment. This represents a direct parallel to the post-independence history of female erotic performance. In this chapter, I continue to emphasise, as with female performers, the importance of history, heritage, culture and skilled labour in matters of inclusion/exclusion, and in the construction of culture, identity, and belonging/not-belonging.

I also look at new dimensions of the dynamics of inclusion/exclusion that have emerged since the 1990s in the context of economic liberalisation and globalisation. From the 1990s, the global gay/queer/LGBT movement has become established in India, and *kothi*s are becoming involved in the fight for rights and belonging and its consequences. This politicisation offers dramatically new forms of inclusion for *kothi*s and other sexual minorities, and can be seen as a parallel movement to the successful campaign against the dance ban for bar girls. However, it is far more complex and problematic since it involves creating a public, legitimate identity for a group that has always been, by definition, liminal and opaque in its social space. These developments also have important implications for performing arts and for *kothi*s as performers, which is in some ways key to their belonging.

Contexts and genres

In South Asia there are a variety of non-elite traditions in which males perform female roles. Some are hereditary and therefore will only include *kothi*s by chance. There are others where males perform as females, but not in specifically erotic guises, and it is difficult to say how much *kothi*s are involved and to what extent the men are just female impersonators. Judging from my own research in Delhi, Mumbai, Uttar Pradesh and Bihar, such roles would certainly appeal to *kothi*s and it seems highly likely they would involve at least some. However, the sexuality of female impersonators has not been broached in any public arena.[14]

The genres and traditions I discuss here involve self-identified *kothi*s either substantially or entirely. The degree of erotic or seductive performance involved in these traditions varies, and some are not erotic at all, but aimed at family audiences. However, *kothi* performers, like female public performers, are still liable to be seen erotically by male audience members, and sexual encounters and/or relationships with male audience members do take place. In most, but not all of these genres, *kothi*s perform alongside or as equivalents to female erotic performers. Below are some of the most widespread genres or contexts in North India in which *kothi*s are involved:

- *Ramlila*: *Ramlila* is the dramatic re-enactment of the story of Rama based on the Ramayana epic, which takes place at the time of the *Dussera* festival. *Ram-*

lilas were traditionally performed only by males and probably the majority still are. They are the most important, prestigious and high status context for professional (and local amateur) *kothi* performers. Both elderly and contemporary performers cite *Ramlila* as a genre for which performers receive respect.[15] Professional *kothi* performers also dance during scene changes or before and after shows, in the past performing film songs or *mujra* style songs. Non-*kothi*, non-professional male performers (often boys from local communities) also enact certain female roles in *Ramlila*. Such performances would not involve explicit eroticism as they are aimed at a mixed or family audience.[16]

- *Nautanki*: *Nautanki* is a form of musical drama based on epics, mythological stories and contemporary themes found in Uttar Pradesh, Bihar, and other parts of North India. Traditionally, like *Ramlila*, it involved only male performers. However, from the early twentieth century, female hereditary performers from groups such as the *Bedia* began to take part.[17] *Kothi*s perform female roles and also extra-narrative dances. Since the 1980s or 1990s, *Nautanki* has been rapidly losing status and economic viability, and involves increasingly erotic performance from *kothi* and female performers. *Nautanki* is seen as lower status than *Ramlila*, and some *kothi*s said they would not perform in it.
- *Badhava*: *Badhava* is the name given to dancing in the groom's wedding procession that goes to the bride's home accompanied by a brass band. This happens across North India and, according to the *kothi*s I spoke to, no girls can take part, since it involves dancing on the street.[18] This is probably the lowest status genre of *kothi* performance, and those with successful performing careers or who performed only for enjoyment said they would never dance in *Badhava*. Only poorer *kothi*s from lower status families were involved, and the wages can be meagre. This, and other genres where boys dance, is known as *launda* ('boy') dance in Eastern Uttar Pradesh and Bihar.
- *Launda nach* / *Bidesia*: This is a dance-drama tradition in Bihar.[19]
- Wedding shows: These are performances at wedding parties. This happens across India. In upper class events troupes from the middle class Bollywood world are hired, as described in chapter four. In the lower socio-economic strata girls and/or *kothi*s are hired.
- *Jagran*: *Jagran*s are all-night devotional Hindu events where mythological stories are enacted and devotional songs sung. These take place in *Chait* (Spring: March/April), and around *Dassera* (in October). *Kothi* and female performers may be involved in these events, with *kothi* performers playing female or male roles and enacting devotional songs with *abhinay*.[20] These are family events and the performance is not eroticised. This kind of *jagran* began in Uttar Pradesh and Bihar in the 1990s and has provided a new context for *kothi* performers. Before then there was only *kirtan*, participative group singing of devotional songs without role play, costumes or professional performers.

- *Melas*: Traditionally, *kothis* and troupes of female dancers would perform in *melas* or 'fairs' with acoustic instruments. Restrictions on 'dance parties' at *melas* have apparently drastically reduced this context in and around Lucknow since around 2005. Performances at *melas* are also now included in the wider term 'orchestra shows'.
- 'Orchestra [shows]': These are performances at events, parties, or in *melas*, on some kind of stage and involving accompaniment by an 'orchestra' (guitar, bass, drums, keyboard). They began in the early 1990s according to *kothis* I spoke to in Lucknow.[21] Taking place in both cities and rural areas, they are notorious for involving increasingly eroticised performance with mini skirts, 'body show' or lewd moves by female and *kothi* performers.
- 'Shows': This is the name given to dance performances to recorded music or any other kind of self-organised show. This may involve fairly high-brow *mujra* or dance performances to a public or elite private audience; or dancing to film songs in a range of other contexts where tickets are sold to the public. Like the 'orchestra shows', increasingly eroticised performance and Western dress are often involved. 'Shows' also include performances at parties for elite gay

Image 16: Advertisement in Balliya for a female dance troupe for wedding and other shows. Similar troupes of *kothi* performers are common in Balliya. (Author's photograph)

men in Delhi, where (lower class) *kothi*s can provide erotic entertainment and (paid-for) sex.

- Dance bars: These are venues at which there is dancing to recorded music; a small number of *kothi*s (and now loosely-defined *hijra*s) danced alongside girls in dance bars in Mumbai.[22]
- *Lavani: Lavani* is a form of Maharashtrian regional 'folk' song and dance that has become a part of much *Tamasha* theatre. It is performed principally by female artistes from the *Kolhati* community. However, on certain occasions, all male 'without women' *(binbaikacha) Lavani* is performed, involving *kothi*s exclusively. Lavani is erotic in a bawdy way, though performed in traditional clothes, and audiences may be mixed.
- *Badhai*: Another increasingly important context for *kothi*s to earn money as performers is in performing *badhai* with the *hijra*s. This is an 'unofficial' context, and represents the increasingly blurred boundaries between *hijra*s and *kothi*s. Dancing with the *hijra*s is extremely low status, and *kothi*s I met in Lucknow who were involved in *badhai* had begun to do so out of financial desperation and concealed it from many of the other *kothi*s. In Balliya, there was more open involvement with *hijra*s. In many areas *hijra*s are also, against the rules of their society, increasingly involved in public, erotic genres traditionally the preserve of *kothi*s or females.
- Other: A number of other traditions or contexts involve *kothi*s. Ones I have cursory information on are forms of celebratory (possibly unpaid) dancing on *Janmastami* (Krishna's birthday) in South India, and dancing during the night of *Holi* in Uttar Pradesh and Bihar (and probably other regions too). *Durbhanga, Dhanush, Panchguiyan* were also mentioned as genres where *kothi*s perform in Uttar Pradesh and Bihar.

The social organisation of kothi *performers*

A large number, if not the majority, of traditional professional performers in South Asia are connected in some way to heredity, caste, or partially familial artistic 'households' or lineages. *Jajmani* relations involve the linking of particular (low) castes as performers (bards, genealogists, entertainers and so on) for particular (high) caste patrons (*jajmans*).[23] In terms of the broad and complex geographical distribution of the classical traditions, social and musical organisation involves musical practices, stylistic schools, lineages, and familial or extra-familial structures. These include *khandan* (extended family), *biradari* (broader regional community), *baj* ('style' or 'school') and *gharana* (literally 'households', a stylistic school based on genealogical lineage).[24] Another pan-Indian tradition at a very different level on the cultural hierarchy is brass band musicians, who are organised according to complex relations of caste and community that vary from region to region.[25]

Figure 1: A comparison of contexts in which girls, *kothi*s and *hijra*s perform, showing in brackets how *kothi*s and *hijra*s are now involved unofficially in contexts previously strictly limited to each group.

	Girls	*Kothis*	*Hijras*
Ramlila	Yes	Yes	No
Nautanki	Yes	Yes	(Yes)
Badhava	Yes	Yes	(Yes)
Wedding shows	Yes	Yes	(Yes)
Jagran	Yes	Yes	No
'Shows'; 'orchestra shows'	Yes	Yes	(Yes)
Dance bars	Yes	Yes	(Yes)
Lavani	Yes	Yes	(Yes)
Badhai	No	(Yes)	Yes
Mujra (based in *kotha*)	Yes	No	No
Private '*mujras*'	Yes	Yes	(Yes)

Female professional performers, although they live outside of marriage, are also organised into tribes, communities and partially familial lineages and establishments. In her historical study of *tawaif*, Sachdeva shows that courtesan lineages were in part hereditary and linked to certain tribes and communities; however, outsiders were also admitted, largely in the form of slave girls, widows or 'fallen women'.[26] *Devadasi*s too were hereditary performers with stable connections to the patronage of particular temples. The question of whether they form a 'caste' has been debated.[27] However, they were also allowed to take in outsiders, with legal permission to adopt girls and bring them up as *devadasi*s. *Hijra*s are also organised into houses or lineages, which may be referred to as *gharana*s, as well as smaller households. Since becoming a *hijra* is not hereditary, these are made up entirely of 'outsiders'.[28]

Comparing *kothi*s to these other kinds of performers, their professional organisation is unusual, since there is no link to any kind of domestic sphere; there are no castes or familial, extra-familial or quasi-familial households; and generally no clearly or formally defined lineages. Each *kothi* has a caste and a natal home and later usually a marital home, all of which are a part of mainstream society. However, generally speaking, this is insignificant to their role or identity as *kothi*s or *kothi* performers, since at home they are not *kothi*s (apart from the very few who are 'open' with their families), but sons/brothers/husbands/fathers. *Kothi*s use familial terms with each other, such as 'mummy' and 'sister', but generally lightly and ephemerally, and often with irony and humour (as I describe in chapter three), since these are roles they move in and out of depending on context. This contrasts with *hijra*s, for whom the separation from mainstream society is total and quasi-familial bonds are therefore more formalised.[29] Hence *kothi*s and *kothi* performers only truly exist as such in certain interstices of public space. The social arrangement of *kothi* performers (and *kothi*s in general) is consequently one of loosely arranged groups, troupes and networks as opposed to formal and public *gharana*s, houses, or castes.

New *kothi*s become part of existing groups as they are recognised by and/or recognise other *kothi*s in public space. This is typically through their effeminate gait or mannerisms.[30] Most *kothi*s have been dancing from early childhood and hence long before they are able to roam around outside and get drawn into *kothi* communities. If they are keen dancers and have some talent (something that can easily be displayed in one of the areas in which they congregate at night with just a few moves of *abhinay*), they may become part of a dancing troupe or be taken on as a disciple (*chela*) of a senior *kothi* dancer. The senior *kothi* will help them not just with dance but with their behaviour on stage and with audiences, and will also give them opportunities to perform and earn money. However, the gurus or 'mothers' are, at least nowadays, rarely dance teachers in the true sense—more mentors or agents—and all the *kothi*s I met largely learned to dance more informally, by imitating films, *Nautanki* or *Ramlila* and gradually getting involved with performing. They tend to describe themselves as 'god gifted' rather than guru-taught.[31] It is to be noted that *kothi*s, like *hijra*s, use the term *chela* for 'disciple' rather than *shishya* (which is used in the classical performing arts traditions). The troupes are also flexible, with *kothi*s sometimes taking individual bookings, perhaps with permission from the group leader depending on the tightness of the group. Many *kothi* performers are not full-time professionals, but moonlight as dancers while carrying on lives and livelihoods in mainstream society.

*Kothi*s may also get experience performing female roles in community-organised *Ramlilas*, where they will get picked to play female roles because of their natural femininity. Matters of gender identity or sexuality are not discussed, but certain boys are seen as having the 'right look', including some non-*kothi* boys. New *kothi*s may therefore be put in contact with professional *kothi* dancers who also take part in these events. Similarly, young *kothi*s may come into contact with professional *kothi* performers at *jagrans*, an ostensibly 'safe', family environment. In this way, *kothi* networks intersect with family space, but they are not based in the family—rather, they are situated in public space with links to the family, and are something the family or wider community only inadvertently mediates.

*Kothi*s and *kothi* performers are defined by liminality and opacity. They do not have a stable social identity like *hijra*s but, at the same time, they are able to be *kothi* in certain public spaces in ways that can appear remarkably unrestricted. The rigid norms of heterosexuality are oppressive of same-sex relationships and transgender activity but, at the same time, this very inflexibility brings freedom. Because same-sex relationships are unthinkable or unsayable, they are, to a significant extent, rendered opaque and thus protected, even while happening in front of people's eyes. The initial process of being drawn into groups and communities of *kothi*s is generally unrestricted by family and community, since it ostensibly just involves roaming around with male friends. Many families and wives of *kothi*s are aware that their son or husband performs professionally as a female. However, this awareness is not linked to knowledge of a female sexuality or sexual relationships with men. I had a sense that some of the wives of *kothi* performers I met knew something was amiss, but did not know what. For example, one commented that when she first saw her husband perform in *Ramlila* soon after their marriage, 'he was more beautiful than me', and said jokingly, though with a certain exasperation, that he always played *rani* ('queen') roles, never *raja* ('king') ones.[32] The liminal space that *kothi*s occupy is becoming more and more fragile, however, and levels of violence are increasing dramatically. I discuss these changes further below.

It is perhaps fair to say that generally speaking, families and communities who are not hereditary performers disapprove of dance as a profession, except within the new arenas of middle class, respectable classical performing arts and Bollywood that I describe in chapter four. Almost all *kothi*s I spoke to described how they used to secretly perform by sneaking off, making excuses to family, or even renting a separate room where they kept performance clothes, makeup and jewellery. Mostly, the objection was to dance itself. For some, however, there was a sense that dancing as a female was even more disgraceful than dancing as a male. It was *kothi*s from lower status homes whose families were more accepting of their roles as a professional (female) performer, although this was almost always after initial heavy resistance, and was often only justified and finally embraced—sometimes with pride—because the work was providing for the family (in some cases handsomely). An upper class male who loved to dance as a female, and hence embraced in many ways a lower class and low status identity and profession, suffered overwhelming conflicts and problems from his family. *Kothi*s also tend to perform away from home (unless they are involved in local *Ramlila*s), often with the conscious intention that they should not disgrace their family. The freedom to perform becomes much more restricted as *kothi*s get married and have children. Their concerns with family status increase, as well as intense concerns over their children finding out or being shamed by their activities. It is also harder to slip away when it is they who are responsible for the family, as fathers. Many give up dancing after their children are born and rely on jobs that are regular and salaried, though often low paid.

The degree and forms of heterosexual normativity also vary from place to place, affecting how *kothi* performers are able to operate. In Lucknow and most places in India, including Delhi and Mumbai, male-to-male sexual relationships are not open and *kothi* networks are somewhat nebulous. In Balliya and certain other places in Eastern Uttar Pradesh and Bihar, however, relationships between local men and *kothi*s are open, though a sensitive topic. Consequently, *kothi* performers and networks are far more clearly defined, with performers able to live together as groups in rented rooms, for example (whereas those in Lucknow tend to live with family). There are also more formal mechanisms for hiring *kothi* performers, as I describe below. Presumably it is also far easier for *kothi*s in Balliya to buy clothes, jewellery and makeup than those in Lucknow, who get teased or, as I witnessed, suffer awkwardness and embarrassment. However, it is crucial to note that even in Balliya there is a clear dissociation of *kothi*s from the domestic sphere. It is *kothi*s from outside of Balliya who perform there and become long-term concubines to local men, with local *kothi*s generally moving elsewhere to avoid disgracing their family. Local *kothi*s are not able to be open. With such an open understanding of *kothi* culture in this area, it is not conceivable that *kothi*s could be professional performers without their families realising.

*Kothi*s and *kothi* networks are also gaining a new organisational force in the form of the various Community Based Organisations (CBOs) who work on MSM issues such as HIV/AIDS. These organisations actively employ fieldworkers and peer educators to meet *kothi*s and distribute condoms and talk to them about safe sex. They also hold, usually weekly, drop-in sessions that include information on safe sex, counselling, getting tested, discussions on relationships, violence, harassment, etc., as well as dancing. In Delhi, Naz India's Milan project holds a number of classes for *kothi*s, including dance. In this way, these CBOs open up a new space for *kothi*s to network and exist as *kothi*s that is outside both the public domain and the family. I discuss the CBOs and NGOs in more detail below.

Sexual relationships

In addition to the freedom for males to roam around in public space, a very high level of male-to-male physical affection or homosociality is acceptable in India.[33] I saw *kothi*s flirting with *giriya*s or *panthi*s (as the 'real' male partners of *kothis* are known), playing with their hair, putting their arms around them, fiddling with their earrings or the chains around their necks, giggling, or giving them looks. This attracted no attention, while a male-female couple or a lone female would cause stares, crowds and questions with much less. While family or community members will quiz a boy or man who goes off with a female dancer, if he goes off with a *kothi*, they will probably just assume that he is roaming around with a male friend.[34] Finding a female to have sex with generally involves going somewhere that is outside of public space. The majority of female sex work proper is brothel-based and female performers are more likely to arrange liaisons by phone than in person. *Kothi* performers and *kothi*s in general are able to engage in far more immediate sexual activity in public space than female performers. It is for these reasons (*kothi*s themselves report) that *kothi*s are sexually more available than female dancers and many brothel-based female sex workers; they are literally 'easier' and they are usually cheaper. Additionally, many *kothi*s cruise for sex anyway, something almost unthinkable for females who are not sex workers. However, the heightened femininity and desirability of *kothi* dancers makes them more expensive and less easily available than non-performers, in the same manner as female performers versus sex workers.[35]

Although a discursive opacity enables *kothi*s to (publicly) dance, seduce, cruise and have sex, it also makes them more vulnerable than female dancers or female sex workers. While members of all these groups get beaten up or raped, there is less protection for *kothi*s since they 'do not exist'. *Hijra*s on the other hand, as a public group, have more organisational protection and links with police. People are also afraid of their ability to curse and *kothi*s have reported adopting the stylised *hijra* mannerisms, such as clapping, when under threat. However, *hijra*s also suffer extensively from police harassment and other forms of discrimination and violence.

Performing leads to a range of fleeting sexual encounters for *kothi*s, some of which are paid for, as well as longer-term sexual relationships and romantic friendships. These relationships involve matters of status, as well as sex, affection and love. In Balliya, where *kothi* culture is very open, in addition to more casual encounters, *kothi* dancers may be formally kept by local men. These men take pride in this as they believe keeping a *kothi* gives them a kind of 'royal' (*shahi*) prestige, paralleling the way that courtesans and other dancing girls have been kept as concubines by elite men. Men may have such relationships in addition to marriage, keeping two separate households. The wife and children will know about the *kothi* but will not talk about them or have any involvement with them. Again, as with courtesans, social censure only comes into play if the man wants to live with the *kothi* instead of, rather than in addition to, marrying. *Kothi*s who enter into these 'kept' relationships often stay with the *giriya* for their whole life, and cannot have relationships with other men (or can do so only secretly). About 10 per cent of these couples are said to enter into a written marriage contract, certified by a stamp paper. Although marriage between two males is illegal, it is possible to get advocates to make the stamp paper contract. There is no problem from local police, since they are local men and in many cases involved with *kothi*s themselves. 'Marrying' in this way is voluntary—a romantic gesture, done out of love—since the couple are able to live together and have sexual relations anyway. It is said that many men feel more masculine having sex (in the 'active' role) with a *kothi* than a female, and this experience of enhanced masculinity is also an important part of the *girya-kothi* relationship in this region. Although *kothi* dancers are also very much a part of the culture of Eastern Uttar Pradesh and Bihar, this degree of openness and institutionalisation is exceptional. By local accounts it has existed like this for generations at least.

Economic factors also play a role in these relationships. Although it is said that the *giriya* keeps the *kothi*, economically speaking, it is often the other way round, since *kothi* dancers and sex workers can earn very good money, especially in a place like Balliya. This can cause tensions. Cynically, I was told (by *kothi*s) that 'one per cent' of *giriya*s do it for love, the rest for money.[36] However, there is no formal arrangement whereby the *kothi* must hand over earnings; what they earn from dance programmes is their own, but they can choose or be compelled to give it to their husband. The *kothi* will also look after the home and carry out many other kinds of domestic services for the *giriya*. Beating of *kothi* wives by *giriya*s is common and, as stated in chapter three, there are not inconsiderable numbers of *kothi*s who expect this kind of treatment, or even in rarer cases 'want' it, as it makes their husband seem more masculine and them more feminine.

Overall, it seems that *kothi*s in Balliya are able to do better from relationships with men, and are far more likely to have a long-term relationship with a man than those in Lucknow, Delhi or Mumbai, where formal and semi-public recognition is impossible. *Kothi*s from Lucknow said the chance of getting a good boyfriend was 'one per cent'—that virtually all men just wanted sex and saw *kothi*s as something to 'use and throw'. While in the short term, *giriya*s may be attached to *kothi*s, the vast majority get married and, except in a place like Balliya, they are unable once they are married to devote a great deal of time to their extra-marital, *kothi* 'wives'. For many men, *kothi*s are a means of getting sexual satisfaction until they get married and can have sex with their wife. In terms of protection from sexual exploitation as well as violence, *kothi*s are generally more vulnerable than women, with no social capital invested in their 'honour' and, except in Balliya and the handful of other places like it, there is no system of norms and expectations in relationships.

On the whole, in all the places I visited, levels of paid sexual transactions are increasing fast. There are complex reasons for this, which I discuss in more detail below.

Livelihoods of kothi *dancers: some glimpses*

Here, I explore the livelihoods of *kothi* dancers in more detail, including a range of contexts in terms of openness of *kothi* culture and current versus retired or semi-retired dancers. *Kothi* performers exist across South Asia, and here I can offer no more than glimpses from Uttar Pradesh, Bihar and, more briefly, Delhi and Mumbai.[37] However, these illustrate to some degree the socio-cultural space of *kothi* performers as well as some of the major factors of change, which I discuss further at the end of this chapter: the decreasing viability in most places of a livelihood as a fully professional dancer; an increased dependency on sex work; an increased involvement with the *hijras*; and increased harassment and violence.

Balliya[38]

Balliya and a small number of other areas of Uttar Pradesh and Bihar are exceptionally open in terms of *kothi* culture and *launda* dance. In Balliya, *kothis* are largely preferred to female dancers and there is a thriving culture of dancing for wedding parties and in the *baraat*—the procession that brings the groom to the bride's house—as well as other shows and private parties. Most of the work is for marriages and is hence seasonal, but a lot of money can be made by *kothis* who are beautiful, young and good at dancing. Most *kothi* dancers are also increasingly making additional money through sex work. *Kothi* dancers in Balliya largely come from or via Calcutta to work during the marriage season. In the off-season they go home or, as is increasingly the case, go to Delhi or Punjab where they have gurus within the *hijras* and can earn extra money doing *badhai*. In Balliya, most dancers operate under contract with a particular band for an entire season, though some freelance work with bands also takes place. The system is highly structured (far more so than the troupes that operate in and around Lucknow, for example), involves formal, written contracts, and can in many ways be called an industry.

There are a small number of 'first rank' agents who bring *kothis* and girls from (most commonly) Calcutta to Raniganj (on the Uttar Pradesh/Bihar border). At Raniganj, bandmasters who also act as 'second rank' agents take around five to fifteen *kothis* and/or girls and contract them onto smaller, local bandmasters for a profit. *Kothis* also work in Balliya through direct contact with the bandmasters there, i.e. without the 'first rank' agents acting as middlemen. Bandmasters choose *kothis* and make written and exclusive contracts with them for a full year. The contracts stipulate the following payments:

- A one-off payment to the *kothi* for the full year, in the region of Rs 15–25,000[39]
- A fee per performance to the *kothi*, which is Rs 700 minimum and Rs 5,900 maximum, but usually around Rs 2,000

The bandmasters also have to arrange lodging and food for the *kothis* as part of the contract. Each band hires two *kothis* per year. The rate at which a *kothi* is paid per event depends on their beauty, youth and performing skills, but also on the particular band, since different bands command different rates, ranging from Rs 20,000 to Rs 50,000 per night.[40] Those arranging the function generally come to see the dancers, choose who they want (for example male or female) and agree a written contract stipulating the date and time of the event and the fees. In addition to the lump sum and per-event payments, dancers also get tips (*bagsheesh*) from the public, which can be a lot of money (Rs 10,000 in a night is not unheard of). The dancer keeps 50 per cent of these tips, and the remainder is shared by the entire band, which may be fifteen or twenty people.[41]

*Kothi*s can therefore earn a great deal of money, since in the marriage season (which runs for about three months in the winter and another three months in spring/summer), they can get work most nights. However, they have to give 50 per cent of the performance fees (i.e. around Rs 1,000 per function) to the 'first rank' agent, if they have one. This agent, known as the 'dance guru', will induct the *kothi* into the world of dance and may show them how to behave on stage and with the audience. These few gurus are immensely rich. The biggest agent, a *hijra* originally from Calcutta, is said to have twenty-five *kothi chelas* ('disciples'); with each earning around Rs 2,000 a night, s/he could receive Rs 25,000 per night.[42] Such 'dance gurus' dominate this performing economy to a large degree.

Balliya is mainly populated by dancers who have come from or via Calcutta.[43] *Kothi*s from other areas come to the city, but do so by directly contacting bandmasters in Balliya or those who have contacts there. Most if not all the *kothi* dancers in Balliya receive a considerable amount of extra money from sex work and this is becoming increasingly common. They can earn anything from Rs 500–1,500 per time, which is a considerable incentive. In this way, *kothi*s can earn in multiple thousands per night most nights of the marriage season. *Kothi*s with gurus among the *hijra*s in Delhi are expected to give the guru some kind of 'present', though no fixed sum or percentage of their earnings from Balliya. The kind of money they earn from *badhai* (and, presumably, sex work) in the off season in Delhi or Punjab would be considerably less than that earned in Balliya from dancing.

Although there are large amounts of money involved, the dance economy in Balliya does not seem to be exploitative. There was one isolated case of a 'trafficked' *kothi* forced to dance in Balliya, but generally *kothi*s are not forced to do sex work by bandmasters, or forced to dance by gurus. *Kothi*s dance from their own enthusiasm, earn very good money, and get involved in sex work because they want additional income. However, there are wider social, economic and cultural changes taking place that are having an impact, as I discuss below.[44]

The *kothi*s in Balliya are in many ways semi-*hijra*s, and the *kothi* and *hijra* communities were becoming increasingly intertwined in all areas I visited. Many *kothi*s in Balliya undergo the emasculation operation. However, they do not live in the *hijra* household in a traditional manner, but continue to work as a '*kothi*' dancer, arriving only seasonally for *badhai*. *Kothi*s who undergo the emasculation operation do so because it is erroneously believed to make the body more feminine in terms of softness of look, skin and muscle tone rather than through a desire to join the *hijra*s in a more absolute way.[45] One *kothi* I met in Balliya who had had the operation described herself as female ('ladies') rather than '*kothi*', and said that, although she had a *hijra* guru in Delhi, she did not like the *hijras* since they had so many rules and restrictions. She stayed with her 'husband' whom she had 'married' in a temple and worked as a dancer. The Balliya *kothis*, due to the openness of the area, also keep their hair long and cross dress permanently, like *hijras*, and unlike most *kothis* of, for example, Lucknow, Delhi or Mumbai.

Nai Kiran, the local Community Based Organisation (CBO) that works with MSMs in Balliya, tries to stop *kothis* from undergoing the emasculation operation. As their staff explained, dance is a very short career, with most retiring by the age of thirty-five or earlier; the advantages of beauty and femininity that emasculation may bring are not therefore of benefit for very long. The operation is of course one-way, highly risky, massively restricts the future of the *kothi* (for example making it impossible for them to (re)join mainstream society and marry or have children) and makes little difference to their preferred sexual activity, which is passive anal penetration. They reported in 2008 managing to dissuade about 30 per cent of *kothis* from undergoing the operation.

Delhi[46]

While the tradition of *launda* dance for weddings is clearly an old one in Eastern Uttar Pradesh and Bihar, *kothis* have only started dancing for wedding processions and in wedding functions in Delhi since around 2000. Before that *kothis* only danced in *Ramlilas* and other local festivals. Like in Balliya, *kothis* in Delhi can now get booked for the entire marriage season with a particular band. Fees in and around the capital are high, with a pair of *kothis* getting paid about Rs 8–10,000 for a night, out of which they will have to pay about 25 per cent in commission to the agent who gets them the contract. Performing for *Ramlilas* (in female roles and providing extra dance entertainment) is also very well paid—up to Rs 50,000 for two *kothis* for the whole week, including food, travel and accommodation (again, with 25 per cent deducted for commission). There are also opportunities for paid dance (and sex) in Delhi linked to the gay network, with *kothis* hired to dance at, for example, parties of rich gay men. Although not a professional engagement, the trend for *kothis* to attend *mehndi* or pre-wedding henna parties as females (and to dance as females) has emerged among circles of friends. Overall, however, a livelihood of dance is limited and seasonal.

One way to earn extra money during the quiet season (apart from doing odd jobs) is to get involved in sex work. Like in Balliya, sex work is becoming far more common in Delhi, and *kothis* can get around Rs 1,000 per encounter—again, a very considerable sum of money. It is now the norm for dancers and *kothis* to be engaged in additional sex work, something that was not the case in the 1990s.

Again, in Delhi, there has recently been an increasing blurring of lines between *kothi*s and *hijra*s, with some *kothi*s having gurus in the *hijra*s and doing *badhai* in the off-season. Some *hijra*s also dance in shows, but performing as an erotic dancer was not common among Delhi *hijra*s in the late 2000s.

Mumbai[47]

Although there is no established tradition of *launda* dance in Mumbai, there are various traditional and modern opportunities for *kothi*s to dance professionally, including at marriage parties (within the lower socio-economic strata). In Mumbai, the rules of the *hijra*s have become very slack, and transgenders who call themselves *hijra*s rather than *kothi*s, and keep close contact with a guru and a household in Mumbai (even if they do not permanently live there), perform as erotic dancers. Up until the ban in 2005, the best earning potential for *kothi*s and *hijra*s (and female dancers) had been dancing in bars. One professional *kothi*/*hijra* dancer in

Image 17: Professional *hijra* dancer, Simran. (Author's photograph)

Image 18: Professional *hijra* dancer, Simran, performing at an *Urs* celebration in Rajasthan. (Author's photograph)

Image 19: Female impersonators for *Binbaikacha Lavani* performance in Mumbai. (Author's photograph)

Mumbai danced in bars for three years and managed to transform her family's economic circumstances, buying two properties in their slum home.

There are also various forms of 'shows' in which *kothis*/*hijras* dance. There are *lavani* performances held at certain festival times with all male performers, known as *binbaikacha lavani* ('without women' *lavani*). There are also shows that groups of dancers organise themselves by booking theatres and selling tickets. Two dancers I met, for example, were planning a series of *mujra* shows, in which they would perform favourite film *mujras* such as those from *Umrao Jaan* and *Pakeezah*. Opportunities in TV and film for cross-dressed dancers are however almost non-existent. Without the bars, a livelihood as a full-time professional performer is very difficult.

Lucknow, past and present[48]

In contemporary Lucknow too, it is difficult to survive from dance alone. A lot of opportunities for dancing are in areas outside of the city, and *kothis* sometimes travel overnight to dance within the extensive *launda* dance culture that exists in Eastern Uttar Pradesh and Bihar. As described with respect to Balliya, however, in places where *launda* dance is very popular, most dancers book in for an entire season, apart from those *kothis* who are not open and are living ostensibly as boys/men with families. In and around Lucknow, *kothis* dance principally for *Ramlila*, *Nautanki*, in *Jagrans*, and in shows and orchestra shows, as well as in *Badhava*, on *Holi* and in other genres I heard mentioned (*Dhanush*, *Durbhanga*, *Panchguiyan*). Dancing and singing used to be a viable profession, with performers earning good money, and being received and treated well. In the last ten years or so, however, it has become almost impossible to survive as a professional performer. More and more *kothi* performers have been performing *badhai* with the *hijras* in order to earn money, even though it is paid very poorly and is extremely low status. Sex work is also reported to have increased in the aftermath of the lifting of ban on same-sex sex (section 377 of the Indian Penal Code) in 2009. Since around 2005 this increasing economy of sex work has also seen a tendency for dance troupe leaders ('dance gurus') to put pressure on *kothis* in their troupes to have sex with men, for which they take half the money (Rs 500 of an average Rs 1,000). Other evidence of cutthroat commercialism includes procurement of *kothis* specifically for sex work and *hijras* using *kothis* for commission purposes. Hence evidence suggests the sex work sector is becoming more organised, and is in part using the same structures as the economy of dance (as has happened to some extent with female hereditary performers). Such changes are reported in other parts of North India too.

A major factor in the dwindling viability of survival as a professional dancer is the demise of *Nautanki*. Once one of the most important contexts for *kothi* performers in and around Lucknow, it is now limited, down-at-heel, and badly paid.[49] Restrictions stipulating that shows at weddings must end at midnight—when they used to continue far into the night—also contribute to decreased earnings as they curtail the scope for dance, for payment, for tips and ultimately for the hosting of these shows. I also heard that shows ('dance parties') at *mela*s had in some way been 'banned' around 2005, causing a marked cut in livelihood for female and *kothi* performers.[50] *Nautanki* and shows rely increasingly on sexualised performance.[51] This seems to be a vicious circle: audiences want more titillation, and performers provide more titillation because they think that is what audiences want, which in turn feeds the expectation that dancers should perform in sexually explicit ways. Teasing and sexual harassment of performers has become common, and dancers do not feel they are respected or that people are interested in their art. This, combined with lower earning potential, has drastically reduced the status of *kothi* performers, as well as female performers. Virtually all the performers I spoke to who had lived through this change complained bitterly about it. Since it is a family occasion, performing in *Ramlila* is still well paid and respected. However, the work is seasonal.

Although *Nautanki* work is not seasonal, it has become very sparse. In the rural areas, *Nautanki* shows usually need four or five female performers (including *kothi*s), and the pay is in the region of Rs 200–500 per performance. Fees for 'shows' are also low, and/or the work is not regular enough to constitute a livelihood. For an orchestra show the pay is Rs 500–800 or, in grander setups, Rs 1,500–2,000, plus tips (half of which go to the group or band). One of the *kothi*s working at Bharosa had started to dance in shows (mostly for weddings), for which s/he got about Rs 1,000–1,500 per night including tips. The work was irregular though—sometimes there would be four or five engagements in a month, sometimes none. For dancing on the night of *Holi*, *kothi*s can get around Rs 400. As in Balliya, dancers for wedding-related shows are booked by the band. However, as the system is less extensive and certainly less open than in Balliya, it is necessary to rely on word of mouth for professional contacts, often provided by gurus or 'mothers' of dance troupes.[52] *Kothi*s also dance in *Badhava*, but the work is seasonal, very low paid and, unlike in Balliya, not very common. In Lucknow, *Badhava* is seen as very low status, and it is the *kothi*s from poorer backgrounds who do it. There is no such distinction in Balliya, where *kothi*s perform in both wedding shows and *Badhava*. In and around Lucknow though, there are rare opportunities for highly accomplished *kothi mujra* dancers to perform in private homes. One *kothi* who performed on such an occasion said it was watched by the entire family. There are also opportunities for *kothi* staff to dance at functions within the NGO/CBO world. However, while increasing a performer's prestige, these occasions are generally not paid, though the dancer may receive some tips. The pay for doing *badhai* with the *hijra*s is very poor—one *kothi* told me s/he got Rs 1,200 per month. While increasing numbers of *kothi*s were involved in *badhai* up until my last visit in 2010, it is not something many would admit to. Several *kothi*s involved in *badhai* did not tell me about it, and two spoke openly only after it became clear I already knew. They had not told other *kothi*s in the office.

The opportunities for *kothi*s in Lucknow are very limited compared to Balliya. There are some extremely talented dancers, but no platform for them beyond badly paid and/or irregular shows, plus a few seasonal festivals and dramatic traditions. A number of *kothi*s I met in the CBO Bharosa were learning *kathak*, since this provides a medium in which they are able to perform in public and gives them the skills and technique to perform proper *mujra* (even if only to film songs). However, as *kathak* dancers, they are only able to perform in public as males; performing in female dress would only be for limited circles of MSM-related people.

The changes in the livelihood of *kothi* dance and the increased pressures and challenges on *kothi*s can be illustrated by some individual stories:

Narendra: Aged around thirty, he had been performing professionally for about fifteen years when I met him in 2010. His family was plunged into poverty after his father died. His brother is distanced from the family, and hence Narendra is the only male. He therefore holds all the financial responsibility and had to marry. He described how he initially danced for Rs 500 per show but, as he became popular, his rate increased to Rs 1,000. He used to be able to comfortably do ten or more shows in a month, which would give him Rs 5,000–10,000. This was a very considerable amount of money around 1990, and was enough for him to run an entire household and build a (modest) house for his family. Now he is often offered only Rs 200–300 per show, which is difficult to accept. He also tells of dramatically increased sexual harassment, teasing, and a lack of respect:

> [about 15 years ago] when I entered the dance line, there was a good craze, at that time there was real respect for artistes. Nowadays, the atmosphere is such, even if the girl/*kothi* is good, even if they are a good artiste, people look at them badly, they don't watch the artistry, they watch [thinking] 'when can I enjoy, when can I get off?' (Interview, 25 January 2010).

He cites the restrictions on dance shows as the reason for his loss of earnings. He also used to perform in *Nautanki*, but that work too has dwindled. Narendra relies on doing *badhai* with the *hijra*s and struggles financially, which has had repercussions on family relations. He did not tell me that he was doing *badhai*, but spoke (perhaps at least partially rhetorically) of joining the *hijra*s, which would mean disgrace for his family:

> Things have been closed down in Lucknow city to such an extent, where can a person go? What can they do? An artiste can't go around robbing and mugging, neither can they drive

a rikshaw. They can't do anything. So if they don't go amongst the *hijras* [becoming emasculated], where can they go?[53]

Munna: Principally a *Nautanki* performer, he had been performing since he was about ten years old and was aged around forty-five when I met him in 2010. He had also performed in Ramlila, 'shows' and *Badhava*. He enjoyed *Nautanki* and singing ghazals from a young age, and started to perform after picking up songs, dance moves and roles from watching *Nautanki*. He met a guru—a female artiste—who recognised his talent and beauty and further trained him in *Nautanki*. He had lived well as a performer and spoke enthusiastically and animatedly about performing in *Nautanki*. When he began his career, he received Rs 20, which was a lot of money then and worth more than the Rs 500 he now receives per show. His family objected strongly, but eventually accepted his choice of work. He married seventeen years ago, and has three children. Fifteen years ago, he took a job as a caretaker in a school, partly out of concern for his status and his family, for which he earns Rs 2,000 per month. He would ideally do about four shows each month to give him a total of Rs 4,000 per month. However, he said he had received no dance work for three months, and was struggling and pessimistic about the future.

Satin: From a very poor family, he was about thirty when I first met him in 2007. He had performed for many years in *Nautanki*, in 'shows', in *Badhava* and on *Holi*, and also performed 'fillers' in *Ramlilas* (dance items during scene changes). He is not well educated and has limited work opportunities. He worked for some time at Bharosa as a peer educator (which provided a salary of Rs 1,700 per month). His parents do not approve of him dancing. He married in about 2008, and his first child was born about 2009. His wife knows he performs as a female, but has no idea that he is *kothi*. When I returned in 2010, he had started to do *badhai* and was becoming more involved in the *hijras*, purely for financial reasons.

Salim and Salman: Two talented dancers who had been making a living from work as outreach workers at Bharosa (for a salary of Rs 5,900 per month). Their families were neither poor nor particularly wealthy. Salim's family is at the upper end of lower middle class, and Salman's middle class, with some of his sisters well-educated and his niece in an English medium school. They are both from Muslim families, where there is apparently more hostility to dance, and especially female dance, as a profession. Salim wanted to follow dance as a profession but his family would not let him. On one occasion, his elder brother found out he was dancing as a female and beat him and ordered him to stop. He still continues secretly and suffers immense conflict between love of his family and his sexuality and passion for dance. He was in his mid-twenties when I met him in 2007, and will have to marry soon. During a financial crisis, he became increasingly involved with the *hijras*, having a guru and doing *badhai* in order to earn money. He stopped once his financial difficulties passed. Salman occasionally did paid dance work, but had not planned to become a professional dancer. He was in his late twenties when I met him in 2007, and is under increasingly heavy pressure to marry. He began dancing in shows during a time when he did not receive a salary from his day job.[54]

Retired dancers I met had far more positive stories:

Anand: A very poor dancer of over sixty years old. He had danced in *Nautanki*, in marriage parties, in *mela*s and in the homes of *zamindar*s (landowners). When he was first performing *Nautanki*, female performers were rare. He spoke of being treated with respect as a dancer, being given food and money by local people after dancing and wearing *ghungroo*s (ankle bells). He emphasised again and again the respect that used to exist in the profession and spoke with joy and enthusiasm of his life as a performer. He did not face resistance from his family. Although now poor, he had earned very good money from dancing and was able to buy some land (which he later lost due to conflict within his performing group, which broke up in the late 1980s or early 1990s). He is married, but is estranged from his wife and lives with his long-term (male) partner in Lucknow. He had a friend in the *hijra*s who had given him a territory that could have brought him a lot of money. However, since he was married he felt unable to join the *hijra*s or get castrated and he has never performed *badhai*.

Gaurang: The eldest performer I met, he was seventy-two when I interviewed him in 2010. He had loved dance from a young age, and started dancing professionally from the age of thirteen or fourteen. His parents had objected strongly, but he kept on dancing secretly ('*karte rehe chori chupke*'), and eventually they gave in. He was trained in *kathak* with a guru from one of the prestigious *kathak gharana*s. He performed female roles in *Ramlila*, in other (non-seasonal) forms of theatre, and also danced in *mela*s. He would also perform light-classical dance during these shows, for example between scene-changes in *Ramlila*, and pure classical if there was appropriate instrumentation.[55] He never performed film songs. He also had a salaried job, but mostly existed through dance. Even at the age of seventy plus, he still performs in *Ramlila*s. When he began, there were very few female performers, and mostly *kothi*s performed. He married when he was twenty-two, but maintained a dancing career. His wife knew he danced as a female but, as with most other married *kothi*s, had no idea that he is *kothi*. She did not like him dancing, because she saw it as low status, and used to tell him to get a salaried job. However, she has more recently accepted it, since (classical) dance has become respectable. She knows he performs in *Ramlila*s and other dramas (as a female) as well as doing some classical shows (as a male), but she did not know he danced more widely as a female, for example in *mela*s. Gaurang is the most senior in a 'family' of *kothi* performers, and he has introduced many *kothi*s to dance. Although these *kothi*s call him guru, or see him as their gurus' guru, he does not see himself as a guru in the classical sense. As stated above, *kothi* performing groups are far more loosely constructed than classical *gharana*s or hereditary traditions, and they do not have formalised teaching processes. Like all the elder performers, Gaurang spoke of receiving great respect as an accomplished performer, and saw today's arena of *kothi* dance as 'dirty' (*ganda nach*) and devoid of respect for art.

Aamir: In his fifties when I met him on several occasions, he died in 2011. He fully retired from dance in 1982 when he got a government job. He was a member of Gaurang's 'family' of dancers, his guru having been a disciple of Gaurang's (again, not a disciple in the formal classical sense). He was from a respectable Muslim family and appears to have had a reasonable standard of living. His family vigorously opposed him dancing as a young boy. However, he just as vigorously pursued his passion, keeping his dresses and jewellery at a friend's house and making excuses to go for dancing engagements (some of which involved staying away several nights and going as far as Bihar, Delhi or Haryana). He performed female roles in *Ramlila* and *Nautanki*, and also danced *mujra* style songs during scene changes in these shows. He recalled how, in the days before cassettes, he and other *kothi*s performed with *ghungroos* in Indian dress to live instruments and sang their own songs. In *Nautanki*, the group he performed with included three *kothi*s and two girls. He danced because he loved dancing, but also used to earn good money. He explained that he and others in his group were treated with great respect as *Ramlila* performers; that ladies were present at performances and it was a 'religious work' (*dharmik kaam*). He also performed for marriage parties, but never for *Badhava*, since that involved dancing on the street and was hence not respectable—he only performed on stage. He was married with two children, who had no idea that he used to dance. He felt it was not suitable for him to be dressing in ladies clothes and dancing as a female as he grew older, and was concerned for his family and children. He also did not like the present-day *kothi* dance scene. He said that, since around the mid-1990s, 'the profession is looked on very badly, it has become very bad, disgraced, ... dancers drink and wear short dresses' and there is no longer respect. Whereas before, dancers used to know a large variety of dances for different genres and different regions, this is no longer the case.

Ayub: Another now-retired *kothi* performer from within Gaurang's 'family', he was fifty-eight when I met him in 2010. He began performing in 1990, and stopped in 2000. Unusually for *kothi*s, he only began performing after getting married. Although he sometimes danced, he was more interested in acting, especially tragic roles, and most of his performances were female roles in dramas. His long-term partner, a *pandit*, fell in love with him after seeing him in a female role. Ayub also performed in *Ramlila*, but would not perform *Nautanki* (saying it was 'cheap') or *Badhava* ('the cheapest of all'). His views reflect the fact that he is from a middle class Muslim family.[56] Even being a classical performer would have been utterly unacceptable for him and, like Aamir, Salim and Salman, it is his *kothi* status that has enabled him to be drawn into (secret) careers of acting, singing and dancing. Ayub rented a separate room where he kept his costumes and was able to change and wash after performances. He also made good money from performing, about Rs 250–300 per night, which was a substantial amount in the 1990s. He too sees a lot of problems in the current world of *kothi* dance, including a lack of respect, with dancers being taunted and called such names as *zanana* ('female', a word for *kothi* in many areas), *gandu* (a derogatory word for a man who takes the passive role in anal sex) or *nachaniya* ('dancer', but implies a low-level and inevitably disreputable female dancer). He dates the start of 'vulgarity' in the profession back to the early 2000s, and sees *kothi* culture in general as declining. Rather than being characterised by a 'feminine touch' such as an involvement in dance, being a *kothi* now seems to be principally 'based on sex'. He considered the time when he was young and performing as a 'golden age' for *kothi*s.

New struggles for socio-cultural space

Loss of livelihood and status as artistes

Nostalgia, age and a degree of class distinction aside, it is clear that a livelihood as a *kothi* dancer is no longer viable in almost the entire region. The same is true of Delhi and Mumbai—though if the dance ban is lifted in Mumbai beer bars, there will be scope for a limited number of *kothi* performers to make a good living there. It is also clear that being a *kothi* dancer involves far more sexually explicit or suggestive performance at the beginning of the second decade of the twenty-first century compared to even the 1990s or the 2000s and is, in many contexts, as likely to result in sexual harassment and taunting as appreciation. *Kothi*s are increasingly relying on transactional sex instead of or in addition to dance for a living and are facing far more violence from members of the general public as well as the police.

These developments represent a close parallel with the post-independence history of female hereditary performers, apart from dance bars. Having been excluded from the newly (re)invented, legitimate realms of classical performing arts, female performers either married and exited the profession or continued to operate below the level of legitimate culture. However, since independence, and in many cases in the twenty-first century, even in these remaining illicit contexts, hereditary female performers have been finding it almost impossible to survive as performers and are involved increasingly in sex work. The stigmatisation of female performers as prostitutes has acted as a self-fulfilling prophecy, changing their identity and limiting their choices increasingly to sex work. With *kothi* performers, there has been no direct or high profile discourse, but given their equivalence to female erotic performers and the fact that they perform alongside them, the identity of female performers inevitably affects them too. There is similarly no recognition of *kothis*' artistic skills within discourses of 'culture' and 'art' in modern India and *kothi* performers are seen increasingly as 'cheap' (even by other *kothis*) and available only for sex.

However, as with female hereditary performers, this loss of livelihood and rise in sex work has emerged not just through the workings of more or less overt forms of naming and discourse, but through the rapid socio-economic development that India has seen since the liberal reforms of the 1990s. There is now a vast increase in the disposable income of certain sectors of Indian society, and an increased willingness to spend this on sex.[57] Payments of around Rs 1,000 'per shot' for sex with a *kothi* is a large expenditure, so would presumably be realistic only for those whose monthly income is into the tens of thousands of rupees. In other words, a vast increase in demand and ability to pay has made sex work a financially rewarding livelihood, although an exceedingly high risk one in the era of HIV/AIDS in particular and one that is socially exceedingly marginal. Economic development has also made life considerably more expensive and radically changed horizons of economic possibility and/or aspiration, and there are *kothis* who are doing sex work not just for survival but as additional income. A number of the older performers said that they used to earn a small amount in terms of rupees but it went a lot further.

This era of post-liberalisation India has also seen the advent of the legitimate zone of Bollywood dance. This financially and socio-culturally highly capitalised new dance arena provides competition for traditional forms of dance in places like Lucknow. People who want to book dance entertainment for weddings and birthdays are likely to opt for the most expensive troupes they can afford, and display wealth and status by so doing. It is no longer necessary to interact with low status traditional performers. Furthermore, the new Bollywood dance scene provides entertainment that is sexy, but with dancers retaining 'respectability'. In this way, there is no need to hire erotic *kothi* or female performers unless there is a particular need for sexually available individuals (or more elite troupes are not affordable). Hence the artistic dimension and function of these performers becomes redundant, whereas the (potential) provision of sex does not. In a process of cultural 'distinction', the advent of this new, upper level of culture has 'raised' the standards of dance and entertainment within the popular sphere, and what has been left behind is seen as 'backward' or 'cheap'. This can be seen as a continuation of the processes of marginalisation of female performers in high status theatre traditions in the late nineteenth or early twentieth centuries amid discourses of reform and modernity. That such cross-dressed performers represent a kind of rural, 'backward' culture is spoken to by the fact that *launda* dance is overwhelmingly popular in the interiors of Eastern Uttar Pradesh and Bihar—the most 'backward' part of North India in terms of hegemonic norms. One elite, transnational Indian to whom I spoke about the extensiveness of *kothi*s and *kothi* dancers admitted with slight reluctance or embarrassment, 'it is very traditional', though not meaning that it was a tradition to be proud of. In this sense, *kothi* performers are marginalised just as much or more by class than by homophobia, and this looks set to increase, given the speed of socio-economic development/disparity in India.

The increase in sex work and in the sexualisation of dance performance represents the disintegration of what is arguably the most important traditional space of belonging for *kothi*s, a space where they can legitimately and to a large degree be openly feminine/female. Although being a performer is a low status activity, it had offered respect, recognition, pleasure, and a good living. While sex, sex work and sexualised performance is an arena in which *kothi*s can be feminine/female, it is one that is marginal and excluded in an absolute sense in comparison with the socially, culturally and economically well-integrated domains of performing arts. The endemic illness, debilitation, and curtailed lifespans that HIV/AIDS has brought constitutes an added force of downward pressure on the earning capacity and social status of the *kothi* community.

Blurring of lines of *hijra*s and *kothi*s

Financial pressures as a result of loss of livelihood from dancing have also been bringing about another major change in *kothi* livelihood and socio-cultural space: the increasing overlap of the *kothi* and *hijra* communities. The *hijra*s are an intensely stigmatised and low status group, and it is considered a disgrace for a son to join them. The blurring of lines of *kothi*s (who are ostensibly 'respectable' citizens of lower class yet mainstream society) with the *hijra*s represents a significant socio-cultural change. Performers such as Gaurang, Aamir and Ayub had absolutely no contact with the *hijra*s. As Aamir stated:

> In those days, we had a different 'getup'. We wore good pants and qameez, and looked like boys. We didn't show that we were *hijra*s. *Hijra*s wore salwaar suit and danced on the streets. In our society, *hijra*s are looked on very badly. Society does not like *hijra*s. Nobody likes them. So our getup was that of boys. But when we were on stage, then we were completely like a girl. … We never, the thought never came in our minds that we would become *hijra*s. We just danced. The dancers of Lucknow had their own way, their way was different, the *hijras*' way was different. Dancers didn't go into the *hijra*s. The *kothi* dancers kept distant from the *hijra*s.[58]

On the whole, it has been boys from families in the very low socio-economic strata who joined the *hijra*s. Those in 'good' families remained *kothi*s and often made a good living from a full–time, moonlighting or supplementary career in dance and performing arts. In contemporary Lucknow, many *kothi*s from 'good' families are now joining or mixing with the *hijras*. This may be definitive, with the *kothi* going to live with the *hijras*; or it may be part-time, with the *kothi* performing *badhai* with the *hijras* during the daytime and returning home in the evenings. The ability to be a 'part-time' *hijra* itself represents a major change in the *hijra* society, which used to involve a total form of belonging and severing from mainstream society. Part-time *hijras* may be married *kothis*, like Satin and Narendra, or those from fairly 'good' families who will go on to get married, such as Salim. As well as *kothis* becoming linked with the *hijras*, more and more *hijras* are involved in what were previously *kothi* genres.[59] Although there has always been some overlap—a *hijra* is a *kothi* before becoming a *hijra*—these new developments affect the core spaces, identities and activities of the two groups.

Like sex work, the involvement of *kothis* with the *hijras* comes mostly from financial desperation but the appeal of earning extra money may also be a factor. In Balliya, as described, some *kothis* who earn extremely good money from performing in marriage parties and *Badhava* also have gurus from the *hijras* and do *badhai* during the off-season. Many also have the emasculation operation. However, this is to enhance femininity and beauty rather than to become a *hijra*. These developments represent a far more commercialised and opportunistic 'pick and mix' attitude to the practices and livelihood options of what has previously been an all-encompassing religious cult. This has been further intensified since the decriminalisation of same-sex sexual relations in 2009, which has released pressure on all communities of MSMs. In Delhi and to a lesser extent in Lucknow, having a guru in the *hijras* has become something of a fashion, with the *hijras* having a certain status and prestige among transgenders.[60] *Kothis* are also deferent and fearful of *hijras* because of the power and recognition they have in mainstream society.[61] Therefore, while linking with the *hijras* has financial motivations for *kothis*, it also appears to be motivated by considerations of status associated with identity and the changing place of transgenders in society, with older contexts crumbling, and newer spaces still heavily contested and/or dangerous. These processes of blurring boundaries between *kothis* and *hijras* have caused problems and conflicts between the two communities.[62]

Violence, identity, advocacy, and questions of culture and livelihood

Another major current in this confluence of social, economic and cultural change and marginalisation is the increase of harassment and violence. Rape and random violence against *kothis* in the form of '*kothi* bashing' has become a major problem, and performers receive a lot of sexual harassment. This can be interpreted as a factor in the narrowing of *kothi* identity into one grounded in sex, sexuality and gender, and the severing of more integrated links to mainstream society. With *kothis* seen as 'cheap' and sex their only purpose—and without having the prestige and power that being a performer can bring—it is easier for men to use and despise them.

However, perhaps a more far-reaching factor is the increased awareness of ideas of homosexuality and gayness that has been spread by the global media. As much work has emphasised, the idea of 'homosexuality' did not traditionally exist in India. *Kothi*s and *hijra*s function as females (although *hijra*s also have an official third gender/asexual identity). The men who have sex with *kothi*s and *hijra*s would not distinguish themselves from other men in any way, and largely see *kothis*/*hijra*s as interchangeable with females. Sexual role, gender and status also intersect, with elite men never (in theory) taking a receptive, 'feminine', subordinate role in anal sexual intercourse. In addition, as discussed in this chapter and chapter three, the place of *kothi*s in society has rested on the discursive impossibility, unsayability or unknowability of male-to-male sex, which has allowed it to take place without being officially 'seen'. However, with the spread of mass media and global Western ideas of gayness, upper middle class men are self-identifying as 'gay'. Being 'gay' is accepted within elite, liberal circles and, to a certain extent, in twenty-first-century Bollywood. Gayness is increasingly talked about openly, particularly in terms of sex/love between two men, and this is breaking down the heterosexual framework and opacity of male-to-male sex that has traditionally given it space. This inevitably leads to conflict. Because of virulent homophobia in many sectors of Indian society, same-sex sexual relations were only decriminalised in 2009, and it is still widely denied in India that 'homosexuality' exists at all. *Kothi*s are increasingly recognised as 'gay' or 'homosexual', and there is immense hostility to them on these grounds. In this context, it is increasingly difficult for *kothi*s to be female impersonators, let alone seductive and effeminate female singer/dancers, without being recognised and named as 'gay', and these traditions therefore survive in parts of the country and society that are less affected by open knowledge of 'homosexuality' and 'gayness'. Thus socio-economic development produces a pressure on the liminal social identity of *kothi*s and, in turn, on their livelihood as performers.

In the West, there have been tensions between the struggle for gay interests based on the right to privacy on the one hand and, on the other, the right to a full, open, gay identity grounded in a person's 'nature', and consequent minority status and rights within the nation state.[63] Since the 1980s, there has been increasing emphasis on gayness as an identity rather than gayness as behaviour. In India, groups have emerged, largely in response to HIV/AIDS from the early 1990s, that have resisted importing the Western identity categories, and have instead focused on behaviour, i.e. 'men who have sex with men' (MSMs), aware of the delicate spaces *kothi*s and *hijra*s occupy.[64] However, this approach is compromised by the spread of global gay identities by the mainstream media where there is an increased interest in 'homosexuality' and no sympathetic representation of *kothi*s or *hijra*s or understanding of their traditional place in society.[65] Also, although these groups avoid identity-based advocacy, some kind of publicity and openness is inevitably necessary to campaign for protection from harassment—especially from the police—and to sensitise politicians and public figures to the need for large-scale funding for the fight against HIV/AIDS. The category of MSM itself is also problematic in that it puts *kothi*s in the category of males, identifying them on the basis of biological sex, whereas much of their livelihood and socio-cultural space has rested on the fact that they are equivalent to females.[66] Furthermore, with other groups involved in identity-based struggles—and even if 'lesbian' and 'gay' is broken down to 'lesbian, gay, bisexual, transgender' (LGBT), or if '*kothi*' and '*hijra*' are added—the same problems emerge with a struggle for openness and recognition for identities, lifestyles and cultures that have existed precisely because of their liminality and opacity.

These groups, along with India's LGBT movement, represent a response to the mounting homophobia and marginalisation of MSMs that has emerged fundamentally through the creation of an overarching homophobic national identity from the late nineteenth century, as well as a necessary response to HIV/AIDS. The movement offers support and protection for *kothi*s and other MSMs. But at the same time, these identity-based initiatives inevitably become a part of larger social, economic and cultural changes that are breaking down the traditional space of *kothi*s. This situation can be interpreted as one of 'fighting fire with fire', a classic problem of nationalism and identity politics. It represents a modern response to the problems that modernity has brought—inevitable and necessary, yet also inevitably and necessarily problematic in certain ways. As social and cultural topographies are restructured amid modern ideologies and in the context of new forms of economic development and disparity, identities are becoming contested more intensely on the grounds of absolute belonging and rights (rather than opacity and liminality), thereby responding to and engendering more absolute forms of discrimination. The situation becomes more black and white and represents radical change for *kothis*' social and cultural existence.

Further complexities can be seen when looking at the role of the CBOs and NGOs working specifically for MSMs. Clearly, they represent welcome new spaces for *kothi*s and other MSMs, as well as urgently needed health and other welfare support. They also provide employment for *kothi*s and *hijra*s in the form of peer educators and field officers and some groups provide vocational training leading to new forms of socio-economic belonging. However, as with all aid and development work, the situation depends on MSMs as a community in need and brings into play the trope of victimhood. As with female hereditary performers, the level of the problems and social marginalisation of the community and the pressure to justify its needs to funders and decision makers in competition with other groups in need, has a tendency to condense *kothi* identity into one of disease, discrimination, tragedy and violence, which can overwhelm other social roles and identities. A 2007 photographic book on *kothi*s, *My body is not mine*, for example, was under considerable pressure from its funders to include a maximum amount of material relating to violence and abuse against *kothi*s.[67] The authors and photographer were keen to resist this and to balance the material with broader images of the *kothi* community.[68] Another recent study frames cross-dressed performing narrowly and polemically in terms of the 'forced migration, trafficking and sexual exploitation' of adolescent boys. This imitates exactly the discourse that has surrounded female performers and bar girls to such devastation of their livelihood and identity, and is missing the nuances of dance as socio-cultural space and economic livelihood.[69] The achievements of groups offering support and advocacy, and their necessity for MSMs, are immeasurable. However, there is a danger that they, and the wider culture of aid, development, and advocacy of which they are a part, contribute to the narrowing of *kothi* public identity to one that revolves around issues of gender, sexuality, rights, injustices and problems.

Performing has historically been the most important livelihood and socio-cultural space for *kothi*s, yet it forms no part of the contemporary discourse surrounding them. Performing arts are seen at best as a decorative background to *kothi* identity. For example, a magazine produced to celebrate the tenth anniversary of Bharosa, *Bharosa: Voices of the unheard*, features an image of a *kothi* dancing on the back cover with a poem about dancing from the point of view of a *kothi* performer. Yet the magazine focused on matters of health and advocacy. Dance has also been spoken of as one of the 'clichéd roles and professions' that *kothi*s are restricted to due to their femininity, something that *kothi*s should be able to move on from.[70] While this view is understandable, it also vastly underestimates the importance of this occupation and activity as a structural part of their social, cultural and economic place. On a practical level, *kothi*s are at present 'moving on' from dance only into sex work, rather than higher status professions. This ignoring or undervaluing of performing is revealing of the ways in which development is focused on 'issues' and 'problems' to the degree that the cultural and historical context that has given rise to these problems, and could potentially help to find integrated solutions to them, is obscured. This parallels the campaign surrounding the bar girls described in chapter five. This undervaluing is particularly ironic and short-sighted given the structural importance of culture as 'soft power' in the form of identity and nationhood in many nation states including India. More specifically, in the case of *kothi*s and female erotic performers, much of their problems are centred on the fact that a new or modern national culture and identity has been formed that excludes them and pretends they never existed. I would certainly argue that while *kothi*s should not be restricted only to their principal traditional role as performing artistes, the level of their contribution to Indian culture (defined narrowly or broadly) should not be ignored either. An approach that includes the historical and cultural place of *kothi*s could potentially form powerful and extremely grounded arguments about the rights of *kothi*s to belong and to be valued in modern India and to help construct a positive and diverse *kothi* identity.[71]

Conclusions

This chapter has outlined a world of erotic male cross-dressed dance in India that is very much a part of traditional culture. However, like hereditary females, there is, in living memory, an undeniable trajectory of exclusion. This has involved an undermining of *kothis*' principal livelihood of performing arts, which has been the central legitimate space for them to exist as females and to engage in eroticism and relationships with men. The exclusion represents a continuity of previous currents of marginalisation that saw erotic male performers and female impersonators disappear from high status performing arts. As with female hereditary performers, the pace of marginalisation appears to be accelerating rapidly, with a dramatic rise in sex work and a collapse in livelihoods in performing occurring only since the 1990s or 2000s.

However, alongside these processes of exclusion, new spaces are being negotiated and fought for through political activism and identity politics. This, too, parallels the bar girls' situation. However, while female hereditary performers in the form of bar girls face the possibility of a dramatic improvement in their status, with a real form of legitimacy and recognition of their labour, livelihood and identity as performers (depending on the judgement of the Supreme Court on the dance ban), this looks less likely for *kothi*s. While it is possible that more secure spaces for *kothi*s and other sexual minorities could be established, as they have been in the Western world, it is not clear how this might structure their involvement in performing arts, or indeed, if performing would remain an important space for them. It is also unclear how a history that rightly places them as an integral part of Indian culture and society can emerge without a focus on their role in performing arts.

CONCLUSION

This book has explored the modern history of India's public/erotic female and transgender dancers, bringing to light worlds of performing arts hidden from mainstream conceptions of 'Indian culture'. It has traced an axis of inclusion/exclusion in Indian modernity, contextualising the formation of bourgeois nationalist social norms and India's nationally and internationally lauded culture in processes of marginalisation. While nationalism as a process of construction or (re)invention in performing arts has been extensively studied, this book looks at nationalism as a project of exclusion as well as inclusion. These processes of inclusion/exclusion go far beyond the legitimisation or valuing of certain traditions at the cost of others; with performing arts tied to communities of people and their livelihood and sociocultural identities, India's traditional female public/erotic performers have suffered devastating loss of place and status from the nineteenth century onwards. Hereditary female and transgender performers are core to the history and heritage of Indian performing arts. However, they are nowadays seen as unrelated to 'culture', but instead related to 'development' problems such as sex work, social exclusion, poverty and HIV/AIDS. This book has thus traced the transformation of their formerly complex, liminal status to a position of more absolute exclusion.

A particularly striking aspect of the processes of inclusion/exclusion is that they have continued unabated from colonial to postcolonial India. It is reasonably well known that courtesans and *devadasi*s were excluded from performing arts, enabling the transformation of these traditions into 'respectable', national culture, embodied largely by middle class, upper caste Indians. However, what is far less known is the postcolonial trajectory of the axis of inclusion/exclusion. The middle class zone of performing arts has continued to expand and, since the 1990s, has incorporated an extensive Bollywood dance craze that spans middle class India and its globalised diaspora and breaks previous rules of cultural and social legitimacy. Meanwhile the hereditary female and transgender performers have found it harder to maintain an identity and livelihood as performers, becoming increasingly involved in sexual transaction and markedly more sexualised performance. Some communities of hereditary performers moved to wholesale commercial sex work only after the loss of both princely patronage and routes into legitimate zones of cultural production, which followed independence. In particular, the period of liberalisation, economic growth and globalisation since the 1990s has been characterised by an acceleration of these processes of inclusion and exclusion, although it also shows some nascent signs of change.

I have sought to locate the origins of these profound changes to the terrain of Indian performing arts in a number of areas relating to modernity and the ways in which it has reconfigured pre-existing cultural and social formations. A fundamental driving force in this respect has been the set of central contraditions that female public/erotic performers represent for patriarchal structures. In India, under pre-modern systems, these performers combined a low status and a lack of 'respectability' with sometimes immense power, importance, and acclaim. While female hereditary performers have been more prestigious and culturally visible on the whole, female impersonators, including transgender erotic cross-dressed performers, have a similarly liminal and complex position. These zones of performing arts were once central to cultural life, and were patriarchally constituted. Yet they were also transgressive of patriarchy and other social hierarchies, and constituted dangerous zones, with an erotic charge fuelled by gender and class dynamics as well as the affective, aesthetic power of song and dance.

Under colonial and bourgeois nationalist modernity, female performers and their 'disreputable' non-married status became unacceptable, and the only category into which they fitted was that of 'prostitute'. Also unacceptable, though not widely talked about, was the intimate nature of the (extra-marital) relationships of low status women with upper class/caste patrons. Female impersonators, too, became gradually more sidelined through discourses that saw their performance as 'unrealistic', 'unmodern', or 'backward'. Homosexuality became actively outlawed, (though the implicit or explicit homoeroticism of female impersonators or transgender erotic performers respectively was not targeted openly on homophobic grounds).

Nationalism, and its effect on the configuration of belonging and not-belonging, has been a fundamental driver of the shifts in the socio-cultural topography of performing arts. As nationalism brings diverse peoples into one nation, formerly different groups and communities become linked far more closely, and the identities of the various parts affect the identity of the whole in radically new ways. Thus under nationalism, the identity of female hereditary performers affects that of the bourgeoisie in a way it never affected that of the upper caste or elite patrons of the pre-nationalist order. Nationalism is ostensibly a project of unification and equalisation. However, it in fact engenders forms of conflict, hierarchy and exclusion, since there is a necessity and imperative to change or deal with those who do not conform to the now shared identity. Performing arts are one of the most important means to represent and embody a nation and, given that they involved so many low status men and 'disreputable' women in India, this was a key zone for reform. Through this (cultural) nationalist ideology, the bourgeoisie appropriated the emblematic performing arts traditions, excluding female hereditary performers, female impersonators and transgender performers as well as many other low status performers.

I have also focused on the role of discourses of liberalism, rights, progress and development in configuring the belonging and not-belonging of female hereditary and transgender performers in modern India. This book constitutes a case study in the materiality of these discourses. At many levels, these powerful but tautological ideologies have pitched modernity against 'backwardness', with only acceptable 'tradition' to be maintained. They have also legitimised moves framed as 'reform', 'progress' or the fight against 'exploitation' at the cost of a wealth of more subtle historical and contextual matters. In certain basic ways, these ideologies form the bedrock of colonial and postcolonial modernities and of liberal democracy across the world. Their use in the framing of discussions of female hereditary performers from the nineteenth to the twenty-first centuries has shown extraordinary blindness to their repetition and consequences. The illicit arena of performing arts was created through drives to reform society and make it respectable—to 'rescue' *devadasi*s and *tawaif* from 'indignity' or 'exploitation', and to 'rescue' performing arts from what was declared to be a degenerated state and return them to their former glory. However, these drives did not rescue the women. The vast majority continued as performers, but in an increasingly illicit, sexualised 'underbelly' of national performing arts that has merged more and more with commercial sex work. These illicit worlds can be seen as a 'monster' created by the exclusionary power of nationalism and liberal, rational modernity. To use Bauman's phrase, they are a form of 'collateral damage' of Indian nationalism and colonial and postcolonial modernity, an 'other' that rational modernity has been unable to control and that instead continues to grow.[1]

This book has focused on describing India's illicit zones of performing arts alongside the legitimate ones, analysing their historical genesis with the aim of understanding the virtually unrelenting patterns of inclusion/exclusion. I have sought to highlight the blind spots of these processes, and thus to outline new and more productive paradigms for discussion. A number of important points have emerged. To begin with, there is a need for a far more interdisciplinary understanding of performing arts and 'culture'. I have outlined the ways in which illicit zones of performing arts have fallen between the gulf of arts scholarship that studies 'culture', 'music' and 'dance' on the one hand, and social-science-oriented scholarship that studies problems such as exclusion, poverty and minority or marginal people on the other. This disciplinary gulf has played a crucial role in the lasting identity of female public/erotic performers as 'prostitutes', feeding the vicious circle of marginalisation and loss of identity, status and livelihood. The more they became 'problems', in need of help or 'development', the less they have been recognised as performers or as people with any useful or valuable role in Indian history and culture.

Thus I argue in this book for a view of artistic and creative culture that integrates it entirely with social and economic questions of development. As large amounts of research—in ethnomusicology and other disciplines—has shown, performing arts are part of the basic fabric of societies, identities, power, place and legitimacy. This is true in traditional and small societies as well as complex post-industrial nation states. Performing arts are therefore far more extensive in social and political function than narrow notions of art, entertainment or expression warrant. In mainstream society, there is increasing understanding of the power of music and performing arts to engender expression, self-esteem and confidence (indeed, the Bollywood dance revolution is a part of this trend). Music therapy is becoming more widespread and recognised. 'Advocacy' and 'applied' ethnomusicology are becoming increasingly prominent, mobilising music and performing arts for projects of development and socio-psychological emplacement and (re)construction.[2] However, such initiatives remain marginal in the world of development despite evidence of their potency and subtlety, and 'harder' and more quantifiable approaches that seek to fight the 'real' issues of 'exploitation', 'trafficking' and so on are given much greater time and energy. The consequences of the dramatic loss of involvement in performing arts on hereditary female and *kothi* performers needs to be seriously considered in this context.[3] This book examines performing arts as a leisure activity in the context of the middle class Bollywood dance craze, looking at effects on health, confidence and well being. The (continuing) history of India's female public/erotic performers represents an almost exact reverse of these processes, a profound socio-cultural displacement. A deeper investigation into what has been lost by the disenfranchised performers on individual and community levels, and what has been gained by the middle classes now able to engage in amateur or professional dance, would be an important angle for future research.

Art and culture become a development issue not only through direct considerations of performing arts as identity and socio-cultural fabric, but also through a consideration of the value of performing arts as labour and the ways in which it constitutes livelihoods. This is particularly important in India where the linking of occupation and social identity through caste make social mobility difficult.[4] The lack of consideration of performing arts as skilled labour has been one of the most damaging blind spots in the modern history of public/erotic female performers. It is imperative that the value of performing arts as a livelihood and as aesthetic, affective, and skilled labour is considered by those working with such performers or ex-performers under programmes targeting sex work or prostitution. At the moment there is little understanding of where dance fits in; at best it is seen as a side issue. This entire book consists of an elaboration and exploration of the value of dance and performing arts in social, cultural and economic terms, both to those who have gained it and those who have lost it. To restate two brief if blunt illustrations of the difference that having performing skills, a context in which to use them and permission to do so can make to these performers. A lodge-based sex worker in Mumbai would take something like Rs 500–600 for sex, and a brothel-based sex worker much less. To have sex with a bar girl could take weeks or months of setting up—wooing, buying gifts, and showering money on her as she dances—and may not even be successful. So sex cannot always be straightforwardly bought, even at a high price (which would run into thousands or tens of thousands of rupees). Similarly, at a meeting of sex workers I attended, they were asked how they were different from *Lavani* performers, who are mostly non-marrying, hereditary, female performers.[5] The sex workers replied that the *Lavani* artistes get more respect, more money, and less harassment than themselves. One sex worker said she had been in the audience at a *Lavani* performance moving along to the music and partially dancing while in her seat. A man who had been sitting behind her later solicited sex from her and she was stunned to be paid Rs 2,000 (ten times her usual rate). She assumed that this was because he thought she was a *Lavani* artiste. A bar girl or a *lavani* dancer must, therefore, on the grounds of labour and socio-economic status, be distinguished from a prostitute. A far more nuanced exploration of labour and social status needs to be addressed in literature on prostitution in India, and should consider ex-performers, disenfranchised performers, or illicit performers, historically and in present day India.

This book has analysed processes of marginalisation, critiquing the internal contradictions of nationalism and liberal discourses and considering how such discourses have made the lives of these particular Indian citizens far worse. The aim has been to fill in denied histories and contexts; to create a more nuanced and grounded debate; and to create awareness of the potential for these discourses to dichotomise, essentialise and create exclusion and 'backwardness'. However, since the start of the globalising era in the 1990s these discourses have also opened up new possibilities. This can be seen on two levels.

I have described the Bollywood dance revolution as a phase two of embourgeoisement, a concretisation of middle class place and confidence. Similarly, the ban on dance bars and the years since 1990 of accelerated marginalisation of female hereditary and *kothi* performers have constituted a parallel solidification of inclusion/exclusion. However, at the same time, potentials have opened up through the very continuity of the liberal trajectory, which appears to be tipping consolidation into change. A twist in the binary topography appears to be taking place due to the fact that the middle class legitimate zone has proceeded so far on the same trajectory that it has paradoxically become close in many ways to the kinds of performing arts declared illicit and wrong. With globalisation and the increased liberalisation of gender and sexual behaviour in middle class India, and the distance of the illicit worlds from the legitimate ones, many girls from 'good' families can now dance in a sexy way. Additionally, there are many sexy or 'vulgar' songs in Hindi films (which have been a solidly legitimate part of culture since the 1990s). These developments have made it difficult for the bar girls' dancing to be declared 'vulgar', 'exploitative' and 'not dance'. This was crucial to their success in the High Court. The continuity and progression of embourgeoisement versus exclusion has resulted in the two sides of the coin no longer being in opposition. Hence, while the tautologies and blind spots of discourses of progress and rights have played a key role in the continuity of the history of exclusion, it is in this case possible to see the progressiveness and dynamism of liberalism as laying potential for change.

On another level, while liberal discourses have the potential to bifurcate their objects into zones of universal good and universal bad, these discourses may at the same time be appropriated, and the terms of debate and zones of agency changed. This has indeed been a pattern throughout their history. This is almost inevitable since liberal and rights-based discourses create their 'others' as objects to transform or bring into the fold. As the two sides continue to interact, appropriation by the other becomes a logical step. In the context of globalisation and increased middle class confidence, women such as sex workers and bar girls have been included among those thought worthy of having rights upheld to some degree on their own terms, overcoming assumptions that they are unable to 'choose' and are under forms of 'false consciousness'. In the case of the bar girls, there has been a successful appropriation of labour rights, too, which has helped to undermine the far more subjective, emotional and easily-manipulated debates concerning 'choice' and 'exploitation'. The LGBT movement also promises radical change to the position of *kothi*s, and a complete restructuring of their social and cultural place—though bringing with it a serious danger of essentialisation, which can compound other processes of marginalisation.

Rather than representing two eternal separate(d) parallels, liberalism's 'forward' momentum can bring about twists. The legitimate versus illicit topography of performing arts that has come into being since the nineteenth century has the potential to gain a character more comparable to a moebius strip with the opposite surfaces running into each other and linking at various points. At this point in the modern history of Indian performing arts, therefore, continuity could tip into change. The use of discourses of labour and of legal rights can be powerfully used to ground some of the particularly slippery and de-contextualising discourses of 'exploitation'. This could benefit both female and transgender performers.

Another approach that binds the zones of arts and development into meaningful and nuanced dialogue is the mobilisation of ideas of cultural heritage and collective or indigenous rights. These are relatively newly-emerged 'rights' that relate to justice, belonging and place in a nation's culture. They could be used to reverse the stigma surrounding these performers and the current view that their communities are 'problems'. Similarly, direct projects of artistic rehabilitation could serve to emplace the performers, and spell out, through embodied performance, the communities' history and potential.[6] Most of the work on arts, heritage, sustainability and indigeneity has focused on protecting small traditions against globalisation or dominant majorities. However, in the case of India's public/erotic female performers (and other traditional performers), it is the traditional performers themselves that have been marginalised, rather than the traditions. These discourses and debates would need to be adapted in new ways. However, new ways of exploring cultural ownership and heritage hold much potential.

Given that even sexy Bollywood dance has become respectable for middle class women in India, a genuine reconsideration of the public/erotic female and transgender performers in terms of heritage and cultural role may be feasible. A revivification of run-down vernacular traditions might also be timely. Government (or other) support would be necessary, as would regulation. If the dance bar ban is defeated in the Supreme Court, bar dancing will become legal and, with the help of the union and other groups, good working conditions would be likely to develop. Similarly, if vernacular traditions such as *Nautanki* were supported and protected, so too would be the status and livelihood of their artistes, as the case of *Lavani* and *Tamasha* in Maharashtra illustrates. However, such initiatives are not watertight. Support often takes the form of folklorisation for touristic purposes, which helps only selected performers rather than the broad communities. Gaining support and legitimacy can also lead to increased appropriation by the middle classes, as Rege has described in the case of Marathi films and *Lavani*.[7] Similarly, dance bars could well begin to draw in middle class girls if they had appropriate working conditions and good enough salaries—such a leap would be no greater in scale than that of the past when 'respectable' women entered the film industry and classical performing arts.

New supportive frameworks for female hereditary performers are also opening up via the National Commission for Denotified, Nomadic and Semi-nomadic Tribes, set up in 2006 by the Government of India Ministry of Social Justice and Empowerment.[8] A report in June 2008 included a range of recommendations including reservations, publicity campaigns against stigma, and initiatives to build better relationships with leaders of these communities. The report also recommended a regular National Commission for Denotified, Nomadic and Semi-nomadic Tribes to provide constitutional safeguards for these groups. The report makes general points about various non-pastoralist nomadic groups losing livelihood and social space since the nineteenth century, and about their services, crafts or skills losing value and respect. However, the only point made regarding female hereditary performers turning to 'prostitution' is that it is a result of loss of livelihood due to loss of patronage and the advent of mass media entertainment. Bar dancing is also reported to lead to 'exploitation'. The specific, long history of stigmatisation of these particular performing groups through social campaigns, and the distinct, non-marrying social structure of the performers themselves, is not explored. Thus, as a door to social justice opens for these acutely marginalised groups, an inner door remains closed due to lack of understanding—of the history of social stigma that has built up against these women, their direct exclusion from classical performing arts and legitimate culture in general, and how this has pushed them into a reliance on sexual transaction.

Approaches to reinstate India's public/erotic performers into history and culture have immense mountains to climb. As I have outlined, these performers are typically seen as 'prostitutes', 'backward', or 'exploited'. At best they are pitied because they 'have no choice' but to dance. On an official level, Indian culture has not begun to rehabilitate these important culture carriers or even squarely acknowledge their existence, identity, history and social structure. In addition to practical campaigns, large amounts of research are still necessary in order to piece together an understanding of these performers, their place in history, and their modern decline. The history and present of female impersonators (whether erotic transgender performers or simply cross-dressed males) has barely begun to be explored. Potentially extremely important aspects of the history of hereditary female performers—for example, the effect of the Criminal Tribes Act—have also been as yet only glimpsed. The post-independence history of female hereditary performers and transgender performers is in urgent need of documentation across a wide range of these communities. Time is limited to do so using oral sources. Compounding this lack of research, marginalisation has occurred through a problem of knowledge transfer. While serious South Asian scholars are unlikely to deny the importance of courtesans in India's past, decision makers in the public realm or those involved in aid and development work do not have such knowledge, and do not see it as relevant to themselves. A basic understanding of modern history still eludes the public sphere. This is also a serious problem with the politics of *kothi* identity: the identity being claimed and reified is one based in gender and sexual orientation rather than broader cultural and social questions, and heavily shaped by Western LGBT categories. Thus better communication of knowledge into these areas could help mitigate some of the essentialising tendencies of these identity politics.

In addition to problems of knowledge and its flows, extreme forms of stigma need to be negotiated. With female performers, these relate to the fact that they live outside of marriage-based respectability, and in many cases, are involved in sex work. However, the stigma also stems from their belonging to ex-criminalised tribes.[9] There are no easy or obvious solutions to these problems. However, looking back at the modern history of the performers, it is clear that new approaches are urgently needed. The furious debates that centre on 'exploitation', 'saving' and 'victimhood' at the expense of details of history and context are particularly problematic. In short, the consequences of these patterns of demonization or 'rescuing' of female performers have been devastating. They have made the problems they sought to solve worse, and taken up considerable time and resources. The same is true of the more silent but equally extensive marginalisation of transgender performers. Loss of identity as performers, loss of skilled and higher-paid labour, an increase in prostitution, poverty, marginality, and lack of choice have formed a vicious circle. In the twenty-first century these female and male transgender performers continue to be marginalised and to be drawn more and more into prostitution. Rising economic, social and cultural disparity following India's economic liberalisation in the 1990s has also fuelled the gulf between these performers and the mainstream. Furthermore, the increased wealth of middle class males means there is more money to pay female performers or *kothi*s for sex. With decreased identity as dancers and fewer salubrious places to perform, this money goes increasingly to pay for sex, rather than to reward skill and prowess in dance.

NOTES

INTRODUCTION: INDIAN PERFORMING ARTS AND MODERNITY'S CULTURES OF EXCLUSION

1. Cousin marriage is common among Muslims.
2. *Maaf kijiega, ittefaqan aapke compartment men chal aaya tha, aapke paonv dekhe, bahut haseen hain, inhen zameen pe mat utaariega, maile ho jaenge, aapke ek humsafar.* The word '*humsafar*' literally means 'fellow traveller', but also has the sense of life partner.
3. Such a questionable status for female performers has been common across much of the world, where comparable or historically related patriarchal systems mean women are restricted in the public domain. See for example Doubleday (1988), Cowan (1990), Sliverman (2003), Austern and Naroditskaya (2006) and Feldman and Gordon (eds) (2006).
4. This interpretation of *Pakeezah* was first presented in Morcom (2004). See Bhaskar and Allen for a longer analysis of *Pakeezah* highlighting images of death and captivity and of freedom and renewal (2009: 171–186). Bhaskar and Allen analyse five courtesan films in the context of their study of Islamicate Bombay cinema.
5. *Dupatta* refers to the scarf worn by women as a symbol of respectability and a means of physically covering the chest.
6. This push towards a definitive and (publicly) performed end of the courtesan and transformation into a bride is also central to the film's ability to make a general, social message.
7. Many courtesans ended up in permanent relationships with just one man, yet this was almost always as a kept woman, not a wife, and usually in addition to the man's wife.
8. See Qureshi's study of hereditary performers in India within a feudal context (2002). She does not study female performers specifically, but how the inequality of the relationship of performer and patron in terms of labour, status and remuneration works out in terms of gender and sexuality with female performers, as I explore here. See also Hansen's work on *Nautanki* theatre of North India (1992: 9–32).
9. Women who perform in husband–wife pairs, who are not specifically erotic performers, exist, but they are low status—for example the *Badi* in the Indian Himalaya (Fiol, 2010). Women as auspicious performers are also common in South Asia. This involves singing

mainly in the company of other women, and only sometimes in front of men for certain public festivities, and has no conflict with marriage or respectability. Brown describes *Domni* and *Dhadhi* women in the Mughal court in these roles (2003: 150, 156–159), and Tingey describes the *Mangalini* in the court of Kathmandu, who are upper caste women (1993).

10. Sachdeva (2008: 74–76, 91, 138, 297, 319, 369)
11. See Soneji's analysis of *devadasis*' marital status (2012: Chapter 1). It is important to note that undedicated women were also performers in South India, and *devadasi*s were by no means just 'temple dancers' (Ibid.: Introduction). See also Srinavasan's discussion of *devadasis* and marriage (1984: 168–181)
12. Srinivasan (1984: 283–289 and 1985: 1870); Gaston (1996); Soneji (2012).
13. *Devadasi*s per se did not constitute a caste prior to reforms. The *devadasi*s or courtesans Soneji discusses in his book are mid-caste. Low caste, Dalit women who are dedicated to temples in a comparable fashion to *devadasi*s also exist—groups such as *jogti*s—but are distinguished from *devadasi*s. Please see Srinivasan (1984: 239–289 and 1985) and Soneji (2012: Introduction).
14. Hansen (1998; 2002).
15. A. Srinivasan (1984: 283–289), Shankar (1990: 16–20), K. Brown (2003: 118–176; and 2006), D. Srinivasan (2006) and Post (1987).
16. Crooke (1896: vol. I, 380).
17. The term *randuwa*, or widower, has no such disreputable connotations. It was suggested that widows could act in Marathi theatre rather than prostitutes in the early twentieth century, see Adarkar (1991: WS89).
18. Banerjee (1998).
19. A. Srinivasan (1984; 1985) and Soneji (2012: Introduction) both critique this persistent discourse.
20. K. Brown explores these matters of gender, status and eroticism at length (2003: 118–176; and 2006).
21. Similarly, having European women performing in front of native audiences was seen as highly unsuitable. Shope (forthcoming) quotes a contemporary source on cabaret in Calcutta from the 1910s: 'for ten years the police imposed a ban, to the relief of most of the influential [British] who heard with concern of the state of undress permitted to performers in London cabarets and considered that the effect on the Indian public of the spectacle of European girls as professional dancers in a public restaurant would be unfortunate'.
22. Oldenburg (1989; 1990); Qureshi (2001; 2006); K. Brown (2003; 2006); Soneji (2012).
23. Brown makes this point in her analysis of performers in Mughal India, a point still very much valid in today's India (2003: 118–176).
24. See K. Brown (2003: 118–176; and 2006) for analysis of cautionary tales.
25. Qureshi,(2006), Rao (1999 [1990]), Brown (2003: 118–176), Hollander (2007: 77–82); Soneji (2012). Remarkable parallels exist in terms of gender, emotion and music in many patriarchal configurations. See, for example, Austern's work on Elizabethan England (1989), Austern and Naroditskaya (eds) (2006), and Doubleday on Afghanistan (1988: 157–213).

26. Shankar (1968: 11–29), Widdess (2004) and Brown (2003: 177–225).
27. Post (1987). The problem of respectability for females performing in public has not been entirely removed through this new configuration. However, it is nationally acceptable. It is also important to note that a large number of low status male musicians also became disenfranchised by this process of embourgeoisement.
28. See Adarkar (1991) and Hansen (1998; 2002).
29. Soneji has described how the art of some communities of *devadasis* has gone underground in a different way in South India, with these women performing in private, for themselves, as a means to retain, in some form, their former status and identities (2012: Ch. 5). Other *devadasis* went into commercial sex work, see Nair (1994) and Soneji (2012: Ch. 5), and the low caste female hereditary performers such as *jogtis* have become far more involved in a livelihood that rests on and is known as prostitution rather than performance, see Jairazbhoy and Caitlin (2008) and Soneji (2012: Introduction).
30. Many low status male hereditary performers have become excluded from the new traditions, and a great range of 'folk' performers struggle to subsist or to have their art validated. They are increasingly poor, due to exclusionary forces based variously on caste/class, nationalism, or the uneven economic development of neoliberalism. See work by Babiracki (2000/2001; 2003), Magriel (2001: 32–37) and Fiol (2010; 2011). Striking parallels also exist between traditional, hereditary musicians and wider artisans working in a range of arts and crafts. I became aware of this after hearing papers given at the British Association for South Asian Studies conference, 2012, by Hacker, Kawlra, Raina and Szanton.
31. The terms 'classical', 'folk' and 'popular' are certainly approximate and problematic. For example, classical music has amalgamated much from vernacular, local traditions over the centuries, see Widdess (1995: 22–28), and some 'folk' traditions have a strong overlap with classical music, such as the virtuosic music of the *Langas* and *Manganiyars* in Rajasthan. Seasonal 'folk' genres such as *kajri* are also performed as light classical music, as are devotional genres (Hindu *bhajans* and Sufi *Qawwali*). 'Popular' film music has drawn from classical and folk music, and folk music has in many cases appropriated film music, in terms of tunes or increasingly, in played back recording, see Marcus (1992/3; 1994/5); Booth (1990) and Manuel (1993). The categories of classical, folk and popular are also as much modern as historical, themselves formed by modern processes of institutionalisation and legitimisation, as has been explored, for example, in the context of studies of the 'invention' of the classical in India, see Bhakhle (2005) and Weidman (2006). Brown, on the other hand, argues for deeper roots of 'classicisation' of Indian music (2010). However, the terms classical, folk and popular are also not without salience. They highlight different levels and types of training, virtuosity, professionalisation, consciousness of 'tradition', aesthetics, functions and involvement of the mass media, which can be useful distinctions.
32. Nye (2004).
33. See Morcom (2009: 135–136). Similarly, while Bollywood has been very much embraced in academia, Indian B films, horror films and porn films, or even low budget regional films such as Bhojpuri, which are not the (official) cinema of the middle classes, are very

little researched. See Hoek (2010) on Bangladeshi B films and porn inserts and Vitali (2011) on the Ramsey brothers' Hindi horror films.

34. See Shresthova's analysis of processes of codification and institutionalisation of Bollywood dance (2008).
35. Maciszewski (2001a).
36. Appadurai and Breckenridge (1988).
37. Pinney (2000: 5).
38. The same problem exists with the term 'public' female performer, hence I term them public/erotic performers, or 'hereditary female performers', or 'traditional female professional performers', or 'transgender female performers'.
39. Mazzarella discusses bar dancing in these terms (forthcoming); See also Dalwai (2012).
40. Gupta (2001). See also Seizer (2005: 12–13).
41. Young (2001: 4).
42. Ibid.
43. Gupta (1998: 7–8) and Duffield and Hewitt (eds) (2009). These issues are also discussed by Kaviraj (1997: 10–16; and 2010).
44. Bauman looks at capitalist and consumerist modernity's production of 'collateral damage' through socio-economic disparity (2011), and also human 'waste' through the progressive notion of 'design' (2004). His earlier work studies broader structural features of progressive modernity and its tendency to engender chaos and intolerance through its search for absolute order and delineation (1991).
45. See Nisbet (1979), Douzinas (2007) and Campbell (2006: 3–21), on the juxtaposition of the extraordinary successes of these ideologies—such as the abolition of slavery—alongside appalling carnage.
46. Gray (2004: 13).
47. Mehta (1999: 7–8).
48. Ibid. (1999: 77).
49. Mutua (2002: 3–4).
50. Mehta (1999: 1–4).
51. Mutua (2002: 32).
52. Ibid. (2002: 10–38) links this metaphor to both the colonial and the Christian legacy of human rights.
53. Žižek discusses this in the context of human rights and liberalism (2008: 126). Post-development and postcolonial critiques of development have been similar.
54. Hunt discusses the 'self-evidence' of fundamental rights, asserted first in the American declaration of Independence in 1776, as emotional at core. She traces the role of literature in making rights self-evident, due to its ability to manoeuvre readers into positions where they identify with characters and empathise with their suffering (2007). The emotionalising work of human rights continues, with shocking stories of suffering, degradation and the violation of rights always a part of debates that are rights-based, as has been the case of anti-*nautch* and also the dance bar ban as I explore in chapters three and five respectively.
55. Campbell cites 'egotism' as one of four fundamental critiques of human rights (2006:

11–14). This is also a problem with nationalism (as I explore later in this chapter) though, in this case, it is in a sense less insidious than with human rights, since any given nationalism explicitly aims to struggle for the statehood, or protection of the statehood, of a given nation.

56. I have been put in this uncomfortable situation many times myself in arguing with people over bar girls and contemporary *tawaif*.
57. Liberalism, following the philosophy of Hobbes and Locke, is founded on ideas of social contract, see Gray (1986: 7–15). Žižek describes the kinds of 'symbolic exchange' that enables people to preserve the ideal and illusion of 'free choice' in everyday social situations, in which compromise and the curtailment of one's choice are typical (2008: 137–138).
58. Quoting Ignatieff (2001b: 21) and Campbell (2006: 15–18) respectively. See Also Gearty's *The Rights Future*, especially Track 1, 'Human rights provide the best platform for progressive politics in our post-political age', that discusses human rights as politics (2010/11).
59. Mutua (2009: 39). It is significant that critiques of human rights are well developed especially in the arena of law, where practitioner-scholars have a grounded understanding of rights as 'the basic building block of Western law' and hence involving conflicts between people, see Douzinas (2007: 9). Similarly, critiques of rights and other universal ideologies are well developed in political theory and philosophy. Within the practice of development-oriented human rights work, however, there is less criticality, and similarly in journalism.
60. Butler (2000: 22–23).
61. The situation with those who do not conform to what is 'scientifically' defined as 'natural' can be similar, and such arguments can be used to fuel homophobia. See also Gupta's classic study on development in postcolonial India, and the creation of notions of 'backwardness' as core to what he terms the 'postcolonial condition' (1998).
62. It is perhaps for this reason there is a far greater literature on the problems of belonging, not belonging and being made to belong that relates to nationalism in terms of people and also culture than with universal ideologies, for example Anderson (1991), Gellner (2006), Hobsbawm (1992), Ignatieff (1998; 2001a). Extensive work on minorities and multiculturalism also focuses on these issues, for example Gilroy's work on the UK (1992), and Gladney's work on China (1994). Literature on the 'invention of tradition', see Hobsbawm and Ranger (1983), and on the problems of cultural belonging and un-belonging that relate to music and performing arts is also extensive.
63. Ignatieff (1998: 51). For Freud's theory of the 'narcissism of minor differences' see Freud (2002 [1930]: 305).
64. Ignatieff (1998: 51). Gilroy makes similar arguments in his chapter 'On living with difference' (2004: 1–28); See also Butler on the exclusion and foreclosure fundamental to discursive formations (1993: 1–23).
65. Ignatieff (1998: 51).
66. Gellner (2006), Anderson (1991), Hobsbawm (1992).
67. Parekh (2008: 8–55) and Sen (2006: 1–17) write of the dangers of essentialised or

mono-identities. Identity politics are increasingly seen as potentially problematic. Following Butler, gender theory and activism has critiqued identities and identity politics, see Wilchins (2004),and Bernstein Sycamore (ed.) (2006). This is also the case of work for MSMs in India, yet in practice, much identity-based work continues, as I discuss in chapter seven.

68. Bauman (1991: 53–74).
69. Ibid.
70. An apparently unique project that aims to see courtesans regain their liminal place in society is described by Macisewski, herself involved in the project (2006; 2007). This is discussed in chapter two.
71. Frank's well-known study 'The development of underdevelopment' argues that the capitalist system as a whole leads to underdevelopment and the 'third world' (1966). See also Escobar (1995) for a classic analysis of the construction of 'backwardness' and the 'third world'.
72. Hobsbawm (1992: 12), quoting Renan, E. 'Qu'est que c'est une nation?', paper given at conference at Sorbonne 11 March 1882.
73. See Hunt's discussion of the expansion of political rights following the French Revolution (2007: 146–175).
74. The traditional Left is strongly against prostitution, or the notion that it can ever be 'work', and see it as the commodification of a woman's body. This has produced strongly abolitionist stances against courtesans and bar girls, who are identified as commodified by capitalism, exploited, and therefore in need of saving. However, if the discussions were grounded more on empirical reality of livelihood, they could become more productive.
75. These kinds of cultural and collective rights are a second (or third) tier in the Human Rights movement, which started with civil and political rights. See Mutua (2002: 192, n. 4). Initiatives and programmes by the UN since the 2000s form a focal point for intangible cultural heritage http://www.unesco.org/culture/ich/index.php?lg=EN&pg=home, last accessed 17 July 2012. However, projects of cultural preservation go back much further.
76. There is a burgeoning literature on these topics. On intangible cultural heritage, see Howard (2006), Ramnarine (2012), Howard (ed.) (2012) and Norton (forthcoming). See also the ESRC-funded Centre for Indigeneity in the Contemporary World: Performance, Politics, Belonging, run by Helen Gilbert at Royal Holloway, University of London, http://www.indigeneity.net/, last accessed 17 July 2012. On copyright see Brown (1998) and Rees (2003).
77. I am grateful to Amrit Srinivasan for raising the notion of 'intangible cultural heritage' in the context of possible rehabilitation for female hereditary performers.
78. In terms of excluded courtesan performers as an issue for contemporary India to address, Maciszewski's work has been groundbreaking (1998; 2001a; 2001b; 2006; 2007). Qureshi's work has also been highly significant (2001; 2006), as have studies of *Kanjar* dancing girls in Lahore by Saeed (2002) and L. Brown (2006). Mehrotra's biography on Gulab Bai is remarkable in its address of wider communities of female hereditary

performers—beyond classical courtesans—and the extreme exclusion they have suffered, in particular in recent decades (2006). Jairazhboy and Caitlin's film on contemporary *jogti* prostitute/performers is groundbreaking (2008), and Soneji's recent book on *devadasis* is a landmark publication that fills a gap between historical studies of *devadasis* and contemporary excluded communities (2012). Agnes' articles on bar girls are also important (2005; 2006; 2007). See chapter one for a fuller discussion of the growing work on female hereditary performers, particularly historical work; and chapters three and six for that relating to transgender performers or female impersonators.

79. In addition to work cited in the above section, key work includes Harvey (2005), M. Fisher (2009), Žižek (2006), Baumann (2004; 2011), and poststructuralist development work, referenced below.
80. Foucault (1979; 1990; 1992; 1998; 2002) and Butler (1990; 1993).
81. Radcliffe (2005: 292).
82. Kothari's work has particularly focused on this aspect of modern development (2005a; 2005b; 2005c). Also significant is critical work on modernisation theory: see Frank (1966), Bernstein (1971), Peet and Hartwick (1999); post-development theory: Escobar (1995), Sachs (ed.) (2010); and postcolonial development studies: Kothari (ed.) (2005), Harris (2005), Sylvester (1999).
83. For example, Seeger's ethnography of the Suya is a classical example of the illustration of music and dance as a structural part of the social and cultural whole (2004 [1987]), and Feld's work on the Kaluli (1988) emphasises social structure and place in the environment. Small's work on 'musicking' focuses on contemporary western society and art music, but similarly shows the role of music in social construction (1998). Turino's work also theorises music as social life more broadly (1999; 2008). The agenda of music in the construction of identity was explicitly raised in ethnomusicology by Turino (1984) and, following Stokes' work (1994), a very extensive literature has formed. Work specifically on nationalism has grown from research into folk music, see Bohlman (1988) as well as studies more specifically focused on cultural nationalism and the importance of music and performing arts, which are too numerous to mention.
84. See Sheehy (1992), Avorgbeda (2006), Hemetek (2006) and Seeger (2006). In terms of its critical attention to music in society and culture, concerns of power, the centrality of participation and performance in research, and the involvement in documentation and preservation, most ethnomusicology can be described as 'applied'. Seeger dates 'applied ethnomusicology' back to the 1930s (before the terms had arisen) with remarkable data of early advocacy (2006). The Applied Ethnomusicology Section of the Society for Ethnomusicology was instituted in 1998, see http://www.ethnomusicology.org/?Groups_SectionsAE last accessed 3 March 2013. Impey has used the term 'advocacy ethnomusicology' to refer to more specific development-oriented initiatives (2002; 2006). See also Maciszewski (2006; 2007) regarding ethnomusicology and advocacy.
85. See, for example, Woolcock, Szreter and Rao (2009), and Radcliffe and Laurie (2006).
86. Following Guha's work on history and nationalism (1988 [1982]), Hansen brought up a subaltern agenda within Indian literary studies and theatre with her article 'The birth of Hindi drama in Banares, 1868–1885' (1989).

1. THE CREATION AND RECREATION OF INDIA'S ILLICIT ZONES OF PERFORMING ARTS: DYNAMICS OF EXCLUSION IN COLONIAL AND POSTCOLONIAL INDIA

1. Maciszewski (2006: 334).
2. Srinivasan (2006: 161).
3. Kumar (1988), Dalmia (2005: xii) and Sachdeva (2008).
4. Erdman's historical studies of the musicians of the Jaipur court in the nineteenth and first half of the twentieth centuries reveals *tawaif* as a central category of professional performers (1978; 1985).
5. Bor (1986/7).
6. Ballhatchet (1980: 157).
7. Oldenburg (1989: 135–136).
8. Sachdeva (2008: 195–306).
9. Ibid.: 218–275.
10. Ibid.: 275–284.
11. See Kinnear (2000: 3) and Farrell (1997: 111–143). See Sachdeva (2008: 284–305) for an overview of *tawaif*, gramophone recording and music markets in the early twentieth century, including biographies of two of the best-known *tawaif* artistes, Gauhar Jan and Janki Bai. In the South, similarly, the maximum number of recordings between 1910 and 1930 were made by *devadasis*, see Weidman (2006: 123), quoted in Sachdeva (2008: 288).
12. Erdman, 1992, p. 163.
13. According to Hansen, female performers existed alongside female impersonators in Parsee theatre 'as early as 1874', in *Tamasha*, and also in Bengal 'from the earliest times' (2002: 168). Female performers entered theatrical traditions in the early twentieth century that had previously been all male, for example, *Nautanki*, which had used only female impersonators, see Mehrotra (2006). Writing of Marathi (urban) theatre, Adarkar reports that mixed groups existed only after 1929, but prior to that there were all female groups (i.e. with women playing male and female parts) since at least 1865 (1991: WS-87).
14. Bhaumik (2001: 75–76).
15. Ibid: 45.
16. Gaisberg (1942: 29), quoted in Sachdeva (2008: 288).
17. Said (2003 [1978]).
18. Cohn (1987), Dirks (2002: 125–227).
19. Sachdeva (2008: 308–309). What Maciszewski describes as 'religious eclecticism' is still to be found with contemporary *tawaif* (2001: 166). It is also found in wider communities of dancing girls/sex workers, such as *Nat*, though processes of Sanskritisation are active.
20. Sachdeva (2008: 315). To describe these female performers as constituting a 'caste' is itself highly problematic, as these groups were fundamentally exogamous. I discuss this in more detail in the next chapter.
21. Ibid.: 321. Performers and prostitutes were also linked due to racially-based categori-

sations of prostitution. This was compounded by the fact that British legal thinkers had no 'satisfactory definition of what was meant by and what could be defined under the rubric of prostitution', see Levine (2000: 6). Ratnabali Chatterjee asserts that colonial rule effectively created categories of the wife versus 'other' women outside the domestic sphere through 'an ideology of domesticity', which led to an amalgamated class of prostitutes (1993: 159). See Bhattacharji (1987) for an overview of the many names and categories of prostitutes and female performers in ancient India.

22. Sachdeva (2008: 319).
23. Ballhatchet (1980: 10–39) and Levine (2003).
24. Ballhatchet (1980: 186). It is interesting to note that regulated prostitution existed in pre-colonial times, and also included laws to protect the abuse of prostitutes or courtesans, as Bhattacharji's article 'Prostitution in ancient India' shows (1987).
25. Oldenburg (1989: 134–144), Sachdeva (2008: 185–193, 321–326). See also Banerjee (1998) on the CDA and other colonial policies regarding prostitutes. Sachdeva describes how courtesans were taxed particularly harshly in order to 'raise funds', including for lock hospitals (2008: 190–192). Hence, 'In a way, the *tawa'if* were paying for the benefit of the health of European soldiers', Sachdeva (2008: 191).
26. Oldenburg (1989: 134–144) and Sachdeva (2008: 189–193, 325).
27. Oldenburg (1989: 141).
28. Levine (2003: 91–119).
29. This exchange is quoted in Sachdeva (2008: 323).
30. See in particular Mutua (2002).
31. Levine (2003: 188), quoted in Sachdeva (2008: 324).
32. See also 'Ideologies of "progress", "freedom", and "rights" in the modern history of female public/erotic performers' in the Introduction to this book.
33. Ballhatchet (1980: 60–63, 68–95) and Pivar (1981: 260–261).
34. Pivar (1981: 265).
35. Ibid.: 264.
36. See Yang (1986), Radhakrishna (2001: 1–26) and Gandhi (2008: 1–20) for overviews of the CTA.
37. Yang (1986: 114–116). See also Radhakrishna for an examination of prejudices against nomadic peoples (2001: 9–15), and Markovits, Pouchepadass and Subrahmanyam (2003) for an analysis of negative views on mobile or itinerant peoples from the point of view of settled society.
38. I explore the status of the menfolk of these communities in more detail in chapter two. It is also significant to note that the eunuchs or *hijras* were also declared a Criminal Tribe.
39. There has recently been a National Commission on DNTs and nomadic and semi-nomadic tribes by the Government of India Ministry of Social Justice and Empowerment, with a report dated 30 June 2008. This Commission could open up far more attention and research on all DNTs. However, the report itself provides little specific information on the female entertainers, and falls into the same kinds of patterns as the overwhelming amount of postcolonial information on female hereditary performers, which I discuss later in this chapter.

40. Agrawal (2008: 29; and 2006).
41. Agrawal (2008: 29).
42. Ibid.: 32–33.
43. Ibid.: 33. As I discuss later in this chapter, Agrawal problematically puts performing under the category of 'prostitution' while describing *Bedia* history.
44. Radhakrishna (2001: 15). Radhakrishna mentions that the practice of bride-price amongst the Koravas had led to charges of buying female children for marriage into the community; the system of polygamous relationships had led to charges of prostitution (2001: 55).
45. Gandhi (2008: 28).
46. Information on performer groups can also be gleaned from Biswas (1960), Yang (1986), and Bhattacharya (2003).
47. Yang mentions in his study of *Magahiya Doms* that in Central and South Indian *Doms* 'worked as "coarse weavers", acrobats, dancers', and in Bihar, they could be 'divided into four broad occupational categories', one of which is 'musicians, mendicants, and tailors' (1986: 120). Brown's study of music in the Mughal court lists female *Doms* or *Dominis* as principally performing for women, i.e., not as erotic performance (2003: 156–157).
48. See for example the legislator Muthulakshmi Reddy's books (1930: 1928–1931). See also *The Wrongs of Indian Womanhood* (1900) by Mrs Fuller, the wife of an English missionary, who was a virulent critic of *nautches*, discussed by Sachdeva (2008: 321–331). See Forbes (1996) for a study of the various movements of reform and mobilisation relating to women, and Gupta for details of wide-ranging pressure on women in the public sphere in the late colonial period (2001).
49. A pamphlet published in 1837 in Calcutta by the Baptist Mission Press is perhaps the earliest document of anti-*nautch* that has been found, see Williams (2012). The title is: 'An Exposition in English and Hindustani of the Evil Tendency of Naches, in corrupting the morals, and especially in supplying money for the further purchase of Innocent Female Children, for the wretched purpose of *Prostitution!* And an appeal to the respectable natives of India, and to all Christians by their influence and example to discountenance so great an evil' [emphasis in the original].
50. Srinivasan (1985: 1873) and Sachdeva (2008: 326).
51. Pivar (1981: 264) and Sachdeva (2008: 328) respectively.
52. Sachdeva (2008: 327).
53. Brown (2003: 118–176).
54. Srinivasan makes essentially this point in relation to *devadasis* when she states that '[the *devadasi*'s] strict professionalism made her an adjunct to conservative domestic society not its ravager' (1985: 1870).
55. See discussion in chapter one.
56. Bhaumik (2001: 86). I discuss the film industry in more detail in chapter four, in the context of the embourgeoisement of performing arts.
57. See Adarkar for commentary of reformers writing about Marathi (urban) theatre and female performers in the early twentieth century (1991). Bor also describes the decline

of courtesans and the sarangi players who taught and accompanied them amid the new climate of morality and reform (1986/7: 106–109).

58. Chatterjee (1993: 166–170).
59. Ibid. Premchand's novel *Sevasadan*, published in Hindi in 1918 and Urdu in 1924, follows a similar trajectory of misery and ruin of a courtesan, though also contains some highly critical views on marriage, see Dalmia (2005).
60. Bhaumik (2001: 66). Adarkar writes how, ironically, troupes of female entertainers themselves were performing Marathi plays on these subjects (1991).
61. Sachdeva (2008: 330–331).
62. See Erdman (1985: 106–112). Erdman reports the changing status and identity of *tawaif* from performer to prostitute in the Jaipur court during the first half of the twentieth century.
63. Srinivasan (1985). Nair describes how the bureaucracy of the princely state of Mysore effectively put a stop to *devadasi*s earlier with a Government Order in 1909 that disenfranchised them from their temple employment and undermined their rights to inherit property (1994). Other states in South India also legislated against *devadasi*s. See Soneji for a comprehensive history of this legislation (2012).
64. Post describes such strategies to raise the 'respectability' of professional female performers in the late nineteenth and early twentieth centuries (1987: 103–107).
65. Post (1987: 105–107) and Adarkar (1991: WS89–90).
66. Qureshi (2001).
67. This is discussed in more detail in the next chapter.
68. The title of Post's 1987 article.
69. Indeed, 'scientific' approaches involving categorisation are a core feature of modern knowledge in general, extending far beyond colonial times. See Bauman (1991) and Fisher (2009).
70. While *kothi* performers have generally been too taboo for any kind of public debate (but see Lahiri and Kar [2007], who outline *kothi* performers almost entirely in terms of 'exploitation' in the same way as female hereditary performers), their representation in literature shows a similar pattern. I discuss representations of *kothi*s in historical and contemporary literature in chapter three.
71. For example, Kersenboom-Story (1987), Meduri (1988), Anandi (1991), Nair (1994), Kannabiran (1995), Gaston (1996), Allen (1997) and Subramanian (1999a).
72. Weidman (2006) and Soneji (2012) respectively.
73. For example, Shankar (1990). The view of *devadasi*s as 'exploited' by Brahmins was also an important part of the non-Brahmin movement in South India. See Soneji (2012).
74. Oldenburg (1989[1984]; 1990), Bor (1986/7), Manuel (1987) and Post (1987). Van der Meer and Bor's Dutch publication *De Roep van de Kokila: Historische en Hedendaagse Aspecten van de Indiase Muziek* appears to constitute the first scholarly material on courtesans in a non-Indian language (1982: 34–60); Bor's chapter in Bor, Joep and Bruguière's French publication *Gloire des princes, louange des dieux: Patrimoine musical de l'Hindoustan du XIVe au XXe siècle* also includes descriptions of courtesans and *nautch* girls (2003: 135–141).

75. On *Thumri* see Manuel (1989) and Rao (1999 [1990]); on *tabla* see Kippen (1988), and on *sarangi* see Qureshi (1997). See also Erdmann's studies of court musicians (1978; 1985).
76. For example Neville (1996), Maciszewski (1998; 2001a; 2001b; 2006; 2007); Qureshi (2001; 2002; 2006), Bhaumik (2001), Magriel (2001: 32–37), Saeed (2002), K. Brown/Schofield (2003; 2006; 2007a; 2007b; forthcoming), Walker (2004), L. Brown (2006) and du Perron (2007). Publications by Bor (2007; 2011; forthcoming) and Bor and Leucci (forthcoming) focus on *devadasis* and courtesans through the eyes of Europeans.
77. See Walker's critical review of the literature on *kathak* (2004: 22–44) and Sachdeva's review of literature on *tawaif* (2008: 15–24). Walker explores the involvement of courtesans in *kathak* history, and how they have been written out of it (2004: 163–194).
78. Macisewski (1998; 2001a; 2001b; 2006; 2007).
79. Oldenburg (1989) and Qureshi (2006).
80. Saeed (2002) and L. Brown (2006).
81. Adarkar's work on women in Marathi theatre (1991) and Rege's work on *Lavani* performers from the *Kolhati* community (1995; 2002) are particularly important. Gargi (1966) and Hollander (2007:75–110) also include information on contemporary *Kolhati* performers in their studies of *Tamasha*. Hansen's study of *Nautanki* raises the question of female performers in terms particularly of reputation, but does not extend to a sociological study (1992: 16–23, 41, 252–258). The relative availability of information on female performers in work on *Tamasha* is related to the fact that *Lavani* is unique amongst erotic performance traditions in receiving support and legitimacy from the (Maharashtra) government, as I discuss in chapter two. Female performers are routinely mentioned in work on *Tamasha*, and their unique lifestyle may also be discussed. A rich literature on *Lavani* and *Tamasha* exists in Marathi. See Rege (1995) for a bibliography of Marathi sources.
82. Bhaumik (2001).
83. Soneji (2012).
84. *Lavani* and *Tamasha* are exceptions to this, as I discuss in chapter two.
85. Saeed's study clearly illustrates problems she faced, as a Pakistani researcher, in working with *tawaif* in Lahore (2002: 13–22). Doubleday faced similar difficulties from 'respectable' friends as she got more involved with and started performing with public female performers in Afghanistan (1988: 194–197).
86. I am grateful to Katherine Schofield for this point (personal communication, 2008). Sociological work on male artistes is also difficult since, as scholarship shows, even now high-caste or high-status performers can be traced back historically to low-caste/low-status groups. Brown's work on the Mughal court of Aurangzeb finds all professional male musicians to be low status, although they were high 'prestige' (2003: 118–176). Walker's work on the *Kathaks* finds tracing a Brahmin lineage and indeed a dance form named 'kathak' problematic (2004). The de-emphasis of sociological research is also due to the heavy emphasis on the Indian classical traditions as high art, which has led to a preponderance on their musical features. The first book-length sociological study of Hindustani classical music was published by Neuman in 1980 (reprinted 1990).

87. Qureshi (2001).
88. Mehrotra (2006).
89. Kidwai (2003: 18–69, particularly 29–30).
90. George (2004: 77–98) and Desai (2007: 8–26) respectively.
91. Mansingh and Pasricha (2007: 21–38, 51–62).
92. Prakash (2007: 76–79).
93. Ibid.: 83–88.
94. See Pinto on vamps in Hindi films, in particular 'Good girls, bad girls' (2006: 85–101) and 'She was dying to become a good girl' (2006: 119–132). See also Kasbekar's examination of how Hindi cinema deals with the conflicting desire to have erotic female performance, yet protect the 'good name' of the heroine, and also save viewers from feeling uncomfortable as voyeurs (2000).
95. Bhattacharji (1987), Banerjee (1998), and Sleightholme and Sinha (1996).
96. Forbes (2004: 157–188).
97. Cox's work studies a hereditary community of performers/prostitutes in Nepal, published significantly before similar work on such communities in India (1990, later printed as a book in 2006 [1993]). Agrawal's work on the *Bedia* constitutes the most detailed study of a hereditary performing/prostitute community available (2006; 2008). Swarankar's work (no date) and O'Neill et al (2004) also present unique, ethnographically-grounded information on *Nat*. Sharma's Hindi book on sex workers also provides information on various (ex-) performing communities (2001: 6–50). Information can also be gleaned on what appear to be hereditary performers now doing mostly sex work in Desai's essay in AIDS sutra (2008). Information on erotic female (ex- or current) performers as sex workers can also be found in development reports produced by a number of government agencies, such as Sen and Nair (2004).
98. Maciszewski (2001a; 2001b; 2006; 2007), Saeed (2002), Qureshi (2006), Brown (2006) and Mehrotra (2006).
99. Kothari (2005b).
100. Theories of 'modernisation' built on evolutionary schema are critiqued by Frank (1966), Bernstein (1971), Peet and Hartwick (1999: 103–140) and Harriss (2005). Post-development represented a radical movement against the enlightenment ideological basis of development, and in places called for an abandoning of it altogether, see Escobar (1995) and Sachs (ed.) (2010). Postcolonial and Marxist critiques of development also address these issues, for example Sylvester (1997), Gupta (1998), Radcliffe (2005), Radcliffe and Laurie (2006), Kothari (2005a; 2005b; 2005c) and Duffield and Hewitt (eds) (2009). Kothari (2005a; 2005b; 2005c) and Duffield and Hewitt (eds) (2009) in particular have highlighted the continuities of colonialism and empire in development.
101. Agrawal (2008: 23, 26).
102. Ibid.: 10.
103. Ibid.: 10.
104. Ibid.: 7.
105. The distinction is made clearly by *Nat* I interviewed, as described in chapter two.
106. Agrawal (2008: 66–75).

107. Ibid.: 8.
108. Qureshi (2006: 313, 326–7).
109. Srinivasan (1984).
110. Qureshi (2006).
111. Mehrotra (2006).
112. Saeed's and Brown's studies of the *Kanjar* dancing girls in Lahore are similar in revealing the differences that are involved with loss of status and livelihood of dancing and increasing reliance on sexual transaction (2002; 2006), as does work on *Deredar* courtesans by Maciszewski (2001a; 2006; 2007) and Qureshi (2006).
113. O'Neil et al. (2004) and Swarankar (no date).
114. For example Srinivasan (1985) and Nair (1994). The only source they cite on courtesans is Oldenburg (1989), with publications such as those by Maciszewski perhaps not sufficiently well known at the time of publication of the article.
115. Cox's publications on the *Badi* in Nepal are similar (1990; 2006). They discuss the *Badi* under a rubric of prostitution, though also mention that they perform. The works include rare detail of religion and customs published as early as 1990, yet no analysis of the balance of, or relationship between, performing and prostitution. The report of the National Commission for Denotified, Nomadic and Semi-nomadic Tribes by the Government of India (30 June 2008: 98–204) is similar, but provides far less specific information on groups of female entertainers, making only generalised and overarching comments about 'gender issues' such as 'exploitation'. It also states that these groups have become involved in prostitution due to generalised loss of livelihood, without entering into the history of stigmatisation and exclusion from culture through social campaigns. The report strongly refutes the idea of 'traditional sex work', stating recourse to sex work has been a result only of loss of livelihood. Thus, like Agrawal's study, it also misses the point that these groups had traditional structures whereby performing women did not marry, that this was not 'prostitution' in terms of sexual transaction; however, as the groups lost livelihood and status as performers, these stable structures of concubinage snowballed into transactional sex.
116. Sen and Nair (2004).
117. Ibid.:194–202.
118. Ibid.: 195.
119. For example Srinivasan (1984; 1985) and Nair (1994).
120. Nair (1994: 3165).
121. Shankar (1990).
122. This myth, along with the one that Aurangzeb 'banned' music, has been clearly disproved in Brown's work, which demonstrates, from a study of Persian sources, that though Aurangzeb himself withdrew from music, music and courtesans flourished in his court (2003). Shankar also describes women as 'the weaker sex' in the introduction to the book (1990: 2).
123. Shankar (1990: 42), quoted in Sen and Nair (2004: 197).
124. The report also confuses (middle or upper caste) *devadasis* with girls dedicated to the goddess Yellama—*jogtis*—who are low caste. Soneji's book clarifies this distinction (2012).

125. Sen and Nair (2004:198).
126. Ignatieff terms human rights as 'moral trump cards' (2001: 21).
127. Bhaumik reports that the Bombay Police Act was amended in 1923 to 'crack down on brothels' under pressure from reformers attempting to 'clean up' the culture of courtesans and actresses (2001: 85). Oldenburg states that the government abolished *zamindari* rights in 1957 and 'declared existing salons illegal' (1989: 137). I do not have further information on these two developments and the specific legalities involved, but in present day India, *kotha*s and *mujra* are not illegal per se.
128. Human Rights Watch (1995:77).
129. Ibid.: 77, n. 16.
130. Ibid.: 72.
131. See also Sen and Nair for an overview of national, regional and international laws relating to trafficking (2004: 232–246).
132. Human Rights Watch (1995: 72–73).
133. The same has been the case with the commencement of sexual relations in marriage in much of India before modern reforms.
134. Gargi (1966: 46).
135. Varsha Kale, personal communication, August 2011.
136. The IPC is available online at www.indiankanoon.org, last accessed 23 July 2010.
137. Bhatia (2004: 19–20, 48–49, 89).
138. Mazzarella (forthcoming).
139. Qureshi reports a 'campaign' launched in 1952 and the closing down of salons in 1958 (2001: 98–111), and Nagar writes of the raids on courtesans in Lucknow in 1958 (1979: 64–69). However, there are no details of the nature of the campaign or legal process.
140. The government of Maharashtra initially tried to ban dancing in dance bars only outside of Bombay, but this was unsuccessful. The government then went ahead with a ban across the state as a whole. In the bar girls case, there has been vigorous opposition to the ban, which was apparently lacking in the late 1950s. The legal aspects of stopping, if not banning, the long-standing and culturally and historically important centres of *mujra* in North Indian cities requires further investigation.
141. Personal communication, Varsha Kale, July 2010 and August 2011.
142. Mazzarella (forthcoming).
143. Mazzarella discusses this tactic in the bar girls case (Ibid). For prosecution under the obscenity laws, 'annoyance' has to have taken place in a 'public place', which becomes complex in the case of bars or cabaret clubs for example, and obscenity charges are difficult to successfully apply (Ibid).
144. See also Gupta's study of the restriction of a variety of lower class / lower culture or more 'vernacular' phenomena on the grounds of obscenity in colonial India, including 'obscene' songs (2001); and Seizer on Special Drama from Tamil Nadu (2005: 62–82).
145. Agnes discusses this (2007: 162–163); non-genuine complainants are also mentioned in the judgement on the appeal in the High Court against the ban (*Indian Hotel and Restaurants Association (AHAR) and others v. State of Maharashtra and others*, 2006).

146. See Agnes on the licensing of Mumbai dance bars (2005; 2007).
147. Liquor cannot be sold to guests, but it would be possible to have an amount reasonable for domestic use in the fridge, for example. A temporary liquor license could be obtained, but it would involve a lot of work (personal communication, Varsha Kale, August 2011).
148. Personal communication, Varsha Kale, July 2010 and August 2011.
149. These licenses may be owned by women who are engaged in prostitution and little or no performing. However, they illustrate in themselves that these communities used to be entertainers.
150. Personal communication, Varsha Kale, July 2010 and August 2011.
151. Agrawa (2008: 227), emphasis in original.
152. Rege, 1995, p. 2002.
153. Mehrotra (2006: 220–232).
154. See Maciszewski (2006; 2007).
155. The use of increased taxation was also used by the State of Maharashtra to put pressure on dance bars a few years prior to the ban, see Agnes (2005).
156. Ibid.: 229–230.
157. Butler (2000: 23).
158. See 'Colonial and postcolonial modernities, inclusion/exclusion, and performing arts' in the introduction to this volume for a fuller discussion of these issues.

2. FEMALE HEREDITARY PERFORMERS IN POST-INDEPENDENCE INDIA: COMMUNITIES, HISTORIES AND LIVELIHOODS

1. *Nachni*, described by Carol Babiracki, have some significant sociological differences setting them apart from the groups I describe here. They do not appear to be hereditary, but are closely linked to *Bhakti*, taking on the role of female consort to Krishna. However, they do exist outside of marriage (2003). There are also women who perform as a part of husband–wife teams who are not erotic performers, at least some of whom are connected to the groups I describe here.
2. Agrawal (2008: 144).
3. Ibid.
4. Ibid.: 146, 153.
5. See the entire chapter on the marriage economy (Ibid.: 141–185), but in particular (Ibid.: 144–153).
6. Ibid.: 145
7. Crooke briefly discusses the language of *Nat*s (1896, vol. III: 76). Cox discusses the *Badi* 'argot' (1990: 170) and (2006 [1993]: 17). In her study of itinerant singers in the Bhojpuri region, Servan-Schreiber mentions 'mobile castes of bards, who were reputed to use a "secret" language for internal communication …' (2003: 281). These bards consist of male musicians or husband–wife teams. Agrawal briefly discusses this language in her study of the *Bedia* and states its commonality across *Bhatu* groups (2008: 146). Secret languages of marginal groups is also in evidence with *hijra*s and *kothi*s. See Nagar (2008).

8. However, taking this as evidence of common group *origin* is potentially problematic. The paradigm of the female erotic performer, living outside of marriage, can be traced back much further than any available evidence of these groups. It can be seen in many ways as being fundamentally linked to South Asian patriarchy, as I discuss in the introduction to this book. It is therefore possible that new communities whose women, for whatever reason, started to perform, also followed this sociological deep structure. As I discuss later in this chapter, there is evidence of much change among *Bhatu* groups in terms of whether their women did or did not perform.
9. This is described by L. Brown in her study of *Kanjar* dancing girls in Lahore (2006: 226–236). See Agrawal also for a detailed description of *nath utarna* amongst the *Bedia* (2008: 49–55). Sachdeva mentions the concretisation of rituals of *nath utarna* amongst these communities in the late nineteenth century, resulting from the increasingly rigid categorisation and definition of female performers by colonial ethnographies and censuses (2008: 314–319). Shankar also outlines colonial sources on *devadasis* and dancing girls including rites of dedication and sexual initiation (1990: 36–64). I describe relationships with patrons/clients in the context of certain performing groups later in the chapter. See Saeed (2002), Mehrotra (2006), Brown (2006), and Agrawal (2008) for ethnographic work describing changing patterns of relationships of female performers with patrons/audiences.
10. Agrawal's research shows *Bhatu* to be a broad category of formerly nomadic tribes that encompasses many occupations. However, I have heard that the term *Bhatu* itself denotes the particular groups whose females perform, now do sex work, and do not marry. *Bazigar* girls were also found performing in bars and are included slightly tentatively in the list. *Bazigar* are not known as a group whose women perform or do sex work, and it appears it may only be a particular subgroup who were, or are, an exception. They may or may not identify as *Bhatu*. The situation with *Bhat*, who are known more as genealogists and whose women do not perform, is similar, in that it is a particular subgroup of *Bhat* in which women perform. Some of these distinctions can be seen in terms of social mobility driven by occupation, as I explore later in this chapter.
11. It is to be noted that *Deredar* are not listed in these sources. Sachdeva interprets the specific category '*Deredar tawaif*' as emerging from an attempt by high status *tawaif* in certain cities in North India to distinguish themselves from the wider communities of dancing girls and prostitutes, which the 1891 census had linked them to (2008: 314–321). Contemporary *Deredar* state that they are the same as *Gandharva*, except that they are Muslim whereas *Gandharva* are Hindu.
12. Carnegie (1868: 15–18).
13. Ibid.: 15.
14. Ibid.: 17–18.
15. Ibid.: 18.
16. Risley (1891: 84).
17. Ibid.
18. Ibid.: 162.
19. Sherring (1874: 386–390).

20. Ibid.: 386.
21. Ibid.: 388.
22. Ibid.: 389.
23. Ibid.: 271–272.
24. Fiol (2010).
25. Cox (1990; 2006) and Shresthova (2008: 200–213).
26. Enthoven (1920: 328–9).
27. Ibid.: 330.
28. Ibid.: 331.
29. Ibid.: 227.
30. Crooke (1896, vol. I: 242).
31. Ibid.: 333.
32. Crooke (1896, vol. II: 136). I have not heard of *Habura* from sources related to the bar girls, which is not to say they are not involved in bar dancing. Agrawal mentions *Haburas* in her study on *Bedia* as a linked group (2008: 145, 148, 173).
33. Crooke (1896, vol. II: 137).
34. Crooke (1896, vol. III: 56–7). As stated earlier in this chapter, in contemporary India, Rajasthani *Nat* have said that *Kolhati* are *Nat*. *Dombaris*, if the same as *Dombari Kolhatis*, are distinguished from *Kolhatis* as not being *Bhatu*, and the women are able to marry after having given up dancing.
35. Ibid.: 57.
36. Ibid.: 59.
37. Ibid.: 59. *Saperu* are a performing group in Rajasthan in which the women perform. However, like *Teratali* and *Kalbelia*, they do not associate themselves as *Bhatu*, and claim their female performers to be 'respectable' (personal communication, Shyam Lacchiya, February 2010).
38. Crooke (1896, vol. III: 60–61).
39. Ibid.: 72. Cox also links Badi to *Nat* and other tribes in India (1990; 2006).
40. Agrawal uses the term 'indolent men' as characterising the *Bedia* (2008: 120–140); Mehrotra also describes the lack of work amongst men folk of the *Bedia* (2006: 35–50). See the description of *Nat* in Rajasthan below, which shows that male members of this community used to be engaged in various work for their patrons, including being musicians.
41. In her study of *kathak*, based on such colonial ethnographies, Walker notes that some female courtesans or nautch girls came from communities where men were also entertainers (2004: 166).
42. Saeed (2002: 54–66). Male musicians in the reformed classical performing arts establishment have dissociated themselves from previous links as teachers or accompanists to dancing girls, despite the fact that such links were effectively universal: dancing girls and courtesans were entirely mainstream prior to modern reforms, with no 'respectable' women performing.
43. Risley (1891: 130).
44. Sherring (1874: 388).

45. Ibid.: 274.
46. Ibid.: 275.
47. Ibid.: 379, 383.
48. 1873–94: 271, quoted in Brown (2003: 152).
49. Brown (2003: 152). *Nat* are also listed as musicians in the *Ain-i-Akbari* (a list is reproduced in Neuman, Chaudhuri and Kothari (2006: 270) as are *Bajigar* (*Bazigar*), *Bahrupi, Bhagtaiya*, and *Hurkiya*, which are connected to contemporary female performer *Bhatu* groups in colonial ethnographies.
50. Servan-Schreiber (2003: 290–293).
51. Carnegie (1868: 15–18).
52. Personal communication, Varsha Kale and Shyam Lacchiya, February 2010.
53. Brown (2003: 150).
54. Ibid.:150, 156–159. She mentions the *Dhadhis* as possibly linked or equivalent to the *Domnis*, as also involved in public auspicious singing at weddings as well as performing for the *harim*. Male *Dhadhis* were musicians and soloists in the Mughal time (Ibid.:153–168), and have been linked to today's *Mirasis*, see Neuman (1990: 129–133)—Neuman spells the name *Dhari*. Although *Mirasi* women are said not to perform in front of men, Neuman mentions sources that cite the contrary (Ibid.: 130).
55. Sherring (1874: 387).
56. Ibid.: 130.
57. Ibid.: 389.
58. Crooke (1896, vol. III: 56–80).
59. Crooke (1896, vol. I: 243).
60. Ibid.: 296.
61. Agrawal (2008: 26–29).
62. Enthoven (1920: 200).
63. See Neuman for a sociological analysis of *Kalawant*, and other male musicians of the classical world (1980).
64. Brown (2003: 152). Neuman also suggests *Kalawant* are linked to *Dhadhi* (*Dhari*) (1990: 129–133), who in turn are linked to *Dom(ni)*, whose women did become courtesans in the eighteenth century, as stated earlier in this chapter.
65. Crooke (1896, vol. III: 364–371).
66. Brown (2003: 152).
67. Crooke (1896, vol III: 365).
68. More detail on *Nat* later in this chapter, Agrawal on *Bedia* (2008), Saeed (2002) and Brown (2006) on *Kanjar*, and Rege (1995) on *Kolhati*.
69. This is supported by Sachdeva's observations of the self-defining of *Deredar tawaif*. Erdman's study of performers in the Jaipur court also shows certain *tawaif* or *baiji* negotiating a superior status for themselves which meant they did not have to perform in events for the general public (1985: 97–98).
70. Crooke (1896, vol. III: 56).
71. Other examples of groups that are probably primarily seen as occupational are *Kalawant*, which literally means 'artist' and *Kathak*, which literally means 'storyteller'. See

Walker's study of *kathak* for an exploration of communities of performers and matters of social mobility into the twentieth century, focusing on the *Kathak*s, but mentioning many other groups (2004).

72. See also Pinch on the purchase of slaves and communities of *tawaif* and ascetics (2004).
73. See also Fiol (2010), Cox (1990; 2006) and Shresthova (2008: 200–213) on the *Badi* in India and Nepal and the processes of exclusion they have undergone. See also Babiracki (2003) on *Nachni*. This is not a hereditary/*Bhatu* group, but another configuration of erotic female performer suffering increasing marginalisation. Aside from *Badi* and the groups I discuss, I am not aware of substantial literature on any other erotic/public female performer *Bhatu* groups, for example *Garara*, *Chari*, *Gwar*. Research on these groups is still in a very early stage relative to the scale of phenomena they represent.
74. It is important to note that, during the second half of the twentieth century, hereditary performers have also been displaced by mediated music and DJs. However, the fact that they continue to be seen as 'prostitutes' or social 'problems' rather than performers and have suffered intense socio-economic marginalisation is itself a significant reason why they have not been able to take advantage of electronic media. The control of media production by upper caste, middle class individuals and the exploitative use of the labour of traditional performing communities has been described by Rege (1995), and more recently, Babiracki (2009) and Fiol (2010). Bhaumik's account of the embourgeoisement of the film industry in the 20s and 30s shows a similar pattern (2001).
75. Exceptions to this are in the Gulf and in the Mumbai dance bars from the 1980s to 2005.
76. Hansen also mentions *Nat* and *Bedia* (*berin* or *natin*) as performers of *Nautanki* in her study of this theatrical tradition, but does not focus further on these groups (1992: 41).
77. Neuman, Chaudhuri and Kothari list *Nat* only as acrobats who are genealogists to the Meghwal (2006: 313). This may be due to regional variation, as their study is on western Rajasthan.
78. Agrawal (2008). I do not know if there are any communities still involved in performing in these states.
79. See introduction.
80. I discuss the matter of *mujra* being 'banned' or restricted in city centres in chapter one.
81. The recent history of *Nat* in Rajasthan can also be compared to other groups—*Teratali*, *Kalbelia*, and *Saperu*—whose women still perform, see Neuman, Chaudhuri and Kothari (2006). These groups are said not to be *Bhatu*, and not to follow the system where girls who dance do not marry. Now at least they are seen in reasonably respectable terms as 'folk' singers/dancers, performing for tourists and also local people in weddings and other functions. However, one member of the *Nat* community said *Kalbelia* were *Bhatu* (he did not know about *Teratali* and *Saperu*) and did follow the same system of non-marrying females, but disguise the fact and are negotiating a mainstream identity. He said that these groups used to be lower status performers than the *Nat*. However, they did not suffer the drastic loss in patronage and livelihood with the abolition of princely courts and have been able to continue performing, similarly to the Sultanpur *Nat*s, but possibly with a more robust socio-cultural space.

82. Mehrotra (2006).
83. See Agrawal (2008) and Sharma (2001). Agrawal traces back community-based sex work in the *Bedia* she studied by only a few generations. The analysis is somewhat confused by the conflation of brothel-based sex work with singing and dancing and concubinage with upper caste men, as I discuss in chapter one. However, Agrawal's evidence shows that almost all of the third generation women of the community she studied had been involved in brothel-based prostitution, whereas half of the second generation had moved elsewhere, implying they did not stay with the natal community and do sex work. Women in the first generation of settlers had stayed in the community engaged in singing, dancing and concubinage (2008: 19–29). Hence, it seems that this *Bedia* community have not followed such a clear-cut transition of performers to sex workers as the Rajasthani *Nat*, i.e., previously some but not all women performed, whereas now all daughters born to the community do sex work.
84. Mehrotra (2006). Gargi also mentions an increasing eroticisation of *Nautanki* in this period (1966: 46).
85. Kotiswaran (2008: 591).
86. Anand Sharma, interview, 18 December 2007.
87. Ibid.
88. Interview, 3 May 2007. The institution of PITA to deal with trafficking or prostitution, as opposed to SITA, is very likely a factor, as I discuss in chapter one.
89. Anand Sharma, interview, 18 December 2007.
90. Saeed (2002) and Brown (2006).
91. As stated earlier in this chapter, Mughal sources list *Kanjari* or *Kanchan/Kanchani* as prestigious courtesans.
92. Neuman, Chaudhuri and Kothari (2006: 307–308, 313).
93. Shyam Lacchiya, interview, 2 February 2010.
94. This information is derived from interviews with two groups of *Kolhati* performers on two different occasions; an interview with *Tamasha* theatre owners; and an interview with Dr Khan, a health worker from an NGO in Pune, as well as more informal conversations and published material.
95. *Dombari Kolhati* also perform *Lavani* and *Tamasha*. They are not *Bhatu*, and can marry after a dancing career.
96. Rege (1995).
97. Ibid.: 31.
98. For example, in propaganda and educational campaigns pre- and post-independence, see Abrams (1975). The eroticism of *Lavani* and *Tamasha* has also been supported against allegations of 'vulgarity' and attempts at 'purification' through a discourse of an anti-Brahmin, vernacular, 'common man' 'Maharashtrian culture', see Hollander (2007: 107–110). Hollander gives an image of *Tamasha* and *Lavani* as still very much a thriving and living culture and an important part of theatre in South Asia.
99. Rege (1995). Processes of exclusion of *Kolhati* women from *Lavani* in Marathi films are marked.
100. See chapter six for a description of *Nautanki* and 'shows' in Uttar Pradesh in the context of *kothi* performers.

101. Mehrotra (2006: 220–232). Interest from the mainstream grew in regional and traditional theatres from the 1960s and elite, urban theatre forms started to borrow from the traditional forms, as Hansen describes (1983). However, this did not translate into practical support.
102. I have heard that there are *Kolhati* women involved in sex work from their villages, but do not know any details about this system, how widespread it is, how long it has been going on for, or if it involves *Lavani* performers.
103. Mehrotra (2006).
104. *Tamasha* parties are owned by *Kolhati* women, in the same way that *Nautanki* troupes were run by female performers, as Mehrotra describes (2006: 173–180), and *kotha*s were run by *tawaif*.
105. According to Agrawal, *Bedia* use this word to describe all outsiders from their community, *Bedia* or *Bhatu* (2008: 145).
106. See also Rege's description of the labour of *Kolhati* women (1995: 32–35).
107. This system was explained to me by a group of *Kolhati* performers in a village in Maharashtra.
108. Rege (1995: 34).
109. Interview, Dr Khan, JPSDP, Pune, 16 January 2010.
110. I was told a story of a man who fell for a *Kolhati* woman, and who eventually arranged and paid to have sex with her as her first sexual partner. Some months later, the woman, now pregnant, appeared with other members of the group and he was told he was obliged to keep her. Although he had thought of the deal in more recreational terms, he was forced to take some responsibility for the woman and child (personal communication, Varsha Kale, January 2010).
111. Rege (1995: 36).
112. See Sachdeva (2008: 314–321).
113. Qureshi (2001: 111). See Nagar for an account of raids on Lucknow salons in 1958 based on interviews with courtesans (1979: 64–69). As stated in chapter three, I cannot confirm how these salons were closed down legally, as *mujra* per se is not illegal, but it was quite likely with anti-nuisance laws.
114. Maciszewski (2001a; 2001b; 2006; 2007).
115. See chapter one.
116. See L. Brown on *Kanjar* dancing girls from Lahore going to the Gulf (2006: 198–200, 226–238, 260, 271–272).
117. Varsha Kale, personal communication, February 2007.
118. See http://www.guriaindia.org/, last accessed 7 July 2011. *Tawaifs* are referred to as 'women in prostitution' by Guria, the problematic nature of which Maciszewski points out in her articles (2006: 333).
119. Another *Bhatu* group in Gujarat has managed to support itself and change its image through a form of artistic rehabilitation. They have started a theatre group and present themselves as thus carrying out their traditional 'caste' occupation of performing arts. They do not mention that they were traditionally a group where the women were erotic performers, or that most of the girls and young women of the community had

been dancing in Bombay's dance bars. In this way, they are achieving promising mobility from stigmatised to socially acceptable performers.

120. Interviews, Balkrishna Sidram Renke, and others, National Commission for Denotified, Nomadic and Semi-Nomadic Tribes, Delhi, 27 March 2007. In a later conversation with Meena Radhakrishnan, head of Research in the Commission, she stated that she was aware that the dance bar ban had left the bar girls worse off and increasingly involved in prostitution (Delhi, 6 December 2007). 'Gender issues' in the report of the National Commission for Denotified, Nomadic and Semi-nomadic Tribes are only discussed in the most general of terms, and bar dancing is clearly identified as something that leads to 'exploitation' (Ministry of Social Justice and Empowerment, Government of India, 30 June 2008, pp. 98–104).

3. TRANSGENDER EROTIC PERFORMERS IN SOUTH ASIA

1. They are also known as *zankhal/jankha*, and *zananal/janana* and there are other terms in other areas (for example, in Nepal they are known as *Metti*). I emphasise that not all female impersonators in Indian performing arts are *kothi*s. Indeed, there are hereditary traditions where young boys perform as females, and hence statistically, only a minority would be likely to be *kothi*. Pani describes in overview a range of theatrical traditions across India in which female impersonators have existed (1977).
2. Cohen claims *kothi*s to be a recent identity, dating from the work of Khan in particular, which refused the importation of western categories of 'homosexuality' (2005). See Nagar's critique of Cohen's conclusions, based on her ethnography of *kothi* language in Lucknow, and interviews with elder *kothi*s (2008: 126). I also interviewed elder *kothi*s in Lucknow, and they said the word was used in their youth. I use the term *kothi* for feminine males, since it is current in the areas in which I was doing fieldwork. I also use the term 'transgender' to describe *kothi*s in their mixing and crossing of male-female boundaries. I use the term MSM more generally for 'men/males who have sex with men/males', which includes *kothi*s, the partners of *kothi*s, *hijra*s and gay men. The term MSM emerged as a response to the inappropriateness of western categories such as 'homosexual' or 'gay' in South Asia. See Khan (1995; 1998; 2001), Seabrook (1999) and Katyal (2002).
3. Hansen (2002). It is sometimes claimed that female impersonators existed only because it was not possible to find female performers, a view that does not stand up to scrutiny for many reasons, not least because female courtesan performers were readily available, see Hansen (2002: 167–169). Kapur also explores questions of desire and the female impersonator in Parsee theatre (2003).
4. Details including the Delhi High Court ruling are available on Naz India's website, http://www.nazindia.org/advocacy.htm, last accessed 31 August 2011.
5. I discuss the implications of these changes in chapter six.
6. A vast source includes publications, reports and websites of the various NGOs and CBOs that work with transgenders, such as Naz, Naz Foundation International (NFI) and Humsafar. NFI in particular has an online knowledge centre with extensive material on MSMs including *kothi*s, and its own publication *Pukaar*, with a range of articles on MSMs in

India and South Asia (http://www.nfi.net, last accessed 1 May 2011). In the mainstream and academic press, growing publications on *kothi*s, male prostitutes and MSMs include Biswas (1997), Seabrook (1999), Khan (2001), Cohen (2005) Kavi (2007), Menon (2007), Shanghvi (2008), and Faleiro (2008).

7. Nagar's study examines processes of identity and community construction through language and is the first book-length, ethnographic study of *kothi*s (2008). Shah and Bandopadhyah's photographically illustrated book incorporates rich representations of *kothi*s and their lives within its focus on the problems they face (2007). Important ethnographically-grounded information on *kothi*s or *zananas* is also to be found in studies of *hijra*s, see Nanda (1999: 11, 14, 54) and Reddy (2005: 15–16, 59–67).
8. Lahiri and Kar (2007) is something of an exception. However, this report understands performing only in terms of exploitation and problems, and contains no broader or sympathetic view of this culture. Thus it follows approaches to female performers such as anti-*nautch* and the dance bar ban campaign of Mumbai in certain fundamental aspects. Reddy also briefly outlines *kothis* as performers (2005: 61–63).
9. See the discussion in chapter one.
10. Hansen's work on the female impersonators of the Parsee, Marathi and Gujarati stage of the late nineteenth and early twentieth century has been the first in modern scholarship to explore issues of homoeroticism in Indian performing arts (1998; 2002). Kapur's work also touches on these issues, but more tangentially (2003). Earlier studies of female impersonators or these theatrical traditions did not breach these issues, for example Adarkar (1991), Pani (1977), Gargi (1966). Walker's study of *kathak* includes a survey of dance and male performers in literature up until the twentieth century, and contains some references to cross-dressed or sexualised male performers (2004: 22–98), including some of those discussed in this chapter (Ibid.: 62–63, 77, 94). Brown's studies, which discuss erotic male performers in Mughal India, are the only ones that explore questions of gender, sexuality and eroticism in the context of male performers (2003: 118–176; 2006; 2007b). However, the present of (non-*hijra*) transgenders and MSMs as performers has been virtually non-existent in scholarship on performing arts, though limited information can be found in L. Brown's study of dancing girls in Lahore (2006), Nagar's study of *kothi*s (2008) (although this study tends to term *kothi*s who are performers as 'sex workers') and studies on *hijra*s, see Nanda (1999) and Reddy (2005). Ugra's 1960 autobiography provides an important and unique source on male *Ramlila* performers and love and sex from his own experiences (2007: 61–68). Prakash's work is groundbreaking in terms of its exploration of an aesthetic of obscenity in the *launda nach* (boys performing as girls) *Bidesia* dance-drama tradition, although it does not explore issues of sexuality and gender directly (2011).
11. Nanda (1999) and Reddy (2005).
12. This is a common combination in traditional performers.
13. The birth of male children is celebrated with songs sung by women as well as the singing and dancing of *hijra*s. The celebration of a female child has no such ritual celebration.
14. Rahul, interview, 13 October 2008.
15. See Nanda's account of the emasculation ritual and its meanings in *hijra* culture (1999: 24–37).

16. In Eastern Uttar Pradesh and Lucknow, where I did much of my fieldwork, they are known as *chibri* (adjective), or as *chibra* (noun, so 'a *chibra*').
17. *Kothis* may be seen as 'fake' *hijras* or 'not yet' *hijras* by *hijras* themselves and in research on *hijras*. See Nagar for a critique of such ideas (2008: 81–86). Throughout the study she explores links between *kothis* and *hijras* and the relationship of the two communities.
18. See also Nagar (2008) on the construction of *kothi* identity and community, in particular through linguistic practices.
19. Vanita (2000: 27).
20. Ibid.
21. Kugle (2000: 137), translation of *Mir'at al-Asrar*.
22. Krishna devotional cults also involve devotees taking the position of Krishna's mother, Yashoda.
23. Kidwai (2000: 117).
24. Vanita and Kidwai (2000: 220–228).
25. Saleem Kidwai, personal communication, October 2008.
26. Kidwai (2000: 175).
27. Ibid.: 124.
28. Ibid.: 176.
29. Ibid.: 180–183.
30. Indeed, their behaviour adapts radically to norms of maleness outside of the spaces in which they can be female/feminine. I explore contemporary *kothi* performing culture in chapter six.
31. Sharar (1994: 142–3), quoted in Brown (2003: 147).
32. Burton, *Scinde* (1851, vol. II: 247), quoted from Dyson (1978: 355) in Walker (2004; 77).
33. Broughton, 1813, quoted in Walker (2004: 118). The possible links between today's *Kathaks* and Hindu dancing boys or other kinds or communities of performers is explored in Walker's thesis. I explore contemporary *kothis* in terms of their social organisation as performers in chapter six. A link with *Kathaks* or other hereditary groups does not seem compelling based on contemporary evidence, since *kothis* are non-hereditary performers.
34. This image of *hijras* implies they were providing non-ritual entertainment, which is no longer their official role. There may be confusion in the use of the word *hijra* or a change in the role of *hijras* in today's India compared to in the context of courts, where they had important roles to play and held powerful positions.
35. Kidwai (2003:75).
36. Butler (2004: 187).
37. Ibid.: 10.
38. Desmond (1999: xiv).
39. See also Kapur's study of the female impersonator of Parsee Theatre, which looks at the art of gender, performance, desire and ambiguity (2003). These stars have never been publicly discussed as anything but consummate artistes and imitators, rather than the *kothis* I write about who were open about their gender/sexual orientation.

40. *Kothis* can also be seen to embody the iconically feminine voices of the famous playback singers as they perform and lip-sync to film songs nowadays, as do the original film stars themselves. See Majumdar on the voice and embodiment in film songs (2001). Before the wide availability of recorded music, *kothis* used to also sing, some in falsetto.
41. Connell (2005 [1995]: 60).
42. Ibid.: 61.
43. Ibid.: 71.
44. Siddarth, interview, 12 October 2008.
45. Butler (1990: 183–193; and 1993: 223–242).
46. Butler (1990: 187).
47. Female hereditary performers, however, have also particularly suffered from a lack of access to gurus due to their stigmatisation—whereas *kothis* are generally self-taught, and performance is more spontaneous or less formally trained.
48. Simran, interview, 13 September 2008. There are also discourses of boys becoming *kothi* after being 'spoiled' through sexual penetration, often in the form of abuse by relatives of other men. These men may be seen as responsible for making them a *kothi*, for 'spoiling' them, see Seabrook (1999: 66) and Nagar (2008: 74–77).
49. Many *kothis* are also violent to their wives, seeing violence as a necessary part of being a man, which they must fulfil when married (Rahul, interview 13 October 2008).
50. Questions of male performers, femininity and (homo)sexuality are explored in Ramsay's classic investigation of 'the trouble with the male dancer' (2007 [1995]), and Fisher and Shay's edited collection of cross-cultural studies (2009). While I focus here on dance as feminising, particularly with a view of *kothi* performers, as both these books explore, gender is involved in very different and often ambiguous or shifting forms in the various traditions of male dance, including female impersonation.
51. Brown (2003: 141).
52. Ibid.: 144–145.
53. Brown (2003: 134). Doubleday, who lived in Afghanistan in the 1970s with her husband who was studying classical music, and herself joined a group of female performers, crossed lines of respectable society in many ways. She chose and was also advised to at least not dance within this female troupe, but only to sing, and thus put some limit on the transgression of codes of respectability that would also affect her husband's standing (2006 [1988]: 210).
54. Ashish, interview 2 December 2007.
55. Mulvey (1975: 11).
56. Qureshi (2006: 321–322). This intense eye contact is a form of erotic seduction but is also broader than that. It encourages some form of action on the part of the person watching, which may be in the form of subsequent romantic or sexual liaisons, but may also serve to encourage tipping or exclamations of appreciation. I have on a number of occasions seen female or *kothi* performers performing specifically to me in this manner, clearly without the intention of erotically seducing me, but more of showing me importance as a guest/friend or someone who has arranged the *mujra*, and making sure they gave me attention and ensured I enjoyed the performance.

57. See Brown (2003: 118–176) on Mughal India. See chapter five on bar girls, and chapter four on the embourgeoisement of performing arts in India, extending into the popular realm of Bollywood dance.
58. I explore this further in chapter six in terms of parallels of socio-cultural marginalisation in recent decades.
59. Brown (2003: 153).
60. Connell (2005 [1995]: 68).
61. I discuss erotic performers and processes of imitation and identification of films and real life in Morcom (2011). This example illustrates a more typical drag performance approach, and could be interpreted as reflecting male ideas of femininity and its imitation, see Case (1985), and also of artifice or the playing with (inadequate) gender categories, see Butler (1990: 183–193; and 1993: 223–242). However, given that as transgenders these performers have a direct stake in and identification with femininity, these kinds of analyses need to be nuanced, and generally, drag is not highly comparable to *kothi* performance.

4. THE BOLLYWOOD DANCE REVOLUTION AND THE EMBOURGEOISEMENT OF INDIAN PERFORMING ARTS

1. Also significant are urban theatre traditions, though many were superseded by the film industry or involved clean breaks with the past, as opposed to a transition from low status performers and feudal models to middle classes and bourgeois performance styles and aesthetics. I focus in this chapter on emblematic, pan-Indian traditions.
2. Bourdieu (1984).
3. See for example Radhakrishnan's work on the Silicon Valley/Bangalore circuit (2008).
4. See Dwyer on the post-liberalisation new middle classes and Hindi cinema (2000). On the process of Bollywoodisation, see Rajadhyaksha (2003), Prasad (2003) and Vasudevan (2011).
5. On *Bhangra*, see Banerji (1998); Bauman (1990); S. Sharma, J. Hutnyk and A. Sharma (eds) (1996); Dudrah (2002) and Leante (2009); on the growth of Bollywood dance in the UK, see David (2007). Girls in Indian communities were dancing to film songs in the UK from at least the 1970s.
6. Radhakrishnan (2008).
7. Studies that focus on this broad shift include Higgins (1976), Neuman (1990[1980]), Post (1987), Kippen (2005[1988]), Sundar (1995), Subramaniam (1999a; 2006), Qureshi (2002), Bakhle (2005) and Weidman (2006).
8. Hereditary Muslim male musicians have also been marginalised in many ways, but not excluded outright. See for example Kippen on the requirement of literacy for staff in teaching institutions (2005: 33–34). However, *sarangi* and *tabla* players have suffered particularly because they were seen to be closely associated with *tawaif*, see Kippen (2005: 24), Bor (1986/7), Qureshi (1997; 2002), and Magriel (2001: 32–37).
9. On the entry of middle classes and the exit of professional hereditary women, see Post (1987), Qureshi (2001; 2002; 2006) and Maciszewski (2001a; 2006; 2007).
10. Srinivasan (1984: 62; and 1985: 1875), Meduri (1988), Allen (1997: 63–64, 88) and

O'Shea (1998), describe this in the case of *Bharatanatyam*. See Rao (1999 [1990]) on *Thumri*, and also du Perron on the 'cleansing' of *Thumri* texts (2007: 27–63).

11. Post (1987).
12. Intense eye contact continues in the illicit world of erotic dance in India, including bar dancing and *mujra*; *kothis* also perform in this manner, as I describe in chapter three.
13. Post (1987) and Qureshi (2001).
14. Kippen (2005 [1988] 24–25) and Bakhle (2005).
15. The sense that classical performing arts were 'rescued' or 'revived' from a degraded past is still one that is widely accepted, and appears even in academic studies (see chapter one).
16. Chinchore (1990: 22), quoted in Bhaumik (2001: 164). Bhatkhande had, however, also approved ideas for schools to teach the daughters of professional female performers, though it would certainly be understood that these girls would not follow in a courtesan lifestyle, but be performers in the modern, bourgeois sense, see Chinchore (1990: 23).
17. Quoted in Luthra (1986), and Qureshi (2006: 312). This policy seems to have later changed, as *tawaif* have performed on AIR. See Maciszewski for biographies of a number of *tawaif* who performed on All India Radio (2001a). This article provides an excellent illustration of the exclusionary pressures *tawaif* were facing in even late twentieth-century India as compared to female artistes from middle class or elite backgrounds.
18. Bhaumik (2001: 7). Barnow and Krishnaswamy tell of how Phalke was unable to persuade even prostitutes to act in his first film (1961: 13–14). Phalke used boy actors for female roles, and later his own daughter. High status courtesans also shunned the cinema initially, see Bhaumik (2001: 73). See Bhaumik (2001) for a history of the first few decades of Bombay cinema, and Majumdar (2009) for a study of female stardom as it emerged from the 1930s-1950s.
19. The creation of reputable exhibition spaces has also been crucial to the embourgeoisement of the cinema, see Bhaumik (2001: 21–23, 92–95, 181–188).
20. See Bhaumik (2001: 84–110, 54–200) in particular. See Majumdar (2009), on female stars.
21. Bhaumik (2001: 85–89).
22. Ibid.: 83.
23. Ibid.: 89–92.
24. Ibid.: 86.
25. Ibid.: 88.
26. Ibid.: 104–5.
27. Ibid.: 146–147.
28. While women of hereditary performer lineages had largely disappeared from the national Hindi film industry by around independence, or had to conceal their family backgrounds and pretend to be middle class, in the case of regional industries, a considerable number of hereditary female performers are still involved, for example in Marathi films. However, in the case of Marathi films, and *lavani* too, *kolhati* women are being marginalised, see Rege (1995). *Deredar* and *Gandharva tawaif* also act in Bhojpuri films,

though I am not aware about the extent of their involvement, or if they are open about their backgrounds.

29. A new watershed was reached for girls from 'good' and elite families with the entry of Karisma Kapoor into a career of acting in 1991. Karisma is granddaughter of Raj Kapoor and great granddaughter of Prithviraj Kapoor, one of the early middle class actors of the film industry, see Bhaumik (2001: 127), and it had been widely thought that she would not be allowed to act.
30. Rachel Dwyer, personal communication, April 2010.
31. The status and reputation of the industry has also changed since the 1930s. For example, the 1930s and 1940s were a relatively high point while the 1970s, and in particular the 1980s, were low points. The history of female performers in the cinema industry is extremely complex and sources still limited; however, hereditary female performers became excluded by around independence.
32. Lataji's performance style is disembodied over and above the splitting of voice and body via playback technology, and the media have played further into this paradigm of disembodiment through the emphasis on her simplicity and her physical unattractiveness, see Majumdar (2001). Lataji is unmarried, and, dressing consistently in a white sari, presents herself as a form of celibate religious devotee, or *brahmacarini* (ibid)—a respectable traditional paradigm for a mature, unmarried woman, as opposed to a courtesan or *devadasi*. In counterpoint to her elder sister Lata, Asha Bhosle has become famous for singing for vamps (though she has also sung for many heroines); she also married and her overall image has been far more colourful. Generally, playback singers have followed at least a 'restrained' style. Since the late 1990s, there has been a rise in the number of singers who flaunt an attractive, sexy image.
33. See Bhaumik on the development of genres in the 1920s (2001: 58–67). See Vitali for a detailed study of the emergence of women in Hindi action cinema in the social and political context of 1920s and 1930s India, and indeed, their disappearance in later decades (2008: 56–118). See also Thomas and Gandhi on the famous (foreign) stunt heroine Fearless Nadia (1991).
34. Bhaumik (2001): 65–66, 88–89.
35. Ibid.: 163–169.
36. Quoted in Ibid: 168.
37. Ibid.: 162.
38. Pinto (2006: 85).
39. Ibid.: 85–101.
40. Kasbekar (2000).
41. Majumdar (2001).
42. Quoted in Morcom (2007: 194). The market for music and thus its commercial importance had also increased dramatically due to the advent of cassette technology, see Manuel (1993).
43. See Shresthova (2008: 27–34) for an introduction and overview of dance in Hindi movies from the 1950s. See Bhaumik (2001) for references to dance throughout the early period of Hindi cinema. See also Pinto (2006) for information on dance in the context of Helen, the famous Hindi film dancer and vamp.

44. Kasbekar (2000). However, the 'item song' exists as a means of inserting particularly sexy songs in the narrative, which go beyond the bounds of acceptability for most heroines in terms of their narrative context and level of erotic display.
45. Produced by BBC World Productions in India.
46. See Shresthova (2008: 22–27) on *Nachle Ve*.
47. Interview, Justine, 21 April 2006.
48. Ibid.
49. Ibid.
50. For example, the choreographer Ganesh Acharya has had a school in Mumbai for many years, catering for the film industry; the choreographer Saroj Khan had a school in Delhi from 1994–1995, as did the actress Padmini Kolhapuri.
51. Interviews, Shiamak Davar, 30 April 2006; Rajesh Mansukhani, SDIPA, 30 April 2006.
52. See Shresthova for a discussion of *Dil To Pagal Hai* and SDIPA (2008: 77–157). Shiamak has a family legacy in the film industry. His great-uncles were JBH Wadia and Homi Wadi, and his great-aunt was Fearless Nadia, the megastar of the 1930s and 1940s who had married Homi Wadia. However, he was not keen to work in films and had already been asked by Yash Chopra to choreograph *Dilwale Dulhania Le Jayenge*, which he refused. He had also received requests for choreography from Mani Ratnam, and from Shekhar Kapoor to act. Gauri, wife of *Dil To Pagal Hai*'s hero Shahrukh Khan, had been a student at SDIPA, and had persuaded Shiamak to discuss the question of choreographing *Dil To Pagal Hai* with Shahrukh Khan, who finally convinced him (Shiamak Davar, interview, 30 April 2006).
53. Shiamak Davar, interview, 30 April, 2006.
54. Interview, Rajesh Mansukhani, 30 April 2006.
55. Kalpana Bhushan, interview, 6 March 2006. This is also the case with classical dance.
56. See Shresthova (2008: 1–75), for an overview of film dance seen as a combination of narrational aspects, as well as more generic moves gathered from classical/folk/foreign sources. This parallels, unsurprisingly, the basic makeup of film song style, see Arnold (1991) and the balance of situational details and more audio-oriented details, see Morcom (2001; 2007: 25–136).
57. Shiamak Davar, interview, 30 April 2006. Interestingly, *seva* directly of the deity was part of the *devadasi*'s role. In fact, devotional Hinduism and Sufism have involved a central thread of erotic engagement and *seva* of deities, part of which has been music and dance. Here, the sense of *seva* is evoked without any romantic/erotic (*sringarik*) connotation, ironically core to devotional Hinduism and Sufism.
58. Interview, Anees, SDIPA, 30 April 2006.
59. Interview, 30 April 2006.
60. Shresthova (2008: 136).
61. Interview, Kainaaz Mistry, VAF, 8 May 2006.
62. Interview, Shiamak Davar, 30 April 2006.
63. Shresthova (2008: 77–157).
64. Interview, Gaggun Bedi, 26 April 2007.
65. Interview, 26 April 2007.

66. Interview, 26 April 2007.
67. Ibid.
68. Interview, 26 April 2007.
69. Interview, 26 April 2007.
70. Shresthova (2008: 112–113).
71. Ibid.
72. Interview, Anchal, 22 April 2006.
73. Interview, Justine, 21 April 2006.
74. Interview, Praveen Shandilya, 16 March 2006.
75. Interview, Anchal, 22 April 2006.
76. Shrestova (2008: 76).
77. A.R. Rahman composed the music for Bombay Dreams, which opened in London in 2002, with choreography by Farah Khan.
78. Interview, Gaysil, 17 April 2006.
79. Ibid; interview, Praveen Shandilya, 16 March 2006.
80. Interviews, Ganesh Hegde, 14 April 2006; Vivek, 23 April 2006.
81. Interview, Ganesh Hegde, 14 April 2006.
82. White girls (often from Russia) are paid considerably more than Indian dancers, which has been the cause of some resentment.
83. Interview, Gaysil, 17 April 2006.
84. Interview, Justine, 21 April 2006.
85. Although the diaspora has been crucial in making the Bollywood dance craze what it is, just being a dancer/performer/teacher of Bollywood dance (let alone an extremely good one) is not enough to earn a living in London, according to interviews I carried out in 2009. It is only those who own their own institutes and get into arranging events and providing dancers and teachers who are realistically able to give up their day jobs. Professional dancers may do some Bollywood dancing alongside other styles, but to survive on performing and peripatetic teaching of Bollywood or *Bhangra* alone in the UK is not possible.
86. Interview, Rajesh Mansukhani, 30 April 2006.
87. Interview, Vivek, 23 April 2006.
88. Interview, Justine, 21 April 2006.
89. Ibid.
90. Ibid.
91. Interview, Kalpana Bhushan, 6 March 2006.
92. Interview, Gaysil, 17 April 2006.
93. In fact, strict rules were in place prohibiting contact between bar dancers and audience members in Mumbai. Traditional *mujra* also had etiquette and codes of practice, though the term is now used loosely to include all kinds of illicit dance performances at private parties that involve touching and semi or full nudity.
94. Pinto (2006).
95. See Morcom on real and 'reel' life synergies of popular music and dance culture (2011).
96. Interview, Kalpana Bhushan, 6 March 2006.

97. In the UK, Bollywood dance shows by dance troupes take place at weddings, and couples also have their 'first dance' choreographed Bollywood style. Hen nights and other functions are also arranged by Bollywood dance institutes.
98. Interview, Gaggun Bedi, 26 April 2007
99. Interview, Kalpana Bhushan, 6 March 2006.
100. Ibid.
101. Ibid.
102. Ibid.
103. Ibid.
104. Ibid.
105. Interview, Praveen Shandilya, 16 March 2006.
106. Ganesh Hegde started his career in circuits of school shows and competitions, and was particularly keen on break dance, hip hop, and stars like Michael Jackson (interview, 14 April 2006).
107. Indeed, there is also extensive illicit and illegal film-making and exhibition in South Asia. See Hoek (2010).
108. I make these arguments in Morcom (2009).
109. Faleiro's book on bar girls, charting the changes following the ban, reveals this vividly (2010). Srinivasan raises the question of the psychological effects of the loss of the profession and activity of dance on *devadasis* in her 1984 ethnography, evocatively describing the prestige and power they had whilst still in office, and their present 'despondency' (1984: 231–2, n. 21; 182–6). However, whilst these matters form a small part of Srinivasan's work, Soneji takes them up as a major focus in his historical and ethnographic study, looking at dance and memory in contemporary *devadasi* communities in the latter part of the book (2012). These sensitive but important questions of the psychological impact of exclusion from performing arts warrant further research.
110. This is also a part of a sexual revolution for certain sectors of the middle class.
111. Personal communication, Varsha Kale (2007). See chapter five for further discussion of the support for the bar girls.

5. MUMBAI DANCE BARS, ANTI-*NAUTCH* II, AND NEW POSSIBILITIES

1. Agnes (2005).
2. See Dalwai on the class background of dance bars (2012).
3. Ibid.
4. Agnes (2005). The figure 75,000 is the most common one used in discussions on dance bars. Some have estimated a greater number, some much less. There were also a small percentage of Bangladeshi girls dancing in bars, which was greatly exaggerated by the pro-ban lobby amid alarmism over 'terrorism' or 'security', and also linked to questions of compensation for bar girls, which the State would not be liable for if they were not Indian (interview, Varsha Kale, 9 April 2005). See Blanchet on the migration of girls from Bangladesh to dance in Mumbai's bars (2010).
5. See Research Centre for Women's studies, SNDT Women's University, Mumbai's survey for a breakdown of average earnings of bar girls (2005: 9). The BBU's letter to Girija

Vyass, Chairperson, National Commission for Women, also gives information on five income categories of bar girl and the proportion of bar girls in each category (16 May 2005).

6. See Dalwai on the fantasy *nawabi* element of dance bars (2012).
7. See Sachdeva for an analysis of *tawaif* as 'celebrity performers' in emerging forms of popular culture in India in the late nineteenth and early twentieth centuries (2008).
8. Agnes (2005).
9. Ibid.
10. Ibid.
11. Ibid.
12. Ibid.
13. Ibid.
14. This is discussed in the High Court ruling on the ban, *Indian Hotel and Restaurants Association (AHAR) and others v. State of Maharashtra and others* (2006: 188–191).
15. Agnes (2005)
16. Ibid.
17. The Ladies Bar and Restaurant Employees Union had seen bar girls organised together with the bar owners prior to 1997, campaigning particularly over the question of working hours. However, this organisation did not retain its momentum, see Chaukar (1997: 45).
18. Agnes (2005).
19. See Mazzarella's description of dance bars in the late 1990s, and his investigation of what constituted 'obscenity' in these bars, especially in comparison to other cases of obscenity allegations, for example, against cabaret artistes from the 1970s (forthcoming). I was unfortunately unable to witness dance bars in full swing in Mumbai as the ban was in force by the time I began fieldwork in early 2006, though I visited some with singers and bands, and also a 'restaurant and bar' where bar girls 'waitressed' and later went to nearby lodges with customers for sex. I witnessed Indian dance bars in Singapore in December 2007, and also dance bars in Kathmandu in May and June 2007.
20. Mazzerella, forthcoming; interview, Praveen Patkar, Prerana, 6 March 2007.
21. For example, see Aiyar's article in *The Economic Times*, 23 March 2005, 'India may face US sanctions in June. The trigger: Not taking action to stop trafficking in women and children'.
22. See Fernandes and Heller on the illiberalism of the post-liberalisation new middle classes (2006). With bar girls, all the threats were made to converge, with accusations that most bar girls were Bangladeshi and so a security threat, and/or the bar girls were outsiders to the city. While it is true that most bar girls came from outside of Mumbai, those from Bangladesh were only a small minority. See Research Centre for Women's studies, SNDT Women's University, Mumbai's publication (2005: 4).
23. Agnes (2005).
24. These attitudes are in many was contradictory, as Agnes points out (2005; 2006). However, with a conflation of women, honour and culture, the violation of women and the violation of culture are one. On the grounds of rights too, as I discuss in the next section, these two arguments serve the same purpose, acting as 'good' and 'bad' cop.

25. In Hindu mythology, Savitri is the wife of Satyavan. Satyavan dies soon after their marriage, but Savitri is so loyal to her husband she visits the lord of death, Yama, and demands he be returned to life. She ultimately manages to persuade Yama.
26. Research Centre for Women's studies, SNDT Women's University, Mumbai's survey reports that only 25.8 per cent of bar girls were earning between Rs 15–30,000 per month (2005: 9).
27. Sen (1894: 3–5), quoted in Sachdeva (2008: 327).
28. Reddy (1930: 56).
29. Ibid.: 117.
30. *Free Press*, 3 September 2005.
31. Prerana, the most important NGO in the pro-ban lobby, which deals with trafficking and prostitution, claimed they had no moral stance at all (interview, Praveen Patkar, 6 March 2007). Other tropes existed around the harm that bars were deemed to cause, for example, that they were a nexus of criminality, or that since most bar girls came from Bangladesh, bars represented a security threat.
32. In particular, the government itself had issued the liquor and performing licenses and made considerable money from the dance bars. See Agnes (2005; 2006) and statements by the BBU (Kale, 9 April 2005 and 16 May 2005).
33. The letter from the BBU to the National Commission for women, New Delhi, for example, includes a section on 'caste class composition of the performers', Kale (2005). Two articles on the ban and a third in an academic publication by Flavia Agnes, the lawyer representing the BBU, are almost unique in their clear historicising of the bar girls (2005; 2006; 2007). However, the mention is relatively brief, since the focus of the articles is legal arguments, and the similarities with anti-*nautch* are not mentioned.
34. I saw it mentioned in only three out of hundreds of press cuttings, two of those relating to Mahasweta Devi, who supported the bar girls specifically due to their background in performing communities (see for example *Asian Age*, 9 September 2009), and one for which I do not have a date or the name of the newspaper. Chapekar mentions performing communities in her paper on bar girls (1997: 7). Faleiro also mentions them in her book on bar girls (2010: 21–22) but does not make the link between the stigmatising of these communities and curtailing their livelihood from the late nineteenth century and the current stigma and restrictions on their livelihood. An article on *tawaif* in *Tehelka* (Gupta, 7 November 2007) mentions the bar girls, citing a short chapter written by myself on the topic, Morcom (2009), the author having contacted Katherine Schofield who advised on the entire article and passed on details of my work. *Tehelka* is a distinctly intellectual, leftist news magazine, and this article was exceptional within Indian journalism concerning the bar girls.
35. Thakraney (2005)
36. Harhari (2005)
37. Ibid.
38. Kotiswaran similarly criticises the debate on the bar girls for its fixation on the question of whether or not the girls were 'prostitutes'. She argues that the argument carries with it a judgement of 'morally "good" and "bad" female labour, namely, bar dancing

and sex work'. She continues that 'This is ironic given their striking sociological similarities and the stigmatization and levels of state abuse inflicted against both' (2010: 105). The attempts to prove or disprove the 'prostitution' of bar girls does tend to carry an implicit disapproval of prostitution. Kotiswaran is also correct in pointing out the similarity of bar girls and sex workers. However, this argument fails to take into account history and causality, or the significance of skilled, artistic labour in terms of earning capacity and also socio-cultural place.

39. Kothari, (2005a; 2005b).
40. 'Sweety v/s Savitri', for example, concludes: 'Finally the issue boils down to this. Either you are for women sexploitation or for women liberation. Please standup and be counted' (13 May 2005).
41. See Ignatieff for a discussion of human rights as 'moral trump cards' (2001: 21).
42. Interview, Praveen Patkar, 6 March 2007.
43. The justification of this stance here with a discussion of democracy is also particularly problematic in this case given that India is a well-functioning democracy and the bar girls had been able to form a registered trade union.
44. When the bar girls were seen in the guise of home-breakers, the victims were wives, or young boys who became 'addicted' to them, and were thus helpless and devoid of their ability to choose.
45. Shrinivasan (2005).
46. Chaukar's report is similar in its focus on general poverty and helplessness (1997).
47. 1, 8, 15, 22, 29 October and 5 November 2005. The last article actually focused on a *hijra* activist and dancer Laxminarayan Tripathi, who had been only an occasional bar girl, though knew many bar girls (5 November 2005).
48. Faleiro (2005e).
49. L. Brown's book on *Kanjar* dancing girls in Lahore is also similar in places (2006).
50. Faleiro's book foregrounds particularly compellingly the collapse of livelihoods and the pressures of survival for bar girls following the ban, with the second half of the book devoted to the aftermath of the ban (2010).
51. Varsha Kale told me how she had to break through such stories from bar girls initially, before they opened up to her about their family backgrounds. I received such stories from bar girls I met in Singapore, to whom I had had no 'insider' introduction (that their fathers had died, had been in the army, or had abandoned them). While they may have been true (I had no way of verifying), they exactly matched the standard excuses told to people from mainstream society.
52. Mehta (2004: 294–344).
53. Sachdeva (2008).
54. Morcom (2009: 134).
55. Mazzerella, forthcoming.
56. The ban was also driven by other factors relating to Maharashtrian politics, which I do not enter into here. See Dalmai (2012).
57. Agnes (2005).
58. Varsha Kale, BBU, personal communication, January 2010. I visited such a 'restaurant

and bar' and saw the large numbers of Lodging and Boarding houses nearby with Varsha Kale in Kalyan (a Central suburb of Mumbai) in January 2010. One of the protagonists in Faleiro's book on bar girls becomes a lodge-based sex worker (2010). See Dalmai for an investigation of the effects of the ban on the livelihoods of bar girls (2012).

59. The English language press and the BBU emphasised heavily that many bar girls would go into transactional sex work following a ban, and the press carried stories after the ban of the destitution bar girls were facing.
60. This is according to 2005 statistics from the World Bank, http://www.worldbank.org.in/WBSITE/EXTERNAL/COUNTRIES/SOUTHASIAEXT/INDIAEXTN/0,,contentMDK:21880725~pagePK:141137~piPK:141127~theSitePK:295584,00.html, last accessed 25 August 2011.
61. See for example Radhakrishnan (2008).
62. Varma (1998: 130–137).
63. Ibid.: 176–177, quoting Gautam Mukherjee in *The Pioneer*, 26 Feb 1996. See also Aiyer (2007) for a swingeing criticism of the growth in disparity under neoliberalism, a remarkable statement by a government minister.
64. 'Backward' refers specifically to 'Backward castes', yet is still not devoid of a civilisational connotation.
65. 'All for the ban. TOI-TNS poll: An overwhelming 87% backs government action on dance bars', *Times City*, 20 April 2006, Mumbai. Fernandes and Heller describe the new middle classes as largely characterised by political and social 'illiberalism' (2006).
66. Pinto (2005).
67. 'Support grows for bar dancers. Actor Soni Razdan says there's more vulgarity in movies than dance bars', 25 April 2005, *Express News Service*.
68. Shekhar (2005).
69. *Times of India* (2005).
70. India was founded in part on a massive civil rights movement (against untouchability), and the constitution offers protection from discrimination by caste. Moral minorities such as the bar girls have struggled to be included in such rights. However, the 'internal logic' of human rights is expansion to more and more groups on the basis of the principle of equality, see Hunt (2007: 146–175).
71. The growth of the sex workers' collectives and also LGBT groups since the 1990s, in many ways in response to AIDS, has brought powerful voices to such moral minorities. Flavia Agnes writes of her own initial reluctance, as a more 'traditional' feminist of the 70s/80s, to work for the bar girls, and also the difficulties in particular of being in opposition to Prerana, which had previously been a 'fellow organisation' (2005).
72. Srinivasan (1985: 1873–1874).
73. Sachdeva (2008: 355–361).
74. Following the ban, the BBU has been campaigning for late-night working hours for ex-bar girls doing waitressing to enable them to work till 1.30am like male staff instead of 9.30pm. The 9.30pm limit has resulted in girls going to lodges with men for paid sex after finishing the waitressing work, whereas the extension of hours for waitressing would allow for more money to be earned in tips than sex work.

75. The background of the girls is stated in summary in all their press releases and, in terms of personal communications, I was given all my initial leads and connections for this project via Varsha Kale and the BBU. This began with bar girls and spread to their home communities (*Deredar* in Muzaffarpur, *Nat* in Rajasthan, *Bedia* in Delhi or Mumbai), and also *Kolhati Lavani* performers, and more indirectly, *kothi* performers.
76. Agnes (2005).
77. See http://www.majlisbombay.org/index.htm, last accessed 15 July 2011.
78. July 2005.
79. The SNDT reports were certainly on the anti-ban side, providing assertions backed up by data. The other lengthy report into bar girls is Chaukar, 1997. Although it also includes statistics and information on bar girls and their working conditions and warned that a ban 'would lead to something still worse', it is at times moralistic and aligned with what became pro-ban views (Ibid.: 47). It includes the extreme right wing Hindu comment: 'Muslim men are especially known for their fondness for wine and women. So their presence in large numbers in bars is not surprising' (Ibid.: 13).
80. See, for example, Harhari (2005).
81. *Asian Age*, 3 September 2005.
82. The dedication of girls to temples to make *devadasi*s was banned, but that was after the institution was thoroughly stigmatised through the anti-*nautch* campaign.
83. As I state in the introduction to this book, the ways in which lawyers (ideally) deal with rights as the basic building blocks of laws and citizenship can be compared to the far more emotionalised discussion of rights and morality more typical of social campaigners.
84. The amendments are reproduced in summary by Agnes (2005).
85. Agnes (2006). Agnes (2007) quotes certain certain key parts of the judgement.
86. Mazzarella interprets this need for distinguishing on the basis of establishment and dance as related to the difficulties of bringing a case successfully under the obscenity laws (forthcoming). However, also underlying this is a less clear social consensus than, for example, in the days of anti-*nautch*.
87. That is, the state justified exempting certain establishments because, although the dances in bars were vulgar, in the exempted establishments, they were not.
88. Indian Hotel and Restaurant Association (AHAR) and others v. State of Maharashtra and others (2006). Paragraph 52, pp. 135–136; Paragraph 88, pp. 239–240.
89. Ibid., Paragraph 58, pp. 151–152.
90. Ibid., Paragraph 58, p. 155.
91. Mazzarella (forthcoming).
92. Indian Hotel and Restaurant Association (AHAR) and others v. State of Maharashtra and others (2006). Paragraph 71, p. 196.
93. Ibid., Paragraph 81, p. 217; paragraph 82, p. 218.
94. Ibid., Paragraph 83, pp. 222–223.
95. Ibid., Paragraph 86, pp. 235–236.
96. Ibid., Pagraph 85, pp. 227–228.
97. Interview, K.P., Singapore, 27 December 2007.

6. THE CONTEMPORARY WORLD OF *KOTHI* PERFORMERS: CHANGING PATTERNS OF LIVELIHOOD AND SOCIO-CULTURAL SPACE

1. Some interviewees have been given pseudonyms in this chapter.
2. This is clearly apparent in a passage from Malka Pukhraj's autobiography, quoted in chapter three, see Kidwai (2003: 75).
3. Hansen (1998; 2002) and Kapur (2003). Female impersonators existed as star performers in Marathi and Gujarati theatre, too.
4. Effeminate or homosexual/bisexual males are common in classical performing arts, especially dance, but classical performing arts are now largely gender neutral, and it is understood that male or female roles are not grounded in the 'nature' of the performer, but in their art, and homoeroticism has no open, discussed role. The upper class '*kothi*' performer in his fifties or sixties whom I had met, and who had studied and performed *kathak*, stated that male *kathak* performers did perform in female dress prior to independence, but that this stopped as women began to perform (interview, Siddharth, 12 October 2008). This would be out of the question now, unless playing a particular dramatic role.
5. Vanita and Kidwai (2000: 191–217) and Bhaskaran (2002).
6. Vanita (2000: xviii).
7. However, vulgarity and obscenity were mentioned as a disagreeable aspect of the performance of female impersonators in Marathi theatre by at least one commentator, Adarkar (1991: WS89).
8. Adarkar (1991) and Hansen (1998; 2005).
9. Adarkar (1991) and Bhaumik (2001: 86–113).
10. Pani (1977: 41–42). Gargi states that the restriction on the livelihood of *mujra* performers via the Suppression of Immoral Traffic Act (SITA) in 1959 saw many more females join the *Nautanki* theatre (1966: 46), which may have been an added pressure on the female impersonators.
11. See discussion in the introduction to chapter three in this book.
12. For example *My Brother Nikhil* (2005, Onir), *Page 3* (2005, Madhur Bhandarkar), *Honeymoon Travels Pvt. Ltd.* (2007, Reema Kagti), *Dostana* (2008, Tarun Mansukhani). Many films contain gay themes or homoeroticism, from *Sholay* (Prakash Mehra, 1975) to *Kal Ho Na Ho* (Karan Johar, 2003), the latter being obvious but not open in its gay plot. There is a growing literature on queerness in Bollywood, for example Dudrah (2008), Henniker (2010) and Shahani (2008). These processes of 'queering' Hindi films in the context of reception by gay and lesbian (NRI or elite) Indians with, for example, emphasis on *yaari* ('love'/'friendship') or *dosti* (typically same sex 'friendship') or *khel* ('play', 'fun') (Dudrah, 2008) is a very different subculture from *kothi* involvement with films and film songs, where there is a far more direct identification with the female heroines and characters.
13. The film *Welcome to Sajjanpur* (Shyam Benegal, 2008) contained a *hijra* as a central character, depicted with remarkable accuracy and sympathy as regards contemporary issues of marginalisation. A less serious though certainly not negative depiction of *hijras* is in *Amar Akbar Anthony* (1979, Manmohan Desai), where they sing a song against

the heroine's father '*Pyar ka dushman*' ('Enemy of love') who is trying to oppose her match to the hero. Otherwise, *hijras*, let alone *kothis*, do not have a role in any forms of mainstream cinema that I am aware of.

14. There are jokes about such female impersonators, which are suggestive. For example the *nacas* of Marathi *Tamasha* are said to be so feminine they 'bathe with women' (*auraton ke saath nahate hain*).
15. See Ugra's description of the reverence of Ramlila performers in his 1960 autobiography (2007: 62).
16. I have heard from a *kothi* performer in Delhi that *Raslila*, the re-enactment of Krishna's story, also involves many *kothis* performing as *gopis* (milkmaids), though again, non-*kothi* boys are also involved (interview, Siddarth, 12 October 2008).
17. Mehrotra (2006: 35–50).
18. Booth states that female performers used to dance *Badhava* some decades ago (2005: 213).
19. See Prakash's work on this tradition (2011).
20. *Abhinay* is the (often seated) expression of textual meaning through facial expression and hand gestures.
21. Marcus mentions 'orchestra' as one of five forms of entertainment in temple festivals known as *shringar* in Banaras, stating they are 'a recent phenomenon in which a band performs imitations of hit film songs; these bands appeared in Banaras in c. 1978' (1989: 104). There is no mention of dance at all.
22. There have been considerable changes to the boundaries of both *kothis* and *hijras* in recent years, which I discuss in more detail later in the chapter.
23. See section on 'performing and caste' in Charsley and Kadekar (2006: 25–122); see also Kothari (1972) and Neuman, Chaudhuri and Kothari (2006) for studies of particular groups in Rajasthan.
24. See Neumann (1990 [1980]), Kippen (1988), Walker (2004). Qureshi also discusses heredity and *biradari* in the context of feudal structures of performance and patronage in Hindustani music (2002).
25. Booth (2005: 33–67; and 2009).
26. Sachdeva (2008: 74–76).
27. Srinivasan (1984: 239–89; and 1985: 1869). See also Soneji's study of historical and contemporary *devadasis*, which cites them as middle or upper caste, as opposed to dalit *jogtis* (2012: Introduction).
28. Nanda (1999: 38–48) and Reddy (2005: 9–11).
29. See Reddy (2005: 154–164). *Kothis* are increasingly taking gurus in the *hijras*, but this is in the context of a new, part-time *hijra* identity—hence the ties remain loose. I discuss these changes later in this chapter.
30. See Seabrook (1999) for a discussion of this process with MSMs, and Nagar (2008: 87–133) regarding *kothis* in particular.
31. Some I met in Lucknow, Delhi and Mumbai have learned classical dance, but that follows an earlier interest in and gift for dance and the desire to take things further by learning more thoroughly. It is not a part of the traditions described here. There is also

a desire to excel at *mujra*, one of the most popular and prestigious dance styles (even if many younger *kothi*s now go for more of an 'item girl' style).

32. Interview, Gaurang, 23 January 2010. The Hindi word '*rani*' does not have any of the same queer connotations of the English term 'queen'.
33. See Seabrook (1999) for a rich ethnographic study of the sexual relationships and identities of MSMs in India. See also publications by Khan (http://www.nfi.net/articles_essays.htm, last accessed 24 June 2011).
34. In an area where *kothi*s are a (more or less) openly acknowledged part of society, people will understand that the relationship is potentially sexual, yet in these areas, these relationships are seen as acceptable.
35. This illustrates the value of the skilled labour of performing arts, key to the different status public/erotic female performers have previously had from prostitutes, something fundamentally misunderstood by the conflation of these performers with prostitutes simply on morality or marriage grounds.
36. This is also the case with *hijra*s, who earn from sex work, *badhai* and begging. There is a hierarchical, pyramid-type system for sharing income from a given territory, and those who are high up can be immensely rich, earning far beyond middle class incomes.
37. I also visited Kathmandu, and met *kothi*s (who are known as *metti*s) there. I cannot comment in detail on Kathmandu/Nepal, but overall, sex work is increasing with the *metti*s there.
38. This information is drawn from conversations with Shailesh Kumar from *Nai Kiran*, the organisation working with MSMs in Balliya, over two visits (12–14 November 2007 and 6–7 October 2008), and a formal interview on 6 October 2008. It is also drawn from a number of conversations with *kothi*s during these trips to Balliya, numerous visits to Lucknow from 2006–2010 and phone conversations with Divya Sagar, Outreach worker at Bharosa, Lucknow.
39. All prices relating to Balliya are those cited in 2008.
40. Freelance *kothi*s get comparable per-event rates from the bands, but no lump sum.
41. Rs 10,000 per month would be a very good monthly salary for people of the lower socio-economic strata, equivalent to some call centre work, with some very poor people earning only Rs 1,500–2,000 for menial jobs. A good middle class salary would be around Rs 15,000–20,000, and a high (though not stratospheric) salary Rs 40,000–50,000. Dancers in Balliya, therefore, earn extremely well.
42. This kind of commission from *chelas* can similarly make *hijra nayaks* astronomically rich.
43. It is interesting to note that *kothi*s who perform in *Ramlila*s in this area are not taken from these circuits of dancers—this is quite likely because they do not have enough knowledge of the genre or the local language, coming from around Calcutta rather than Uttar Pradesh or Bihar.
44. This is very different from the culture of dancing boys in Afghanistan, where boys are bought, sold and 'owned' by patriarchs (see Quraishi's 2009 film). Some of the boys are *kothi* and are naturally drawn to the role of female dancer, but many are feminine because of their age (as they are 'beardless') and are released aged 18 to be able to marry, see

Ibrahimi (2008), Khan (2008), Abdul-Ahad (2009). See also Baldauf (1990), Rahman (1989) and Schild (1988) on boy love and dance in Central Asia and the Middle East. There is some pressure by group leaders on *kothi* dancers in Lucknow to have sex with audience members. I discuss this later in this chapter. However, *kothi* or *launda* dance is not forced per se.

45. More *kothis* are now having sex change operations, becoming 'female' or 'transgender' (TG). Thus such TGs are emerging as another (overlapping) group alongside *kothis* and *hijras*.
46. This information is drawn from a formal interview with Rahul (13 October 2008), who runs Naz India's MSM project Milan, and from conversations with *kothis* at Milan drop-in sessions.
47. This information is drawn from interviews with Simran, a *hijra* dancer (13 September 2008), Laxmi, a *hijra* dancer and activist (12 September 2008), and more informal conversations with *kothis* at a drop-in session of Humsafar, the Mumbai-based MSM organisation.
48. This information is drawn from formal interviews with a number of *kothis* and *kothi* performers, as well as many informal conversations over several trips to Lucknow between 2006 and 2010. Figures relate to information given between 2007 and 2010.
49. See Mehrotra (2006) for a rich account of *Nautanki* in the late twentieth century, and its collapse in status and financial viability.
50. As I discuss in chapter one, it is almost certainly not a legal ban on dance that has taken place, but restrictions or revoking of licenses on grounds of obscenity. The reason for the stopping (if not 'banning') of dance shows at *melas* was said by several performers to be related to the fact that the shows had become obscene, including 'body show', 'shower dances' (when performers literally dance under a shower), and explicitly sexual gestures.
51. Garga writes in 1966 that *Nautanki* had become 'increasingly lewd' (1966: 46). Mehrotra also describes the increasing sexualisation of *Nautanki* in the 1990s (2006). Prakash similarly reports on increasingly sexualised performance in *Bidesia* (2011).
52. The situation in Benares appears to be similar, with opportunities for performance rapidly dwindling and the entire scene becoming seedier. I met a *kothi* in Benares who performed at private gatherings in female dress singing film songs in falsetto voice with *abhinay*. S/he was also acting as an agent for bookings for *kothis* to perform in Benares and surrounding areas.
53. Interviews, Narendra, 22 and 25 January 2010.
54. I became acutely aware of the fragility of the lives of *kothis* when funding problems hit Bharosa in 2010 and staff could not be paid. In addition to Salim and Salman turning to *badhai* and dance shows respectively, another *kothi* joined the *hijras* more definitively and two had started to do sex work. The hierarchy for *kothi* occupation clearly seems to be 1) some kind of a salaried job, 2) dance, 3) doing *badhai* with the *hijras*, 4) joining the *hijras*, 5) sex work.
55. In *Ramlila* and *Nautanki* generally the *dholak* is used. This does not allow for pure classical *kathak*, which requires the tabla.

56. His views may also reflect the fact that he began performing only in the 1990s, after *Nautanki* was in decline.
57. When I asked about the reasons for the increase in sex work, Rahul, from Milan in Delhi, stated this was because there was more money to spend on sex now (interview, 13 October 2008).
58. Interview, Aamir, 9 October 2008.
59. However, I met a *hijra* guru who was fifty or sixty years old and had performed in *Nautanki* and 'shows' for many years prior to these recent changes, so there clearly has been overlap in the past. The description of the performers as *hijra*s in the excerpt from Malka Pukhraj's biography also suggests previously blurred lines, or certainly differences from the current or recent identities and social organizations of *hijra*s and *kothi*s, see Kidwai (2003: 75). Without further research, it is not possible to comment in more detail.
60. Interview, Rahul, 13 October 2008.
61. Nagar (2008: 78–80).
62. Shailesh Kumar, personal communication, 4 September 2011.
63. Katyal (2002).
64. Ibid.
65. See Kole on the globalization of LGBT discourses and institutions in India since the 1990s (2007).
66. See also Khan on the problems of categorisations, including the category MSM (1998).
67. Book produced in collaboration with Naz Foundation International.
68. Shah and Bandopadhay (2007). Personal communication, Vidya Shah and Parthiv Shah (2007).
69. Lahiri and Kar (2007). This approach perhaps also arises from knowledge of such practices of dancing boy catamites in Afghanistan, for example as depicted in Quraishi's film (2009). However, *bacha bazi* or 'boy play' in Afghanistan is structured very differently from *launda* dance in India, with zero consent.
70. Shah and Bandopadhay (2007: 62).
71. Parallel arguments are made by Impey about the use of musical traditions and the re-emplacement of displaced communities in South Africa, in particular, in opposition to narrow and essentialist cultural tourism (2002, 2006). This approach formed the basis of advocacy and development initiatives working with these groups.

CONCLUSION

1. Bauman (2004; 2011).
2. See in particular Maciszewski's advocacy projects to rebuild performing identity and roles for *tawaif* (2006; 2007), Impey's work on music, emplacement and memory (2002; 2006), and Soneji's study of music, memory and identity in the case of contemporary *devadasi*s (2012).
3. Srinivasan raises this question in her ethnography on *devadasi*s, though does not focus on it (1984). Maciszewski's work on *tawaif* (1998; 2001a; 2006; 2007), and Soneji's monograph on *devadasi*s both explore these questions (2012).

4. Marginalised, disenfranchised traditional (hereditary) performers extend far beyond female hereditary or *kothi* performers. Vast numbers of traditional artisans have become displaced or marginalised in different stages of social, cultural and technological change.
5. See the discussion of contemporary *kolhati* performers in chapter two.
6. Issues of cultural heritage and cultural (re)integration have been raised in connection to classical *tawaif*, Maciszewski (2006; 2007). This has been the exception rather than the rule.
7. Rege (1996).
8. Ministry of Social Justice and Empowerment, Government of India, 30 June 2008.
9. Laxman Mane, an established fighter for Denotified Tribes, in a response to the DNT Commission's report, amongst other criticisms, objected to the naming of DNT groups as involved in bar dancing, since this further stigmatises them (25 September 2008), http://laxmanmane.blogspot.com/2008/09/national-commission-for-de-notified_25.html, last accessed 9 August 12. The report made a generalised comment about girls from DNTs making up around 80 per cent of bar dancers, rather than naming the very specific groups of female hereditary performers.

BIBLIOGRAPHY

Abdul-Ahad, Ghaith, 'The dancing boys of Afghanistan', *The Guardian*, 12 September 2009.

Abrams, Tevia, 'Folk theatre in Maharashtrian social development programs', *Educational Theatre Journal*, Vol. 27, No. 3 (1975), pp. 395–407.

Adarkar, Neera, 'In search of women in history of Marathi theatre, 1843 to 1933', *Economic and Political Weekly*, Vol. 26, No. 43 (1991), pp. WS87–WS90.

Agnes, Flavia, 'State control and sexual morality: The case of the bar dancers of Mumbai' in John, Mathew and Kakarala, Sitharamam (eds), *Enculturing Law: New Agendas for Legal Pedagogy*, New Delhi: Tulika Books, 2007.

——— 'Hypocritical morality', *Manushi*, October 2005, http://www.indiatogether.org/manushi/issue149/index.htm, last accessed 5 May 2008.

——— 'The right to dance', *Manushi*, July 2006, http://www.indiatogether.org/2006/jul/soc-dancebar.htm, last accessed 5 May 2008.

Agrawal, Anuja, 'Family, migration and prostitution: The case of Bedia community of North India' in Agrawal, Anuja (ed.), *Migrant Women and Work*, New Delhi: Sage Publications, 2006, pp. 177–194.

——— *Chaste Wives and Prostitute Sisters: Patriarchy and Prostitution Among the Bedias of India*, New Delhi: Routledge, 2008.

Aiyar, Swaminathan S., 'India may face US sanctions in June. The trigger: Not taking action to stop trafficking in women and children', *The Economic Times*, 23 March 2005.

Aiyer, Mani Shankar, 'I was always Leftist. Economic reforms made me completely Marxist', edited extracts from a speech at the CII Northern Region annual meeting, 2006–07, New Delhi, April 4 2007, *Indian Express*, 24 April 2007, http://www.indianexpress.com/story/29112._.html, last accessed 6 May 2008.

Akhavi, Negar (ed.), *AIDS Sutra: Untold Stories from India*, London: Vintage Books, 2008.

Alexander, Jeffrey C. and Sztompka, Piotr (eds), 'Introduction' in *Rethinking Progress: Movements, Forces, and Ideas at the End of the Twentieth Century*, Boston: Unwin Hyman, 1990.

Allen, Matthew, 'Rewriting the script for South Indian dance', *The Drama Review*, Vol. 41, No. 3 (1997), pp. 63–100.

BIBLIOGRAPHY

Anandi, S., 'Representing devadasis: Dasigal Mosavalai as a radical text', *Economic and Political Weekly*, Vol. 26, Nos 11–12 (1991), pp. 739–46.

Anderson, Benedict, *Imagined Communities: Reflections on the Origin and Spread of Nationalism*, New York: Verso, 1991.

Appadurai, Arjun and Breckenridge, Carol, 'Why public culture?', *Public Culture*, Vol. 1, No. 1 (1988), pp. 5–10.

Arnold, Alison, *Hindi Filmi Git: On the History of Indian Popular Music*, PhD thesis, University of Illinois at Urbana-Champaign, 1991.

Austern, Linda Phyllis and Naroditskaya, Inna (eds), *Music of the Sirens*, Bloomington, IN: Indiana University Press, 2006.

Austern, Linda Phyllis, '"Sing again syren": The female musician and sexual enchantment in Elizabethan life and literature', *Renaissance Quarterly*, Vol. 42, No. 3, (1989), pp. 420–448.

Avorgbedor, Daniel K., 'The impact of rural-urban migration on a village music culture: Some implications for applied ethnomusicology', *African Music*, Vol. 7, No. 2 (1992), pp. 45–57.

Babiracki, Carol, '"Saved by dance" the movement for autonomy in Jharkhand', *Asian Music*, Vol. 32, No. 1 (2000/2001), pp. 35–58.

——— 'The Illusion of India's "Public" Dancers' in Jane Bernstein (ed.), *Women's Voices Across Musical Worlds*, Boston: Northeastern University Press, 2003.

——— '"Traditional" musicians in Jharkhand and the limits of boundless opportunity', paper presented at South Asian Music and Dance Forum 'Caste, class and social mobility', Institute for Musicological Research, Senate House, University of London, 2 December 2009.

Bakhle, Janaki, *Two Men and Music: Nationalism in the Making of an Indian Classical Tradition*, New York: Oxford University Press, 2005.

Baldauf, Ingeborg, 'Bacabozlik: Boylove, folksong and literature in Central Asia', *Paedika*, No. 2 (1990), pp. 12–31.

Ballhatchet, Kenneth, *Race, Sex and Class Under the Raj: Imperial Attitudes and Policies and Their Critics, 1793–1905*, London: Weidenfeld and Nicolson, 1980.

Banerjee, Sumanta, *Dangerous Outcast: The Prostitute in Nineteenth Century Bengal*, Calcutta: Seagull Books, 1998.

Banerji, Sabita, 'Ghazals to bhangra in Great Britain', *Popular Music*, Vol. 7, No. 2 (1988), pp. 207–213.

Barnouw, Eric and Krishnaswamy, S., *Indian film*, Second Edition, New York: Oxford University Press, 1980.

Bauman, Gerd, 'The re-invention of bhangra: Social change and aesthetic shifts in a Punjabi music in Britain', *The World of Music*, Vol. 32, No. 2 (1990), pp. 81–95.

Baumann, Zygmunt, *Modernity and Ambivalence*, Cambridge: Polity Press, 1991.

——— *Wasted lives: Modernity and its Outcasts*, Cambridge: Polity Press, 2004.

——— *Collateral Damage: Social Inequalities in a Global Age*, Cambridge: Polity Press, 2011.

Bernstein, Henry, 'Modernization theory and the sociological study of development', *Journal of Development Studies*, Vol. 7, No. 2 (1971), pp. 141–160.

Bernstein Sycamore, Mattilda (ed.), *Nobody Passes: Rejecting the Rules of Gender and Conformity*, Berkeley, CA: Seal Press, 2006.

Bhaskar, Ira and Allen, Richard, *Islamicate Cultures of Bombay Cinema*, New Delhi: Tulika Books, 2009.

Bhaskaran, Suparna, 'The politics of penetration: Section 377 of the Indian Penal Code' in Vanita, Ruth (ed.), *Queering India: Same-Sex Love and Eroticism in Indian Culture and Society*, New York and London: Routledge, 2002, pp. 15–29.

Bhatia, Nandi, *Acts of Authority/Acts of Resistance: Theater and Politics in Colonial and Postcolonial India*, Michigan: University of Michigan Press, 2004.

Bhattacharji, Sukumari, 'Prostitution in ancient India', *Social Scientist*, Vol. 15, No. 2 (1987), pp. 32–61.

Bhattacharya, Neeladri, 'Predicaments of mobility: Peddlers and itinerants in nineteenth century northwestern India' in Markovits, C., Pouchepadass J. and Subrahmanyam S. (eds), *Society and Circulation: Mobile People and Itinerant Cultures in South Asia 1750–1950*, Delhi: Permanent Black, 2003, pp. 163–214.

Bhaumik, Kaushik, *The Emergence of the Bombay Film Industry 1913–1936*, PhD thesis, University of Oxford, 2001.

Biswas, P.C., *The Ex-Criminal Tribes of Delhi State*, Delhi: Department of Anthropology, University of Delhi, 1960.

Biswas, Soutik, 'Out of the shadows', *Outlook* (6 October 1997), pp. 76–79.

Blanchet, Thérèse, 'Migration to the bars of Bombay: Women, village religion and sustainability', *Women's Studies International Forum*, Vol. 33 (2010), pp. 345–353.

Bohlman, Philip V., *The Study of Folk Music in the Modern World*, Bloomington: Indiana University Press, 1988.

Booth, Gregory, 'Brass bands: tradition, change, and the mass media in Indian wedding music', *Ethnomusicology*, Vol. 34, No. 2 (1990), pp. 245–262.

——— *Brass Baja: Stories from the World of Indian Brass Bands*, New Delhi: Oxford University Press, 2005.

——— 'Constructing the local: Migration and cultural geography in the Indian brass band trade' in Wolf, Richard K. (ed.), *Theorizing the Local: Music, Practice, and Experience in South Asia and Beyond*, Oxford and New York: Oxford University Press, 2009, pp. 81–96.

Bor, Joep, 'The voice of the sarangi: An illustrated history of bowing in India', *National Centre for the Performing Arts Quarterly Journal*, Vol. 15, Nos 3–4 (1986); Vol. 16, No. 1 (1987), pp. 1–183.

——— 'Bardes et baladins' in Bor, Joep and Bruguière, Philippe (eds), *Gloire des Princes, Louange des Dieux: Patrimoine Musical de l'Hindoustan du XIVe au XXe Siècle*, Paris: RMN and Musée de la Musique, 2003, pp. 135–141.

——— 'The social status of bowers, musicians and dancers', reprinted in Joshi, O.P. (ed.), *Sociology of Oriental Music: A Reader*, Jaipur: ABD Publishers, 2004, pp. 270–294.

——— 'Mamia, Ammani and other Bayaderes: Europe's portrayal of India's temple dancers' in Clayton, Martin and Zon, Bennet (eds), *Music and Orientalism in the British Empire, 1780s-1940s*, 2007, pp. 39–70.

——— 'On the dancers or devadasis: Jacob Haafner's account of the eighteenth-century

Indian temple dancers' in Kouwenhoven, Frank and Kippen, James (eds), *Music, Dance and the Art of Seduction*, Delft: Eburon Academic Publishers, 2013.

Bor, Joep and Leucci, Tiziana, *Indian Courtesans Through European Eyes: Five Devadasis in Europe, 1838–1839*, forthcoming.

Bose, Brinda and Subhabrata Bhattacharya (eds), *The Phobic and the Erotic: The Politics of Sexualities in Contemporary India*, London, New York and Calcutta: Seagull Books, 2007.

Bourdieu, Pierre, *Distinction: A Social Critique of the Judgment of Taste*, London: Routledge and Kegan Paul, 1984.

Broughton, Thomas Duer, *The Costume, Character, Manners, Domestic Habits and Religious Ceremonies of the Mahrattas*, London: John Murray, 1813.

Brown, Louise, *The Dancing Girls of Lahore: Selling Love and Saving Dreams in Pakistan's Pleasure District*, New York: HarperCollins Publishers, 2006.

Brown, Michael, 'Can culture be copyrighted?', *Current Anthropology*, Vol. 39, No. 2 (1998), pp. 193–222.

Brown/Schofield, Katharine Butler, *Hindustani Music in the Time of Aurangzeb*, PhD thesis, School of Oriental and African Studies, University of London, 2003.

——— '"If music be the food of love": Masculinity and eroticism in the Mughal *mehfil*' in Orsini, Francesca (ed.), *Love in South Asia: A Cultural History*, Cambridge: Cambridge University Press, 2006.

——— 'Introduction: Liminality and the social location of musicians', *Twentieth-Century Music*, Vol. 3, No. 1 (2007a), pp. 5–12.

——— 'The social liminality of musicians: Case studies from Mughal India and beyond', *Twentieth-Century Music*, Vol. 3, No. 1 (2007b), pp. 13–49.

——— 'Reviving the golden age again: "Classicization", Hindustani music, and the Mughals', *Ethnomusicology*, Vol. 54, No. 3 (2010), pp. 484–517.

——— 'The courtesan tale: Female musicians and dancers in Mughal historical chronicles', *Gender & History*, Vol. 24, No. 1 (2012).

Burt, Ramsay, *The Male Dancer: Bodies, Spectacle, Sexualities*, London and New York: Routledge, 2007 [1995].

Butler, Judith, *Gender Trouble: Feminism and the Subversion of Identity*, Second Edition, New York and London: Routledge, 1990.

——— *Bodies that Matter: On the Discursive Limits of 'Sex'*, London and New York: Routledge, 1993.

——— 'Restaging the universal: Hegemony and the limits of formalism' in Butler, J., Laclau, E. and Žižek S. (eds), *Contingency, Hegemony, Universality: Contemporary Dialogues on the Left*, London and New York: Verso, 2000, pp. 11–43.

Campbell, Tom, *Rights: A Critical Introduction*, London and New York: Routledge, 2006.

Carnegie, Patrick, *Notes on the Races, Tribes and Castes Inhabiting the Province of Avadh*, Lucknow: Oudh government Press, 1868.

Case, Sue-Ellen, 'Classic drag: The Greek creation of female parts', *Theatre Journal*, Vol. 37, No. 3 (1985), 'Staging Gender', pp. 317–327.

Charsley, Simon and Kadekar, Laxmi Narayan (eds), *Performers and Their Arts: Folk, Popular and Classical Genres in a Changing India*, New Delhi and London: Routledge, 2006.

Chatterjee, Ratnabali, 'Prostitution in nineteenth century Bengal: Construction of class and gender', *Social Scientist*, Vol. 21, Nos 9–11 (1993), pp. 159–172.

Chaukar, Shubhada, *Problems of Mumbai's Bargirls*, Wadala, Mumbai: Vinay Sahasrabuddhe, 1997.

Chinchore, Prabhakar, 'Pandit Bhatkande's thoughts on Thumri' in Mehta, R.C. (ed.), *Thumri Tradition and Trends*, Bombay: Indian Musicological Society, 1990, pp. 22–25.

Clapham, Andrew, *Human Rights: A Very Short Introduction*, Oxford and New York: Oxford University Press, 2007.

Clifford, James, *The Predicament of Culture: 20th Century Ethnography, Literature and Art*, Cambridge, Mass: Harvard University Press, 1988.

Cohen, Lawrence, 'The *Kothi* wars: AIDS cosmopolitanism and the morality of classification' in Adams, Vincanne and Pigg, Stacy Leigh (eds), *Sex in Development: Science, Sexuality, and Morality in Global Perspective*, Durham and London: Duke University Press, 2005, pp. 269–303.

Cohn, Bernard, 'The census, social structure and objectification in South Asia' in *An Anthropologist Among the Historians and Other Essays*, Delhi and London: Oxford University Press, 1987.

——— *Colonialism and Its Forms of Knowledge: The British in India*. Princeton, NJ: Princeton University Press, 1996.

Connell, R.W., *Masculinities*, Second Edition, Cambridge: Polity Press, 2005 [1995].

Cowan, Jane, *Dance and the Body Politic in Northern Greece*, Princeton: Princeton University Press, 1990.

Cox, Thomas, 'The Badi: Prostitution as a social norm among an untouchable caste of west Nepal', *Kailash*, Vol. 16, Nos 3–4 (1990), pp. 165–186.

——— *The Badi of West Nepal: Prostitution as a Social Norm Among an Untouchable Caste*, Second Edition, Causebay, PO: Orchid Press, 2006 [1993].

Creppell, Ingrid, *Toleration and Identity: Foundations in Early Modern Thought*, New York and London: Routledge, 2003.

Crooke, William, *Tribes and Castes of the North-Western Provinces and Oudh*, Volumes I-IV, Calcutta: Office of the Supt. of Govt. Print, 1896.

Dalmia, Vasudha, 'The house of service or the chronicle of an un/holy city', 'Introduction' in Premchand, Munshi, *Sevasadan*, New Delhi: Oxford University Press, 2005.

Dalwai, Sameena, 'Performing caste: the ban on bar dancing in Mumbai', PhD thesis, Keele University, 2012.

David, Ann R., 'Beyond the sliver screen: Bollywood and *filmi* dance in the UK', *South Asia Research*, Vol. 27, No. 1 (2007), pp. 5–24.

de Alwis, Malathi (1999) '"Respectability", "modernity", and the policing of "culture" in colonial Ceylon' in Burton, Antoinette (ed.), *Gender, Sexuality, and Colonial Modernities*, London and New York: Routledge, pp. 177–92.

Desai, Kiran, 'Night claims the godivari', in *AIDS Sutra: Untold Stories from India*, London: Vintage Books, 2008, pp. 37–56.

Desmond, Jane C., *Staging Tourism: Bodies on Display from Waikiki to Seaworld*, Chicago and London: University of Chicago Press, 1999.

Dirks, Nicholas B., *Castes of Mind: Colonialism and the Making of Modern India*, New Delhi: Permanent Black, 2002.

Doubleday, Veronica, *Three Women of Herat*, London: Cape, 1988.

Douzinas, Costas, *Human Rights and Empire: The Political Philosophy of Cosmopolitanism*, Oxford and New York: Routledge-Cavendish, 2007.

Dudrah, Rajinder, 'Drum 'n' dhol: British bhangra music and diasporic South Asian identity formation' *European Journal of Cultural Studies*, Vol. 5, No. 3 (2002), pp. 363–383.

——— 'Queer as desis: Secret politics of gender and sexuality in Bollywood films in diasporic urban ethnoscapes' in Gopal, Sangita and Moorti, Sujata (eds), *Global Bollywood: Travels of Hindi Song and Dance*, Minneapolis and London: University of Minnesota Press, 2008, p. 288–307.

Duffield, Mark and Hewitt, Vernon (eds), *Empire, Development and Colonialism: The Past in the Present*, Woodbridge, Suffolk and Rochester, NY: James Currey, 2009.

du Perron, Lalita, *Hindi Poetry in a Musical Genre*, Abingdon: Routledge, 2007.

Dwyer, Rachel, *All You Want is Money, All You Need is Love: Sex and Romance in Modern India*, London and New York: Cassell, 2000.

Dyson, Ketaki Kushari, *A Various Universe: A Study of the Journals and Memories of British Men and Women in the Indian Subcontinent, 1765–1856*, Delhi: Oxford University Press, 1978.

Enthoven, Reginald Edward, *The Tribes and Castes of Bombay*, Bombay: Government Central Press, 1920.

Erdman, Joan, 'The maharaja's musicians: Performance at Jaipur in the nineteenth century' in Vatuk, Sylvia (ed.), *American Studies in the Anthropology of India*, Delhi: Manohar, 1978, pp. 342–67.

——— *Patrons and Performers in Rajasthan: The Subtle Tradition*, Delhi: Chanakya Publications, 1985.

——— 'Petitions to the patrons: Changing culture's substance in twentieth century Jaipur' in Erdman, Joan (ed.), *Art Patronage in India: Methods, Motives and Markets*, New Delhi: Manohar Publications, 1992, pp. 143–176.

Escobar, Arturo, *Encountering Development: The Making and Unmaking of the Third World*, Princeton, New Jersey: Princeton University Press, 1995.

Faleiro, Sonia, 'The dying of the evening stars, the lives of Mumbai's bar girls, 1: The circus girl lost in a dance bar', *Tehelka*, Vol. 2, No. 39 (2005).

——— 'The dying of the evening stars, the lives of Mumbai's bar girls, 2: Camera, camera, who's the saddest of us all?', *Tehelka*, Vol. 2, No. 40 (2005).

——— 'The dying of the evening stars, the lives of Mumbai's bar girls, 3: Bawdy, beautiful, not yet damned', *Tehelka*, Vol. 2, No. 41 (2005).

——— 'The dying of the evening stars, the lives of Mumbai's bar girls, 4: Gali no. 2, street despair', *Tehelka*, Vol. 2, No. 42 (2005).

——— 'The dying of the evening stars, the lives of Mumbai's bar girls, 5: My love encloses a plot of roses', *Tehelka*, Vol. 2, No. 43 (2005).

——— 'The dying of the evening stars, the lives of Mumbai's bar girls, 6: Come, I am your lucky chance dance', *Tehelka*, Vol. 2, No. 44 (2005).

——— 'Maarne ka, bhagane ka' in *AIDS sutra: Untold stories from India*, London: Vintage Books, 2008, pp. 77–98.

——— *Beautiful Thing: Inside the Secret World of Bombay's Dance Bars*, New Delhi: Penguin, 2010.

Farrell, Gerry, *Indian Music and the West*, Oxford: Clarendon Press, 1997.

Feld, Steven, 'Aesthetics as iconicity of style or "lift-up-over-sounding": Getting into the Kaluli groove', *Yearbook of Traditional Music*, Vol. 20 (1988), pp. 74–113.

Feldman, M. and Gordon, B. (eds), *The Courtesan's Arts: Cross-Cultural Perspectives*, New York: Oxford University Press, 2006.

Fernandes, Leela and Heller, Patrick, 'Hegemonic aspirations: New middle class politics and India's democracy in comparative perspective', *Critical Asian Studies*, Vol. 38, No. 4 (2006) pp. 495–522.

Fiol, Stefan, 'From folk to popular and back: Assessing feedback between studio recordings and festival dance-songs in Uttarakhand, North India', *Asian Music*, Vol. 42, No. 1 (2011).

——— 'Sacred, inferior, and anachronous: Deconstructing liminality among the *Baddī* of the central Himalayas', *Ethnomusicology Forum* 19 (2010).

——— 'Dual framing: Locating authenticities in the music videos of himalayan possession rituals' *Ethnomusicology*, Vol. 54, No. 1 (2010) pp. 28–53.

Fisher, Jennifer and Shay, Anthony, *When Men dance: Choreographing Masculinities Across Borders*, New York: Oxford University Press, 2009.

Fisher, Mark, *Capitalist Realism: Is There no Alternative?*, Winchester, UK and Washington, USA: O Books, 2009.

Forbes, Geraldine, *Women in Modern India*, New York: Cambridge University Press, 2004 [1996].

Foucault, Michel, *Discipline and Punish: The Birth of the Prison*, New York: Vintage Books, 1979.

——— *The Care of the Self: The History of Sexuality, Three*, London: Penguin, 1990.

——— *The Use of Pleasure: The History of Sexuality, Two*, London: Penguin, 1992.

——— *The Will to Knowledge: The History of Sexuality, One*, London: Penguin Books, 1998.

——— *The Archaeology of Knowledge*, London and New York: Routledge, 2002.

Frank, Andre Gunder, 'The development of underdevelopment', *Monthly Review*, Vol. 18, No. 4 (1966), pp. 17–31.

Freud, Sigmund, *Civilization and its Discontents*, London: Penguin Group, 2002 [1930].

Fuller, Marcus B., *The Wrongs of Indian Womanhood*, Edinburgh and London: Oliphant Anderson and Ferrier, 1900.

Gaisberg. F.W, *The Music Goes Round*, New York: The Macmillan Company, 1942.

Gandhi, Malli, *Denotified Tribes: Dimensions of Change*, New Delhi: Kanishka Publishers, Distributors, 2008.

Gargi, Balwant, *Folk Theatre of India*, Seattle and London: University of Washington Press, 1966.

Gaston, Anne-Marie, *Bharata Natyam: From Temple to Theatre*, New Delhi: Manohar, 1996.

Gearty, Conor, *Can Human Rights Survive?*, Cambridge: Cambridge University Press, 2005.

——— *The Rights Future*, collaborative web-based publication, 2010–11, http://therights-future.com/, last accessed 11 April 2011.

Gellner, E., *Nations and Nationalism*, Second Edition, Oxford: Blackwell Publishing, 2006.

George, T.J.S., *MS: A Life in Music*, India: HarperCollins, 2004.

Gilroy, Paul, *There Ain't No Black in the Union Jack: The Cultural Politics of Race and Nation*, London and New York: Routledge, 1992.

——— *After Empire: Melancholia or Convivial Culture?*, Oxford: Routledge, 2004.

Gladney, Dru, 'Representing nationality in China: Refiguring majority/minority identities', *The Journal of Asian Studies*, Vol. 53, No. 1 (1994), pp. 92–123.

Gopal, Santita and Moorti, Sujata (eds), *Global Bollywood: Travels of Hindi Song and Dance*, Minnesota: University of Minnesota Press, 2008.

Gray, John, *Liberalism*, Milton Keynes: Open University Press, 1986.

——— 'An illusion with a future', *Daedalus*, Vol. 133, No. 3 (2004), pp. 10–17.

Guha, Ranajit, 'Methodology' in Guha, Ranajit and Spivak, Gayatri Chakravorty (eds), *Selected Subaltern Studies*, New York: Oxford University Press, 1988 [1982], pp. 35–88.

Gupta, Akhil, *Postcolonial developments: agriculture in the making of modern India*, Durham, London: Duke University Press, 1998.

Gupta, Charu, *Sexuality, obscenity, community: women, Muslims, and the Hindu public in colonial India*, Delhi: Permanent Black, 2001.

Gupta, Trisha, 'Bring on the dancing girls', *Tehelka*, Vol. 6, No. 44 (2009).

Haldanker, Vaishali, *Barbala*, Mumbai: Mehta Publishing House, 2010.

Hansen, Kathryn, 'Indian folk traditions and the modern theatre', Asian Folklore Studies, Vol. 42, no. 1 (1983), pp. 77–89.

——— 'The birth of Hindi drama in Banaras, 1868–1885' in Freitag, Sandra B. (ed.), *Culture and Power in Banaras: Community, Performance, and Environment, 1800–1980*, 1989, pp. 62–92.

——— *Grounds for Play: The Nautanki Theatre of North India*, Berkeley: University of California Press, 1992.

——— '*Stri bhumika*: Female impersonators and actresses on the Parsi stage', *Economic and Political Weekly*, 29 August 1998, pp. 2291–2300.

——— 'A different desire, a different femininity: Theatrical transvestism in the Parsi, Gujarati, and Marathi theaters 1850–1940' in Vanita, Ruth (ed.), *Queering India: Same-Sex Love and Eroticism in Indian Culture and Society*, New York and London: Routledge, 2002, pp. 163–180.

Harhari, Santosh, 'Our secret probe into dance bars. Mid Day reporter becomes a dancer to find the truth. Mr Home Minister, read this before you change the law', *Mid Day*, 11 April 2005.

Harris, John, 'Great promise, hubris and recovery: A participant's history of development studies' in Kothari (ed.), *A Radical History of Development Studies: Individuals, Institutions and Ideologies*, 2005, pp. 17–46.

Harvey, David, *A Brief History of Neoliberalism*, Oxford: Oxford University Press, 2005.

Hemetek, Ursula, 'Applied ethnomusicology in the process of the political recognition of a minority: A case study of the Austrian Roma', *Yearbook for Traditional Music*, Vol. 38 (2006), pp. 35–57.

Henniker, Charlie, 'Pink rupees or gay icons? Accounting for the camp appropriation of male Bollywood stars', *South Asia Research*, Vol. 30, No. 10 (2010), pp. 25–41.

Heywood, Andrew, *Political Theory: An Introduction*, Second Edition, Basingstoke and London: Macmillan Press Ltd, 1999.

Higgins, Jon B., 'From prince to populace: Patronage as a determinant of change in South Indian (Karnatak) music', *Asian Music*, Symposium on the Ethnomusicology of Culture Change in Asia, Vol. 7, No. 2 (1976), pp. 20–26.

Hobsbawm, E.J., *Nations and Nationalism Since 1780: Programme, Myth, Reality*, Cambridge: Cambridge University Press, 1992.

Hobsbawm, E.J, and Ranger, T.O. (eds), *The Invention of Tradition*, Cambridge: Cambridge University Press, 1983.

Hoek, Lotte, 'Cut-pieces as stag film: Bangladeshi pornography in action cinema', *Third Text*, Vol. 24, No. 1 (2010), pp. 133–146.

Hollander, Julia, *Indian Folk Theatres*, London and New York: Routledge, 2007.

Howard, Keith (ed.), *Music as Intangible Cultural Heritage: Policy, Ideology and Practice in the Preservation of East Asian Traditions*, SOAS Musicology Series, Farnham, Surrey: Ashgate, 2012.

Howard, Keith, *Preserving Korean Music: Intangible Cultural Properties as Icons of Identity*, Aldershot: Ashgate, 2006.

Hunt, Lynn, *Inventing Human Rights: A History*, New York and London: W.W. Norton and Company, 2007.

Ibrahimi, Sayed Yaqub, 'Dancing boys of the north', *Pukaar*, No. 60 (2008), p. 8.

Iggers, Georg G., 'The idea of progress: A critical reassessment', *The American Historical Review*, Vol. 71, No. 1 (1965), pp. 1–17.

Ignatieff, Michael, *The Warrior's Honor: Ethnic War and the Modern Conscience*, London: Chatto and Windus, 1998.

——— *Blood and Belonging: Journeys into the New Nationalism*, London: Vintage, 2001a.

——— *Human Rights: As Politics and Idolatry*, Princeton and Oxford: Princeton University Press, 2001b.

Impey, Angela, 'Culture, conservation and community reconstruction: Explorations in advocacy ethnomusicology and participatory action research in northern Kwazulu Natal', *Yearbook for Traditional Music*, Vol. 34 (2002), pp. 9–24.

——— 'Sounding place in the western Maputaland borderlands', *Journal of the Musical Arts in Africa*, Vol. 3 (2006), pp. 55–79.

Kale, Varsha, Bhartyiya Bargirls Union 'Struggle for the complete rehabilitation of bargirls and other hotel employees', 9 April 2005.

——— Bhartyiya Bargirls Union, letter to Girija Vyass, Chairperson, National Commission for Women, New Delhi, 16 May 2005.

Kannabiran, Kalpana, 'Judiciary, social reform, and debate on "religious prostitution" in colonial India', *Economic and Political Weekly*, Vol. 30, No. 43 (1995), pp. 59–69.

Kapur, Anuradha, 'Impersonation, narration, desire and the Parsee theatre' in Blackburn, Stuart and Dalmia, Vasudha (eds), *India's Literary History: Essays in the Nineteenth Century*, New Delhi: Permanent Black, 2003, pp. 87–118.

Kasbekar, Asha, 'Hidden pleasures: Negotiating the myth of the female ideal in popular Hindi cinema' in Pinney and Dwyer (eds), *Pleasure and the Nation: The History, Politics and Consumption of Public Culture in India*, New Delhi: Oxford University Press, 2000, pp. 286–308.

Katyal, Sonia K., 'Exporting identity', *Yale Journal of Law and Feminism*, Vol. 14, No. 1 (2002), pp. 97–176.

Kavi, Ashok Row, '*Kothis* versus other MSM: Identity versus behaviour in the chicken and egg paradox' in *The Phobic and the Erotic: The Politics of Sexualities in Contemporary India*, London, New York and Calcutta: Seagull Books, 2007, pp. 437–450.

Kaviraj, Sudipta, 'On the construction of colonial power: Structure, discourse, hegemony' in Kaviraj, Sudipta (ed.), *Politics in India*, New Delhi: Oxford University Press, 1997, pp. 141–158.

——— *The imaginary institution of India: Politics and ideas*, New York: Columbia University Press, 2010.

Kawlra, Aarti, 'Handloom weaving—Tamil Nadu', paper given at the British Association of South Asian Studies annual conference, School of Oriental and African Studies, London, April 2012.

Kersenboom-Story, Saskia, *Nityasumangali: Devadasi Tradition in South India*, Delhi: Motilal Banarsidass, 1987.

Khan, Shivananda, 'Cultural constructions of male sexualities in India', 1995, http://www.nfi.net/downloads/knowledge_centre/NFI%20publications/articles%20and%20essays/1995_Cultural%20Constructions.pdf, last accessed 4 May 11.

——— 'The risks of categorisation', 1998, http://www.nfi.net/downloads/knowledge_centre/NFI%20publications/articles%20and%20essays/1998_risks%20of%20categorisation%20.pdf, last accessed 4 May 11.

——— 'Culture, sexualities and identity: Men who have sex with men in India' in Sullivan, Gerard and Jackson, Peter A. (eds), *Gay and Lesbian Asia: Culture, Identity, Community*, New York: Harrington Press, 2001, pp. 99–116.

——— 'Everybody knows, but nobody knows: Desk review of current literature on HIV and male-male sexualities, behaviours and sexual exploitation in Afghanistan', 2008, http://www.nfi.net/downloads/knowledge_centre/Useful%20documents/2008-Everybody%20knows-AfghanLitReview-final.pdf, last accessed 27 June 2011.

Kidwai, Saleem, *Song Sung True: A Memoir. Malka Pukhraj*, New Delhi: Kali for Women, 2003.

Kinnear, Michael S., *The Gramophone Company's Indian Recordings 1908–1910*, Victoria: Bajakhana, 2000.

Kippen, James, *The Tabla of Lucknow: A Cultural Analysis of a Musical Tradition*, Cambridge: Cambridge University Press, 2005 [1988].

Kole, Subir, 'Globalizing queer? AIDS, homophobia and the politics of sexual identity in India', *Globalization and Health*, Vol. 3, No. 8 (2007), pp. 1–16.

Koskoff, Ellen, 'An introduction to women, music, and culture' in Koskoff (ed.), *Women and Music in Cross-Cultural Perspective*, New York: Greenwood Press, 1987, pp. 1–23.

Kothari, Uma, 'A radical history of development studies: Individuals, institutions and ideologies', in Kothari (ed.), *A Radical History of Development Studies: Individuals, Institutions and Ideologies*, London: Zed Books, 2005a, pp. 1–13.

——— 'From colonial administration to development studies: A post-colonial critique of the history of development studies' in Kothari (ed.), *A Radical History of Development Studies: Individuals, Institutions and Ideologies*, London: Zed Books, 2005b, pp. 47–66.

——— 'Authority and expertise: The professionalization of international development and the ordering of dissent', *Antipode*, Vol. 37, No. 3 (2005c), pp. 425–446.

Kotiswaran, Prabha, 'Born unto brothels: Toward a legal ethnography of sex work in an Indian red-light area', *Law and Social Enquiry*, Vol. 33, No. 3 (2008), pp. 579–629.

——— 'Labours in vice or virtue? Neo-liberalism, sexual commerce, and the case of Indian bar dancing', *Journal of Law and Society*, Vol. 37, No. 1 (2010), pp. 105–24.

Kugle, Scott, 'The mirror of secrets: *"Akhi" Jamshed Rajgiri*', commentary and translation, in Vanita and Kidwai (eds), *Same-Sex Love in India*, New York: Palgrave, 2000, pp. 136–139.

Kumar, Nita, *The Artisans of Banaras: Popular Culture and Identity, 1880–1986*, Princeton: Princeton University Press, 1988.

Lahiri, Agniva and Kar, Sarika, *Dancing Boys: Traditional Prostitution of Young Males in India: Situational assessment Report on Adolescents and Young Boys Vulnerable to Forced Migration, Trafficking and Sexual Exploitation in India*, Kolkata: Plus, 2007.

Leante, Laura, 'Urban myth: Bhangra and the dhol craze in the UK' in Clausen, B., Hemetek, U. and Saether, E. (eds), *Music in Motion: Diversity and Dialogue in Europe*, New Brunswick and London: Transaction Publishers, 2009, pp. 191–208.

Levine, Philippa, 'Orientalist sociology and the creation of colonial sexualities', *Feminist Review*, No. 65 (2000), pp. 5–21.

——— *Prostitution, Race and Politics: Policing Venereal Disease in the British Empire*, New York and London: Routledge, 2003.

Luthra, H.R., *Indian Broadcasting*, New Delhi: Publications Division, 1986.

Maciszewski, Amelia, *Gendered Stories, Gendered Styles: Contemporary Hindustani Music as Discourse, Attitudes, and Practice*, PhD thesis, University of Texas, 1998.

——— 'Stories about selves: selected north Indian women's musical (auto)biographies', *The World of Music*, Vol. 43, No. 1 (2001a), pp. 39–172.

——— 'Multiple voices, multiple selves: Song style and North Indian women's identity', *Asian Music*, Vol. 32, No. 2 (2001b), pp. 1–40.

——— 'Tawa'if, tourism, and tales: The problematics of twenty-first-century musical patronage for north India's courtesans' in Feldman, M. and Gordon, B. (eds), *The Courtesan's Arts: Cross-Cultural Perspectives*, New York: Oxford University Press, 2006, pp. 332–351.

——— 'Texts, tunes, and talking heads: Discourses about socially marginal North Indian musicians', *Twentieth-Century Music*, Vol. 3, No. 1 (2007), pp. 121–144.

Magriel, Nicolas, *Sarangi Style in North Indian Art Music*, PhD thesis, School of Oriental and African Studies, University of London, 2001.

Majumdar, Neepa, 'The embodied voice: Song sequences and stardom in popular Hindi cinema', in Robertson Wojcik, Pamela and Knight, Arthur (eds), *Soundtrack Available: Essays on Film and Popular Music*, Durham and London: Duke University Press, 2001.

——— *Wanted Cultured Ladies only! Female Stardom and Cinema in India, 1930s-1950s*, Urbana: University of Illinois Press, 2009.

Mane, Laxman, 'National Commission for De-Notified, Nomadic and Semi-Nomadic Tribes, 30 June, 2008: comment on report Vol. 1', 25 September 2008, http://laxman-mane.blogspot.co.uk/2008/09/national-commission-for-de-notified_25.html, last accessed 9 August 2008.

Mansingh, Sonal and Pasricha, Avinash, *Incredible India: Classical Dances*, New Delhi: Wisdom Tree, by arrangement with Department of Tourism, Ministry of Culture, Government of India, 2007.

Manuel, Peter, 'Courtesans and Hindustani music', *Asian review*, Vol. 7, No. 1 (1987), pp. 12–17.

——— *Thumri in Historical and Stylistic Perspective*, Delhi: Motilal Banarsidass, 1989.

——— *Cassette Culture: Popular Music and Technology in North India*, Chicago: University of Chicago Press, 1993.

Marcus, Scott L., 'Recycling Indian film-songs: Popular music as a source of melodies for North Indian folk musicians', *Asian Music*, Vol. 24, No. 1 (1992/3), pp. 101–110.

——— 'Parody-generated texts: The process of composition in Biraha', *Asian Music*, Vol. 26, No. 1 (1994/5), pp. 95–147.

Markovits, C., Pouchepadass, J. and Subrahmanyam, S., 'Introduction: Circulation and society under colonial rule' in *Society and Circulation: Mobile People and Itinerant Cultures in South Asia 1750–1950*, Delhi: Permanent Black, 2003, pp. 1–22.

Mazzarella, William, '"A Different Kind of Flesh": Public Obscenity, Globalization, and the Mumbai Dance Bar Ban', in B. Bose and S. Phadke (eds), *Explode Softly: Sexualities in Contemporary Indian Visual Cultures*, Calcutta and London: Seagull Books, forthcoming.

Medhasandana, Swami, *Varanasi at the Crossroads: A Panoramic View of Early Modern Varanasi and the Story of its Transition*, Kolkata: The Ramakrishna Mission Institute of Culture, 2001.

Meduri, Avanti, 'Bharatha Natyam—what are you?', *Asian Theatre Journal*, Vol. 5, No. 1 (1988), pp. 1–22.

Mehrotra, Deepti Priya, *Gulab Bai: The Queen of Nautanki Theatre*, New Delhi: Penguin Books India, 2006.

Mehta, Suketu, *Maximum City: Bombay Lost and Found*, London: Review, 2004.

Mehta, Uday Singh, *Liberalism and Empire: A Study in Nineteenth-Century British Liberal Thought*, Chicago and London: University of Chicago Press, 1999.

Menon, Nivedita, 'Introduction' in *Issues in Contemporary Indian Feminism: Sexualities*, New Delhi: Women Unlimited (an associate of Kali for Women), 2007, pp. xiii-lv.

Menon, Nivedita (ed.), *Issues in Contemporary Indian Feminism: Sexualities*, New Delhi: Women Unlimited (an associate of Kali for Women), 2007.

Monzini, Paola, *Sex traffic: Prostitution, Crime and Exploitation*, London and New York: Zed Books, 2005.

Morcom, Anna, 'The pure voice: Disembodied performance and playback singing in Hindi films', paper presented at British Forum for Ethnomusicology One-day conference 'Music and the Body', 2004.

——— 'Indian popular culture and its "others": Bollywood dance and anti-*nautch* in twenty-first century global India' in Gokulsing, Moti and Dissanayake, W. (eds), *Popular Culture in a Globalised India*, Oxford and New York: Routledge, 2009, pp. 125–38.

——— 'Film songs and the cultural synergies of Bollywood in and beyond South Asia' in Dwyer, Rachel and Pinto, Jerry (eds), *Beyond the Boundaries of Bollywood: The Many Forms of Hindi Cinema*, New Delhi: Oxford University Press, 2011, pp. 156–187.

Mulvey, Laura, 'Visual pleasure and narrative cinema', *Screen*, Vol. 16, No. 3 (1975), pp. 6–18.

Mutua, Makau, *Human Rights: A Political and Cultural Critique*, Philadelphia, Pennsylvania, University of Pennsylvania Press, 2002.

Nagar, Anantlal, *Yeh Kothewaliyan*, Allahabad: Lok Bharati Prakashan, 1979.

Nagar, Ila, *Language, Gender and Identity: The case of Kotis in Lucknow*, India, PhD dissertation, Ohio State University, 2008.

Nair, Janaki, 'The Devadasi, dharma, and the state', *Economic and Political Weekly*, 10 December 1994, pp. 3157–67.

——— '"Imperial reason", national honour and new patriarchal compacts in early twentieth-century India', *History Workshop Journal*, Vol. 66 (2008), pp. 208–266.

Nanda, Serena, *Neither Man nor Woman: The Hijras of India*, Canada: Wadsworth Publishing Company, 1999.

Neville, Pran, *Nautch Girls of India: Dancers, Singers, Playmates*, New Delhi: Ravi Kumar Publisher, 1996.

Neuman, Daniel, *The Life of Music in North India: The Organization of an Artistic Tradition*, Chicago and London: University of Chicago Press, 1990 [1980].

Neuman, Daniel, Chaudhuri, Shubha and Kothari, Komal, *Bards, Ballades and Boundaries: An Ethnographic Atlas of Music Traditions in West Rajasthan*, Calcutta: Seagull Books, 2006.

Nisbet, Robert, 'The idea of progress', *Literature of Liberty: A Review of Contemporary Liberal Thought*, Vol. 2, No. 1. (1979), available at http://oll.libertyfund.org/index.php?Itemid=259&id=165&option=com_content&task=view, last accessed 10 April 2011.

Norton, Barley, 'Musical revival, Ca Tru ontologies, and intangible cultural heritage in Vietnam' in Bithell, Caroline and Hill, Juniper (eds), *The Oxford Handbook of Music Revivals*, New York: Oxford University Press, forthcoming.

Nye, Joseph S., *Soft Power: The Means to Success in World Politics*, New York: PublicAffairs, 2004.

Oldenburg, Veena, *The Making of Colonial Lucknow, 1856–1877*, Princeton, N.J.: Princeton University Press, 1989 [1984].

——— 'Lifestyle as resistance: The case of the courtesans of Lucknow', *Feminist Studies*, No. 16 (1990), pp. 259–88.

O'Neil, J., Orchard, T., Swarankar, R.C., Blanchard, J.F., Gurav, K. and Moses, F., 'Dhandha, dharma and disease: Traditional sex work and HIV/AIDS in rural India', *Social Science and Medicine*, Vol. 59 (2004), pp. 851–860.

Orsini, Francesca (ed.), *Love in South Asia: A Cultural History*, Cambridge: Cambridge University Press, 2006.

O'Shea,'"Traditional" Indian Dance and the Making of Interpretive Communities', *Asian Theatre Journal*, Vol. 15, No. 1 (1998), pp. 45–63.

Pani, Jiwan, 'The female impersonator in traditional Indian theatre', *Sangeet Natak*, Vol. 45 (1977), pp. 37–42.

Parekh, Bhikhu, *A New Politics of Identity: Political Principles for an Interdependent World*, Hampshire: Palgrave Macmillan, 2008.

Parker, Kunal, '"A corporation of superior prostitutions": Anglo-Indian legal conceptions of temple dancing girls, 1800–1914', *Modern Asian Studies*, Vol. 32, No. 3 (1998), pp. 559–633.

Peet, Richard, and Hartwick, Elaine, *Theories of Development*, New York and London: The Guilford Press, 1999.

Pinch, Vijay, 'Gosain tawaif: Slaves, sex and ascetics in Rasdhan, ca. 1800–1857', *Modern Asian Studies*, Vol. 38, No. 3 (2004), pp. 559–597.

Pinney, C., 'Introduction: Public, popular and other cultures' in Pinney, C. and Dwyer, R. (eds), *Pleasure and the Nation: The History, Politics and Consumption of Public Culture in India*, New Delhi: Oxford University Press, 2000, pp. 1–34.

Pinto, Jerry, *Helen: The Life and Times of an H-Bomb*, India: Penguin, 2006.

——— 'Dirty dancing: Corruption is the dance partner in the government's decision to close dance bars, writes Jerry Pinto', *Sunday Mid Day*, 3 April 2005, p. 8.

Pivar, David J., 'The military, prostitution, and colonial peoples: India and the Philippines, 1885–1917', *The Journal of Sex Research*, Vol. 17, No. 3 (1981), pp. 256–269.

Post, Jennifer, 'Professional women in Indian music: The death of the courtesan tradition' in Koskoff, Ellen (ed.), *Women and Music in Cross-Cultural Perspective*, New York: Greenwood Press, 1987, pp. 97–109.

Prakash, Brahma, '"Mind it! Folk is always fucking": Aesthetic of obscene in Bidesia travelling troupe performing', paper presented at CHIME-APAF conference, Royal Holloway, University of London, 8 July 2011.

Prakash, H.S., *Incredible India: Traditional Theatres*, New Delhi: Wisdom Tree, by arrangement with Department of Tourism, Ministry of Culture, Government of India, 2007.

Prasad, Madhav 'This thing called Bollywood', 2003, http://www.india-seminar.com/2003/525/525%20madhava%20prasad.htm, last viewed 20 August 2011.

Premchand, Munshi, *Sevasadan*, New Delhi: Oxford University Press, 2005.

Pukhraj, Malka, *Song Sung True: A Memoir*, translated by Kidwai, Saleem, New Delhi: Zubaan, 2002.

Qureshi, Regula, 'The Indian sarangi: Sound of affect, site of conquest', *Yearbook for Traditional Music*, Vol. 29 (1997), pp. 3–38.

——— 'In search of Begum Akhtar: Patriarchy, poetry, and twentieth-century Indian music', *The World of Music*, Vol. 43, No. 1 (2001), pp. 97–137.

——— 'Mode of production and musical production: Is Hindustani music feudal?' in Qureshi, Regula Burkhardt (ed.), *Music and Marx: Ideas, Practice and Politics*, New York: Routledge, 2002, pp. 81–105.

——— 'Female agency and patrilineal constraints: Situating courtesans in twentieth-century India' in Feldman, M. and Gordon, B. (eds), *The Courtesan's Arts: Cross-Cultural Perspectives*, New York: Oxford University Press, 2006, pp. 312–331.

Radcliffe, Sarah, 'Development and geography: Towards a postcolonial development geography?', *Progress in Human Geography*, Vol. 29, No. 3 (2005), pp. 291–198.

Radcliffe, Sarah and Laurie, Nina, 'Culture and development: Taking culture seriously in development for Andean indigenous people', *Environment and Planning D: Society and Space*, Vol. 24 (2006), pp. 231–248.

Radhakrishna, Meena, *Dishonoured by History: 'Criminal Tribes' and British Colonial Policy*, Hyderabad: Orient Longman, 2001.

Radhakrishnan, Smitha, 'Examining the "global" Indian middle class: Gender and culture in the Silicon Valley/Bangalore circuit', *Journal of Intercultural Studies*, Vol. 29, No. 1 (2008), pp. 7–20.

Rahman, Tariq, 'Boy love in the Urdu *ghazal*', *Paidika* (Amsterdam), Vol. 2, No. 1 (1989), pp. 10–27.

Raina, Neelam, 'The importance of craft to the reconstruction of Kashmir', paper given at the British Association of South Asian Studies annual conference, School of Oriental and African Studies, London, April 2012.

Rajadhyaksha, Ashish, 'The Bollywoodisation of Indian cinema: Cultural nationalism in a global arena', *Inter-Asian Cultural Studies*, Special Issue on 'Cinema, Culture Industry and Political Societies, Vol. 4, No. 1 (2003), pp. 25–39.

Ramnarine, Tina K., 'Musical creativity and the politics of utterance: Cultural ownership and sustainability in Amoc's Inari Sámi raps' in Andersson, Kajsa (ed.), *L'Image du Sápmi Vol. 2*, Göteburg: Örebro University, 2012.

Rao, Anupama (ed.), *Gender and Caste*, New Delhi: Kali For Women, 2003.

Rao, Vidya, 'Thumri as feminine voice' in Menon, Nivedita (ed.), *Gender and Politics in India*, New Delhi: Oxford University Press, 1999 [1990], pp. 475–93.

Reddy, Gayatri, *With Respect to Sex: Negotiating Hijra Identity in South India*, Chicago and London: University of Chicago Press, 2005.

Reddy, Muthulakshmi, *Should the Devadasi System in the Hindu Temples be Abolished?*, Madras: Lodhra Press, 1928–31.

——— *My Experience as a Legislator*, Madras: Current Thought Press, 1930.

Rees, Helen, 'The age of consent: Traditional music, intellectual property and changing attitudes in the People's Republic of China', *British Journal of Ethnomusicology*, Vol. 12, No. 1 (2003), pp. 137–171.

Rege, Sharmila, 'The hegemonic appropriation of sexuality: The case of the *lavani* performers of Maharashtra', *Contributions to Indian Sociology*, Vol. 29, Nos 1–2 (1995).

——— 'Conceptualising popular culture: "*Lavani*" and "*powada*" in Maharashtra', *Economic and Political Weekly*, March 16 2002, pp. 1038–1046.

Risley, Herbert Hope, *The Tribes and Castes of Bengal. Ethnographic Glossary*, Calcutta: Bengal Secretariat Press, 1891.

Ruswa, Mirza Hadi, *Umrao Jan Ada*, translated by David Matthews, New Delhi: Rupa & Co, 1996.

Sachdeva, Shweta, *In Search of the Tawa'if in History: Courtesans, Nautch Girls and Celebrity Entertainers in India (1720s-1920s)*, PhD dissertation, School of Oriental and African Studies, 2008.

Sachs, Wolfgang (ed.), *The Development Dictionary: A Guide to Knowledge as Power*, Second Edition, London and New York: Zed Books, 2010.
Saeed, Fouzia, *TABOO! The Hidden Culture of a Red Light Area*, Pakistan: Oxford University Press, 2002.
Said, Edward, 'Foreword' in Guha, Ranajit and Spivak, Gayatri Chakravorty (eds), *Selected Subaltern Studies: v-x*, Delhi: Oxford Univeristy Press, 1988.
——— *Orientalism*, London: Penguin, 2003 [1978].
Sangari, Kumkum and Vaid, Sudesh (eds), *Recasting Women: Essays in Indian Colonial History*, New Brunswick, NJ: Rutgers University Press, 1990.
Schild, Maarten, 'The irresistible beauty of boys: Middle Eastern attitudes about boy-love', *Padaika*, Vol. 1, No. 3 (1988), pp. 37–48.
Seabrook, Jeremy, *Love in a Different Climate: Men Who Have Sex With Men in India*, London: Verso, 1999.
Seeger, Anthony, *Why Suya Sing: A Musical Anthropology of an Amazonian People*, Urbana and Chicago: University of Illinois Press, 2004 [1987].
——— 'Lost lineages and neglected peers: Ethnomusicologists outside academia', *Ethnomusicology*, Vol. 50, No. 2 (2006), pp. 214–235.
Seizer, Susan, *Stigmas of the Tamil Stage: An Ethnography of Special Drama Artistes in South India*, Durham and London: Duke University Press, 2005.
Sen, Amartya, *Identity and Violence: The Illusion of Destiny*, New York and London: W.W. Norton and Company, 2006.
Sen, Babu Keshub Chunder, *Opinions on the Nautch Question: Collected and Published by the Punjab Purity Association*, Lahore: New Lyall Press, 1894.
Sen, Sankar and Nair P.M., *A Report on Trafficking in Women and Children in India 2002–2003. Volume I*, New Delhi: National Human Rights Commission, UNIFEM, Institute of Social Sciences, 2004.
Servan-Schreiber, Catherine, 'Tellers of tales, sellers of tales: Bhojpuri peddlers in Northern India' in Markovits, Claude, Pouchepadass, Jacques and Subrahmanyam, Sanjay (eds), *Society and Circulation: Mobile People and Itinerant Cultures in South Asia 1750–1950*, Delhi: Permanent Black, 2003, pp. 275–305.
Shah, Vidya and Bondyopadhyay, Aditya, *My Body is Not Mine: Stories of Violence and Tales of Hope. Voices from the Kothi Community in India*, India: Naz Foundation International (NFI) and Centre for Media and Alternative Communication (CMAC), 2007.
Shahani, Parmesh, *Gay Bombay: Globalization, Love and (Be)longing in Contemporary India*, Thousand Oaks, CA: Sage Publications, 2008.
Shanghvi, Siddharth Dhanvant, 'Hello, darling' in *AIDS Sutra: Untold Stories from India*, London: Vintage Books, 2008, pp. 57–76.
Shankar, Jogan, *Devadasi Cult: A Sociological Analysis*, New Delhi: Ashish Publishing House, 1990.
Shankar, Ravi, *My Music, My Life*, Delhi: Vikas Publications, 1968.
Sharar, Abdul Halim, *Lucknow: The Last Phase of an Oriental Culture*, Harcourt, E.S. and Hussain, Fakhir (eds and translated), New Delhi: Oxford University Press, 1994.
Sharma, Anand, *Yaunkarmiyan: Kamini ya kulta*, Kolkatta: Durbar Prakashani, 2001.

Sharma, Sanjay, Hutnyk, John, and Sharma, Ashwini (eds), *Dis-Orienting Rhythms: The Politics of the New Asian Dance Music*, London and New Jersey: Zed Books, 1996.

Sheehy, Daniel, 'A few notions about philosophy and strategy in applied ethnomusicology', *Ethnomusicology*, Vol. 36, No. 3, Special Issue: Music and the Public Interest (1992), pp. 323–336.

Shekhar, Mayank, 'Ban Bollywood now! The issue is not that dance bars in Mumbai are no more, but how easily we can let go of our freedom', *Mumbai Mirror*, 26 August 2005.

Sher Singh, 'Sher', *The Sansis of Punjab (A Gypsy and De-Notified Tribe of Rajput Origin)*, Delhi: Munshiram Manoharlal, 1965.

Shope, Bradley, *Entertaining the Imperium: Popular music and Britain's Raj*, Bloomington, IN: Indiana University Press, forthcoming.

Shresthova, Sangita, *Between Cinema and Performance: Globalizing Bollywood Dance*, PhD dissertation, University of California, Los Angeles, 2008.

Shrinivasan, Rukmini, 'Women vs women: The bar that divides us', *The Times of India*, 29 April 2005.

Silverman, Carol, 'The Gender of the profession: Music, dance and reputation among Balkan, Muslim Rom Women' in Magrini, T. (ed.), *Music and Gender: Perspectives from the Mediterranean*, Chicago and London: University of Chicago Press, 2003.

Simhadari, Y.C., *The Ex-Criminal Tribes of India*, New Delhi: National Publishing House, 1979.

Sleightholme, Carolyne and Sihna, Indrani, *Guilty Without Trial: Women in the Sex Trade in Calcutta*, Calcutta: Stree, 1996.

Small, Christopher, *Musicking: The Meanings of Performing and Listening*, Middletown, Connecticut: Wesleyan University Press, 1998.

Soneji, Davesh, *Unfinished Gestures: Devadasis, Memory, and Modernity in South India*, Chicago and London: University of Chicago Press, 2012.

Sorrel, Neil and Narayan, Ram, *Indian Music in Performance: A Practical Introduction*, Manchester: Manchester University Press, 1980.

Srinivasan, Amrit, *Temple 'Prostitution' and Community Reform: An Examination of the Ethnographic, Historical and Textual Context of the Devadasi of Tamil Nadu, South India*, PhD thesis, Wolfson College, Cambridge University, 1984.

——— 'Reform and revival: The devadasi and her dance', *Economic and Political Weekly*, Vol. 20, No. 44 (1985), pp. 1869–76.

Srinivasan, Doris M., 'Royalty's courtesans and god's mortal wives: Keepers of culture in colonial India' in Feldman, M. and Gordon, B. (eds), *The Courtesan's Arts: Cross-Cultural Perspectives*, New York: Oxford University Press, 2006, pp. 161–181.

Stokes, Martin, 'Introduction: Ethnicity, identity and music' in Stokes (ed.), *Ethnicity, Identity and Music: The Musical Construction of Place*, Oxford and New York: Berg, 1994.

Subramanian, Lakshmi, 'Gender and the performing arts in nationalist discourse: An agenda for the Madras Music Academy, 1930–1947' in *The Book Review*, Vol. 23, Nos 1–2 (1999a), pp. 81–84.

——— 'The reinvention of tradition: nationalism, Carnatic music, and the Madras Music Academy', *Indian Economic and Social History Review*, Vol. 36, no. 2 (1999b), pp. 131–63.

——— *From the Tanjore Court to the Madras Music Academy: A Social History of Music in South India*, New Delhi: Oxford University Press, 2006.

Sullivan, Gerard and Jackson, Peter A. (eds), *Gay and Lesbian Asia: Culture, Identity, Community*, New York: Harrington Press, 2001.

Sunder, Pushpa, *Patrons and Philistines: Arts and the State in British India, 1773–1947*, New Delhi: Oxford University Press, 1995.

Swarankar, R.C., 'Traditional female sex workers of Rajasthan, India: An ethnographic study of Nat community', home.eckerd.edu/~lucasle/EC371/CourseMaterials/13SwarankarFinal.doc, last accessed 30 April 2011.

Sylvester, Christine, 'Development studies and postcolonial studies: Disparate tales of the "third world"', *Third World Quarterly*, Vol. 20, No. 4 (1999), pp. 703–721.

Szanton, David, 'The politics of Mithila painting: Or when is a Mithila painting not a Mithila painting?', paper given at the British Association of South Asian Studies annual conference, School of Oriental and African Studies, London, April 2012.

Thakraney, Anil, 'They did not sleep with me, Mr Patil. Four bargirls turn down correspondent Anil Thakraney. Still think dance bars are a front for prostitution, Mr Home Minister?', *Mid Day*, 15 April 2005, pp. 1, 6.

Thomas, Rosie and Gandhy, Behroze, 'Three Indian film stars' in Gledhill, Christine (ed.), *Stardom: Industry of Desire*, London and New York: Routledge, 1991, pp. 107–131.

Tingey, Carol, 'Auspicious women, auspicious songs: Mangalini and their music at the court of Kathmandu', *British Journal of Ethnomusicology*, Vol. 2 (1993), pp. 55–74.

Turino, Thomas, 'The urban-Mestizo Charango tradition in southern Peru: A statement of shifting identity', *Ethnomusicology*, Vol. 28, No. 2 (1984), pp. 253–270.

——— 'Signs of imagination, identity, and experience: A Peircian semiotic theory for music', *Ethnomusicology*, Vol. 43, No. 2 (1999), pp. 221–255.

——— *Music as Social Life: The Politics of Participation*, Chicago and London: University of Chicago Press, 2008.

'Ugra'; Sharma, Pandey Bechan, *About Me* (*Apni Khabar*), translated and with an introduction by Vanita, Ruth, New Delhi: Penguin Books, 2007.

Van der Meer, Wim and Bor, Joep, *De Roep van de Kokila: Historische en Hedendaagse Aspecten van de Indiase Muziek*, Gravenhage: Martinus Nijhoff, 1982.

Vanita, Ruth, 'Preface' in Ruth Vanita and Saleem Kidwai (eds), *Same-Sex Love in India*, New York: Palgrave, 2000, pp. viii–xxiv.

Vanita, Ruth (ed.), *Queering India: Same-Sex Love and Eroticism in Indian Culture and Society*, New York and London: Routledge, 2002.

Vanita, Ruth and Kidwai, Saleem (eds), *Same-Sex Love in India*. New York: Palgrave, 2000.

Vasudevan, Ravi, 'The meanings of "Bollywood"' in Dwyer, Rachel and Pinto, Jerry (eds), *Beyond the Boundaries of Bollywood: The Many Forms of Hindi Cinema*, New Delhi: Oxford University Press, 2011, pp. 3–29.

Vitali, Valentina, *Hindi Action Cinema: Industries, Narratives, Bodies*, New Delhi: Oxford University Press, 2008.

——— 'The evil I: Realism and scopophilia in the horror films of the Ramsay brothers' in Dwyer, Rachel and Pinto, Jerry (eds), *Beyond the Boundaries of Bollywood: The Many Forms of Hindi Cinema*, New Delhi: Oxford University Press, 2011, pp. 77–101.

Wallace, Robert M., 'Translator's introduction' in Blumenberg, Hans, *The Legitimacy of the Modern Age*, Cambridge Massachusetts; London: MIT Press, 1983, pp. xi–xxxi.

Walker, Margaret, *Kathak Dance: A Critical History*, PhD dissertation, University of Toronto, 2004.

Weidman, Amanda J., *Singing the Classical, Voicing the Modern: The Postcolonial Politics of Music in South India*. Calcutta: Seagull books Pvt Ltd in arrangement with Duke University Press, 2006.

Widdess, Richard, *The Rāgas of Early Indian Music: Modes, Melodies, and Musical Notations from the Gupta Period to c. 1250*, Oxford: Clarendon Press, 1995.

——— 'Raga' in Dwyer, Rachel (ed.), *Keywords in South Asia*, 2004, http://www.soas.ac.uk/southasianstudies/keywords/, last accessed 3 September 2011.

Wilchins, Riki, *Queer Theory, Gender Theory: An Instant Primer*, Los Angeles: Alyson Books, 2004.

Williams, Richard David, 'Baptist missionaries, their translators, and the *nautch* in 1837', paper presented at 'Before nautch girl was a racehorse: Indian music and dance 1800–1857', symposium of the South Asian Music and Dance Forum, Institute for Musical Research, School of Advanced Studies, University of London, 21 May 2012.

Wolf, Richard K. (ed.), *Theorizing the Local: Music, Practice, and Experience in South Asia and Beyond*, Oxford and New York: Oxford University Press, 2009.

Woolcock, M., Szreter, S. and Rao, V., 'How and why does history matter for development policy?', Brooks World Poverty Institute, University of Manchester, working paper 68, 2009, http://www.bwpi.manchester.ac.uk/resources/Working-Papers/working-papers-2009.html, last accessed 3 September 2011.

Yang, Anand (ed.), *Crime and Criminality in British India*, Tucson: University of Arizona Press, 1986.

Yang, Anand, 'Dangerous castes and tribes: The Criminal Tribes Act and the Magahiya Doms of Northeast India' in *Crime and Criminality in British India*, Tucson: University of Arizona Press, 1986, pp. 108–127.

Young, Robert C., *Postcolonialism: An Historical Introduction*, Malden, M.A., USA; Oxford, UK; Victoria, Australia: Blackwell Publishing Ltd, 2001.

Žižek, Slavoj, *How to Read Lacan*, London: Granta Books, 2006.

——— *Violence: Six sideways reflections*, London: Profile Books, 2008.

Publications with non-specified authors

Reports

Human Rights Watch, *Rape for profit: Trafficking of Nepali girls and women to India's brothels*, New York, Washington, Los Angeles, London, Brussels: Human Rights Watch, 1995.

'Working women in Mumbai bars: Truths behind the controversy. Results from survey among 500 women dancers across 50 bars', Research Centre for Women's studies, SNDT Women's University, Mumbai, 2005.

'After the ban: Women working in dance bars', Research Centre for Women's studies, SNDT Women's University, Mumbai, 2006.

Indian Hotel and Restaurants Association (AHAR) and others v. State of Maharashtra and others, 2006.
Bharosa: Voices of the unheard, Lucknow, India: NFI, 2007.
Report, volume I, National Commission for Denotified, Nomadic and Semi-nomadic Tribes, Ministry of Social Justice and Empowerment, Government of India, 2008.

Short articles

'Do Mumbai's bar girls corrupt morals?', *Times of India*, 24 April 2005.
'Support grows for bar dancers. Actor Soni Razdan says there's more vulgarity in movies than dance bars', *Express News Service*, 25 April 2005.
'Sweety v/s Savitri. Should dance bars be banned or not? Is it a fight between bar owners and R.R. Patil? Or a fight between bar culture and Indian culture?', *Mid Day*, 13 May 2005.
'The bar girls issue: The exploitation behind the tinsel and the makeup', Maharashtra State Commission for Women, in *Indian Express*, 22 August 2005.
'Dance bar ban has saved these…', *Free Press*, 3 September 2005.
'All for the ban. TOI-TNS poll: An overwhelming 87% backs government action on dance bars', *Times City*, Mumbai, 20 April 2006.
'Mahasweta royalty to help bar girls', *Asian Age*, 9 September 2009.

Filmography

Amar Akbar Anthony (1979, Manmohan Desai).
Dilwale Dulhania Le Jayenge (1995, Aditya Chopra).
Dostana (2008, Tarun Mansukhani).
Honeymoon Travels Pvt. Ltd. (2007, Reema Kagti).
Kabhi Kabhie (1976, Yash Chopra).
Kal Ho Na Ho (2003, Karan Johar).
Lamhe (1991, Yash Chopra).
Music for a goddess (DVD, 2005, Amy Catlin and Nazir Jairazbhoy, Apsara Media).
My Brother Nikhil (2005, Onir).
Page 3 (2005, Madhur Bhandarkar).
Pakeezah (1971, Kamal Amrohi).
Raja Hindustani (1996, Dharmesh Darshan).
Rangeela (1995, Ram Gopal Varma).
Sholay (1975, Prakash Mehra).
Slumdog Millionaire (2008, Danny Boyle, Loveleen Tandan).
The Dancing Boys of Afghanistan (2009, Najibullah Quraishi).
Welcome to Sajjanpur (2008, Shyam Benegal).

Online resources

Bombay Police Act www.mahasecurity.com/pdf/the_bombay_police_act_1951.pdf.
The Indian Penal Code (1860) www.indiankanoon.org.
The Indian Constitution http://indiacode.nic.in/coiweb/welcome.html.
Naz India; advocacy and the case against IPC 377 http://www.nazindia.org/advocacy.htm.

Naz Foundation International (NFI) http://www.nfi.net/.
Naz Foundation International (NFI) publication, *Pukaar* http://www.nfi.net/pukaar.htm.
Shiamak Davar and Shiamak Davar's Institute for Performing Arts (SDIPA) http://www.shiamak.com/.

List of interviews and fieldwork visits

Fieldwork specifically for this project was completed while in India and Nepal over five visits: March–May 2006; February–May 2007; November–December 2007; September–October 2008; and January–February 2010.

Informal conversations too numerous to be listed took place with Varsha Kale, Ankush Deshpande (in Mumbai), Divya Sagar, Salman, Salim, Mahesh and other *kothis* in Lucknow, centred around Bharosa Trust.

1. March–May 2006

Kalpana Bhushan, dancer, dance teacher, event organiser, owner of a dance school in Delhi. Delhi, 6 March 2006.
Praveen Shandilya, dancer, dance teacher, event organiser, owner of a dance school in Delhi, Delhi, 16 March 2006.
Ganesh Hegde, dancer, singer, Hindi film choreographer, Mumbai, 14 April 2006.
Gaysil, freelance dancer (in shows and in Hindi films) and singer, Mumbai, 17 April 2006.
Justine, freelance dancer (in shows and in Hindi films); owner of a dance school in Pune, Bandra, Mumbai, 21 April 2006.
Anchal, dancer, owner of dance school in Mumbai, Mumbai, 22 April 2006.
Vivek, union dancer and assistant choreographer in the Hindi film industry, Mumbai, 23 April 2006.
Shiamak Davar, dancer, choreographer, actor, singer, owner of Shiamak Davar's Institute for Performing Arts (SDIPA), Mumbai, 30 April 2006.
Rajesh Mansukhani, Manager, PR, SDIPA, Mumbai, 30 April 2006.
Anees, dancer, dance instructor and administrator, SDIPA, Mumbai, 30 April 2006.
Kainaaz Mistry, Assistant Project Manager, Shiamak's Victory Arts Foundation, Mumbai, 8 May 2006.

2. February–May 2007

Praveen Patkar, *Prerana*, Mumbai, 6 March 2007.
Pinky Madhiwal (first interview), *Nat* bar girl from Tonk, Rajasthan, Mumbai, 10 March 2007.
Balkrishna Sidram Renke, Chairman, National Commission for Denotified, Nomadic and Semi-nomadic Tribes, Delhi, 27 March 2007.
Manoj, *kothi* performer, Lucknow, 7 April 2007.
Gaggun Bedi, dancer, dance instructor, event organiser, choreographer, owner of dance institute in Jalandhar, Jalandhar, 26 April 2007.
Various students of Gaggun Bedi, Jalandhar, 26 April 2007.
Gani Jail Singh, *Bedia mujra* performer in GP road, Delhi, 3 May 2007.

3. November–December 2007

Jagdish Jadhav, National Commission for Denotified, Nomadic and Semi-Nomadic Tribes, Pune, 20 November 2007.
Ashish, *kothi* performer, Delhi, 2 December.
Meena Radhakrishnan, DNT Commission, Delhi, 6 December 2007.
Anand Sharma, GP Road, Delhi, 18 December 2007.
KP, Bollywood and *Bhangra* dancer, Singapore, 27 December 2007.

4. September–October 2008

Madhukar Niralea, *Tamasha* theatre owner, Mumbai, 9 September 2008.
Laxminarayan Tripathi, *hijra* activist and performer, Mumbai, 12 September 2008.
Simran, *hijra* performer, Mumbai, 13 September 2008.
Mamaji, male member of *Deredar* family, Mira Road, Mumbai, 19 September 2008.
Shabana, *Deredar mujra* performer, Fores Road, Mumbai, 15 September 2008.
Shailesh Kumar, Nai Kiran CBO working with MSMs in Balliya, Balliya, 6 October 2008.
Satin, *Kothi* performer, Lucknow, 8 October 2008.
Aamir, retired *kothi* performer, Lucknow, 9 October 2008.
Siddarth, upper class effeminate male dancer, Delhi, 12 October 2008.
Rahul, Milan project, Naz India, Delhi, 13 October 08.

5. January–February 2010

Pinky Madhiwal (second interview), *Nat* bar girl from Tonk, Rajasthan, Mumbai, 4 January 2010.
Yogesh Patkar, Bollywood dance teacher, owner of dance institute, Dombivli, Mumbai.
Dr Khan, John Paul's Slum Development Project, Pune, 16 January 2010.
Kolhati performers, with Dr Khan, *Tamasha* theatre (Aaryabhushan Theatre) Pune, 16 January 2010.
Anees, *kothi* performer, Lucknow, 17 January 2010.
Narendra, *kothi* performer (first interview), Lucknow, 22 January 2010.
Gaurang, *kothi* performer, Lucknow, 23 January 2010.
Ayub, *kothi* performer, Lucknow, 25 January 2010.
Narendra, *kothi* performer (second interview), Lucknow, 25 January 2010.
Munna, *kothi* performer, Lucknow, 27 January 2010.
Ramesh, *hijra* performer, Lucknow, 27 January 2010.
Anand, *kothi* performer, Lucknow, 29 January 2010.
Gulab, *hijra*, previously *kothi*, performer, Lucknow, 29 January 2010.
Shyam Lacchiya, *Nat*, Tonk, Rajasthan, 2 February 2010.
Hamir, *Nat* community elder (male), Tonk, Rajasthan, 2 February 2010.

Short visits to events/places/meetings during all five visits

Visit to Mira road and visit to (former) dance bar with Varsha Kale, February 2007.
Entertainment Workers Conference, Calcutta, 26 February—1 March 2007 (full conference: 25 February–3 March 2007); visit to orchestra bar in Calcutta.

Deredar kothas, first visit, Muzaffarpur, 2–3 March 2007 and 25–26 March 2007.
Mujra, Deredar performers, Congress House, Mumbai, 8 March 2007.
Deredar tawaif stage performance; visit to NGO working on prostitution, Muzaffarpur, 2–3 March 2007 and 25–26 March 2007.
Nat village (first village), Sultanpur District, Uttar Pradesh, 6 April 2007.
Bedia kotha, GP Road, 3 May 2007.
Kathmandu Blue Diamond Society, Kathmandu, Nepal, 6 May 2007.
Visit to nightclub in Kathmandu with *mettis*, Kathmandu, Nepal, 7 May 2007.
Balliya (first visit), 12–14 November 2007.
Milan, MSM project, Naz India, Delhi, 2 December 2007.
Visit to dance bars in Singapore, 26 December 2007; visits to dance classes, Singapore, 19–27 Dec 2007.
Mujra, Fores Road, Mumbai, 15 September 2008.
Humsafar, MSM project, Mumbai, drop-in meeting, including dancing, 16 September 2008.
Jagran, Lucknow, September 2008.
Ramlila, Lucknow, 8 October 2008.
Balliya (second visit), Utter Pradesh, 6–7 October 2008.
Visit to 'restaurant and bars' and lodges in Dombivli/Thane, Mumbai, 2–3 January 2010.
Kolhati homes, Pune district, Kunner Block, Maharashtra, 11 January 2010.
Government Tamasha Cultural Centre (Tulajabhavani Kala Kendre), *Lavani* performance, Aalephata Village, Kunner Block, Pune district, Maharashtra, 11 January 2010.
Meeting of sex workers, including ex-bar girls, John Paul's Slum Development Project, Pune, 16 January 2010.
Aryabhushan Theatre, Pune, Maharashtra, 16 January 2010.
Nat village (second village), Sultanpur District, Uttar Pradesh, 28 January 2010.
Nat villages, Tonk, Rajasthan, 31 January–2 February 2010.

INDEX

Aawaz-e-Nishan: 162
abhinay: 97–9, 112, 125, 174, 178; concept of, 97
Agnes, Flavia: 142–3, 155; representation provided for bar girls, 162
Agrawal, Anuja: 37, 47–8, 57
Akhtar, Begum: 41
Akshara: 162
Ali, Swati: 149
All India Performing Arts: founding of (1916), 113
All India Radio: 113
All Indian Democratic Women's Association (AIDWA): 152–3
Amrohi, Kamal: *Pakeezah* (1971), 1–3, 6, 12
Aurangzeb: 52
Australia: 110, 121; Commonwealth Games (2006), 12, 131

badhai: 90, 190; concept of, 176
Badhava: 189, 191, 193; concept of, 174
Badi: 65–6; group dynamics of, 67–8
baijis: 69, 75–6, 83; communities of, 32
baithak: concept of, 80
Bai, Gulab: biography of, 44, 48–50, 58, 79
Bangladesh: 62, 71, 77, 157
bar girls: 15, 19–20, 24–5, 39, 47, 82, 141, 145, 155, 158, 188; backgrounds of, 149, 153; banning of (2005), 16–17, 23, 32, 71, 74, 76, 143–8, 151–2, 154–6, 162–3, 167–70, 186–7, 194; media depiction of, 146, 152–5, 159, 164; support for, 160–5, 170; use of obscenity laws against, 56
Baumann, Zygmunt: 205; analysis of modernity's view of ambivalence, 23–4
Bedia: 37–8, 49–51, 57–8, 62–5, 68–71, 74, 76, 165; caste structure of, 65–6; forms of, 47; involvement in *Nautanki*, 77; involvement in prostitution, 47–8, 75–6; notification as Criminal Tribe (1913), 37
Bharatanatyam: 43, 45, 121
Bhartiya (Indian) Bargirls Union (BBU): 63–4, 74, 144, 154, 165; formation of (2004), 160, 162; members of, 62, 81, 160; rallies organised by, 142; support provided for bar girls, 160–4, 170
Bharosa Trust: 100–1, 190, 200
Bhatkhande, Narayan: 112; founder of All India Performing Arts conferences, 113
Bhatu: 71, 73, 83, 85; concept of, 62–3; examples of, 63–4, 78–9
Bhaumik, Kaushik: 39–40, 45
Bhojpuri (language): 67
Bhusan, Kalpana: 136–7; family of, 136
Bollywood dancing: 27, 29, 44, 59, 98, 109–10, 113, 118–19, 129, 132–3, 140, 144, 167, 170, 172, 174, 179, 198, 203, 206; legitimisation of, 12, 15, 111, 117, 120, 131, 134–5, 138–9, 195; music, 14, 136–8; popularity amongst Indian middle class, 98, 103, 109, 117, 132; presence of LGBT in, 103; *sangeets*,

136–8; sexy, 25, 120, 135, 168; teaching of, 122–5, 130, 134, 158; troupes, 132
Bor, Joep: 43
Boyle, Danny: *Slumdog Millionaire* (2008), 131
Brijwasi: 56, 66
British Raj: 86; Cantonment Regulations (1864), 35–6; Contagious Diseases Act (CDA) (1868), 35–6; Criminal Tribes Act (CTA) (1871), 37; Madras, 39; regulation of prostitution in, 35
Brown, Louise: 45, 67–9, 78, 102–3, 105
Butler, Judith: 21, 28, 96, 98–100

Canada: 121; Vancouver, 124
Care International: funding provided by, 84
Carnegie, Patrick: *Notes on the races, tribes and castes inhabiting the province of Avadh* (1868), 64–5, 67
caste/class system: 6–7, 25–6, 32–5, 58, 62–3, 65–9, 70, 72, 77, 83, 89–90, 98, 103–5, 109–15, 121–3, 130, 132, 153, 158–60, 166, 172–4, 176–7, 203–4, 206; impact on performing arts, 11–12, 204, 206–9, 211; intercaste relations, 10, 17–18, 44, 48, 76, 136–44, 179, 191, 196, 203; involvement in anti-*nautch* movement, 29, 39–40; LGBT culture in, 103, 198; social status, 7, 10
Catlin, Amy: *Music for a goddess* (2005), 44
Chopra, Yash: *Dil to Pagal Hai* (1997), 120–1, 125; *Kabhi Kabhie* (1976), 136; *Lamhe* (1991), 136
Christianity: 21, 92; missionaries, 39; morality, 146
Cine Dancers Union: opposition to use of non-union dancers, 120
City Dancers Association: members of, 133
commercial sexual exploitation (CSE): categorisation of, 52
Community Based Organisation (CBO): 97–8, 107, 185, 189; HIV/AIDS, 91, 96, 180; MSMs, 199
Connell, R.W.: 98, 106
Contagious Diseases Act (CDA): debates regarding special status under, 35–6; passing of (1864/1868), 35
courtesan: 2, 6–7, 34, 39, 41, 45, 48, 52, 56, 74–5, 112, 171, 203; and Muslim patronage, 43; cultural origins of, 6–7, 49; perception as prostitutes, 34; prominence in Hindu cinema, 6; restrictions on, 111–12
Criminal Tribes Act (CTA): creation of DNTs following repeal of, 37; impact on hereditary female performers, 210; provisions of, 37; repeal of (1952), 37
criminalisation: impact on performing acts, 38
Crooke, William: 7, 10; *Tribes and Castes of the North-Western Provinces and Oudh* (1896), 64, 67

dance bars: 176; banning of, 54, 145, 147, 156, 159, 165, 209; cultural image of, 141–2; potential re-legalisation of, 209; social opposition to, 147, 156, 159
Datta, Sri Nabakumar: *Swarnabai* (1888), 40
Davar, Shiamak: 124–5, 132, 134, 140; background of, 122–3; founder of SDIPA, 121
Denotified Tribes (DNTs): 38, 85; concept of, 37; creation following repeal of CTA, 37
Deredar: 58, 62–3, 71, 78, 82; communities of, 84–5; cultural background of, 83
devadasi: 19, 43–5, 48–9, 51, 78, 112, 121, 147, 150, 158, 160, 171, 177, 203; concept of, 7; degeneration of, 52, 56; perception as prostitutes, 34; reform of, 51; targeting of, 11, 39–41
Devi, Mahasweta: 165
Dhanavat: 165
Dhawale, Mariam: State Secretary of AIDWA, 152–3
Dixit, Madhuri: 116
Dom: 38; subgroups of, 67
Durbar Mahila Samanwaya Committee (DMSC): 50, 77
Dutt, Nargis: family of, 45
Dutt, Sunil: family of, 45

Ekta Self Help Group: 162
Enthoven, Reginald Edward: *Tribes and*

Castes of the Bombay Presidency, The (1920), 64, 68

Farsi (*hijra*/*kothi* language): 90
female impersonation: 87, 172, 188, 204
female public performers: 18; *classical courtesans*, 6–7, 34, 41; *devadasis*, 7, 10–11, 19, 34, 39, 40–1, 43, 48–9, 51; *transgender/female impersonator*, 7, 10–12, 15
feminism: 28, 159–60; Marxist-, 146
Fight for the Rights of Bar Owners Association (FRBOA): 165; formation of (1999), 142; rallies organised by, 142
film industry: 139; change in performance styles, 113–16; impact of commercial cable television on, 118–19; presence of hereditary female performers in, 121; social film, 115
Forbes, Geraldine: *Women in Modern India*, 46
Forum Against Oppression of Women (FAOW): 162–3
Foucault, Michel: 28
Freud, Sigmund: concept of 'narcissism of minor differences', 22

Gaisberg, F.W.: *The music goes round* (1942), 33
Gandharba: 7, 10, 64, 66–7, 165
Gandhi, Malli: study of DNTs, 38
Gandhi, Sonia: 165
Gargi, Balwant: 54
gender: 102–4; as performance, 96–7; norms, 98; sociological emphasis of, 98
giriya: 91; relationships with *kothis*, 180–2
Guria: objectives of, 85

Haldankar, Vaishali: *Barbala* (2010), 153
Hegde, Ganesh: 133; background of, 122
hereditary female performers: 21, 26–9, 31, 42, 58, 61, 64, 85–6, 111–12, 121, 150, 166, 168, 199, 201, 206; equation with prostitutes, 15–16, 31–2, 35, 40, 42, 53–4, 57–8; exclusion of, 28; presence in film industry, 121; presence in sex work industry, 17; role in *Lavani*/*Nautanki*, 27
hijras: 25, 88–91, 95, 105, 176–8, 181, 184, 186, 190–1, 198; concept of, 88–9; link to *kothis*, 90, 196–7; *nirvana* ritual, 90; transgenders as, 89, 105
Hindi (language): 2, 43; cinematic culture, 6, 12, 106, 116, 119–20, 130, 136, 208
Hinduism: deities of, 44, 90, 93, 112, 176; devotional, 92–4, 123; 174; Diwali, 131–2; *Dussera*, 173–4; *Holi*, 92, 95, 176, 189
HIV/AIDS: 51, 82, 85, 88, 162, 165, 195, 198, 203; CBOs, 91, 96, 180

ideal womanhood: film depiction of, 116; Hindu concept of, 145–6
India: 3, 6, 11–12, 15–16, 18–19, 21, 23, 25–7, 29, 33, 35–7, 41, 51, 59, 61, 63–4, 67, 75, 77, 85–6, 91–4, 102, 109–10, 112, 131, 144, 165, 168, 171, 174, 180, 195, 198, 203, 205–6, 209–11; Andhra Pradesh, 38; Awadh, 34; Balliya, 101, 176, 179–81, 182–5; Bihar, 55, 83, 173–4, 176, 180, 182–3, 185, 193, 196; Bombay, 33; Calcutta, 10, 50, 71, 77, 82, 136, 183–4; Constitution of, 53, 166; Delhi, 55, 77, 90, 93–4, 103, 122, 136, 138, 173, 176, 179–80, 182–6, 193–4, 197; government of, 45, 169, 209; Gujarat, 154; Haryana, 193; Hindustan, 65, 112; income disparity in, 156–8; independence of (1947), 15, 28–9, 31, 41–2, 53, 61–2, 71, 75, 204; Jalandhar, 125; LGBT movement in, 24, 199, 208; Lucknow, 43, 56, 64, 75, 83, 92, 94, 100, 179–80, 182–3, 185, 188–9, 197; Madhya Pradesh, 74, 76; Maharashtra, 55, 57–8, 65, 71, 78–9, 81, 83, 85, 141, 143–4, 162, 176, 209; Mumbai, 17, 23, 41, 53, 56, 62, 72, 74, 76–9, 83–5, 101, 130, 140, 148, 157, 162–3, 165, 167, 170, 173, 179, 182, 185–6, 188, 194; Muzaffarpur, 84; New Delhi, 164; Pune, 80–1, 94; Rajasthan, 51, 69, 71, 74, 76, 78; Sultanpur, 74, 76; Supreme Court, 144, 169–70, 201, 209; Uttar Pradesh, 55, 71, 76, 79, 83, 173, 176, 180, 182–3, 185, 196; West Bengal, 76
Indian Hotel and Restaurants Association: 165

Indian Penal Code (IPC): 53; Article 377, 23; prohibitions against obscenity in, 55–6; Sections 292–294, 54; Section 377, 88, 188; use against public performers, 55
Institute of Social Sciences: 51
Iraq: Operation Iraqi Freedom (2003–11), 152
Islam: 91, 102, 112, 115; Sufism, 92–4, 123

Jagran: 188; concept of, 174
Jairazbhoy, Nazir: *Music for a goddess* (2005), 44
Jammu and Kashmir: 95
Jan, Gauhar: recording of (1902), 33
Johar, Karan: *Kal Ho Na Ho* (2003), 119, 137
John Paul's Slum Development Project (JPSDP): 80–1; personnel of, 82

kaja: relationships of, 79–80
Kakkar, Prahlad: 159
Kalawant: branches of, 68
Kale, Varsha: 85, 140; founder of WPI, 160; leader of BBU, 62, 81, 160
Kanchan: 67–9
Kanjar: 63–5, 69, 71; communities of, 77–8; group dynamics of, 67, 78; student/teacher dynamic of, 66
Kathak: 95, 103
Kaviraj, Sudipta: 17
Keskar, B.V. Indian Broadcasting Minister, 113
Khan, Ahmed: 120
Khan, Dargah Quli: *Muraqqa i Delhi*, 93–4
Khan, Farah: 120
Khan, Saroj: 119
Kidwai, Saleem: 44–5; *Same Sex Love in India* (2000), 91–2
Kolhati: 48, 64, 71, 82; association with prostitution, 82–3; forms performed by, 78; income of performers, 79
Koravars: 37–8
kothas: 81, 84; closure under obscenity laws, 55
kothis: 25–7, 48, 56, 71–2, 90–3, 95–7, 101–3, 106–7, 125, 171–80, 183–5, 190, 194–5, 200–1, 206; as MSMs, 88, 107, 199; as transgressive, 99–100, 104–5, 107; concept of, 87–8; dancing in bars, 170; emasculation operations undertaken by, 184–5; erotic, 98; exclusion/restrictions of, 28, 53; financial income of, 184–6, 188–9, 191–2, 194; hire by bandmasters, 183–4; involvement in LGBT activism, 24, 88, 140, 173; involvement in sex work, 100, 182–3, 185–6, 196, 211; *jajmani*, 176; link to *hijras*, 90, 196–7; payment of, 49; performance, 185, 189–93; relationship with *giriya*, 180–2; sexual relationships of, 180–2; student/teacher dynamic of, 178; target for violence, 197–8
Kshatriya: concept of, 68

Lacchiya, Shyam: 62–4
launda: 186; dance culture of, 188; popularity of, 195–6
Launda nach I Bidesia: concept of, 174
Lavani: 45, 58, 83, 207, 209; concept of, 176; state promotion of, 78–9; use of obscenity laws against performers of, 56
legislation: Bombay Police Act (1951), 54–6, 165–6; Bonded Labour System (Abolition) Act, 53; Contagious Diseases Act (CDA), 35–6; Criminal Tribes Act, 37, 210; Dramatic Performance Act (1876), 54, 57; Immoral Traffic in Persons Prevention Act (ITPPA/PITA) (1986), 53–4, 56–7, 76, 84; Madras Devadasis Prevention of Dedication Act (1947), 40; Rules for Licensing and Controlling Places of Public Amusement (other than Cinemas) and Performances for Public Amusement including Melas and Tamasha (1960), 57; Suppression of Immoral Traffic in Women and Girls Act (SITA) (1956), 53–4, 56–7, 76
Levine, Philippa: 36
liberalism: 15, 18, 24, 28, 205, 208; colonial, 19
Lloyd Weber, Andrew: *Bombay Dreams* (2002), 131

Madras Christian Literature Society: role in anti-*nautch* movement, 39

Maharashtra State Commission for Women: 145–6
Majumdar, Neepa: 117
Malaysia: 155
males who have sex with males / men who have sex with men (MSMs): 96, 180, 185, 190, 198, 200; CBOs/NGOs targeting, 199; communities of, 197; *kothis* as, 88, 107, 199; transgenders, 89
Mangeshkar, Lata: 117
Manuel, Peter: 43
Marathi (language): 156
Marwari (language): 75
Marxism: language of, 19
Mehrotra, Deepti Priya: 44, 45, 48–50, 79
Mehta, Suketa: *Bombay: Maximum City*, 154
melas: attempted restriction under obscenity laws, 55–6; concept of, 175
Mirasi: student/teacher dynamic of, 66
Mughal Empire: 39, 68, 102–5; impact on *devadasis*, 52
mujra: 15, 27, 73, 104, 125; cultural origins of, 14; *kotha*-based, 76; performance in private residences, 57; restrictions of, 53, 55–6, 75–6; sexualisation of, 14, 77
Mutua, Makau: 20–1; concept of 'victim-savage-saviour' metaphor, 19

Nagar, Ila: 43
Nai Kiran: objectives of, 185
Nat: 51, 62–7, 69, 74, 78, 156; caste structure of, 66; communities of, 71–2, 74–5; concept of, 71; identification of groups as, 69–70; involvement in prostitution, 51, 75
nath utarna: concept of, 63
National Commission for Denotified, Nomadic and Semi-nomadic Tribes: establishment of (2006), 209–10
National Commission for Women: 164
National Congress Party (NCP): 142; members of, 143
National Human Rights Commission: 51
nationalism: 11, 15, 24–5, 28, 39, 112–14, 160, 203; focus on identity, 131, 204; group dynamics of, 22–3; Indian, 23, 150; problems of, 21–2
Nautanki: 14–15, 27, 33, 44–5, 54, 58, 76, 81, 97, 178, 188–9, 191–2, 209; *Bedia* involvement in, 77; concept of, 174; decline of, 188–90; sexual politics of, 62, 189
nautch: 32, 39, 48, 88, 113, 135, 143, 160; depictions of, 146; opposition to, 11, 23, 31–2, 37–40–1, 44, 51–3, 83, 144–5, 147–8, 150, 152, 159, 165–6, 168
Naz India: Milan project, 180
Nepal: 62, 68
non-governmental organisations (NGOs): 23, 29, 80, 84–5, 107, 142, 151, 180, 189; MSMs, 199
non-resident Indians (NRIs): markets of, 110; popularity of *sangeets* amongst, 136; role in development of Bollywood dance culture, 117–18, 131

Oldenburg, Veena Talwar: 43

Pakistan: 62, 71, 77; Lahore, 43, 77–8
Paluskar, Vishnu Digambar: 112
Patil, R.R.: 145; Deputy Chief Minister and Home Minister of Maharashtra, 143, 149
Patkar, Praveen: 151
performing femininity: 7, 18, 20, 91; cultural role of, 25, 203; erotic, 45, 59, 105, 203, 210; exclusion of, 15, 17, 89; religious, 93; transgender performers, 3, 10–12, 14–17, 22–3, 25, 29, 89, 105, 171, 178, 204, 208–11
Phalke, Dadasaheb: *Raja Harishchandra* (1913), 113
Pradhesh, Madhya: 62
Prerana: objectives of, 142–3; personnel of, 151
public culture: concept of, 14–15
Pukhraj, Malka: autobiography of, 44–5, 95

Qureshi, Regula Burkhardt: 43–4, 49, 83, 104

Radhakrishnan, Meena: works on *Koravars*, 37–8
raga: concept of, 11
Ramjani: 68–9
Ramlila: 178–9; concept of, 173–4; *kothi* dancing in, 185, 189–93
randi: concept of, 10

Razdan, Soni: 159
Reddy, Mutthulakshmi: 147
Report on Trafficking in Women and Children in India 2002–3: findings of, 51
Risley, Herbert Hope: *Tribes and Castes of Bengal. Ethnographic Glossary, The* (1891), 64
Robert, Lord Frederick: Commander-in-chief of British Army in India, 35; support for regulated prostitution, 35–6

Sachdeva, Shweta: 32–5, 39, 45
Salvation Army: involvement in reformatory settlements, 37
Sanmitra Trust: 162
Sansi: 69
Second World War (1939–45): 19
sex workers: 50, 77, 80–1, 85, 100, 161; brothel-based, 74, 80, 180–1; family-based, 47; *kothis* as, 182–3, 185–6, 196, 211; legislation targeting, 53–4, 56–7, 76; relationship with performing arts genres, 81–2
Shankar, Jogan: *Devadasi Cult: A Sociological Analysis*, 52
Sherring, Matthew Atmore: *Hindu Tribes and Castes as Represented in Benares* (1872), 64–5
Shiamak Davar's Institute of Performing Arts (SDIPA): 121–3, 125, 132; classes of, 124; founding of (1985), 121; members of, 124; Victory Arts Foundation (VAF), 124
Shilappadikaram: 92
Shreemati Nathibai Damodar Thackersey (SMDT) Women's University: Research Centre for Women's Studies (RCWS), 163
Sikhism: 103
Singapore: 100, 155, 170
Sparkling Pearlz Institute of Fine Dances and Grooming: 125; founding of (2004), 125; students of, 128–9
Srinivasan, Amrit: 32, 43
St Denis, Ruth: 33
Subbalakshmi, M.S.: biography of, 45

Tamasha: 45, 58, 81–2, 176, 209; *Sangeet Baree*, 78; relationship with sex workers, 81–2; sexual politics of, 62; state promotion of, 78–9, 82, 85; theatres, 79–80, 82; use of obscenity laws against performers of, 56
Tamil (language): 92
tawaif: 20, 32, 34–5, 43–4, 70, 73, 113, 158, 160, 177; marginalisation of, 83–4; popularity of, 33
Thakur: 72
trafficking: 42, 46, 51–2, 143, 150, 156; prohibition of, 35, 53; use of legislation to target female performers, 53–4
transgender: 29, 59, 88–9, 203, 208; as MSMs, 89; as *hijras*, 89, 105; exclusion of, 15–16; *kothi*, 22, 96, 105; public recognition of, 17; religious subject position, 93

United Kingdom (UK): 110, 121; Bollywood Proms (2009), 131; Contagious Diseases Act (CDA) (1864), 35–6; London, 122, 131, 155
United Nations (UN): Development Fund for Women (UNIFEM), 51; Global Initiative to Fight Human Trafficking, 53
United States of America (USA): 110, 143, 155–6
universal ideology: concept of, 18–19; examples of, 19; focus of, 21–2; limitations of, 20
Urdu (language): 73, 75, 92; poetry, 93

Vanita, Ruth: *Same Sex Love in India* (2000), 91–2
Varma, Pavan: 157
Varma, Ram Gopal: *Rangeela* (1995), 134–5
Vijayantimala: 116

Walker, Margaret: 94–5
Womanist Party of India (WPI): founding of (2003), 160
Women's Action and Research Group: 162
Women's Centre: 162